M000195251

# GREAT ADVENTURES IN ARCHAEOLOGY

EDITED AND
WITH AN INTRODUCTION BY

*Robert Silverberg*

UNIVERSITY OF NEBRASKA PRESS

LINCOLN AND LONDON

To my wife
BARBARA

First Bison Books printing: 1997
Most recent printing indicated by the last digit below:
10   9   8   7   6   5   4   3   2   1

Library of Congress Cataloging-in-Publication Data
Great adventures in archaeology / edited and with an introduction by Robert Silverberg.
p.   cm.
Originally published: New York: Dial Press, 1964.
Includes index.
ISBN 0-8032-9247-3 (pbk.: alk. paper)
1. Antiquities.   2. Archaeology—History.   I. Silverberg, Robert.
CC165.G74   1997
930.1—dc21
97-18513   CIP

## ACKNOWLEDGMENTS

The task of editing an anthology of this sort turned out to be both more pleasant and more
arduous than I had expected—the pleasant part being the long sessions of bookstore-
prowling as I collected the books from which the selections were taken, and the arduous part
being the collating, the compiling, and the obtaining of publication rights. A number of
people made these tasks easier for me. I offer thanks here to Henry Morrison of the Scott
Meredith Literary Agency and to Carole S. Lewis of The Dial Press for various forms of
assistance and suggestion; to Ernest Benn, Ltd., to the Houghton Mifflin Company, to
Macmillan & Co., Ltd., and to Cassell & Co., Ltd., for granting permission to reprint material included herein; and to my wife Barbara, for relieving me of a great deal of unfortunately necessary drudgery involved in making the book.

The poetic excerpts used to preface the sections on Ur and Nippur are from *Ancient Near
Eastern Texts*, edited by James B. Pritchard, and are reprinted by permission of the pub-
lisher, the Princeton University Press.

# CONTENTS

A man has no more right to think of the people of old as dust than he has to think of his contemporaries as lumps of meat. The true archaeologist does not take pleasure in skeletons as skeletons, for his whole effort is to cover them decently with flesh and skin once more, and to put some thoughts back in the empty skulls. Nor does he delight in ruined buildings because they are ruined buildings; rather he deplores that they are ruined. . . . In fact, the archaeologist is so enamored of life that he would raise all the dead from their graves. He will not have it that the men of old are dust; he would bring them forth to share with him the sunlight which he finds so precious. He is such an enemy of Death and Decay that he would rob them of their harvest; and for every life that the foe has claimed he would raise up, if he could, a memory that would continue to live.

—ARTHUR WEIGALL
*The Glory of the Pharaohs*

# INTRODUCTION

W HAT is the source of archaeology's great popular fascination?

Partly, I think, it stems from some puritan prompting within us. We have an abhorrence of waste. The sight of a waterfall wildly plunging impels us to think of hydroelectric power. The sight of a barren desert stirs thoughts of irrigation schemes. A collection of decaying shacks leads to plans for urban renewal.

So, too, with the past. There, on the horizon, bulks an ugly, shapeless mound. Within it—perhaps—are relics of a lost yesterday, not only works of art but records of departed captains and kings. So long as the mound remains untapped, those relics are hidden, lost from sight and from use. But to uncover them is to lay bare the past, to reclaim it from waste. Certainly there is a powerful appeal here, and a great pleasure, as our museums fill with retrieved treasure and our libraries swell with regained knowledge of our past.

But there is a less subtle fascination as well. Archaeology offers the delights of detection. Schliemann's account of the finding of Troy, Thompson's tale of discovering a Maya city in the jungle—these provide much the same sort of pleasure as the latest Simenon, the latest Agatha Christie. There is the same keen excitement as the first clues are uncovered, the moments of suspense as reverses are encountered, the triumphant climax as the detective-archaeologist displays his proofs.

The detection of criminals, however necessary it may be, strikes me as rather an ignoble profession. It is otherwise with archaeology. The archaeologist deals not with unsavory bludgeonings or poisonings, but with the most glorious moments of the human past. He deals with clues not moments old, but thousands of years. They are scanty clues, too, often fragmentary in the extreme, and only a Holmes or a Nero Wolfe would enjoy much success deciphering the faint, time-riddled clues that a field archaeologist accepts as his daily lot.

And so, of all the sciences, archaeology is the one that can reach out most dramatically toward the layman. It takes the discovery of a new planet or the launching of an interplanetary expedition to arouse much public interest in astronomy, for example—but the opening of the Tomb of Tutankhamen monopolized the front pages of the world's newspapers for months, while the writings of Layard and Schliemann were bestsellers of their day.

Archaeology as a science is not very old though men have been digging up antiquities for a long time. 3500 years ago, a Pharaoh of Egypt had the Sphinx cleared of sand—but he did it to fulfill a religious vow, not to make it accessible for study. Another celebrated "archaeologist" of ancient times was Nabonidus, who succeeded Nebuchadnezzar on the throne of Babylon in 555 B.C. It was Nabonidus who ordered excavations to be made at the sites of ruined temples, for the purpose of determining the names of their builders. And it was Nabonidus who proudly reported finding, eighteen cubits below the contemporary pavement, the foundation-stone of Naram-Sin, grandson of Sargon of Akkad, "which for 3,200 years no previous king had seen." (We know now that Nabonidus overestimated the foundation-stone's age by a millenium and a half.)

These early excavations were for religious purposes. And the later excavations of the Renaissance were done chiefly to provide handsome statuary for the estates of kings and nobles. All during the 16th and 17th centuries, the soil of Italy yielded treasures in profusion—but this was not really archaeology.

Nor was it archaeology in 1709, when an Austrian prince named D'Elboeuf began to sink shafts into the solidified mud that entombed the Roman city of Herculaneum. D'Elboeuf was simply looking for treasure. His workmen smashed their way through the buried buildings in search of fine marbles and lovely bronzes. But treasure-hunting was transformed into archaeology a generation later, when Charles of Bourbon, King of the Two Sicilies, ordered D'Elboeuf's old shafts to be reopened.

Charles brought along an antiquarian expert, the Marchese Don Marcello Venuti, keeper of the royal library. When work began in 1738, Venuti was on hand to supervise the excavations and to prevent the workmen from doing damage to the ruins. It was Venuti who entered the shafts, translated the inscriptions, and revealed that the buried city was, indeed, Herculaneum. Modern scientific archaeology began in that year.

The excavation of Pompeii followed, beginning in 1748. Again, there was a period of casual bashing about belowground, until another scholar, the Prussian-born Johann Joachim Winckelmann, could bring matters under control.

Meanwhile, adventurous travellers were roaming the Near East. Pietro della Valle, in the early part of the 17th century, saw the ruins of Babylon. John Cartwright, in 1611, reported on his visit to what he thought was the ruin of Nineveh. (He was right.) Dozens of others visited sites in Greece, in Egypt, in Crete. One of the most influential was an English divine named Richard Pococke, who travelled through the entire Near East, and who recorded his impressions in two ponderous folio volumes published in 1743 and 1745.

These men were not archaeologists. They came to look, not to dig. But they stirred the enthusiasm of others, and by the early part of the 19th century, men were beginning to thrust spades into the mounds of Mesopotamia and the sand-blown ruins of Egypt. The great age of archaeology was about to open.

The work of these early archaeologists was often crude and clumsy. The flamboyant Giovanni Belzoni, whose adventures within a pyramid at Gizeh form our first chapter, explored the tombs of the kings at Thebes, and described his activities this way:

"After the exertion of entering into such a place . . . I sought a resting-place, found one, and contrived to sit; but when my weight bore on the body of an Egyptian, it crushed it like a band-box. I naturally had recourse to my hands to sustain my weight, but they found no better support; so that I sunk altogether among the broken mummies, with a crash of bones, rags, and wooden cases, which raised such a dust as kept me motionless for a quarter of an hour, waiting till it subsided again. I could not remove from the place, however, without increasing it, and every step I took I crushed a mummy in some part or other."

Today's archaeologists are more careful. But had Belzoni and the other heavy-handed pioneers not caught the public fancy with their work, there would be only scanty funds for modern excavation.

One might wish that the early archaeologists had not been quite so successful in locating lost cities. Again and again, we read in their accounts that some remarkable object was discovered, "but it crumbled upon exposure to the air." The modern methods of preservation were unknown then, and what a wealth of wonders perished, after thousands of years of repose, because discovered a century too soon! Then, too, the pioneers were harassed by local authorities, and had to work in haste, often destructively. And so we read in horror of the methods of excavation, and of the woeful losses—as of the 1855 disaster in which 308 cases of sculpture from Assyrian ruins went to the bottom of the Tigris when native rafts bearing them were capsized by bandits.

The loss of museum-bound treasures, serious enough, was minor compared with the damage done by archaeologists who paid no attention to stratification. In a mound of ruins, successive buildings are found one atop the other; the city-dwellers simply built on the foundations of what had gone before. The first archaeologists, scrambling for antiquities, paid no attention to the order of stratification. They dug down helter-skelter, feverishly hunting for glamorous objects of art.

Only belatedly was it realized that the best way of dating a find was to compare it with other objects found in the same stratum—which meant carefully peeling back each layer of deposit. Heinrich Schliemann, who excavated Troy and Mycenae, was the first digger to show any awareness of the importance of such care. He was able to see that the mound of Hissarlik, the site of Troy, contained clear-cut levels reflecting different periods of occupation. Schliemann recognized seven different cities, one atop the other, at Hissarlik. Later he corrected his figure to nine, which modern stratigraphy has shown to be a considerable underestimate. But in his writings, we see great care expended to identify the objects found with the different strata.

Schliemann's work, though, was coarse and haphazard by latterday standards. Other refinements were yet to come. The English archaeologist Flinders Petrie expanded on Schliemann's work, showing how pottery could be used to date each succeeding stratum. An American, George Andrew Reisner, introduced the practice of recording everything found by the excavator, no matter how trivial, in the order found.

Archaeology today has been placed on a scientific footing. The archaeologist strips back each layer of debris as though he were skinning an onion, carefully photographing and recording everything before he goes deeper. The responsibility is a grave one. The man who digs today is all too thoroughly aware of the archaeological crimes committed by his well-meaning predecessors, and all too uncomfortably fearful that future excavators may heap imprecations on *his* head for destroying irreplaceable evidence.

For, as Leonard Woolley tells us, "All excavation is destruction. The archaeologist unearths a building, perhaps removing two or three later constructions in order to do so; its walls remain and can be seen or, if the wind-blown sand covers them again, they can be dug out a second time, but all the evidence given by stratification, by the position of objects, by traces of wood ash or by fallen brickwork, this has gone, and can never be recovered . . . and evidence that he has failed to note has gone for ever, and unless his record is scientifically complete he has defrauded science, and had better not have dug at all."

Not only has the method of archaeology changed over the last century, but the form in which the archaeologist's findings have been presented to the public has altered as well. The early writers—Belzoni, Layard, and the rest until about 1875— presented their findings in books of a semi-popular nature, which were as much travel accounts as works of science. They make fascinating reading for the layman, but are of only minor value to the professional.

Schliemann, with his heightened awareness of the scientific methodology of excavating, changed the pattern. His many books are part travel report, part scientific publication—and the two do not greatly overlap. Long pages of Schliemann's works are devoted to a painstaking account of everything that was found, down to the merest potsherd. He was the first archaeologist to publish his findings in anything resembling modern form.

Today, the usual procedure is to offer two separate publications: a frankly popular, or semi-popular, work for the public, and a detailed report for the profession. The popular work usually comes first. Thus, Leonard Woolley offered his *Ur of the Chaldees* to the public in 1929, but the official publication, in large and costly quarto volumes, is still going on, the fifth volume having appeared as recently as 1955. In some cases the official report never appears, to archaeology's great loss. Howard Carter published three semi-popular books on his excavations of the Tomb of Tutankhamen, between 1923 and 1937. But he was unable to publish his formal report before his death, and it remains unpublished today, though the notes and photographs are still filed and waiting for someone to assemble them (and—more important—for someone to underwrite the cost of publication. Those scientific reports, thick with photo plates and intended for a highly limited audience, run their publishers into huge deficits.)

This present volume is intended for an audience of laymen. It is edited by one. I have not, therefore, drawn on scientific reports for any of the sections of this book, though some of the technical reports are very well written indeed. Even the best of them are too narrowly specialized to offer much to the reader seeking the glamor, the romantic sweep of archaeological investigation. And they assume much too much prior knowledge on the part of the reader. I was not eager to stud these pages with footnotes.

In making my selections, I attempted to provide a broad view of the archaeological triumphs of the past, but not a total view. In a book of this length, the editor confronts the choice between giving a short snippet of everything, or substantial chunks of a few works. I chose the latter. And so there is nothing here of Sir Arthur Evans' great work at Crete, or of John Marshall's at Mohenjo-Daro and Harappa, or of those archaeologists responsible for recreating the Hittite Empire, and much else is missing as well. It cannot be helped. Perhaps their turn will come in a later volume.

I have tried to present whole chapters wherever possible, with a minimum of editorial elisions. My own deletions are represented by (. . .), and my interpolations by [brackets]. I have removed, without noting the fact in the text, most footnotes and references to illustrations. Where I have deleted, it has been to cut material not self-evident out of the context of the entire book in which it appeared, or to trim away digressions. Many of the conjectures put forth by the ten writers are wrong, as time has proven—most particularly in the matter of dating. I have not presumed to alter texts to provide the latest opinions on chronology, of course. I have changed spellings where necessary to conform to modern American usage, but grammar has been left unmodified. There are certain inevitable inconsistencies, particularly in the spelling of ancient names. The spelling I would prefer, for example, for the name of a Mesopotamian step-tower is *ziggurat;* but Koldewey uses *zikurrat,* Hilprecht *ziggurrat,* and other writers other spellings. I have not attempted to bring such terms into conformity.

Archaeology in the field is not a very glamorous pursuit. The best sites are generally in tropical or semi-tropical climates, and the archaeologist must prepare to perspire a great deal. Most of his time is spent in waiting, or in digging, or in the most taxing form of drudgery. Obviously archaeologists find their profession a rewarding one, but most of us prefer to savor its pleasures vicariously.

I am of the ranks of the armchair archaeologists myself. This volume is humbly offered for the pleasure of those others who respond with chilled spines to the names Babylon and Tutankhamen and Troy, but who are willing to take at second hand the labors of the great excavators.

— ROBERT SILVERBERG

# PART ONE.

---

# *The Valley of the Nile*

Giovanni Batista Belzoni

# 1. BELZONI:

# *Within the Pyramid*

The pyramids themselves, doting with age, have forgotten
the names of their founders.

— THOMAS FULLER, 1642

> *Nile shall pursue his changeless way:*
> *Those Pyramids shall fall;*
> *Yea! Not a stone shall stand to tell*
> *The spot whereon they stood.*
> *Their very site shall be forgotten,*
> *As is their builder's name.*

— SHELLEY, *Queen Mab.*

Few figures in the history of archaeology are more appeal-
ing, and certainly none is more bizarre, than Giovanni Bat-
tista Belzoni, the Italian-born giant who was the first man in
modern times to explore the interior of the Pyramid of
Chephren, the second of the three great pyramids at Gizeh.

Belzoni was no scientist, though he was something of an
educated man, and knew what he was about. He regarded
himself, and we so regard him, as an adventurer, a profiteer

of archaeology. Although his archaeological methods were hair-raising—for example, a mummy-crunching episode—his achievements were such that Howard Carter, the man who found the Tomb of Tutankhamen, was able to call Belzoni "one of the most remarkable men in the whole history of Egyptology."

Belzoni was born in Padua in 1778. The exploration of Egypt had already begun. Dr. Pococke's huge volume of 1743 had excited the European world with its talk of pyramids and temples, and other travellers had since visited the Valley of the Nile and sent back their own glowing reports. James Bruce had been there, en route to his famous journey toward the source of the Blue Nile. Napoleon had been there—to conquer, not to explore—and had brought with him a horde of savants who gave the world the first detailed scientific report on the antiquities of Egypt.

Belzoni's first ambition was to enter the church. But a man of such great gusto could never have been happy in priestly garb, and he abandoned the idea in favor of a career in mechanical engineering. He began his studies in Rome, but in 1803, after Napoleon's soldiers invaded Italy, Belzoni slipped abroad to avoid a political entanglement, and continued his preparation in London. To support himself, he worked as a circus strong man, for he stood six feet seven, and, as Sir Richard Burton wrote of him, "He was a magnificent specimen of a man, strong as a Hercules, handsome as an Apollo; the various portraits taken about this time show the fine features which rarely, except in statues, distinguish the professional athlete."

He passed nine years in England, touring the circuses and music halls as the "Italian Giant." Then, having taken a wife, he travelled eastward, arriving in Egypt in June, 1815. Egypt was then ruled by Mohammed Ali, a colorful figure as unusual as Belzoni himself—a swashbuckler of Albanian extraction who had maneuvered his way to the throne of Egypt, as khedive, or viceroy, to the Turkish Sultan. Belzoni had invented a water-wheel that he hoped to peddle to Mohammed

Ali for use in irrigation and flood control.

The khedive, however, was not interested in Belzoni's hydraulic device, and the giant was left stranded in Egypt without capital. The resourceful Belzoni decided to join the ranks of those who were growing wealthy by digging for antiquities in the land of the Pharaohs. He attached himself to Henry Salt, the British consul-general in Egypt, a great collector of Egyptian relics. Belzoni's first assignment for Salt was to oversee the transport down the Nile of a huge bust of Rameses II, often called "Young Memnon," which Salt had purchased at Thebes. Belzoni saw the colossus safely to Alexandria, where it was shipped to the British Museum.

Salt was impressed by Belzoni's thoroughness, and invited the Italian to continue collecting on his behalf. Belzoni roved Egypt, acquiring antiquities small and large for the Englishman. Among the large ones was an obelisk twenty-two feet high which he removed from the Island of Philae. The operation was a troublesome one. As he was about to embark with the obelisk, the pier on which it rested gave way, and the great monolith slipped into the Nile. The Italian strong man devised a way of fishing it out again, only to run into new difficulties: a band of Arabs, hired by an Italian collector who coveted the obelisk, attacked him. Belzoni fought them off—knocking down one attacker, seizing his ankles, and using him as a club to beat away the others—and continued on his way with his obelisk.

In October, 1817, Belzoni visited Thebes and explored the Valley of the Kings, which we will meet again several chapters hence. Here, many of the Pharaohs of the Middle Kingdom had been buried, and Belzoni explored the tombs, which had earlier been visited by Pococke and Bruce, among others. He spent a year there, opening the tombs, which had all been plundered in antiquity but which had not been entered since.

Belzoni's methods, as noted, were straightforwardly blunt. He opened sealed doors with battering-rams, and flailed about him mightily in his search for marketable antiquities. Of his discoveries in the Valley of the Kings, the most significant was that of the Pharaoh Seti (Sethos) I, father of Rameses the Great. The mummy of the Pharaoh had been removed long ago, but Belzoni found an extraordinary alabaster sarcophagus, which he turned over to Salt, and which Salt sold to Sir John Soane in 1824 for £2000. The sarcophagus is in the Soane Museum, London, today.

Belzoni's work in the Valley of the Kings was the most extensive—and, despite its vandalisms, the most scientific—archaeological exploration performed in Egypt at that time. He brought back countless sketches, wax imprints, and measurements. He was convinced, too, that he had exhausted the Valley: "It is my firm opinion that in the Valley of Beban el Malook, there are no more [tombs] than are now known, in consequence of my late discoveries; for, previously to my quitting that place, I exerted all my humble abilities in endeavoring to find another tomb, but could not succeed." Belzoni was wrong about the Valley, as we shall see.

From Thebes, he turned to Gizeh, and the Pyramids. He worked there during the early part of 1818, and succeeded in entering the Second Pyramid. His experiences are related in the extract reprinted here. Belzoni's other great Egyptian accomplishment was the exploration of the Red Sea port of Berenike, which dated from the Greco-Roman era of Egypt under the Ptolemies.

Belzoni left Egypt forever in 1819. He returned to London, where he wrote—in English, his adopted language—the book of memoirs he called *Narrative of the Operations and Recent Discoveries within the Pyramids, Temples, Tombs, and Excavations, in Egypt and Nubia*. The London publishing house of John Murray, which throughout the 19th century was foremost in bringing the writings of archaeologists to the public, brought the book out in 1820, accompanied by a volume of plates, and carrying an appendix entitled "Mrs. Belzoni's Trifling Account of the Women of Egypt, Nubia, and Syria." The book almost immediately went into a second edition.

Also in 1820, Belzoni set up an exhibition in the Egyptian Hall that had been built in Piccadilly. The main attraction of the exhibit was the sarcophagus of Seti, and a model of the burial chamber. The tomb of Seti was known as "Belzoni's Tomb" for many years thereafter.

In 1823, Belzoni made another voyage of exploration, this time in search of the city of Timbuktoo. His strength was still great, his endurance remarkable, but he was 45, and no longer the casual lifter of obelisks. Several months after his entry into equatorial Africa, he was dead of dysentery, on December 3, 1823. He was buried at the town of Gwato, in what is now Nigeria. Sir Richard Burton, visiting Belzoni's grave in 1862, was unable to find any marker, and a hasty excavation failed to locate the giant's bones.

Belzoni, who smashed mummies by the score and scratched his name into many of the monuments of Egypt, was scarcely a scientific archaeologist. But he was conscientious in his way, and he worked at a time when archaeology was a fledgling discipline without any code of conduct. His account of his findings gave impetus to the great Egyptologists who followed him.

## WITHIN THE PYRAMID

Before my departure for Thebes I visited the pyramids in company with two other persons from Europe. On our arrival at these monuments they went into the first pyramid, while I took a turn round the second. I seated myself in the shade of one of those stones on the east side, which form part of the temple that stood before the pyramid in that direction. My eyes were fixed on that enormous mass, which for so many ages has baffled the conjectures of ancient and modern writers. Herodotus himself was deceived by the Egyptian priests, when told there were no chambers in it. The sight of the wonderful work before me astonished me as much, as the

From *Narrative of the Operations and Recent Discoveries within the Pyramids, Temples, Tombs, and Excavations, in Egypt and Nubia* (London: John Murray, 1820) by Giovanni Belzoni

total obscurity in which we are of its origin, its interior, and
its construction. In an intelligent age like the present, one of
the greatest wonders of the world stood before us, without our
knowing even whether it had any cavity in the interior, or
if it were only one solid mass. The various attempts which have
been made by numerous travellers to find an entrance into
this pyramid, and particularly by the great body of French
savants, were examples so weighty, that it seemed little short
of madness, to think of renewing the enterprise. . . .

With all these thoughts in my mind I arose, and by a natural
impulse took my walk toward the south side of the pyramid.
I examined every part, and almost every stone. I continued
to do so on the west,—at last I came round to the north.
Here the appearance of things became to my eye somewhat
different from that at any of the other sides. The constant
observations I made on the approach to the tombs at Thebes
perhaps enabled me to see what other travellers did not: indeed,
I think this ought to be considered as a standing proof, that
in many cases practice goes farther than theory. Other travellers had been also in various places where I had been, and
came often to the same spot where I was, but perhaps did
not make the observations I did. I certainly must beg leave
to say, that I often observed travellers who, confident of their
own knowledge, let slip opportunities of ascertaining whether
they were correct in their notions; and if an observation was
made to them by any one, who had not the good fortune of
having received a classical education, they scorned to listen
to it, or replied with a smile, if not a laugh of disapprobation,
without investigating whether the observation were just or not.
I had often the satisfaction of seeing such travellers mortified
by the proof of being wrong in their conjecture. I do not
mean to say, that a man, who has had a classical education,
should think himself under a disadvantage in regard to knowing such things, compared with him who has not; but that a
man, who thinks himself well informed on a subject, often
does not examine it with such precision as another, who is
less confident in himself.

I observed on the north side of the pyramid three marks, which encouraged me to attempt searching there for the entrance into it. Still it is to be remarked, that the principal signs I discovered there were not deduced solely from the knowledge I had acquired among the tombs of the Egyptians at Thebes; for any traveller will acknowledge, that the pyramids have little in common with the tombs, either in their exterior appearance, or in any shape whatever:—they are two different things, —one is formed by a vast accumulation of large blocks of stones;—the other is entirely hewed out of the solid rock. My principal guide, I must own, was the calculation I made from the first pyramid, and such was my assurance on this point, that I then almost resolved to make the attempt. I had been at the pyramids various times before, but never with any intention of examining into the practicability of finding the entrance into them, which was deemed almost impossible. The case was now different,—I saw then what I had not seen before.—I observed, that just under the center of the face of the pyramid the accumulation of materials, which had fallen from the coating of it, was higher than the entrance could be expected to be, if compared with the height of the entrance into the first pyramid, measuring from the basis. I could not conceive how the discovery of the entrance into the second pyramid could be considered as a matter to be despaired of, when no one had ever seen the spot, where it must naturally be presumed to exist, if there were any entrance at all. I farther observed, that the materials which had fallen exactly in the center of the front were not so compact as those on the sides; and hence concluded, that the stones on that spot, had been removed after the falling of the coating. Consequently I perceived the probability of there being an entrance into the pyramid at that spot. Encouraged by these observations, I rejoined my companions in the first pyramid. We visited the great sphinx, and returned to Cairo the same evening.

I resolved to make a closer examination the next day, which I did accordingly, without communicating my intention to any one, as it would have excited great inquiry among the

Franks at Cairo, and in all probability I should not have obtained permission to proceed in my design. The next day's examination encouraged me in the attempt. I was confident, that, if my purpose had been known to certain persons, who had influence at the court of the Bashaw, I should never succeed in obtaining permission. On the following day therefore I crossed the Nile to Embabe, as the Cacheff who commanded the province which includes the pyramids resided there. I introduced myself to him, and acquainted him with my intention to excavate the pyramids, if it met his approbation. His answer was, as I expected, that I must apply to the Bashaw, or to the Kakia Bey, for a firman, without which it was not in his power to grant me permission to excavate at the harrans, or pyramids. I asked him, whether he had any other objection, provided I obtained the firman from the Bashaw; he replied, "none whatever." I then went to the citadel, and as the Bashaw was not in Cairo, I presented myself to the Kakia Bey . . . who, on my request for permission to excavate at the pyramids, had no other objection, than that of not being certain, whether round the harrans there were any ploughed grounds, on which he could not grant permission to dig. He sent a message to the above Cacheff at Embabe, who assured him, that round the harrans there was no cultivated land, but that on the contrary it was solid rock.

With such an assurance I obtained a firman to the Cacheff, to furnish me with men to work at the pyramids. My undertaking was of no small importance: it consisted of an attempt to penetrate into one of the great pyramids of Egypt, one of the wonders of the world. I was confident, that a failure in such an attempt would have drawn on me the laughter of all the world for my presumption in undertaking such a task: but at the same time I considered, that I might be excused, since without attempting we should never accomplish any thing. However, I thought it best to keep my expedition as secret as possible; and I communicated it only to Mr. Walmas, a worthy Levantine merchant of Cairo, and partner in the house of Briggs. It is not to be understood, that I intended to conceal the attempt I wished to make on the pyramids, for the effects of my work would plainly show themselves; but being near the capital, where many Europeans resided, I could not prevent myself from being interrupted during my operations; and as I knew too well how far the influences and intrigues of my opponents could be carried, I was not certain, that the permission I had procured might not have been countermanded, so as to put an end to all my proceedings. Accordingly having provided myself with a small tent, and some provision, that I might not be under the necessity of repairing to Cairo, I set off for the pyramids.

My sudden departure from Cairo was supposed to be an expedition to the mountain of Mokatam, for a few days, as I had given out. At the pyramids I found the Arabs willing to work, and immediately set about the operation.

My purse was but light, for very little remained of what I received as a present from Mr. Burckhardt, and the consul; and though it had been a little strengthened by the two statues I lately disposed of to the Count de Forbin, who had paid me one third of the money on account, my whole stock did not amount to two hundred pounds, and if I did not succeed in penetrating the pyramid before this was exhausted, I should have been at a stand, before the accomplishment of my undertaking, and perhaps prepared the way for others stronger than myself in purse.

Two points principally excited my attention: the first was on the north side of the pyramids, and the second on the east. There is on the latter side part of a portico of the temple which stood before the pyramid, and which has a causeway descending straight towards the great sphinx. I thought, that by opening the ground between the portico and the pyramid I should necessarily come to the foundation of the temple, which in fact I did. I set eighty Arabs to work, forty on the above spot, and forty in the center of the north side of the pyramid, where I observed the earth not so solid as on the east and west. The Arabs were paid daily one piastre each, which is sixpence English money. I had also several boys and girls to carry away

Gizeh Pyramid and Sphinx, Cairo

the earth, to whom I gave only twenty paras, or three pence, a day. I contrived to gain their good will by trifles I gave as presents, and by pointing out to them the advantage they would gain, if we succeeded in penetrating into the pyramid, as many visitors would come to see it, and they would get bakshis from them. Nothing has so much influence on the mind of an Arab as reasoning with him about his own interest, and showing him the right way to benefit himself. Any thing else he seems not to understand. I must confess, at the same time, that I found this mode of proceeding quite as efficacious in Europe.

The works on each side continued for several days without the smallest appearance of any thing. On the north side of the pyramid, the materials which were to be removed, consisting of what had fallen from the coating, notwithstanding the appearance of having been removed at a later period than the first, were so closely cemented together, that the men could scarcely proceed. The only instrument they had to work with was a kind of hatchet or spade, which being rather thin, and only fit to cut the soft ground, could not stand much work among stones and mortar, which latter I suppose, as it fell from the pyramid, had been moistened by the dew, and gradually formed itself almost into one mass with the stones.

On the east side of the pyramid, we found the lower part of a large temple connected with the portico, and reaching within fifty feet of the basis of the pyramid. Its exterior walls were formed of enormous blocks of stone, as may now be seen. Some of the blocks in the porticoes are twenty-four feet high. The interior part of this temple was built with calcareous stones of various sizes, but many finely cut at the angles, and is probably much older than the exterior wall, which bears the appearance of as great antiquity as the pyramids. In order to find the basis of the pyramid on this side, and to ascertain whether there were any communication between it and the temple, I had to cut through all the material there accumulated, which rose above forty feet from the basis, and consisted of large blocks of stone and mortar, from the coating, as on the north side. At last we reached the basis, and I perceived a flat pavement cut out of the solid rock. I caused all that was before me to be cut in a right line from the basis of the pyramid to the temple, and traced the pavement quite to the back of it, so that there was evidently a spacious pavement from the temple to the pyramid; and I do not hesitate to declare my opinion, that the same pavement goes all round the pyramid. It appeared to me, that the sphinx, the temple, and the pyramid, were all three erected at the same time, as they all appeared to be in one line, and of equal antiquity. On the north side the work advanced toward the basis; a great number of large stones had been removed, and a great part of the face of the pyramid was uncovered, but still there was no appearance of any entrance, or the smallest mark to indicate that there ever had been one.

The Arabs had great confidence in the hopes I had excited among them, that if any entrance into the pyramid were found, I would give great bakshis, in addition to the advantage they would derive from other strangers. But after many vain expectations, and much hard labor in removing huge masses of stone, and cutting the mortar, which was so hard that their hatchets were nearly all broken, they began to flag in their prospect of finding any thing, and I was about to become an object of ridicule for making the attempt to penetrate a place, which appeared to them, as well as to more civilized people, a mass of solid stone. However, as long as I paid them they continued their work, though with much less zeal. My hopes did not forsake me, in spite of all the difficulties I saw, and the little appearance of making the discovery of an entrance into the pyramid. Still I observed, as we went on with our work, that the stones on that spot were not so consolidated as those on the sides of them, and this circumstance made me determine to proceed, till I should be persuaded that I was wrong in my conjecture. At last, on the 18th of February, aften sixteen days of fruitless labor, one of the Arabian workmen perceived a small chink between two stones of the pyramid. At this he was greatly rejoiced, thinking we had found the entrance so eagerly sought for. I perceived the aperture was small, but I thrust a long palm-stick into it upwards of two yards. Encouraged by this circumstance, the Arabs resumed their vigor on the work, and great hopes were entertained among them. I was aware, that the entrance to the pyramid could not be between two stones in this manner; but I was in hopes, that the aperture would furnish some clew by which the right entrance would be discovered. Proceeding farther, I perceived, that one of the stones, apparently fixed in the pyramid, was in fact loose. I had it removed the same day, and found an opening leading to the interior. This sort of .ough entrance was not more than three feet wide, and was choked up with smaller stones and sand, which being removed, it proved to be much wider within. A second and third day were employed in clearing this place; but the farther we advanced, the more materials we found. On the fourth day I observed, that sand and stones were falling from the upper part of this cavity, which surprised me not a little. At last I found, that there was a passage from the outside of the pyramid by a higher aperture, which apparently was thought to have had no communication with any cavity. When all the rubbish was taken out, and the place cleared, I continued the work in the lower part beneath our feet; and in two days more we came to an opening inward. Having made it wide enough, I took a candle in my hand, and, looking in, perceived a spacious cavity, of which I could not form any conjecture. Having caused the entrance to be cleared of the sand and stones, I found a tolerably spacious place, bending its course towards the center. It is evidently a forced passage, executed by some powerful hand, and appears intended to find a way to the center of the pyramid. Some of the stones, which are of an enormous size, are cut through, some have been taken out, and others are on the point of falling from their old places for want of support. Incredible must have been the labor in making such a cavity, and it is evident, that it was continued farther on towards the center; but the upper part had fallen in, and filled up the cavity to such a degree, that it was impossible for us to proceed any farther than a hundred feet. Half this distance from the entrance is another cavity, which descends forty feet in an irregular manner, but still turns toward the center, which no doubt was the point intended by the persons who made the excavation. To introduce many men to work in this place was dangerous, for several of the stones above our heads were on the point of falling; some were suspended only by their corners, which stuck between other stones, and with the least touch would have fallen, and crushed any one that happened to be under them. I set a few men to work, but was soon convinced of the impossibility of advancing any farther in that excavation. In one of the passages below, one of the men narrowly escaped being crushed to pieces. A large block of stone, no less than six feet long and four wide, fell from the top, while the man was digging under it; but fortunately it rested on two other stones, one on each side of him, higher than himself, as he was sitting at his work. The man was so incarcerated, that we had some difficulty in getting him out; yet, happily, he received no other injury than a slight bruise on his back. The falling of this stone moved many others in this passage: indeed, they were so situated, that I thought it prudent to retreat out of the pyramid, or we might have reason to repent when too late; for the danger was not only from what might fall upon us, but also from what might fall in our way, close up the passage, and thus bury us alive. My expectation in this passage was not great, as I perceived from the beginning it could not be the true entrance into the pyramid, though I had strong hopes that it would lead to some clew for the discovery of the real entrance; but, alas! it gave me none, and I remained as ignorant of it as I was before I began.

Having spent so many days at the pyramids without being discovered by any of the people at Cairo, I did not expect, that my retreat could be concealed much longer, as there were constantly Franks from Cairo making a Sunday's excursion to the pyramids, or travellers, who, of course, made it a point to see these wonders on their first arrival at the metropolis. In fact, the very day I was to have quitted this work, I perceived, in the afternoon, some people on the top of the first pyramid. I had no doubt they were Europeans, as the Arabs or Turks never go up, unless to accompany somebody, to gain money. They saw part of my men at work at the second pyramid, and concluded that none but Europeans could be conducting such an operation. They fired a pistol as a signal, and I returned another. Then they descended the angle which led towards us; and on their arrival proved to be Monsieur L'Abbé de Forbin, who had accompanied his cousin, the celebrated Count, into Egypt, but did not proceed higher. With him were the father superior of the convent of Terra Santa, Mr. Costa, an engineer, and Mr. Gaspard, vice-consul of France, by whom I was introduced to the Abbé. They all entered into the newly discovered passage; but it gave the Abbé less pleasure than a cup of coffee, which he honored me by accepting in my humble tent. Naturally, after such a visit, all the Franks in Cairo knew what I was doing; and not a day passed without my having some visitors.

I was determined to proceed still farther with my researches, the recent disappointment making me rather more obstinate than I was before. I had given a day's rest to the Arabs, which I dedicated to a closer inspection of the pyramid. It often happens, that a man is so much ingulfed in the pursuit of his views, as to be in danger of losing himself, if he do not quickly find the means either of an honorable retreat, or of attaining the accomplishment of his intended purpose. Such was my case. The success of my discovery of the false passage was considered as a failure. I cared little what was thought of it, but I was provoked at having been deceived by those marks, which led me to the forced passage, with the loss of so much time and labor. However, I did not despair. I strictly noticed the situation of the entrance into the first pyramid, and plainly saw, that it was not in the center of the pyramid. I observed that the passage ran in a straight line from the outside of the pyramid to the east side of the king's chamber; and this chamber being nearly in the center of the pyramid, the entrance consequently must be as far from the middle of the face as the distance from the center of the chamber to the east side of it.

Having made this clear and simple observation, I found, that, if there were any chamber at all in the second pyramid, the entrance or passage could not be on the spot where I had excavated, which was in the center, but calculating by the passage in the first pyramid, the entrance into the second would be near thirty feet to the east.

Satisfied with this calculation, I repaired to the second pyramid to examine the mass of rubbish. There I was not a little astonished when I perceived the same marks, which I had seen on the other spot in the center, about thirty feet distant from where I stood. This gave me no little delight, and hope returned to cherish my pyramidical brains. I observed in this spot also, that the stones and mortar were not so compact as on the east side, which mark had given me so much encouragement to proceed in the first attempt; but what increased my hopes was an observation I made on the exterior of the front where the forced passage is. I observed the stones had been removed several feet from the surface of the pyramid, which I ascertained by drawing a line with the coating above to the basis below, and found the concavity was inclined to be deeper towards the spot where I intended to make my new attempt. Any traveller, who shall hereafter visit the pyramids, may plainly perceive this concavity above the true entrance. Such has been the effect of two different hints; first my old guide from Thebes, I mean the spots where the stony matter is not so compact as the surrounding mass; and, secondly, the concavity of the pyramid over the place where the entrance might have been expected to be found, according to the distance of the entrance into the first pyramid from its center.

I immediately summoned the Arabs to work the next day. They were pleased at my recommencing the task, not in hopes of finding the entrance into the pyramid, but for the continuation of the pay they of course were to receive. As to expectation that the entrance might be found, they had none; and I often heard them utter, in a low voice, the word *"magnoon,"* in plain English, madman. I pointed out to the Arabs the spot where they had to dig, and such was my measurement, that I was right within two feet, in a straight direction, as to the entrance into the first passage; and I have the pleasure of reckoning this day as fortunate, being that on which I discovered the entrance into the great tomb of Psammethis at Thebes. The Arabs began their work, and the rubbish proved to be as hard as that of the first excavation, with this addition, that we found larger blocks of stone in our way, which had belonged to the pyramid, besides the falling of the coating. The stones increased in size as we went on.

A few days after the visit of the Abbé de Forbin I was surprised by the appearance of another European traveller. It was the Chevalier Frediani, who, on his return from the second cataract of the Nile, came to visit the great pyramids. I had known him at Thebes on his ascending the Nile, and was much pleased to see him, as I thought he might be an impartial spectator of the event of my operations, which in fact he was. He greatly approved of my undertaking, but after being two days with me was ready to take his departure. I suppose he had as much expectation, that I should open the pyramid, as the Arabs who named me the *magnoon*. It happened, that on the very day he was to set off for Cairo, I perceived in the excavation a large block of granite, inclining downward at the same angle as the passage into the first pyramid, and pointing towards the center. I requested the Chevalier to stay till the morrow, thinking perhaps he might have the pleasure of being one of the first who saw the entrance into the pyramid. He consented, and I was pleased to have a countryman of my own to be witness of what passed on this important occasion. The discovery of the first granite stone occurred on the 28th of February, and on the 1st of March we uncovered three large blocks of granite, two on each side, and one on the top, all in an inclined direction toward the center. My expectation and hope increased, as to all appearance, this must prove to be the object of my search. I was not mistaken, for on the next day, the 2nd of March, at noon, we came at last to the right entrance into the pyramid. The Arabs, whose expectation had also increased at the appearance of the three stones, were delighted at having found something new to show to the visitors, and get bakshis from them. Having cleared the front of the three stones, the entrance proved to be a passage four feet high, three feet six inches wide, formed of large blocks of granite, which descended towards the center for a hundred and four feet five inches at an angle of twenty-six degrees. Nearly all this passage was filled up with large stones, which had fallen from the upper part, and as the passage is inclined downwards, they slid on till some larger than the rest stopped the way.

I had much ado to have all the stones drawn out of the passage, which was filled up to the entrance of the chamber. It took the remainder of this day and part of the next to clear it, and at last we reached a portcullis. At first sight it appeared to be a fixed block of stone, which stared me in the face, and said *ne plus ultra,* putting an end to all my projects as I thought; for it made a close point with the groove at each side, and on the top it seemed as firm as those which formed the passage itself. On a close inspection however I perceived, that, at the bottom, it was raised about eight inches from the lower part of the groove, which is cut beneath to receive it; and I found, by this circumstance, that the large block before me was no more than a portcullis of granite, one foot three inches thick.

Having observed a small aperture at the upper part of the portcullis, I thrust a long piece of barley straw into it, and it entered upwards of three feet, which convinced me, that there was a vacuum ready to receive the portcullis. The raising of it was a work of no small consideration. The passage is only four feet high, and three feet six inches wide. When two men are in it abreast of each other they cannot move, and it required several men to raise a piece of granite not less than six feet high, five feet wide, and one foot three inches thick. The levers could not be very long, otherwise there was not space in the four feet height to work with them; and if they were short, I could not employ men enough to raise the portcullis.

The only method to be taken was, to raise it a little at a time; and by putting some stones in the grooves on each side, to support the portcullis while changing the fulcrum of the levers, it was raised high enough for a man to pass. An Arab then entered with a candle, and returned saying, that the place within was very fine. I continued to raise the portcullis, and at last made the entrance large enough to squeeze myself in; and after thirty days exertion I had the pleasure of finding myself in the way to the central chamber of one of the two great pyramids of Egypt, which have long been the admiration of beholders. The Chevalier Frediani followed me, and after passing under the portcullis we entered a passage not higher or wider than the first. It is twenty-two feet seven inches long, and the works including the portcullis occupy six feet eleven inches in all. Where the granite work finishes at the end of this passage, there is a perpendicular shaft of fifteen feet, and at each side of the passage, an excavation in the solid rock, one of which, on the right as you enter, runs thirty feet in an upward direction, approaching the end of the lower part of the forced passage. . . . Before us we had a long passage running in a horizontal direction toward the center. We descended the shaft by means of a rope. At the bottom of it I perceived another passage running downward at the same angle of 26° as that above, and toward the north. As my first object was the center of the pyramid, I advanced that way, and ascended an inclined passage, which brought me to a horizontal one, that led toward the center. I observed, that after we entered within the portcullis, the passages were all cut out of the solid rock. The passage leading toward the center is five feet eleven inches high, and three feet six inches wide.

As we advanced farther on we found the sides of this passage covered with arborizations of nitre; some projecting in ropes, some not unlike the skin of a white lamb, and others so long as to resemble an endive leaf. I reached the door at the center of a large chamber. I walked slowly two or three paces, and then stood still to contemplate the place where I was. Whatever it might be, I certainly considered myself in the center of that pyramid, which from time immemorial had been the subject of the obscure conjectures of many hundred travellers, both ancient and modern. My torch, formed of a few wax candles, gave but a faint light; I could, however, clearly distinguish the principal objects. I naturally turned my eyes to the west end of the chamber, looking for the sarcophagus, which I strongly expected to see in the same situation as that in the first pyramid; but I was disappointed when I saw nothing there. The chamber has a painted ceiling; and many of the stones had been removed from their places, evidently by some one in search of treasure. On my advancing toward the west end, I was agreeably surprised to find, that there was a sarcophagus buried on a level with the floor.

By this time the Chevalier Frediani had entered also; and we took a general survey of the chamber, which I found to be forty-six feet three inches long, sixteen feet three inches wide, and twenty-three feet six inches high. It is cut out of solid rock from the floor to the roof, which is composed of large blocks of calcareous stone, meeting in the center, and forming a roof of the same slope as the pyramid itself. The sarcophagus is eight feet long, three feet six inches wide, and two feet three inches deep in the inside. It is surrounded by large blocks of granite, apparently to prevent its removal, which could not be effected without great labor. The lid had been broken at the side, so that the sarcophagus was half open. It is of the finest granite; but, like the other in the first pyramid, there is not one hieroglyphic on it.

Looking at the inside, I perceived a great quantity of earth and stones, but did not observe the bones among the rubbish till the next day, as my attention was principally bent in search of some inscription that would throw light on the subject of this pyramid. We examined every part of the walls, and observed many scrawls executed with charcoal, but in unknown characters, and nearly imperceptible. They rubbed off into dust at the slightest touch; and on the wall at the west end of the chamber I perceived an inscription in Arabic . . . and the various interpretations given of it compel me to explain some points, which will perhaps lead to a satisfactory explanation. It appears to me, that all the difficulty lies in the last letters of the inscription, which are supposed to be obscure. This is indeed the fact; but I must say, that these letters were so blotted on the wall, that they were scarcely visible. The transcriber was a Copt, whom I had brought from Cairo for the purpose, as I would not trust to my own pen; and not being satisfied of his protestations of accuracy, though it was copied under my own eyes, I invited many other persons, who were considered as the best skilled in the Arabic language of any in Cairo, and requested them to compare the copy with the original on the wall. They found it perfectly correct, except the concluding word, which indeed appeared obscure; but if it be considered how much that word resembles the right one, we shall find a correct sense, and the whole inscription made out.

### Translation of the Inscription by Mr. Salame.

"The Master Mohammed Ahmed, lapicide, has opened them; and the Master Othman attended this (*opening*); and the King Alij Mohammed at first (*from the beginning*) to the closing up."

I must add, that the circumstance of the pyramid having been again closed up agrees with what I have said of my finding it so.

On several parts of the wall the nitre had formed many beautiful arborizations like those in the passage, but much larger and stronger. Some were six inches long, resembling in shape a large endive leaf, as I mentioned before. Under one of the blocks that had been removed, I found something like the thick part of a hatchet, but so rusty, that it had lost its shape. At the north and south sides are two holes, which run in an horizontal direction, like those that are seen in the first pyramid, but higher up.

Returning out of this chamber we reached the passage below. At the bottom of the perpendicular shaft were so many stones as nearly to choke up its entrance, and after removing these we found the passage running to the north, at the same inclination as above, an angle of 26°. This passage is forty-eight feet six inches in length, when it joins an horizontal passage of fifty-five feet still running north. Half-way up this passage on the right is a recess eleven feet long and six feet deep. On the left, opposite to it, is another passage, running twenty-two feet with a descent of 26° towards the west. Before we proceeded any farther toward the north, we descended this passage, and entered a chamber thirty-two feet long, nine feet nine inches wide, and eight feet six inches high. This chamber contains many small blocks of stone, some not more than two feet in length. It has a pointed roof like that before mentioned, though it is cut out of the solid rock; for it is to be understood, as I before observed, that, after we entered through the portcullis, all the passages, and the large chamber, as high as the roof, are cut out of the solid rock of calcareous stone. On the walls and roof of this chamber are several unknown inscriptions, as there are in the upper chamber. They are perhaps Coptic. Reascending into the horizontal passage, at the end of it we found grooves for a portcullis like the former; but the stone of granite which served for this purpose had been taken down, and is to be seen under the rubbish and stones near the place. Passing the portcullis we entered into a passage, which ascended in a direction parallel with that above. This passage runs up forty-seven feet six inches. Here we found a large block of stone, placed there from the upper part; and by calculation I found, that this passage ran out of the pyramid at its basis, as, from the upper part of this square block, I could perceive other stones, which filled up the passage to the entrance, so that this pyramid has two entrances to it. Half-way up the horizontal passage, which leads into the large chamber, is some mason's work; but I believe it to be only the filling up of a natural cavity in the rock.

Having made all my observations, we came out of the pyramid with no small degree of satisfaction; and I was highly gratified with the result of my labor, of very little more than a month, the expense of which did not amount in all to £150, though I had accomplished a task, which was supposed would have required several thousands.

The Chevalier Frediani went to Cairo the same day, and the news of the opening of the pyramid soon brought the Franks to visit its interior. As I had no fear that the Arabian women would break the pyramid, I left the entrance open (*pro bono publico*); and in that place where the perpendicular descent, just inside the portcullis, is, I made a stone step for the accommodation of visitors, leaving half of the passage to enter into the lower chamber.

A young man of the name of Pieri, employed in the counting-house of Briggs and Walmas in Cairo, came the next day to visit the pyramid, and, having rummaged the rubbish inside of the sarcophagus, found a piece of bone, which we supposed to belong to a human skeleton. On searching farther, we found several pieces, which, having been sent to London, proved to be the bones of a bull. Some consequential persons, however, who would not scruple to sacrifice a point in history, rather than lose a *bon mot*, thought themselves mighty clever in baptizing the said bones those of a cow, merely to raise a joke. So much for their taste for antiquity. It has been stated also, that it might be supposed these large sarcophagi were made to contain the bones of bulls, as the sarcophagus which we found in the tombs of the kings at Thebes was of enormous size, and more fit for a bull than a human body. I cannot agree in this opinion, however, for if the person who made the observation had an opportunity of seeing and examining the cases and sarcophagi in which the Egyptians were buried, he would find, that the better classes of people had cases within cases, some nearly double the size requisite to contain one person; and it is natural therefore to suppose, that the kings of Egypt had more cases than one or two, consequently the sarcophagus, which was the outer case, must have been much larger than the rest, to contain them all.

Outside of the pyramid I observed the rock surrounding it on the north and west sides to be on a level with the upper part of the chamber; and, as the rock is evidently cut all round, it appeared to me, that the stones taken from it must have been applied to the erection of the pyramid. Accordingly I am of opinion, that the stones which seem to form these enormous edifices were not all taken from the east side of the Nile, as is supposed and mentioned by ancient writers. I cannot conceive why the Egyptians should be thought so simple, as to fetch stones at seven or eight miles distance, and across the Nile, when they could have them from much nearer points; indeed from the very spot where the pyramids stand. It is evident, that stones of an enormous size have been cut out of the very rocks around the pyramids; and for what purpose were these stones extracted? It might as well be asserted, that they were cut to build old Babylon of Egypt, or to fill up the vacancies in the quarries of the Mokattam. If any traveller will go within less than half a mile of the pyramids, particularly on the east and south sides, he may see many places, where the rock has been formerly quarried to a great length; and he will find that there is stone enough to build many other pyramids if required. It is true, that Herodotus says the stones to erect the pyramids were brought from quarries on the other side of the Nile; but I firmly believe he was misinformed on this subject, unless what he asserts is to be understood of the granite alone. And as to the causeways in front of the pyramids, said to have been made to convey the stones for the erection of these masses, I believe they were intended for the accommodation of visitors, particularly at the time of high Nile; for if they were only to convey stones, the labor of making them must have been nearly equal to the erection of the pyramids.

So much has been already said about the pyramids, that very little is left to observe respecting them. Their great appearance of antiquity certainly leads us to suppose, that they must have been constructed at an earlier period than any other edifices to be seen in Egypt. It is somewhat singular, that Homer does not mention them; but this is no proof that they did not exist in his time; on the contrary, it may be sup-

posed they were so generally known, that he thought it useless to speak of them. It appears, that in the time of Herodotus
as little was known of the second pyramid as before the late
opening, with this exception, that in his time the second pyramid was nearly in the state in which it was left when closed
by the builders, who must have covered the entrance with
the coating, so that it might not be perceived. But at the time
I was fortunate enough to find my way into it, the entrance
was concealed by the rubbish of the coating, which must have
been nearly perfect at the time of Herodotus: notwithstanding
this we were as much in the dark in this present age, as he was
in his. We know, however, now, that it has been opened by
some of the rulers or chiefs of Egypt; a fact that affords no
small satisfaction to the inquirer on the subject of these monuments. Some persons, who would rather let this circumstance
remain in obscurity, regretted, that I should have found the
inscription on the wall, which proved it to have been opened
at so late a period, as very little more than a thousand years
ago; but I beg them to recollect, that the present opening has
not only made known this very interesting circumstance, but
has thrown much light on the manner in which these enormous
masses were erected, as well as explained the occasion of
them.

The circumstance of having chambers and a sarcophagus
(which undoubtedly contained the remains of some great
personage), so uniform with those in the old pyramid, I think
leaves very little question, but that they were erected as
sepulchres; and I really wonder that any doubt has ever existed, considering what could be learned from the first pyramid,
which has been so long open. This contains a spacious chamber with a sarcophagus; the passages are of such dimensions
as to admit nothing larger than the sarcophagus; they had
been closely shut up by large blocks of granite from within,
evidently to prevent the removal of that relic. Ancient authors
are pretty well agreed in asserting, that these monuments
were erected to contain the remains of two brothers, Cheops
and Cephren, kings of Egypt. They are surrounded by other

smaller pyramids intermixed with mausoleums on burial-grounds. Many mummy-pits have been continually found there; yet with all these proofs, it has been asserted, that they were erected for many other purposes than the true one, and nearly as absurd as that they served for granaries.

Some consider them as built for astronomical purposes, but there is nothing in their construction to favor this supposition. Others maintain, that they were meant for the performance of holy ceremonies by the Egyptian priests. Any thing in short for the sake of contradiction, or to have something new to say, finds its advocate. If the ancient authors had advanced, that they were erected for treasuries, the moderns would have agreed perhaps more in conformity with the truth, that they were made for sepulchres; and they would not have failed to see plainly those circumstances, which clearly prove the facts, and which are not noticed as they ought to be. I will agree with others thus far, that the Egyptians, in erecting these enormous masses, did not fail to make their sides due north and south, and consequently, as they are square, due east and west. Their inclination too is such to give light to the north side at the time of the solstice. But even all this does not prove in the least, that they were erected for astronomical purposes; though it is to be observed, that the Egyptians connected astronomy with their religious ceremonies, as we found various zodiacs, not only among the temples, but in their tombs also.

By the measurement I took of the second pyramid I found it to be as follows.

|  | Feet |
|---|---|
| The basis ................................................................................ | 684 |
| Apotome or central line down the front, from the top to the basis | 568 |
| Perpendicular ......................................................................... | 456 |
| Coating from the top to the place where it ends ........................... | 140 |

The circumstances of not finding hieroglyphics in or out of it makes is appear, that they were erected before this mode of writing was invented; for, strange as it may seem, not a single hieroglyphic is found in all these enormous masses.

Yet I must beg leave to remark a circumstance, which perhaps will lead to the conjecture, that it might not have been the custom of the Egyptians in that part of the country, who might perhaps be even of a different religion from their countrymen, to put hieroglyphics on their monuments; for there are many mausoleums round the pyramids, and some of them very extensive, without an hieroglyphic to be seen within or without them; and I observed, that those which contain chambers with hieroglyphics are evidently of a later date than the former. All this would seem to prove, that till a certain period subsequent to the building of the pyramids hieroglyphics were not known. But what can be said when I assure the reader, that in one of these mausoleums, which stands on the west of the first pyramid, and which is so decayed that it has fallen in, and is in a very ruinous state, I saw and made others observe some hieroglyphics and figures reversed in one of the blocks, which formed that mausoleum; and the hieroglyphics so preserved within, as if they were to be hidden from the view? It certainly must be concluded, that this stone had been employed in a building, which was adorned with hieroglyphics, and consequently proves, that they were known previous to the erection of these mausoleums, though they were without any of these ornaments or inscriptions. This being the case, it may be supposed that the people who built the pyramids were of the same way of thinking as those who built the mausoleums; consequently nothing can be inferred respecting the age of the pyramids from the circumstance of their not having any hieroglyphics.

It has been supposed, that the first pyramid, or that of Cheops, was not coated. I must agree in this opinion, for there is not the slightest mark remaining of any coating. As to the coating of the second pyramid, I had an opportunity of investigating this subject in the excavation I made on the east side of it, where I found the lower part as rough as any of the upper, below the remaining coating, which confirms the account of Herodotus in this respect, who says, that the coating was begun from above; and I believe myself that it was never quite finished to the basis, for if it had, I should have met with some below, as the accumulation of rubbish over the basis would have kept the stones in their places, or at least enough of them to show there was a coating, as was the case in the third pyramid, of which I shall have to speak presently.

It is supposed, that the inundation of the Nile surrounded the pyramids, so that they remained like islands. I cannot say that was not so, for the situation of the pyramids is like an island of rocks, separated from those on the west only by a valley of sand, which might naturally have been accumulated by the wind in the course of so many centuries. I think we cannot have a stronger proof of this than the sphinx itself, the basis of which is so much below the present surface, that if all the sand around the pyramids were on a level with it, I have no doubt the Nile must have run round them, which probably was the case in the early ages.

Having thus finished my operation on the second pyramid, I felt a great inclination to have a cursory view of the third. I observed, that some one had made an attempt to penetrate it by excavations on the east side. I commenced my labors on the north side, and after removing a great quantity of materials, found a considerable accumulation of enormous blocks of granite, which had evidently formed the coating.—Proceeding yet lower, as I cleared away the rubbish I found, that part of the coating still remained in its place down to the bases. The removal of these blocks would evidently have brought me to the entrance into the pyramid, but it required more money and time than I could spare.

By this time the consul, who was at Thebes, hearing of the opening of the pyramid, wrote to me, that he was coming down the Nile; and at the same time Lord Belmore and family arrived at Cairo. It is somewhat singular, and I mention it with much satisfaction, that his Lordship arrived at Thebes one month after my discovery of the celebrated tomb of Psammethis, and was the first British traveller who entered it. On his return from Nubia, he arrived at Cairo a little more than a month after my opening the second pyramid, and was the first British traveller who entered this also. His Lordship and family had been at Thebes for some time, and had accumulated no small collection of antiquities; indeed, I esteem it the largest ever made by any occasional traveller. . . .

The Earl and family set off for Jerusalem by way of the Desert; and I prepared for my departure from Thebes, my old residence, which I knew better than any other place in Egypt. A few days after, the consul arrived, and, in half an hour after him, Colonel Fitzclarence, with despatches from India for England. The consul, Mr. Salt, would have been kind enough to have paid all the expenses I had incurred in opening the pyramid; but this I positively refused, as I thought it would not be fair and right that he should pay for what he had nothing to do with.

I had the pleasure of accompanying the Colonel in a visit to the pyramid, as described by himself in his account of his journey from India to England through Egypt. He had suffered many hardships on his journey, but did not appear fatigued in the least. His short stay in Cairo did not permit me to write a full account of my labors; but at night I made a hasty sketch as well as I could, and addressed it to the Antiquarian Society of London, which he was kind enough to take to England for me. Mr. Salt, the consul, took the same opportunity of sending an official account of my operations in Egypt and Nubia to the ministers in England, I suppose because he had no opportunity of sending any correct account before that time.

My next and principal object was to make a small collection on my own account, and to take drawings of the tomb of Psammethis, with impressions in wax of all the figures, emblems, and hieroglyphics, the whole of which are in basso relievo; noting the colors exactly as in the originals, so as to enable me to erect a facsimile in any part of Europe. This project deserved my serious consideration, not only in calculating the time that it would require to complete it, but in the expense I must incur. However, though I was only in Cairo, I did not want means of finding supplies for what I intended to execute, and in a few days all was ready for my departure on my third voyage up the Nile; when, having arranged my affairs with the consul, I set off for my old habitation among the tombs of Thebes.

# 2. FLINDERS PETRIE:

# *A Lifetime of Digging*

As for the pyramids, there is nothing to wonder in at them so much as the fact that so many men could be found degraded enough to spend their lives constructing a tomb for some ambitious booby, whom it would have been wiser and manlier to have drowned in the Nile, and then given his body to the dogs.

—THOREAU, *Walden.*

Nearly three quarters of a century separates the work of Belzoni from that of Flinders Petrie. It was a time of great changes, both in archaeology in general and Egyptology in particular. The mounds of Mesopotamia had been explored; Schliemann had found Troy; hieroglyphics and cuneiform had both been deciphered. And some glimmerings of archaeological method had developed out of the chaos of indiscriminate digging.

It was William Matthew Flinders Petrie, however, who first put archaeology and its subdivision Egyptology on a fully scientific basis. Many men had come to dig in Egypt after Belzoni, and some of them, such as the Frenchman Auguste Mariette, were diligent and careful workers. They worked, though, within the earlier tradition. Flinders Petrie wrote of the highly respected Mariette's work, "Nothing was done with any uniform plan, work is begun and left unfinished, no regard is paid to future requirements of exploration and no civilized or labor-saving appliances are used. It is sickening to see the rate at which everything is being destroyed, and the little regard paid to preservation."

Flinders Petrie transformed Egyptology. He spent 46 of his 89 years in Egypt and surrounding lands, and his long life extended through the entire developmental period of archaeology. He was born in 1853, in Charlton, Kent. His father was greatly interested in Egyptology, chiefly in the alleged mystic properties of the Great Pyramid, and from boyhood on, young Flinders Petrie dreamed of exploring Egypt. It appears that his ideas on technique were formed early, too: he wanted to study Egypt methodically, to excavate with care and precision, to measure exactly, to record everything as it came from the ground. "The earth ought to be pared away inch by inch to see all that is in it and how it lies," the eight-year-old Flinders Petrie declared.

His first archaeological work was done in England, at Stonehenge. He published his results in 1880, when he was 27, and toward the end of that year headed for Egypt. He was appalled at the quality of the work being conducted there. "It was like a house on fire," he said, "so rapid was the destruction going on."

Mariette, the doyen of Egyptologists, died the year of Flinders Petrie's arrival, and the way was clear for the young Englishman to introduce his new methods. He worked first at the Pyramids, intending to test his father's much-loved theories about their numerical properties. Soon he lost all interest in numerology—"the ugly little fact killed the beautiful theory"— and turned to excavation.

There was nothing colorful about him. Belzoni, perhaps, might have been bored by the quiet little man. But, year after year, Flinders Petrie poured forth his excavation reports, building a bibliography that ultimately would total 90 volumes. He did much of his work in the Nile Delta, where little digging had occurred. He uncovered the Greek colonial town Naukratis, the older city of Tanis, and many other untouched sites. He discovered pre-dynastic tombs and tombs of the First and Second Dynasties, thereby filling a 400-year gap in Egyptian history. His other archaeological contributions were numerous and significant, although he avoided the spectacular and concentrated on work that would answer important historical questions. Flinders Petrie's primary concern was not in uncovering showy displays for museums, but in recovering from the jaws of time the historical information that would clarify the records of the past.

He is noted, therefore, as much for his methodological accomplishments as for his actual findings. He dug, compared, dated, dug again. He recorded everything with minute attention to detail. His techniques provided the foundation for the work that followed after.

In 1892, Flinders Petrie was appointed full professor of Egyptology at University College, London. It was a post he held for forty-one years, though how he managed to maintain his chair while still undertaking the enormous volume of writing and field work he did is a mystery that parallels the construction of the Pyramids. In 1893, the Religious Tract Society of London published a slim volume called *Ten Years' Digging in Egypt (1881-1891)*, which became the most popular of his many books. Four of that book's thirteen chapters are reprinted here.

Petrie's other books include two more that are largely autobiographical: *Methods and Aims in Archaeology* (1904) and *Seventy Years of Archaeology* (1931). He left Egypt in 1926, and did little field work after that year, but he continued writing until his death in 1942.

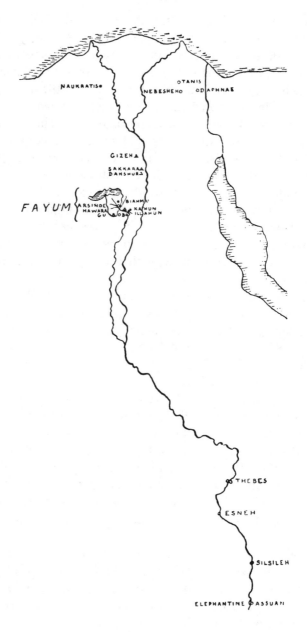

Flinders Petrie's Egyptian Excavation Sites, 1881-1891

# A LIFETIME OF DIGGING

W hen, in the end of 1880, I first started for Egypt, I had long been preparing for the expedition; during a couple of years before that measuring instruments, theodolites, rope-ladders, and all the *impedimenta* for scientific work, had been prepared and tested. To start work under circumstances so different from those of any European country, and where many customary appliances were not to be obtained, required necessarily much prearrangement and consideration; though on the whole my subsequent experience has been that of decreasing the baggage, and simplifying one's requirements.

The first consideration on reaching Egypt was where to be housed. In those days there was no luxurious hotel close to the pyramids; if any one needed to live there, they must either live in a tomb or in the Arab village. As an English engineer had left a tomb fitted with door and shutters I was glad to get such accommodation. When I say a tomb, it must be understood to be the upper chamber where the Egyptian fed his ancestors with offerings, not the actual sepulchre. And I had three rooms, which had belonged to separate tombs originally; the thin walls of rock which the economical Egyptian left between his cuttings, had been broken away, and so I had a doorway in the middle into my living-room, a window on one side for my bedroom, and another window opposite for a store-room. I resided here for a great part of two years; and often when in draughty houses, or chilly tents, I have wished myself back in my tomb. No place is so equable in heat and cold, as a room cut out in solid rock; it seems as good as a fire in cold weather, and deliciously cool in the heat.

I lived then, as I have since in Egypt, independent of servants. The facilities of preserved provisions, and the convenience of petroleum stoves, enable one to do without the annoyance of having some one about meddling with every-

From *Ten Years' Digging in Egypt* (London: The Religious Tract Society, 1893) by W. M. Flinders Petrie

thing. I had one of the most intelligent men of the place, Ali Gabri, to help me with the work, and his nephew and slave used to sleep in the next tomb as my guards at night. Such was my first taste of sweet independence from civilization.

The object in view for which the work was undertaken was to decisively test the various theories concerning the pyramids, which were then being widely discussed on very insufficient knowledge. If all, or any, of these theories were correct, there were some very tough questions to be picked over between different parties; but the first question to be settled was whether the theories agreed with the actual facts of the case, as if they did not there was no need of further discussion. They must pass the test of fact before they could be further considered on the grounds of their abstract probability or metaphysical coherence. One of the most obvious of all the facts, and most deeply concerned in the various theories, was the actual size of the great pyramid; yet this was not known with any accuracy, the best measurements varying by several feet. Most of the theories involved the notion of extreme accuracy of workmanship, yet we were entirely ignorant of the amount of accuracy in the form of the pyramid, and in most of its internal construction.

It may not be amiss here to point out what is the meaning of accuracy. One often hears that something is 'quite accurate.' If I ask a workman if his work is accurate, he will indignantly refer to his footrule to prove it; but if you were to ask if his footrule is accurate he would doubt your sanity. What is accuracy for one purpose is inaccuracy for another. Children build castles on the sand, and make them perhaps tidy enough; but their accuracy would not do for laying out a garden; nor would the garden bed quite do to regulate the straightness of a tennis court. When a house is planned, still further particularity is needed for the accuracy of its squareness and straightness; and yet the joiner needs a better straight edge than the bricklayer. In turn the joiner's ideas would never suffice for the accuracy of putting together a Forth bridge, with its lengths of furlongs of steel, needed to exactly fit into place. And even beyond that, the telescope maker, dividing his circles, or polishing his object glasses, must attend to quantities which are quite beyond the accuracies of the engineer. There are as many kinds of accuracy as there are of cleanliness, from the cleanness of a clean-swept path, up to the absolute lifelessness and chemical purity of some tedious preparation in the laboratory.

There is, therefore, no such thing as absolute accuracy; what is called accuracy in each business is that amount of inaccuracy which is insignificant. If we want to understand what kind of precision the ancients aimed at, our errors in examining their work must be so small as to be insignificant by the side of their errors. If they went to the nearest hundredth of an inch, we must go to the nearest thousandth, in order to know what their ideas of accuracy were.

The main work of the first season, therefore, consisted in making a very precise triangulation all over the hill of Gizeh; including points around all the three pyramids, and on the temples and walls belonging to them. A fine theodolite was used, by which single seconds of angle could be read; and the observations were repeated so many times, that if I finished the work at a single station in one day I was well satisfied. The result of all this mass of checked observations, after duly reducing and computing, was that there was scarcely a point about which one quarter inch of uncertainty remained, and most of the points were fixed to within one-tenth of an inch. These points were, however, only arbitrary marks put on suitable spots of the rock; and it needed a good deal of less elaborate work to connect these with the traces of the ancient constructions near them. The second season I obtained permission from Prof. Maspero to search for the ancient casing and points of construction of the pyramids. Many points were found easily enough; but some required long and dangerous work. To reach the casing, which still remains at the middle of each side of the great pyramid, was a hard matter; it was heaped over with broken chips a dozen to twenty feet deep, and they lay so loosely that they soon fell into any hole that we dug. It was needful therefore to begin with a very wide space, and gradually taper the hole, walling the sides roughly with loose blocks. Thus we succeeded in finding the casing on each of the three sides, where it was as yet unknown; the north casing having been cleared by a huge excavation of Col. Vyze over forty years before. These holes were very ticklish places, make them as we would; the Arabs dared not work them, and I had to get Negroes to face the business. As it was, we could not venture to knock a bit of the stone, for fear of the vibration loosening the sides; and I was all but buried once, when—just as I had come out of the bottom of the hole—many tons of stones went pouring down the pit from the loose stuff above.

At the third pyramid the difficulty was varied; there the pyramid was encumbered with loose blocks lying on a bed of sand. So soon then as we dug into the sand, the blocks came sliding down into our hole. But here the matter was settled by adding more stones, and so wedging all the blocks around into a ring; thus they balanced around the hole, and kept each other out.

The casing of the third pyramid has never been finished.

The outer sides of the granite blocks were left with an excess of stone, in order to protect them in transport from Assuan, and this was never removed by dressing down, as had been intended. Thus in some examples the stone sticks out far beyond where the face was to be. In the granite temple the same method was followed, but there the wall was dressed, and hence each stone at the corners of the chambers turns a little way round the adjacent walls, so that the corner is cut out of solid stone all the way up.

The temple of the third pyramid is the most complete, and gives the best notion of the enclosures around the cell or chamber, in which the offerings to the deceased king were presented. This view is from the top of the pyramid, looking down into it. At the end of its causeway are a few trees, and a hill on the right, with remains of another causeway leading from it to the plain.

Of the inside of the pyramids there were already numerous

measurements recorded, which showed that small differences and errors existed in the work; but some fresh and more accurate methods of examination were needed. Instead then of simply measuring from wall to wall, and remaining in ignorance of where the discrepancies lay, I always used plumb-lines for measuring all upright faces, and a levelling instrument for all horizontal surfaces. By hanging a plumb-line in each corner of a room, and measuring from it to the walls at many parts of the height, and then observing the distances of the plumb-lines on the floor, it is easy to find the dimensions of the room at any level, and to know exactly where the faults of construction lie. The same principle gives us the readiest way of examining a solid, such as a sarcophagus; and we can thus, in a few hours, do more than in as many days' work with elaborate apparatus. Some thread, and a piece of wax to stick it on with, are all that is needed beside the plain measuring rods.

The results of thus attacking the subject were, that on the one hand most brilliant workmanship was disclosed, while on the other hand it was intermingled with some astonishing carelessness and clumsiness. The laying out of the base of the great pyramid of Khufu is a triumph of skill; its errors, both in length and in angles, could be covered by placing one's thumb on them; and to lay out a square of more than a furlong in the side (and with rock in the midst of it, which prevented any diagonal checks being measured) with such accuracy shows surprising care. The work of the casing stones which remain is of the same class; the faces are so straight and so truly square, that when the stones were built together the film of mortar left between them is on an average not thicker than one's thumb nail, though the joint is a couple of yards long; and the levelling of them over long distances has not any larger errors. In the inside of the pyramid the same fine work is seen: the entrance passage joints are in many cases barely visible when searched for; in the Queen's chamber, when the encrusting salt is scraped away, the joints are found with cement not thicker than a sheet of paper; while in the King's chamber the granite courses have been dressed to a fine equality, not

Tomb at Gizeh Used as Flinders Petrie's Residence

varying more than a straw's breadth in a furlong length of blocks.

Side by side with this splendid work are the strangest mistakes. After having levelled the casing so finely, the builders made a hundred times the error in levelling the shorter length of the King's chamber, so that they might have done it far better by just looking at the horizon. After having dressed the casing joints so beautifully, they left the face of the wall in the grand gallery rough chiselled. The design was changed, and a rough shaft was cut from the side of the gallery, down through the building and the rock, to the lower end of the entrance passage. The granite in the ante-chamber is left without its final dressing. And the kernel of the whole, the sarcophagus, has much worse work in it than in the building, or than in other sarcophagi of the same period. The meaning of this curious discrepancy seems to be that the original architect, a true master of accuracy and fine methods, must have ceased to superintend the work when it was but half done. His personal influence gone, the training of his school was not sufficient to carry out the remainder of the building in the first style. Thus the base and the casing around it, the building of the Queen's chamber, and the preparation of the granite for the King's chamber, must all have had the master's eye; but the carelessness of the pupils appears so soon as the control was removed. Mere haste will not account for egregious mistakes, such as that of the King's chamber level, which the skillful architect would have remedied by five minutes' observation. This suggests that the exquisite workmanship often found in the early periods, did not so much depend on a large school or wide-spread ability, as on a few men far above their fellows, whose every touch was a triumph. In this way we can reconcile it with the crude, and often clumsy, work in building and sculpture found in the same ages. There were no trades union rules against 'besting one's mates' in those days, any more than in any business at present where real excellence is wanted.

The results were decidedly destructive for the theories. The fundamental length of the base of the pyramid does not agree to any of the theoretical needs: and though no doubt some comfort has been extracted from hypothetical lengths of what the pyramid base would be if continued down to levels below the pavement (such as the different sockets), yet no such bases ever existed, nor could even be guessed at or theorised on, so long as the pyramid base was intact, as the sockets were entirely covered by casing and pavement. Various other theories fare as badly; and the only important one which is well established is that the angle of the outside was such as to make the base circuit equal to a circle struck by the height as a radius. . . .

The second pyramid was built by Khafra. His name was first found with it on the piece of a mace-head of white stone, which I found in the temple. The form is here completed from another head of the twelfth dynasty; and drawings of maces from Medum show the head and stick entire. In accuracy Khafra's work is inferior to that of Khufu. The errors of the pyramid length are double, and of angle quadruple that found in the earlier work, and the bulk of its masonry is far rougher. But the sarcophagus in it is of much better work, without any mistakes, and generally showing more experience and ability. The third pyramid, of Menkaura, is again inferior to the second, in both its outer form and internal work. It has moreover been most curiously altered; originally intended to be of small size, it has been greatly enlarged, not by repeated coatings, but at one operation. The original entrance passage was abandoned, and the chamber was deepened, another passage cut from the inside outwards so as to emerge lower down, and another chamber excavated below the level of the first, and lined with granite.

Some very usual fallacies with regard to the pyramids were also disposed of. The passages are commonly supposed to have been blocked up by plugs of stone; whereas in both the great and second pyramids there is proof in the passages that no such blocks ever existed. The entrances are supposed to have been concealed by the solid masonry; whereas at Dahshur, and in Strabo's account of the great pyramid, it is evident that a flap-door of stone filled the passage mouth, and allowed of its being passed. The pyramids are supposed to have been built by continuous additions during a king's life, and ended only by his death; whereas there is no evidence of this in any of them, and it is clearly disproved by the construction and arrangement of the interiors; the plan was entire originally, and the whole structure begun at once. The sarcophagi are often supposed to have been put in to the pyramids at the king's burial, with his body inside; whereas in the great and second pyramids they will not pass through the passages, and must have been built in. The casing is supposed to have been all built in the rough, and cut to its slope afterwards; whereas the remaining blocks at the base slightly differ in angle side by side, proving that they were dressed before building in.

Besides examining the pyramids, the remains of the temple of the great pyramid were cleared, and the granite temple of Khafra was thoroughly measured and planned. But perhaps the most interesting part of the subject was tracing how the work was done. The great barracks of the workmen were found, behind the second pyramid, capable of housing four thousand men; and such was probably the size of the trained staff of skilled masons employed on the pyramid building. Besides these a large body of mere labourers were needed to move the stones; and this was probably done during the inundation, when water carriage is easier, and the people have no work. Herodotos gives the echo of this, when he says that the relays of labourers only worked for three months at a time. It would be quite practicable to build the great pyramid in the time, and with the staff of labourers assigned by Herodotos.

Tools are needed as well as labour; and the question of what tools were used is now settled by evidence, to which modern engineers cordially agree. I found repeatedly that the hard stones, basalt, granite, and diorite, were sawn; and that the saw was not a blade, or wire, used with a hard powder, but was set with fixed cutting points, in fact, a jewelled saw. These saws must have been as much as nine feet in length, as the cuts run lengthwise on the sarcophagi. One of the most usual tools was the tubular drill, and this was also set with fixed cutting points; I have a core from inside a drill hole, broken away in the working, which shows the spiral grooves produced by the cutting points as they sunk down into the material; this is of red granite, and there has been no flinching or jumping of the tool; every crystal, quartz, or felspar, has been cut through in the most equable way, with a clean irresistible cut. An engineer, who knows such work with diamond drills as well as any one, said to me, 'I should be proud to turn out such a finely cut core now;' and truth to tell, modern drill cores cannot hold a candle to the Egyptians; by the side of the ancient work they look wretchedly scraped out and irregular. That such hard cutting points were known and used is proved by clean cut fine hieroglyphs on diorite, engraved without a trace of scraping; and by the lathe work, of which I found pieces of turned bowls with the tool lines on them, and positive proof that the surface had not been ground out. The lathe tools were fixed as in modern times, to sweep regular arcs from a centre; and the work is fearless and powerful, as in a flat diorite table with foot, turned in one piece; and also surpassingly delicate, as in a bowl of diorite, which around the body is only as thick as stout cord. The great granite sarcophagi were sawn outside, and hollowed by cutting rows of tube drill holes, as may be seen in the great pyramid. No doubt much hammer-dressing was also used, as in all periods; but the fine work shows the marks of just such tools as we have only now re-invented. We can thus understand, far more than before, how the marvellous works of the Egyptians were executed; and further insight only shows plainer the true skill and ability of which they were masters in the earliest times that we can trace.

After a year in England, for the working out and publication of the survey at the pyramids, described in the last chapter, I undertook to excavate for the Egypt Exploration Fund. And as great things were then expected from Tanis, and a special fund of £1000 was in course of being raised for its clearance, the most desirable course was to ascertain what prospects really existed there. A preliminary exploring trip was made to several places in the Delta, in course of which I discovered Naukratis; and as soon as the marshes had somewhat dried I went in February to Tanis. It is an out-of-the-way place, inaccessible except by water during some months, twenty miles from a post or station; on three sides the marshy plains stretch away to the horizon, only a little cultivation existing on the south. When I arrived the mounds were almost impassable for the mud, and continual storms threatened my tent. But gradually I built a house on the top of the mounds, and from thence looked down over the work on one side, and over the village on the other.

Tanis is a great ring of mounds, around the wide plain in which lie the temple ruins. And the first day I went over it I saw that the temple site was worked out; the limits of the ruins had been reached, and no more statues or buildings should be hoped for, by the side of what was already known. But such were the large expectations about the site, that I had to prove the case, by a great amount of fruitless trenching in all directions. The only monuments that we unearthed were far out of the temple, in a Ptolemaic shrine; this contained a fine stele of Ptolemy II and Arsinoe, which was entirely gilt when discovered, and two or three other steles, the recess containing the large stele being flanked by two sphinxes. The main stele and sphinxes are now in the British Museum.

But though digging was not productive in the temple, yet I found two important monuments which had been exposed by Mariette's excavators, and yet were never noticed by himself, De Rougé, or others who studied the remains. One was a part of an obelisk of the thirteenth dynasty, with an inscription of a king's son, Nehesi, perhaps the son of the king Nehesi-Ra. The other was the upper part of the well-known stele of Tirhaka: this I found lying face up; and on searching every block of the same quality for the remainder of it, I turned up the lower half, which Mariette had hidden; thus the unknown led me to the known.

There was, however, plenty of work to do in examining thoroughly, and planning, all the remains, which—as we have just noticed—were but scantily attended to before. The fallen blocks of the granite pylon needed to be turned over, as they were all cut out of older sculptures; and to do this without tackle, I dug a trench on one side of the heap of blocks, and then rolled them over one by one into it, so as to turn them. In this way I examined every block, and discovered the fragments of the enormous colossus of Ramessu II in red granite, which must have been about 80 feet high, and have towered far above the temple roofs, amid the forest of obelisks which adorned the city. The toe alone is as large as a man's body. Some large statues were also found by the road leading up to the temple. And every block of the hundreds which strew the ground here was examined on all sides, by mining beneath it where needful; every fragment of inscription was copied; and finally a plan was made, showing the place of each block, with numbers affixed referring to the inscriptions. Thus anyone can draw their own conclusions as to the arrangement of the place, and the positions of the monuments, better in their arm-chair than by wandering over the chaos of dilapidation in the plain of Zoan.

Finding that no great discoveries could reward me in the temple, I tried the outskirts of the town, but only found a very late cemetery of no importance. I tried also sinking pits, in hopes of reaching the early town of the Ramessides or the Hyksos; but in vain, as the accumulation of Greek and Roman remains blocked the way, after descending even thirty feet. Then the houses of the Roman period on the surface were examined. One yielded a jar in the corner of the cellar, in which the lady had hidden away a large silver chain, a necklace of fine stones, and a gold ring.

But the burnt houses were the real prize of the season, as the owners had fled and left most of their goods; and the reddened patches of earth attracted us usually to a profitable site. In one house there was a beautiful marble term, of Italian work; and the fragments of a very curious zodiac, painted on a sheet of clear glass over a foot square, each sign or month having an emblematic head to represent it; unhappily, it was broken in a hundred and fifty pieces, and as I uncovered them it was cruel to see the gold foil work which was on them peel off on to the earth, leaving the glass bare in many parts. A yet more heartrending sight was the pile of papyrus rolls, so rotted that they fell to pieces with a touch, showing here and there a letter of the finest Greek writing. The next house, also burnt, was the best of all. Here we found the limestone statuette of the owner, Bakakhuiu, inscribed in demotic on the base; a sensible, sturdy-looking, active man, who seems to have been a lawyer or notary, to judge by his documents. Many household objects of pottery and stone were found, jars, mortars, &c., and a beautiful blue-glazed jar, perhaps the largest such known, and quite perfect. The rich result, however, was in his waste; for in a recess under the cellar stairs had been five baskets of old papyri. Though many had utterly perished by being burnt to white ash, yet one basketful was only carbonized; and tenderly undermining the precious black mass, I shifted it out

Egyptian Mummy Portrait—Encaustic on Wood (Fayyum)

and carried it up to my house with fear and reverent joy. It took ten hours' work to separate safely all the documents, twisted, crushed, and squeezed together, and all as brittle as only burnt papyrus is; a bend, or a jerk, and the piece was ruined. At last, I had over a hundred and fifty documents separated; and, each wrapped apart, and put in tin boxes, they traveled safely. They have now all been opened, and glazed; and two of them already prove to be of the greatest interest. One is a book of hieroglyphic signs in columns, followed by their hieratic equivalents, and the school-name by which they were learned: the greater part of this is preserved, and shows us, for the first time, the system on which the hieroglyphics were arranged and taught.

The other is a geographical papyrus, forestalling Brugsch's great work on the geography and the name divisions of Egypt; though defective in part all through, it is of the greatest value. Most of the other papyri are in demotic, and still await reading, while some are in Greek. Of course, being carbonized, the whole mass is black, and it is only by reflected light that it is possible to read anything; when the illumination is properly arranged, the duller surface of the ink can be seen on the brighter face of the papyrus. It is seldom such a treasure as this basketful of knowledge is so narrowly saved from destruction; a little more air in the burning, a little less care in the unearthing, the separation, the packing, or the opening, and these documents would have disappeared. Of course, under the usual system of leaving Arab overseers to manage excavations, all such discoveries are utterly destroyed.

When in the end of 1886 I went to Egypt, I had no excavations in prospect, having bid good-bye to the Fund; but I had promised to take photographs for the British Association, and I had much wished to see Upper Egypt in a more thorough way than during a hurried dahabiyeh trip to Thebes in 1882. To this end my friend Mr. Griffith joined me. We hired a small boat with a cabin at Minia, and took six weeks wandering up to Assuan, walking most of the way in and out of the line of cliffs. Thus we saw much that is outside of the usual course, and spent afterwards ten days at Assuan, and three weeks at Thebes, in tents. On coming down the Nile I walked along the eastern shore from Wasta to Memphis, but found it a fruitless region. Lastly, I lived several weeks at Dahshur, for surveying the pyramids there.

Assuan proved a most interesting district, teeming with early inscriptions cut on the rocks; and to copy all of these was a long affair. Every day we went out with rope-ladder, bucket, and squeeze-paper, as early as we could, and returned in the dusk; so at last some two hundred inscriptions were secured, many of which were of importance, and quite unnoticed before. These carvings are some of them notices of royal affairs, but mostly funereal lists of offerings for the benefit of various deceased persons. They abound most in the eleventh, twelfth, and thirteenth dynasties, though some of them are later; and one records queen Amenardus, and another Psamtik II, of the twenty-sixth dynasty. Their main interest is in the great number of personal names which they preserve, and the relationships stated. We see that the father is often not named at all, and the father's family is scarcely ever noticed; while on the mother's side the relations extend even to second cousins. To decipher these records is sometimes a hard matter, when they are very rudely chipped—or rather bruised —on the rough granite rocks; and continually we used to consult and dispute about some sign for long enough to copy all the rest of the inscription. Some of them are, however, beautifully engraved, and quite monumental in style. The most striking, perhaps, is a rock on the island of Elephantine, which had never been noticed before, although in the pathway. It was a sort of royal album begun by Ra-kha-nefer (fifth dynasty); followed by Unas (fifth), who carved a handsome tablet. Then Ra-meri Pepi (sixth) appropriated Ra-kha-nefer's inscription; Ra-nefer-ka Pepi next carved a tablet; in later times, of the eleventh dynasty, Antef-aa II followed with another tablet; and lastly Amenemhat I (twelfth dynasty) placed the sixth inscription here.

Not only were there these granite inscriptions to be copied, but also a great number of *graffiti* and travellers' names on the sandstone rocks, principally at Gebel Silsileh. Among these was a Phoenician inscription, one of the very few known in Egypt; and some curious quarry records of Roman age. The main inscription of this region is, however, one very seldom seen, even by antiquaries, as it is in a valley where no one stops. It portrays Antef V and his vizier Khati worshipping Mentuhotep IV and his wife. Near it is another, smaller, tablet with the worship of the same king; and up the valley we discovered a tablet with the worship of Sankh-ka-ra, all of the eleventh dynasty. All over this district are many rude figures of animals, marked on the rocks by hammering: they are of various ages, some perhaps modern, but the earlier ones certainly before the eighteenth dynasty; and, to judge by the weathering of the rock, it seems probable that they were begun here long before any of the monuments of Egypt that we know. The usual figures are of men, horses, and boats, but there are also camels, ostriches and elephants.

On the desert hills behind Esneh I found what is—so far—the oldest thing known from Egypt. In prehistoric days the Nile used to fill the whole breadth of the valley, to a depth of a couple of hundred feet, fed with the heavy rainfall that carved back the valleys all along the river by great waterfalls, the precipices of which now stand stark and arid in the bleaching sun. Many parts of the valley are above the present river, and are now desert, so that at Esneh the hills are several miles from the Nile, and on a spur of one—where probably no man sets foot for centuries at a time—I found lying a palaeolithic wrought flint. It was about a couple of hundred feet above the Nile, and being clearly a river-worn object, it had been left there in the old time of the Great Nile. The flints found by General Pitt-Rivers at Thebes belong to a later age, when the Nile had fallen to almost its present level. But those are far older than any monuments known to us. We see then two stages before the beginning of what we can call history.

At Thebes my main work was in obtaining casts and photo-graphs of all the types of foreign races on the monuments. For making ethnographical comparisons we were, until then, dependent on drawings, which were often incorrect. Now we have nearly two hundred photographs, all with the same size of head, giving several examples of each race that was repre-sented by the Egyptians.

In most cases it would have been difficult to photograph the sculptures directly, owing to the difficulties of placing the camera, and the exact time of the day required for the oblique sunlight. Paper squeezes were therefore taken in preference, and a box of these, weighing a few pounds, served as moulds for producing in England a set of plaster casts which weighed a hundred times as much. By waxing the paper several suc-cessive casts can be made from one mould, and from a set of the casts I took photographs, which can be printed in-terminably, and which are far more clear and distinct than if they were made directly from the stained and darkened sculp-tures. The paintings were of course photographed directly; where near the outer air enough light was obtained by re-flectors of tinned plate; but in distant interiors, such as the tombs of the kings, an explosion of the proper amount of magnesium powder, mixed with chlorate of potash, gave ex-cellent results for light.

Having finished the Theban work, I then went to Dahshur, and there made a survey around the two large pyramids; but unfortunately I could not obtain the permission to uncover the bases of the pyramids in time to measure more than the south-ern one. This pyramid is interesting, as it retains the original casing over most of it, and gives us some idea of what the other pyramids looked like before the plundering by Arabs, and perhaps older thieves. The outside is peculiar, as being of a steeper angle below than above, and hence it is often called the 'blunted pyramid.' . . .

When considering the places favourable for future excava-tions I had named Hawara and Illahun, amongst other sites, to M. Grébaut; and he proposed to me that I should work in the Fayum province in general. The exploration of the pyramids of this district was my main object, as their arrangement, their date, and their builders were quite unknown. Hawara was not a convenient place to work at, as the village was two miles from the pyramid, and a canal lay between; I therefore determined to form a camp of workmen to live on the spot, as at Daphnae. For this purpose I needed to recruit a party from a little distance, and began my work therefore at the ancient Arsinoe or Crocodilopolis, close to Medinet el Fayum. Here I cleared the pylon of the temple, of which a few disturbed blocks remain, and found a second mention of Amenemhat II beside that already known; but his work had all been altered and rebuilt, probably by Ramessu II. Four or five different levels of building and reconstruction could be traced, and the depth of rubbish over the approach to the temple in the shallowest part of the mounds was twenty-four feet. Within the great enclosure of mudbrick wall, the site of the temple could be traced by following the bed of sand, on which the foundations had been laid; but scarcely a single stone was left. One re-used block had a figure of a king of the nineteenth dynasty, probably Ramessu II; and this leads us to date as late as Ptolemy II the temple which we can trace here. He doubtless built a large temple, as the place received much attention in his time, and was dedicated to his sister-wife Arsinoe; she was specially worshipped along with the great gods, as we know from the stele of Pithom. The only early objects found here were flint knives in the soil of the temple; these belong to the twelfth dynasty, as we know from later discoveries.

A short work of a few days at Biahmu resolved the questions about the so-called pyramids there. So soon as we began to turn over the soil we found chips of sandstone colossi; the second day the gigantic nose of a colossus was found, as broad as a man's body; then pieces of carved thrones, and a fragment of inscription of Amenemhat III. It was evident that the two great piles of stone had been the pedestals of colossal seated monolithic statues, carved in hard quartzite sandstone, and brilliantly polished. These statues faced northward, and around each was a courtyard wall with sloping outer face, and red granite gateway in the north front. The total height of the colossi was about sixty feet from the ground. The limestone pedestal rose twenty-one feet, then the sandstone colossus had a base of four feet, on which the figure, seated on its throne, rose to a height of thirty-five feet more. Thus the whole statue and part of its pedestal would be visible above the enclosing courtyard wall, and it would appear from a distance as if it were placed on a truncated pyramid. The description of Herodotos, therefore, is fully accounted for; and it shows that he actually saw the figures, though from a distance, as any person who visited them closely would not have described them in such a manner.

Having by this time formed and organised a good body of workmen, I moved over to Hawara, with as many men as I wanted; and the only difficulty was to restrain the numbers who wished to work. The pyramid had never been entered in modern times, and its arrangement was wholly unknown; explorers had fruitlessly destroyed much of the brickwork on the north side, but yet the entrance was undiscovered. In Roman times the stone casing had been removed, and as the body of the structure was of mud bricks, it had crumbled away somewhat; each side was therefore encumbered with chips and mud. After vainly searching the ground on the north side for any entrance, I then cleared the middle of the east side, but yet no trace of any door could be found. As it was evident then that the plan was entirely different to that of any known pyramid, and it would be a hopeless task to clear all the ground around it, I therefore settled to tunnel to the midst. This work was very troublesome, as the large bricks were laid in sand, and rather widely spaced; hence as soon as any were removed, the sand was liable to pour out of the joints, and to loosen all the surrounding parts. The removal of each brick was therefore done as quietly as possible, and I had to go in three times a day and insert more roofing boards, a matter which needed far more skill and care than a native workman would use. After many weeks' work (for there was only room for one man), I found that we were halfway through, but all in brick. On one side of the tunnel, however, I saw signs of a built wall, and guessing that it had stood around the pit made for the chamber during the building, I examined the rock-floor, and found that it sloped down slightly, away from the wall. We turned then to the west, and tunnelling onwards, we reached the great roofing beams of the chamber in a few days. No masons of the district, however, could cut through them, and I had to leave the work till the next season. Then, after a further search on all the four sides for the entrance, the masons attacked the sloping stone roof, and in two or three weeks' time a hole beneath them was reported; anxiously I watched them enlarge it until I could squeeze through, and then I entered the chamber above the sepulchre; at one side I saw a lower hole, and going down I found a broken way into the sandstone sepulchre, but too narrow for my shoulders. After sounding the water inside it, a boy was put down with a rope-ladder; and at last, on looking through the hole, I could see by the light of his candle the two sarcophagi, standing rifled and empty. In a day or two we cleared away the rubbish from the original entrance passage to the chamber, and so went out into the passages, which turned and wandered up and down. These were so nearly choked with mud, that in many parts the only way along them was by lying flat, and sliding along the mud, pushed by fingers and toes. In this way, sliding, crawling, and wading, I reached as near to the outer mouth of the passage as possible; and then by measuring back to the chamber, the position of the mouth on the outside of the pyramid was pretty nearly found. But so deep was it under the rubbish, and so much encumbered with large blocks of stone, that it took about a fortnight to reach it from the outside.

The pyramid had been elaborately arranged so as to deceive and weary the spoiler, and it had apparently occupied a great amount of labour to force an entrance. The mouth was on the ground level, on the south side, a quarter of the length from the south-west corner. The original explorers descended a passage with steps to a chamber, from which apparently there was no exit. The roof consisted of a sliding trap-door, however, and breaking through this another chamber was reached at a higher level. Then a passage opened to the east, closed with a wooden door, and leading to another chamber with a trap-door roof. But in front of the explorer was a passage carefully plugged up solid with stone; this they thought would lead to the prize, and so all the stones were mined through, only to lead to nothing. From the second trap-door chamber a passage led northward to the third such chamber. From that a passage led west to a chamber with two wells, which seemed as if they led to the tomb, but both were false. This chamber also was almost filled with masonry, which all concealed nothing, but had given plenty of occupation to the spoilers who removed it in vain. A filled-up trench in the floor of the chamber really led to the sepulchre; but arriving there no door was to be found, as the entrance had been let down into place to close the chamber. So at last the way had been forced by breaking away a hole in the edge of the glassy-hard sandstone roofing block, and thus reaching the chamber and its sarcophagi. By a little widening of the spoilers' hole I succeeded in getting through it into the chamber. The water was up to the middle of my body, and so exploration was difficult; but the floor was covered with rubbish and chips, which might contain parts of the funereal vessels, and therefore needed searching. The rubbish in the sarcophagi I cleared out myself; and then I set some lads to gather up the scraps from the floor on the flat blade of a hoe (as it was out of arms' reach under water), and after searching them they threw them into the sarcophagi. Thus we anxiously worked on for any inscribed fragments; my anxiety being for the cartouche of the king, the boys' anxiety for the big bakhshish promised, at *per* hieroglyph found, extra value given for cartouches. The system worked, for in the first day I got the coveted prize, a piece of an alabaster vessel with the name of Amenemhat III, proving

Bakakhuiu, the Notary of Tanis

finally to whom the pyramid belonged; and other parts of inscribed vessels were found. Still there was a puzzle as to the second sarcophagus, which had been built up between the great central one and the chamber side. On clearing in the chamber which led to the sepulchre, however, they found a beautiful altar of offerings in alabaster, covered with figures of the offerings all named, over a hundred in all, and dedicated for the king's daughter, Neferuptah; near it were parts of several bowls in the form of half a trussed duck, also bearing her name: so doubtless the second interment was hers; and she must have died during her father's life, and before the closing of the pyramid. Of the actual bodies I found a few scraps of charred bones, besides bits of charcoal and grains of burnt diorite in the sarcophagi; also a beard of lazuli for inlaying was found in the chamber. The wooden inner coffins, inlaid with hard stone carving, had therefore been burnt. The chamber itself is a marvellous work; nearly the whole height of it is carved out of a single block of hard quartzite sandstone, forming a huge tank, in which the sarcophagus was placed. In the inside it is twenty-two feet long and nearly eight feet wide, while the sides are about three feet

thick. The surface is polished, and the corners so sharply cut
that I mistook it for masonry, until I searched in vain for the
joints. Of course it was above water level originally; but all this
region has been saturated by a high level canal of Arab times.
Afterwards I had all the earth removed from the pyramid
passages as far as practicable, but nothing further was found
there. No trace of inscription exists on either the walls or
sarcophagi; and but for the funereal furniture, even the very
name would not have been recovered.

Though the pyramid was the main object at Hawara, it was
but a lesser part of my work there. On the south of the pyramid lay a wide mass of chips and fragments of building, which
had long been generally identified with the celebrated labyrinth. Doubts, however, existed, mainly owing to Lepsius
having considered the brick buildings on the site to have been
part of the labyrinth. When I began to excavate the result was
soon plain, that the brick chambers were built on the top of
the ruins of a great stone structure; and hence they were only
the houses of a village, as they had at first appeared to me
to be. But beneath them, and far away over a vast area, the
layers of stone chips were found; and so great was the mass
that it was difficult to persuade visitors that the stratum was
artificial, and not a natural formation. Beneath all these fragments was a uniform smooth bed of *beton* or plaster, on which
the pavement of the building had been laid: while on the
south side, where the canal had cut across the site, it could
be seen how the chip stratum, about six feet thick, suddenly
ceased, at what had been the limits of the building. No trace
of architectural arrangement could be found, to help in iden-
tifying this great structure with the labyrinth: but the mere
extent of it proved that it was far larger than any temple
known in Egypt. All the temples of Karnak, of Luxor, and
a few on the western side of Thebes, might be placed together
within the vast space of these buildings at Hawara. We know
from Pliny and others, how for centuries the labyrinth had
been a great quarry for the whole district; and its destruction
occupied such a body of masons, that a small town existed

there. All this information, and the recorded position of it, agrees so closely with what we can trace, that no doubt can now remain regarding the position of one of the wonders of Egypt.

The cemetery of Hawara was a great resource for discoveries, and it proved to be one of the richest fields that I have found, although it was entirely an unexpected prize. The oldest tombs, of the pyramid time, had all been ruined ages ago, and the pits re-used for the nineteenth dynasty, the Ptolemaic times, and crocodile burial of the Roman age. But some slabs from the stone chapels on the surface had fallen down the tomb shafts, and were thus preserved.

The oldest unravaged tomb was of about the end of the twenty-sixth dynasty; and that was a treasury of amulets, being the funeral vault of the family of a great noble, Horuta. It was half inundated, the water being thigh deep, and though all woodwork and stucco was spoilt, yet the amulets of stone, and some of pottery, were uninjured. The great interment was that of Horuta himself. In a side chamber, branching from the large chamber, a huge sarcophagus of hard and tough limestone had been placed, containing three successive coffins of wood. This was built in solidly with masonry all around it, filling up the whole chamber, so that its very existence was hardly to be suspected by any one in the large chamber. To clear this out in such a position was hard work; a party of good hands were steadily labouring at it, mainly by contract, for two or three months. Down a well, forty feet deep, and in a pitch-black chamber, splashing about in bitter water, and toiling by candle-light, all the work had to be done; and dragging out large blocks of masonry in a very confined space in such circumstances is slow and tedious. While thus mining the way to the expected burial, we lit on a hole in the masonry filled with large ushabtis standing in rows, two hundred in all, of the finest workmanship; and, before long, on the other side of the sarcophagus, two hundred more were found in a similar recess. But the sarcophagus itself was most difficult to open. The lid block was nearly two feet thick, and almost under water. It was far too heavy for us to move entire, so some weeks were spent in cutting it in two. One piece was then raised, but it proved to be the foot end; and though I spent a day struggling with the inner coffins, sitting in the sarcophagus up to my nose in water, I yet could not draw them out from under the rest of the stone lid. So after some days the men raised that, enough to get one's head in between the under side of it and the water; and then I spent another gruesome day, sitting astride of the inner coffin, unable to turn my head under the lid without tasting the bitter brine in which I sat. But though I got out the first coffin lid, the inner one was firmly fastened down to its coffin; and though I tried every way of loosening the coffin, it was so firmly set in a bed of sand that crowbars and mining with the feet were useless, and it was so low in the water as to be out of arms' reach. The need of doing everything by feeling, and the impossibility of seeing what was done under the black water, made it a slow business. A third day I then attacked it, with a helpful friend, Mr. Fraser. We drilled holes in the coffin, as it was uninscribed, and fixed in stout iron bolts. Then, with ropes tied to them, all our party hauled again and again at the coffin; it yielded; and up came an immense black mass to the surface of the water. With great difficulty we drew it out, as it was very heavy, and we had barely room for it beneath the low ceiling. Anxiously opening it, we found a slight inner coffin, and then the body of Horuta himself, wrapped in a network of beads of lazuli, beryl, and silver, the last all decomposed. Tenderly we towed him out to the bottom of the entrance pit, handling him with the same loving care as Izaak his worms. And then came the last, and longed-for scene, for which our months of toil had whetted our appetites,—the unwrapping of Horuta. Bit by bit the layers of pitch and cloth were loosened, and row after row of magnificent amulets were disclosed, just as they were laid on in the distant past. The gold ring on the finger which bore his name and titles, the exquisitely inlaid gold birds, the chased gold figures, the lazuli statuettes delicately wrought, the polished lazuli and beryl and carnelian amulets finely engraved, all the wealth of talismanic armoury, rewarded our eyes with a sight which has never been surpassed to archaeological gaze. No such complete and rich a series of amulets has been seen intact before; and as one by one they were removed all their positions were recorded, and they may now be seen lying in their original order in the Ghizeh Museum. The rest of the family of Horuta lay in the large chamber, some in stone sarcophagi, some only in wooden coffins. They also had their due funereal wealth; and a dozen other sets of amulets rewarded our search, some of them as fine a series as any known before, but not to compare for a moment with those of the walled-in patriarch.

Of rather later age, perhaps Ptolemaic, was a large wooden coffin that we found; the body and the lid were two equal parts, plainly rectangular; and they lay where some old spoiler had left them, separated, and afterwards buried under a heap of stuff thrown out in digging later tombs. The whole surface of this sarcophagus was stuccoed, inside and outside, top and bottom, and every part of it finely painted and inscribed. The top of the lid had the deities of the district, the hawk, the Osiris-crocodile, and the bennu, with inscriptions; the lower part inside bore other animals, the vulture, the cow, and white hippopotamus; the inside of the lid had the two crocodile-headed Sebeks and the ape; and underneath the lower part, or body, was a long inscription, partly biographical. I had a terrifying experience with this coffin; when I found it much of the stucco was loose, and any amount of trouble was worth while to preserve so beautiful and important an object. I observed in copying it that parts had been waxed, to heighten the colour, and this suggested to me to fasten down the stucco by wax. I tried melting it on with a plate of hot iron, but could scarcely do it without blackening it with smoke. In course of this I poured a layer of wax over the surface; but what was my horror to see as the wax cooled that it contracted into saucerformed patches, lifting up with it the stucco, and leaving bare wood beneath! To touch these wax patches must irrevocably ruin all hopes of replacing the stucco; so I covered it

with sheets of paper, and thought on it for some days, a spectre
of dismal failure. I tried in vain to buy a brazier at Medinet;
so at last, making a grating of wire, I filled it with red-hot
charcoal, and supported it over part of the unlucky coffin.
As I watched it, the wax softened, flattened, and dropped
exactly into place again; patch after patch settled down, the
wax melted and ran in under the stucco; and at last I saw
the whole surface completely relaid, and fixed so firmly that
even the fearful rattle of an Egyptian railway wagon, in the
long journey to Bulak, did not injure it.

But perhaps the greatest success at Hawara was in the
direction least expected. So soon as I went there I observed
a cemetery on the north of the pyramid; on digging in it
I soon saw that it was all Roman, the remains of brick tomb-
chambers; and I was going to give it up as not worth working,
when one day a mummy was found, with a painted portrait
on a wooden panel placed over its face. This was a beautifully
drawn head of a girl, in soft grey tints, entirely classical in
its style and mode, without any Egyptian influence. More men
were put on to this region, and in two days another portrait-
mummy was found; in two days more a third, and then for
nine days not one; an anxious waiting, suddenly rewarded by
finding three. Generally three or four were found every week,
and I have even rejoiced over five in one day. Altogether sixty
were found in clearing this cemetery, some much decayed and
worthless, others as fresh as the day they were painted.

Not only were these portraits found thus on the mummies,
but also the various stages of decoration that led up to the
portrait. First, the old-fashioned stucco cartonnage coverings,
purely Egyptian, of the Ptolemies. Next, the same made more
solidly, and with distinct individual differences, in fact, modelled masks of the deceased persons. Then arms modelled in
one with the bust, the rest of the body being covered with
a canvas wrapper painted with mythologic scenes, all purely
Egyptian. Probably under Hadrian the first portraits are found,
painted on a canvas wrapper, but of Greek work. Soon the
canvas was abandoned, and a wooden panel used instead; and

then the regular series of panel portraits extends until the decline in the third century. All this custom of decorating the mummies arose from their being kept above ground for many years in rooms, probably connected with the house. Various signs of this usage can be seen on the mummies, and in the careless way in which they were at last buried, after such elaborate decoration.

Though only a sort of undertaker's business, in a provincial town of Egypt, and belonging to the Roman age, when art had greatly declined, yet these paintings give us a better idea of what ancient painting was, and what a high state it must have reached in its prime, than anything yet known, excepting some of the Pompeian frescoes. Mannerism is evident in nearly all of these, and faults may be easily detected; yet there is a spirit, a sentiment, an expression about the better examples which can only be the relic of a magnificent school, whose traditions and skill were not then quite lost. A few indeed of these heads are of such power and subtlety that they may stand beside the works of any age without being degraded. If such was Greek painting still, centuries after its zenith, by obscure commercial artists, and in a distant town of a foreign land, we may dimly credit what it may have been in its grandeur. The National Gallery now begins its history of paintings far before that of any other collection; the finest examples left, after the selection of the Bulak Museum, being now at Trafalgar Square.

The technical methods of these paintings have been much discussed. Certainly the colours were mixed with melted wax as a medium, and it seems most likely that both the brush and hard point were used. The backing is a very thin cedar panel, on which a coat of lead colour priming was laid, followed by a flesh-coloured ground where the face was to come. The drapery is freely marked in with bold brushfuls of colour, while the flesh is carefully and smoothly laid on with zigzag strokes. In some portraits the boldness of the work is almost like some modern romanticist's; at a foot distance the surface is nearly incomprehensible, at six or eight feet it produces a perfect effect.

Several of these pictures when found were in a perilous state; the film of wax paint was scaled loose from the panel, and they could never be even tilted up on edge without perishing. After finding several in this tender state, and pondering on their preservation, I ventured to try the same process as for the stucco coffin. The wire-grating was filled with red-hot charcoal, and then the frail portrait was slid in beneath it, a few drops of melted wax laid on it, and watched. In a few seconds the fresh wax began to spread, and then at once I ladled melted wax all over the surface; a second too long, and it began to fry and to blister; too sharp a tilt to drain it when it came out, and the new wax washed away the paint. But with care and management it was possible to preserve even the most rotten paintings with fresh wax; and afterwards I extended this waxing to all substances that were perishable, woodwork and leather, as well as stucco and paint.

This custom, however, of preserving the mummies above ground, adorned with the portraits, gave way about the time of Constantine, or perhaps a little earlier, and immediate burial was adopted. Probably this was partly due to the progress of Christianity.

Instead, therefore, of finding the portraits of the persons, we have their embroidered and richly woven garments; for they were buried in the finest clothes they had when alive. And their possessions were buried with them. In one grave was a lady's casket made of wood inlaid with ivory panels, on which figures were carved and coloured with inlaying. The fine cut-glass vase from another grave is of the whitest glass, and excellently cut with the wheel; perhaps the finest example of such work from Roman times. The toys were also buried with the children, and dolls, with all their furniture,—bedstead, mirror, table, toilet-box, clothes-basket, and other paraphernalia—were placed with the little ones who had died. ven more elaborate toys were laid here, such as the curious rra cotta of a sedan chair, borne by two porters, with a lady seated inside; a loose figure that can be removed.

In one instance a far more valuable prize accompanied a body; under the head of a lady lay a papyrus roll, which still preserved a large part of the second book of the Iliad, beautifully written, and with marginal notes. A great quantity of pieces of papyrus, letters and accounts, of Roman age, were also found scattered about in the cemetery. In a large jar buried in the ground lay a bundle of title-deeds: they recorded the sale of some monastic property, and were most carefully rolled, bound up with splints of reed, to prevent their being bent, and wrapped in several old cloths.

In yet another respect Hawara proved a rich field. In the coffins, in the graves, and in the ruins of the chambers, were still preserved the wreaths with which the dead had been adorned, and the flowers which the living had brought to the tombs. These wreaths were often in the most perfect condition, every detail of the flowers being as complete as if dried for a herbarium. They illustrate the accounts of Pliny and other writers about ancient wreaths, and the plants used for them, and show what a careful and precise trade the wreathmaker's was. Beside the decorative plants there were many seeds, and remains of edible fruits and vegetables, which had been left behind in the surface chambers of the tombs after the funereal feasts. Altogether, the cemetery of Hawara has doubled the extent of our list of ancient Egyptian botany, under the careful examination given by Mr. Newberry to the boxes full of plants which I brought away.

Few places, then, have such varied interest as Hawara; the twelfth dynasty pyramid, the labyrinth, the amulets of Horuta, the portraits, the botany, and the papyri, are each of special interest and historical value.

In this year also I visited the other side of the lake of the Fayum, now known as the Birket Kerun. There, at some miles back in that utter solitude, stands a building of unknown age and unknown purport. It is massively constructed, but without any trace of inscription, or even ornament, which would tell its history. That it cannot be as late as the Kasr Kerun, is probable from its being at a much higher level. There would be no object in making a building at some miles distant in the desert, as it now is; and we must rather suppose it to belong to the age when the lake was full, and extended out so far. But where it comes before the Ptolemaic age we cannot say. The front doorway leads into a long court, which has a chamber at each end, and seven recesses in the long side opposite the entrance. These recesses have had doors, of which the pivot holes can be seen. There are no traces of statues or of sarcophagi about; and the place has been keenly tunnelled and explored by treasure-seekers.

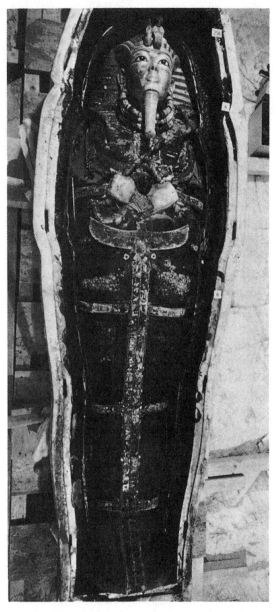

Full Mummy of King Tut-ankh-Amen

# 3. CARTER:

# *The Tomb of Tutankhamen*

If a man do not erect in this age his own tomb ere he dies, he shall live no longer in monument than the bell rings, and the widow weeps.

—SHAKESPEARE, *Much Ado About Nothing*

No other single archaeological discovery has ever touched the popular imagination as did the finding of the Tomb of Tutankhamen, and it is quite likely that no possible find of the future will be greeted the way the world welcomed the report from Thebes in 1922. We live in an age of wonders taken for granted, today, and little short of turning up a live Pharaoh would arouse real interest. But the finding of "King Tut's" tomb penetrated to every level of society. It was headline news for months. The great drama of the story—the long years of failure, the legend of a curse, the unbelievable splendor of the tomb—all this created unparalleled excitement. It is an excitement that has not abated even today, as was seen when the treasures of Tutankhamen's Tomb toured the United States in 1961 and 1962, on loan from Cairo, and attracted heavy crowds in many cities.

The tomb was found in the Valley of the Kings, Thebes. There the Pharaohs, hoping to avoid the grave robberies of the pyramid age, had begun building their tombs in the time of the Middle Kingdom. Preservation of the physical body was an important element of Egyptian religious thought— hence the highly developed art of embalming—but grave robbers were thwarting the hopes of the pharaohs for immortality by stealing mummy and tomb-jewelry as well.

The Valley of the Kings was chosen for its inaccessibility. The indefatigable Pococke, who visited there in 1738, wrote, "We then turned to the north west, enter'd in between the high rocky hills, and went in a very narrow valley. We after turn'd towards the south, and then to the north west, going in all between the mountains about a mile or a mile and a half. . . . We came to a part that is wider, being a round opening like an amphitheatre and ascended by a narrow step passage about ten feet high, which seems to have been broken down thro' the rock, the ancient passage being probably from the Memnonium under the hills. . . . By this passage we came to Biban-el-Meluke, or Bab-el-Meluke, that is, the gate or court of the kings, being the sepulchres of the Kings of Thebes."

Here the Pharaohs of the Middle Kingdom sought to hide their tombs, rather than in conspicuous pyramids. Thothmes I, third Pharaoh of the great 18th Dynasty, was the first to have a tomb carved out of the rock, and then king after king came to rest there—the numerous Thothmeses and Amenhoteps and Rameseses that occupied the throne through the 18th, 19th, and 20th Dynasties.

The hopes that the kings entertained of resting undisturbed

were frustrated. Most of the tombs were robbed in antiquity, the rest plundered over the years by the local Egyptians, who sold their finds to dealers or travellers. Pococke visited 14 tombs, all of them looted. Belzoni entered several others, but they had all been rifled centuries earlier. He concluded that the Valley was exhausted.

Dozens of explorers surveyed the Valley in the succeeding decades, and they tended to confirm Belzoni's opinion. Then, in 1898, the French archaeologist Loret uncovered several new tombs, including that of Amenhotep II, which contained not one but thirteen royal mummies—Pharaohs of past centuries, transferred to Amenhotep's tomb to spare them from further indignities. Even though all these new tombs had been plundered by grave robbers, there was reason to hope that other sepulchres still remained unfound in the Valley—and perhaps one would turn out to be intact as it was on the day it was sealed.

In 1922 came the long-awaited news out of Thebes: a sealed tomb had been found! It was the tomb of a little-known king of the 18th Dynasty, Tutankhamen. The men excavating it soon found that Tutankhamen's tomb had been entered by thieves shortly after the Pharaoh's funeral, but that they had been discovered and little damage had been done. For the first time, a nearly intact burial had been recovered, and a wealth of treasure came to light.

It is ironic that Tutankhamen should be the Pharaoh best known to the 20th century. He was a minor ruler, a boy king who died in his teens, last of his dynasty. He succeeded Amenhotep IV (Akhnaten), the strange and brilliant "heretic pharaoh" who had temporarily imposed a monotheistic religion on Egypt, and there is some reason to think that Tutankhamen was Akhnaten's son as well as his son-in-law and heir. Certainly the boy king held no power in Egypt during his own brief reign. The priests of the sun-god Amon, forced from power during Akhnaten's reign, reduced the new Pharaoh to the status of a puppet.

Yet Tutankhamen was buried with the pomp and splendor

that befitted the greatest among kings. And that pomp and splendor remained, virtually untouched, to dazzle the eyes of men more than three thousand years later.

The man who found Tutankhamen's tomb was an Englishman, Howard Carter (1873-1939). He began his career as a draftsman, employed at the British Museum to ink in the tracings of tomb sketches made by the Egyptologist Percy Newberry. Carter did so well at this task that he was sent to Egypt the following year, 1892, as Newberry's assistant. He worked as draftsman to the archaeological survey under Newberry, and also had his first taste of actual excavation under Flinders Petrie.

Carter soon was in the front ranks of Egyptologists himself. By 1899, he held the post of Inspector in Chief of the Monuments of Upper Egypt and Nubia. Three years later, a wealthy American, Theodore M. Davis, commenced work in the Valley of the Kings, and Carter helped carry out the Davis excavations.

In 1907 another wealthy amateur of archaeology arrived in Egypt: George Herbert, fifth Earl of Carnarvon (1866-1923). A sportsman who relished the new thrills of automobile racing, Carnarvon had suffered serious injuries in a racing accident in 1903, and had gone to Egypt to recuperate. Four years later he had returned to excavate. Young Howard Carter was brought to his notice, and the two men went into archaeological partnership.

The rest of the story—the years of no results, the sudden spectacular discovery—is told by Carter himself in the pages that follow. Carter—with Lord Carnarvon's financial and moral support—was destined to make archaeology's most astonishing single find.

The discovery was no accident. Carter's working methods, derived from Flinders Petrie, were meticulous and exacting, and it would have been surprising if nothing had resulted from them. In *Pioneer to the Past,* the biography of the American Egyptologist James Henry Breasted, Dr. Breasted's son has this to say of Carter's methods: "To make absolutely certain that not a square inch of [the valley] floor should escape examination, he [Carter] made a large-scale map of it upon which he subdivided the terrain into convenient sections; and as his excavations of an actual area progressed and he had satisfied himself that it contained nothing of value, he checked off the corresponding sections on the map."

One consequence of the discovery was the popular legend of the Curse of the Pharaohs that supposedly would smite the foolhardy disturbers of Tutankhamen's tomb. This myth sprang from the circumstance of Lord Carnarvon's death in April, 1923—only months after the opening of the tomb—of the complications that ensued from an infection. *"Revenge of the Pharaohs!"* screamed the newspapers. As members of the expedition followed Carnarvon to the grave, the public frenzy grew. Twenty-one victims were claimed. One newspaper account of Victim 19 read, "Today the 78-year-old Lord Westbury jumped from the window of his seventh-story London apartment and was instantly killed. Lord Westbury's son, who was formerly the secretary of Howard Carter, the archaeologist at the Tutankhamen diggings, was found last November dead in his apartment, though when he went to bed he appeared to be in the best of health. The exact cause of his death has never been determined."

The victims of the Pharaoh, however, seem more to have fallen to natural mortality than to any mysterious curse. Of the five men present at the opening of the tomb, only Carnarvon died within the succeeding decade. Carter was 66 when the curse gathered him up, in 1939. Of the other prominent figures present in the early days of the excavation, Percy Newberry died in 1949, at 80; Dr. Derry, who performed the autopsy on the pharaoh's mummy, was still alive in 1951, at 76; Sir Alan Gardiner, who helped decipher the tomb inscriptions, was still an active 73-year-old Egyptologist in 1962. The curse does not seem to have been overly effective.

Howard Carter published his first report on the expedition in 1923, almost immediately after the discovery. It is from this volume that our excerpt is taken. Carter's collaborator on the work was A. C. Mace of the Metropolitan Museum of Art. A second report followed in 1927, and the third and final one a decade later. Carter's records are kept at the Griffith Institute, Oxford. In 1951 Penelope Fox of the Griffith Institute published a book, *Tutankhamen's Tomb,* based partly on Carter's notes, but to this date there has been no formal scientific publication of Carter's work.

## THE TOMB OF TUTANKHAMEN

Ever since my first visit to Egypt in 1890 it had been my ambition to dig in The Valley, and when, at the invitation of Sir William Garstin and Sir Gaston Maspero, I began to excavate for Lord Carnarvon in 1907, it was our joint hope that eventually we might be able to get a concession there. I had, as a matter of fact, when Inspector of the Antiquities Department, found, and superintended the clearing of, two tombs in The Valley for Mr. Theodore Davis, and this had made me the more anxious to work there under a regular concession. For the moment it was impossible, and for seven years we dug with varying fortune in other parts of the Theban necropolis. . . .

In 1914 our discovery of the tomb of Amen·hetep I, on the summit of the Drah abu'l Negga foothills, once more turned our attention Valleywards, and we awaited our chance with some impatience. Mr. Theodore Davis, who still held the concession, had already published the fact that he considered The Valley exhausted, and that there were no more tombs to be found, a statement corroborated by the fact that in his last two seasons he did very little work in The Valley proper, but spent most of his time excavating in the approach thereto, in the neighbouring north valley, where he hoped to find the

From *The Tomb of Tut·ankh·amen* (London: Cassell, 1923) by Howard Carter and A. C. Mace. Copyright 1923 by Cassell & Co., Ltd., and reprinted by permission of the publishers.

tombs of the priest kings and of the Eighteenth Dynasty queens, and in the mounds surrounding the Temple of Medinet Habu. Nevertheless he was loath to give up the site, and it was not until June, 1914, that we actually received the long-coveted concession. Sir Gaston Maspero, Director of the Antiquities Department, who signed our concession, agreed with Mr. Davis that the site was exhausted, and told us frankly that he did not consider that it would repay further investigation. We remembered, however, that nearly a hundred years earlier Belzoni had made a similar claim, and refused to be convinced. We had made a thorough investigation of the site, and were quite sure that there were areas, covered by the dumps of previous excavators, which had never been properly examined.

Clearly enough we saw that very heavy work lay before us, and that many thousands of tons of surface debris would have to be removed before we could hope to find anything; but there was always the chance that a tomb might reward us in the end, and, even if there was nothing else to go upon, it was a chance that we were quite willing to take. As a matter of fact we had something more, and, at the risk of being accused of *post actum* prescience, I will state that we had definite hopes of finding the tomb of one particular king, and that king Tut·ankh·Amen.

To explain the reasons for this belief of ours we must turn to the published pages of Mr. Davis's excavations. Towards the end of his work in The Valley he had found, hidden under a rock, a faïence cup which bore the name of Tut·ankh·Amen. In the same region he came upon a small pit-tomb, in which were found an unnamed alabaster statuette, possibly of Ay, and a broken wooden box, in which were fragments of gold foil, bearing the figures and names of Tut·ankh·Amen and his queen. On the basis of these fragments of gold he claimed that he had actually found the burial place of Tut·ankh·Amen. The theory was quite untenable, for the pit-tomb in question was small and insignificant, of a type that might very well belong to a member of the royal household in the Ramesside period, but ludicrously inadequate for a king's burial in the Eighteenth Dynasty. Obviously, the royal material found in it had been placed there at some later period, and had nothing to do with the tomb itself.

Some little distance eastward from this tomb, he had also found in one of his earlier years of work (1907-8), buried in an irregular hole cut in the side of the rock, a cache of large pottery jars, with sealed mouths, and hieratic inscriptions upon their shoulders. A cursory examination was made of their contents, and as these seemed to consist merely of broken pottery, bundles of linen, and other oddments, Mr. Davis refused to be interested in them, and they were laid aside and stacked away in the store-room of his Valley house. There, some while afterwards, Mr. Winlock noticed them, and immediately realized their importance. With Mr. Davis's consent the entire collection of jars was packed and sent to the Metropolitan Museum of Art, New York, and there Mr. Winlock made a thorough examination of their contents. Extraordinarily interesting they proved to be. There were clay seals, some bearing the name of Tut·ankh·Amen and others the impression of the royal necropolis seal, fragments of magnificent painted pottery vases, linen head-shawls—one inscribed with the latest known date of Tut·ankh·Amen's reign—floral collars, of the kind represented as worn by mourners in burial scenes, and a mass of other miscellaneous objects; the whole representing, apparently, the material which had been used during the funeral ceremonies of Tut·ankh·Amen, and afterwards gathered together and stacked away within the jars.

We had thus three distinct pieces of evidence—the faïence cup found beneath the rock, the gold foil from the small pit-tomb, and this important cache of funerary material—which seemed definitely to connect Tut·ankh·Amen with this particular part of The Valley. To these must be added a fourth. It was in the near vicinity of these other finds that Mr. Davis had discovered the famous Akh·en·Aten cache. This contained the funerary remains of heretic royalties, brought hurriedly from Tell el Amarna and hidden here for safety, and that it was Tut·ankh·Amen himself who was responsible for their removal and reburial we can be reasonably sure from the fact that a number of his clay seals were found.

With all this evidence before us we were thoroughly convinced in our own minds that the tomb of Tut·ankh·Amen was still to find, and that it ought to be situated not far from the centre of The Valley. In any case, whether we found Tut· ankh·Amen or not, we felt that a systematic and exhaustive search of the inner valley presented reasonable chances of success, and we were in the act of completing our plans for an elaborate campaign in the season of 1914-15 when war broke out, and for the time being all our plans had to be left in abeyance. . . .

In the autumn of 1917 our real campaign in The Valley opened. The difficulty was to know where to begin, for mountains of rubbish thrown out by previous excavators encumbered the ground in all directions, and no sort of record had ever been kept as to which areas had been properly excavated and which had not. Clearly the only satisfactory thing to do was to dig systematically right down to bed-rock, and I suggested to Lord Carnarvon that we take as a starting-point the triangle of ground defined by the tombs of Rameses II, Mer·en·Ptah, and Rameses VI, the area in which we hoped the tomb of Tut·ankh·Amen might be situated.

It was rather a desperate undertaking, the site being piled high with enormous heaps of thrown-out rubbish, but I had reason to believe that the ground beneath had never been touched, and a strong conviction that we should find a tomb there. In the course of the season's work we cleared a considerable part of the upper layers of this area, and advanced our excavations right up to the foot of the tomb of Rameses VI. Here we came on a series of workmen's huts, built over masses of flint boulders, the latter usually indicating in The Valley the near proximity of a tomb. Our natural impulse was to enlarge our clearing in this direction, but by doing this we should have cut off all access to the tomb of Rameses above, to visitors one of the most popular tombs in the whole Valley.

Tablets of Kings,
Fifth to Twelfth Dynasties. 1:40.

We determined to await a more convenient opportunity. . . .

We resumed our work in this region in the season of 1919-20. Our first need was to break fresh ground for a dump, and in the course of this preliminary work we lighted on some small deposits of Rameses IV, near the entrance to his tomb. The idea this year was to clear the whole of the remaining part of the triangle already mentioned, so we started in with a fairly large gang of workmen. By the time Lord and Lady Carnarvon arrived in March the whole of the top debris had been removed, and we were ready to clear down into what we believed to be virgin ground below. We soon had proof that we were right, for we presently came upon a small cache containing thirteen alabaster jars, bearing the names of Rameses II and Mer·en·Ptah, probably from the tomb of the latter. As this was the nearest approach to a real find that we had yet made in The Valley, we were naturally somewhat excited, and Lady Carnarvon, I remember, insisted on digging out these jars—beautiful specimens they were—with her own hands.

With the exception of the ground covered by the workmen's huts, we had now exhausted the whole of our triangular area, and had found no tomb. I was still hopeful, but we decided to leave this particular section until, by making a very early start in the autumn, we could accomplish it without causing inconvenience to visitors.

For our next attempt we selected the small lateral valley in which the tomb of Thothmes III was situated. This occupied us throughout the whole of the two following seasons, and, though nothing intrinsically valuable was found, we discovered an interesting archæological fact. The actual tomb in which Thothmes III was buried had been found by Loret in 1898, hidden in a cleft in an inaccessible spot some way up the face of the cliff. Excavating in the valley below, we came upon the beginning of a tomb, by its foundation-deposits originally intended for the same king. Presumably, while the work on this low-level tomb was in progress, it occurred to Thothmes or to his architect that the cleft in the rock above was a better side. It certainly presented better chances of concealment, if that were the reason for the change; though probably the more plausible explanation would be that one of the torrential downpours of rain which visit Luxor occasionally may have flooded out the lower tomb, and suggested to Thothmes that his mummy would have a more comfortable resting-place on a higher level.

Near by, at the entrance to another abandoned tomb, we came upon foundation-deposits of his wife Meryt·Re·Hat·shep·sût, sister of the great queen of that name. Whether we are to infer that she was buried there is a moot point, for it would be contrary to all custom to find a queen in The Valley. In any case the tomb was afterwards appropriated by the Theban official, Sen·nefer.

We had now dug in The Valley for several reasons with extremely scanty results, and it became a much debated question whether we should continue the work, or try for a more profitable site elsewhere. After these barren years were we justified in going on with it? My own feeling was that so long as a single area of untouched ground remained the risk was worth taking. It is true that you may find less in more time in The Valley than in any other site in Egypt, but, on the other hand, if a lucky strike be made, you will be repaid for years and years of dull and unprofitable work.

There was still, moreover, the combination of flint boulders and workmen's huts at the foot of the tomb of Rameses VI to be investigated, and I had always had a kind of superstitious feeling that in that particular corner of The Valley one of the missing kings, possibly Tut·ankh·Amen, might be found. Certainly the stratification of the debris there should indicate a tomb. Eventually we decided to devote a final season to The Valley, and, by making an early start, to cut off access to the tomb of Rameses VI, if that should prove necessary, at a time when it would cause least inconvenience to visitors. That brings us to the present season and the results that are known to everyone.

The history of The Valley, as I have endeavoured to show in former chapters, has never lacked the dramatic element, and in this, the latest episode, it has held to its traditions. For consider the circumstances. This was to be our final season in The Valley. Six full seasons we had excavated there, and season after season had drawn a blank; we had worked for months at a stretch and found nothing, and only an excavator knows how desperately depressing that can be; we had almost made up our minds that we were beaten, and were preparing to leave The Valley and try our luck elsewhere; and then— hardly had we set hoe to ground in our last despairing effort than we made a discovery that far exceeded our wildest dreams. Surely, never before in the whole history of excavation has a full digging season been compressed within the space of five days.

Let me try and tell the story of it all. It will not be easy, for the dramatic suddenness of the initial discovery left me in a dazed condition, and the months that have followed have been so crowded with incident that I have hardly had time to think. Setting it down on paper will perhaps give me a chance to realize what has happened and all that it means.

I arrived in Luxor on October 28th, and by November 1st I had enrolled my workmen and was ready to begin. Our former excavations had stopped short at the north-east corner of the tomb of Rameses VI, and from this point I started trenching southwards. It will be remembered that in this area there were a number of roughly constructed workmen's huts, used probably by the labourers in the tomb of Rameses. These huts, built about three feet above bed-rock, covered the whole area in front of the Ramesside tomb, and continued in a southerly direction to join up with a similar group of huts on the opposite side of The Valley, discovered by Davis in connexion with his work on the Akh·en·Aten cache. By the evening of November 3rd we had laid bare a sufficient number of these huts for experimental purposes, so, after we had planned and noted them, they were removed, and we were ready to clear away the three feet of soil that lay beneath them.

Hardly had I arrived on the work next morning (November 4th) than the unusual silence, due to the stoppage of the work, made me realize that something out of the ordinary had happened, and I was greeted by the announcement that a step cut in the rock had been discovered underneath the very first hut to be attacked. This seemed too good to be true, but a short amount of extra clearing revealed the fact that we were actually in the entrance of a steep cut in the rock, some thirteen feet below the entrance to the tomb of Rameses VI, and a similar depth from the present bed level of The Valley. The manner of cutting was that of the sunken stairway entrance so common in The Valley, and I almost dared to hope that we had found our tomb at last. Work continued feverishly throughout the whole of that day and the morning of the next, but it was not until the afternoon of November 5th that we succeeded in clearing away the masses of rubbish that overlay the cut, and were able to demarcate the upper edges of the stairway on all its four sides.

It was clear by now beyond any question that we actually had before us the entrance to a tomb, but doubts, born of previous disappointments, persisted in creeping in. There was always the horrible possibility, suggested by our experience in the Thothmes III Valley, that the tomb was an unfinished one, never completed and never used: if it had been finished there was the depressing probability that it had been completely plundered in ancient times. On the other hand, there was just the chance of an untouched or only partially plundered tomb, and it was with ill-suppressed excitement that I watched the descending steps of the staircase, as one by one they came to light. The cutting was excavated in the side of a small hillock, and, as the work progressed, its western edge receded under the slope of the rock until it was, first partially, and then completely, roofed in, and became a passage, 10 feet high by 6 feet wide. Work progressed more rapidly now; step succeeded step, and at the level of the twelfth, towards sunset, there was disclosed the upper part of a doorway, blocked, plastered, and sealed.

A sealed doorway—it was actually true, then! Our years of patient labour were to be rewarded after all, and I think my first feeling was one of congratulation that my faith in The Valley had not been unjustified. With excitement growing to fever heat I searched the seal impressions on the door for evidence of the identity of the owner, but could find no name: the only decipherable ones were those of the well-known royal necropolis seal, the jackal and nine captives. Two facts, however, were clear: first the employment of this royal seal was certain evidence that the tomb had been constructed for a person of very high standing; and second, that the sealed door was entirely screened from above by workmen's huts of the Twentieth Dynasty was sufficiently clear proof that at least from that date it had never been entered. With that for the moment I had to be content.

While examining the seals I noticed, at the top of the door-way, where some of the plaster had fallen away, a heavy wooden lintel. Under this, to assure myself of the method by which the doorway had been blocked, I made a small peephole, just large enough to insert an electric torch, and discovered that the passage beyond the door was filled completely from floor to ceiling with stones and rubble—additional proof this of the care with which the tomb had been protected.

It was a thrilling moment for an excavator. Alone, save for my native workmen, I found myself, after years of com-paratively unproductive labour, on the threshold of what might prove to be a magnificent discovery. Anything, literally any-thing, might lie beyond that passage, and it needed all my self-control to keep from breaking down the doorway, and investigating then and there.

One thing puzzled me, and that was the smallness of the opening in comparison with the ordinary Valley tombs. The design was certainly of the Eighteenth Dynasty. Could it be the tomb of a noble buried here by royal consent? Was it a royal cache, a hiding-place to which a mummy and its equip-ment had been removed for safety? Or was it actually the tomb of the king for whom I had spent so many years in search?

Once more I examined the seal impressions for a clue, but on the part of the door so far laid bare only those of the royal necropolis seal already mentioned were clear enough to read. Had I but known that a few inches lower down there was a perfectly clear and distinct impression of the seal of Tut·ankh·Amen, the king I most desired to find, I would have cleared on, had a much better night's rest in consequence, and saved myself nearly three weeks of uncertainty. It was late, however, and darkness was already upon us. With some reluc-tance I re-closed the small hole that I had made, filled in our excavation for protection during the night, selected the most trustworthy of my workmen—themselves almost as excited as I was—to watch all night above the tomb, and so home by moonlight, riding down The Valley.

Naturally my wish was to go straight ahead with our clearing to find out the full extent of the discovery, but Lord Carnarvon was in England, and in fairness to him I had to delay matters until he could come. Accordingly, on the morning of November 6th I sent him the following cable:—"At last have made wonderful discovery in Valley; a magnificent tomb with seals intact; re-covered same for your arrival; congratulations."

My next task was to secure the doorway against interference until such time as it could finally be re-opened. This we did by filling our excavation up again to surface level, and rolling on top of it the large flint boulders of which the workmen's huts had been composed. By the evening of the same day, exactly forty-eight hours after we had discovered the first step of the staircase, this was accomplished. The tomb had vanished. So far as the appearance of the ground was concerned there never had been any tomb, and I found it hard to persuade myself at times that the whole episode had not been a dream.

I was soon to be reassured on this point. News travels fast in Egypt, and within two days of the discovery congratulations, inquiries, and offers of help descended upon me in a steady stream from all directions. It became clear, even at this early stage, that I was in for a job that could not be tackled single-handed, so I wired to Callender, who had helped me on various previous occasions, asking him if possible to join me without delay, and to my relief he arrived on the very next day. On the 8th I had received two messages from Lord Carnarvon in answer to my cable, the first of which read, "Possibly come soon," and the second, received a little later, "Propose arrive Alexandria 20th."

We had thus nearly a fortnight's grace, and we devoted it to making preparations of various kinds, so that when the time of re-opening came, we should be able, with the least possible delay, to handle any situation that might arise. On the night of the 18th I went to Cairo for three days, to meet Lord Carnarvon and make a number of necessary purchases, returning to Luxor on the 21st. On the 23rd Lord Carnarvon

Burial Mask of King Tut-ankh-Amen

arrived in Luxor with his daughter, Lady Evelyn Herbert, his devoted companion in all his Egyptian work, and everything was in hand for the beginning of the second chapter of the discovery of the tomb. Callender had been busy all day clearing away the upper layer of rubbish, so that by morning we should be able to get into the staircase without any delay.

By the afternoon of the 24th the whole staircase was clear, sixteen steps in all, and we were able to make a proper examination of the sealed doorway. On the lower part the seal impressions were much clearer, and we were able without any difficulty to make out on several of them the name of Tut·ankh·Amen. This added enormously to the interest of the discovery. If we had found, as seemed almost certain, the tomb of that shadowy monarch, whose tenure of the throne coincided with one of the most interesting periods in the whole of Egyptian history, we should indeed have reason to congratulate ourselves.

With heightened interest, if that were possible, we renewed our investigation of the doorway. Here for the first time a disquieting element made its appearance. Now that the whole door was exposed to light it was possible to discern a fact that had hitherto escaped notice—that there had been two successive openings and re-closings of a part of its surface: furthermore, that the sealing originally discovered, the jackal and nine captives, had been applied to the re-closed portions, whereas the sealings of Tut·ankh·Amen covered the untouched part of the doorway, and were therefore those with which the tomb had been originally secured. The tomb then was not absolutely intact, as we had hoped. Plunderers had entered it, and entered it more than once—from the evidence of the huts above, plunderers of a date not later than the reign of Rameses VI—but that they had not rifled it completely was evident from the fact that it had been re-sealed.[1]

Then came another puzzle. In the lower strata of rubbish

---

[1] From later evidence we found that this re-sealing could not have taken place later than the reign of Hor·em·heb, i.e. from ten to fifteen years after the burial.

that filled the staircase we found masses of broken potsherds and boxes, the latter bearing the names of Akh·en·Aten, Smenkh·ka·Re and Tut·ankh·Amen, and, what was much more upsetting, a scarab of Thothmes III and a fragment with the name of Amen·hetep III. Why this mixture of names? The balance of evidence so far would seem to indicate a cache rather than a tomb, and at this stage in the proceedings we inclined more and more to the opinion that we were about to find a miscellaneous collection of objects of the Eighteenth Dynasty kings, brought from Tell el Amarna by Tut·ankh· Amen and deposited here for safety.

So matters stood on the evening of the 24th. On the following day the sealed doorway was to be removed, so Callender set carpenters to work making a heavy wooden grille to be set up in its place. . . .

On the morning of the 25th the seal impressions on the doorway were carefully noted and photographed, and then we removed the actual blocking of the door, consisting of rough stones carefully built from floor to lintel, and heavily plastered on their outer faces to take the seal impressions.

This disclosed the beginning of a descending passage (not a staircase), the same width as the entrance stairway, and nearly seven feet high. As I had already discovered from my hole in the doorway, it was filled completely with stone and rubble, probably the chip from its own excavation. The filling, like the doorway, showed distinct signs of more than one opening and re-closing of the tomb, the untouched part consisting of clean white chip, mingled with dust, whereas the disturbed part was composed mainly of dark flint. It was clear that an irregular tunnel had been cut through the original filling at the upper corner on the left side, a tunnel corresponding in position with that of the hole in the doorway.

As we cleared the passage we found, mixed with the rubble of the lower levels, broken potsherds, jar sealings, alabaster jars, whole and broken, vases of painted pottery, numerous fragments of smaller articles, and water skins, these last having obviously been used to bring up the water needed for the plastering of the doorways. These were clear evidence of plundering, and we eyed them askance. By night we had cleared a considerable distance down the passage, but as yet saw no sign of second doorway or of chamber.

The day following (November 26th) was the day of days, the most wonderful that I have ever lived through, and certainly one whose like I can never hope to see again. Throughout the morning the work of clearing continued, slowly perforce, on account of the delicate objects that were mixed with the filling. Then, in the middle of the afternoon, thirty feet down from the outer door, we came upon a second sealed doorway, almost an exact replica of the first. The seal impressions in this case were less distinct, but still recognizable as those of Tut·ankh·Amen and of the royal necropolis. Here again the signs of opening and re-closing were clearly marked upon the plaster. We were firmly convinced by this time that it was a cache that we were about to open, and not a tomb. The arrangement of stairway, entrance passage and doors reminded us very forcibly of the cache of Akh·en·Aten and Tyi material found in the very near vicinity of the present excavation by Davis, and the fact that Tut·ankh·Amen's seals occurred there likewise seemed almost certain proof that we were right in our conjecture. We were soon to know. There lay the sealed doorway, and behind it was the answer to the question.

Slowly, desperately slowly it seemed to us as we watched, the remains of passage debris that encumbered the lower part of the doorway were removed, until at last we had the whole door clear before us. The decisive moment had arrived. With trembling hands I made a tiny breach in the upper left hand corner. Darkness and blank space, as far as an iron testing-rod could reach, showed that whatever lay beyond was empty, and not filled like the passage we had just cleared. Candle tests were applied as a precaution against possible foul gases, and then, widening the hole a little, I inserted the candle and peered in, Lord Carnarvon, Lady Evelyn and Callender standing anxiously beside me to hear the verdict. At first I could see nothing, the hot air escaping from the chamber causing the candle flame to flicker, but presently, as my eyes grew accustomed to the light, details of the room within emerged slowly from the mist, strange animals, statues, and gold—everywhere the glint of gold. For the moment—an eternity it must have seemed to the others standing by—I was struck dumb with amazement, and when Lord Carnarvon, unable to stand the suspense any longer, inquired anxiously, "Can you see anything?" it was all I could do to get out the words, "Yes, wonderful things." Then widening the hole a little further, so that we both could see, we inserted an electric torch.

I suppose most excavators would confess to a feeling of awe—embarrassment almost—when they break into a chamber closed and sealed by pious hands so many centuries ago. For the moment, time as a factor in human life has lost its meaning. Three thousand, four thousand years maybe, have passed and gone since human feet last trod the floor on which you stand, and yet, as you note the signs of recent life around you—the half-filled bowl of mortar for the door, the blackened lamp, the finger-mark upon the freshly painted surface, the farewell garland dropped upon the threshold—you feel it might have been but yesterday. The very air you breathe, unchanged throughout the centuries, you share with those who laid the mummy to its rest. Time is annihilated by little intimate details such as these, and you feel an intruder.

That is perhaps the first and dominant sensation, but others follow thick and fast—the exhilaration of discovery, the fever of suspense, the almost overmastering impulse, born of curiosity, to break down seals and lift the lids of boxes, the thought —pure joy to the investigator—that you are about to add a page to history, or solve some problem of research, the strained expectancy—why not confess it?—of the treasure-seeker. Did these thoughts actually pass through our minds at the time, or have I imagined them since? I cannot tell. It was the discovery that my memory was blank, and not the mere desire for dramatic chapter-ending, that occasioned this digression.

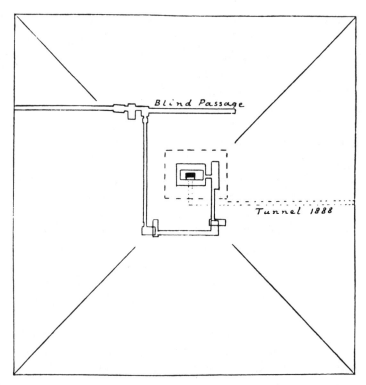

Blind Passage

Tunnel 1888

Plan of the Pyramid of Amenemhat III, Hawara

Surely never before in the whole history of excavation had such an amazing sight been seen as the light of our torch revealed to us. . . . The effect was bewildering, overwhelming. I suppose we had never formulated exactly in our minds just what we had expected or hoped to see, but certainly we had never dreamed of anything like this, a roomful—a whole museumful it seemed—of objects, some familiar, but some the like of which we had never seen, piled one upon another in seemingly endless profusion.

Gradually the scene grew clearer, and we could pick out individual objects. First, right opposite to us—we had been conscious of them all the while, but refused to believe in them —were three great gilt couches, their sides carved in the form of monstrous animals, curiously attenuated in body, as they had to be to serve their purpose, but with heads of startling realism. Uncanny beasts enough to look upon at any time: seen as we saw them, their brilliant gilded surfaces picked out of the darkness by our electric torch, as though by lime-light, their heads throwing grotesque distorted shadows on the wall behind them, they were almost terrifying. Next, on the right, two statues caught and held our attention; two life-sized figures of a king in black, facing each other like sentinels, gold kilted, gold sandalled, armed with mace and staff, the protective sacred cobra upon their foreheads.

These were the dominant objects that caught the eye at first. Between them, around them, piled on top of them, there were countless others—exquisitely painted and inlaid caskets; ala-baster vases, some beautifully carved in openwork designs; strange black shrines, from the open door of one a great gilt snake peeping out; bouquets of flowers or leaves; beds; chairs beautifully carved; a golden inlaid throne; a heap of curious white oviform boxes; staves of all shapes and designs; beneath our eyes, on the very threshold of the chamber, a beautiful lotiform cup of translucent alabaster; on the left a confused pile of overturned chariots, glistening with gold and inlay; and peeping from behind them another portrait of a king.

Such were some of the objects that lay before us. Whether we noted them all at the time I cannot say for certain, as our minds were in much too excited and confused a state to register accurately. Presently it dawned upon our bewildered brains that in all this medley of objects before us there was no coffin or trace of mummy, and the much-debated question of tomb or cache began to intrigue us afresh. With this question in view we re-examined the scene before us, and noticed for the first time that between the two black sentinel statues on the right there was another sealed doorway. The explanation gradually dawned upon us. We were but on the threshold of our discovery. What we saw was merely an antechamber.

Behind the guarded door there were to be other chambers, possibly a succession of them, and in one of them, beyond any shadow of doubt, in all his magnificent panoply of death, we should find the Pharaoh lying.

We had seen enough, and our brains began to reel at the thought of the task in front of us. We re-closed the hole, locked the wooden grille that had been placed upon the first doorway, left our native staff on guard, mounted our donkeys and rode home down The Valley, strangely silent and subdued.

It was curious, as we talked things over in the evening, to find how conflicting our ideas were as to what we had seen. Each of us had noted something that the others had not, and it amazed us next day to discover how many and how obvious were the things that we had missed. Naturally, it was the sealed door between the statues that intrigued us most, and we debated far into the night the possibilities of what might lie behind it. A single chamber with the king's sarcophagus? That was the least we might expect. But why one chamber only? Why not a succession of passages and chambers, leading, in true Valley style, to an innermost shrine of all, the burial chamber? It might be so, and yet in plan the tomb was quite unlike the others. Visions of chamber after chamber, each crowded with objects like the one we had seen, passed through our minds and left us gasping for breath. Then came the thought of the plunderers again. Had they succeeded in penetrating this third doorway—seen from a distance it looked absolutely untouched—and, if so, what were our chances of finding the king's mummy intact? I think we slept but little, all of us, that night.

Next morning (November 27th) we were early on the field, for there was much to be done. It was essential, before proceeding further with our examination, that we should have some more adequate means of illumination, so Callender began laying wires to connect us up with the main lighting system of The Valley. While this was in preparation we made careful notes of the seal-impressions upon the inner doorway and then removed its entire blocking. By noon everything was ready and

(photograph by Harry Burton, The Metropolitan Museum of Art)

Full View of Tut-ankh-Amen's Throne

Lord Carnarvon, Lady Evelyn, Callender and I entered the tomb and made a careful inspection of the first chamber (afterwards called the Antechamber). . . .

By the aid of our powerful electric lamps many things that had been obscure to us on the previous day became clear, and we were able to make a more accurate estimate of the extent of our discovery. Our first objective was naturally the sealed door between the statues, and here a disappointment awaited us. Seen from a distance it presented all the appearance of an absolutely intact blocking, but close examination revealed the fact that a small breach had been made near the bottom, just wide enough to admit a boy or a slightly built man, and that the hole made had subsequently been filled up and re-sealed. We were not then to be the first. Here, too, the thieves had forestalled us, and it only remained to be seen how much damage they had had the opportunity or the time to effect.

Our natural impulse was to break down the door, and get to the bottom of the matter at once, but to do so would have entailed serious risk of damage to many of the objects in the Antechamber, a risk which we were by no means prepared to face. Nor could we move the objects in question out of the way, for it was imperative that a plan and complete photographic record should be made before anything was touched, and this was a task involving a considerable amount of time, even if we had had sufficient plant available—which we had not—to carry it through immediately. Reluctantly we decided to abandon the opening of this inner sealed door until we had cleared the Antechamber of all its contents. By doing this we should not only ensure the complete scientific record of the outer chamber which it was our duty to make, but should have a clear field for the removal of the door-blocking, a ticklish operation at best.

Having satisfied to some extent our curiosity about the sealed doorway, we could now turn our attention to the rest of the chamber, and make a more detailed examination of the objects which it contained. It was certainly an astounding experience. Here, packed tightly together in this little chamber, were scores of objects, any one of which would have filled us with excitement under ordinary circumstances, and been considered ample repayment for a full season's work. Some were of types well enough known to us; others were new and strange, and in some cases there were complete and perfect examples of objects whose appearance we had heretofore but guessed at from the evidence of tiny broken fragments found in other royal tombs.

Nor was it merely from a point of view of quantity that the find was so amazing. The period to which the tomb belongs is in many respects the most interesting in the whole history of Egyptian art, and we were prepared for beautiful things. What we were not prepared for was the astonishing vitality and animation which characterized certain of the objects. It was a revelation to us of unsuspected possibilities in Egyptian art, and we realized, even in this hasty preliminary survey, that a study of the material would involve a modification, if not a complete revolution, of all our old ideas. That, however, is a matter for the future. We shall get a clearer estimate of exact artistic values when we have cleared the whole tomb and have the complete contents before us.

One of the first things we noted in our survey was that all of the larger objects, and most of the smaller ones, were inscribed with the name of Tut·ankh·Amen. His, too, were the seals upon the innermost door, and therefore his, beyond any shadow of doubt, the mummy that ought to lie behind it. Next, while we were still excitedly calling each other from one object to another, came a new discovery. Peering beneath the southernmost of the three great couches, we noticed a small irregular hole in the wall. Here was yet another sealed doorway, and a plunderers' hole, which, unlike the others, had never been repaired. Cautiously we crept under the couch, inserted our portable light, and there before us lay another chamber, rather smaller than the first, but even more crowded with objects.

The state of this inner room (afterwards called the Annexe) simply defies description. In the Antechamber there had been some sort of an attempt to tidy up after the plunderers' visit, but here everything was in confusion, just as they had left it. Nor did it take much imagination to picture them at their work. One—there would probably not have been room for more than one—had crept into the chamber, and had then hastily but systematically ransacked its entire contents, emptying boxes, throwing things aside, piling them one upon another, and occasionally passing objects through the hole to his companions for closer examination in the outer chamber. He had done his work just about as thoroughly as an earthquake. Not a single inch of floor space remains vacant, and it will be a matter of considerable difficulty, when the time for clearing comes, to know how to begin. So far we have not made any attempt to enter the chamber, but have contented ourselves with taking stock from outside. Beautiful things it contains, too, smaller than those in the Antechamber for the most part, but many of them of exquisite workmanship. Several things remain in my mind particularly—a painted box, apparently quite as lovely as the one in the Antechamber; a wonderful chair of ivory, gold, wood, and leather-work; alabaster and faience vases of beautiful form; and a gaming board, in carved and coloured ivory.

I think the discovery of this second chamber, with its crowded contents, had a somewhat sobering effect upon us. Excitement had gripped us hitherto, and given us no pause for thought, but now for the first time we began to realize what a prodigious task we had in front of us, and what a responsibility it entailed. This was no ordinary find, to be disposed of in a normal season's work; nor was there any precedent to show us how to handle it. The thing was outside all experience, bewildering, and for the moment it seemed as though there were more to be done than any human agency could accomplish.

Moreover, the extent of our discovery had taken us by surprise, and we were wholly unprepared to deal with the multitude of objects that lay before us, many in a perishable condition, and needing careful preservative treatment before they could be touched. There were numberless things to be done before we could even begin the work of clearing. Vast stores of preservatives and packing material must be laid in; expert advice must be taken as to the best method of dealing with certain objects; provision must be made for a laboratory, some safe and sheltered spot in which the objects could be treated, catalogued and packed; a careful plan to scale must be made, and a complete photographic record taken, while everything was still in position; a dark-room must be contrived.

These were but a few of the problems that confronted us. Clearly, the first thing to be done was to render the tomb safe against robbery; we could then with easy minds work out our plans—plans which we realized by this time would involve, not one season only, but certainly two, and possibly three or four. We had our wooden grille at the entrance to the passage, but that was not enough, and I measured up the inner doorway for a gate of thick steel bars. Until we could get this made for us—and for this and for other reasons it was imperative for me to visit Cairo—we must go to the labour of filling in the tomb once more.

Meanwhile the news of the discovery had spread like wildfire, and all sorts of extraordinary and fanciful reports were going abroad concerning it; one story, that found considerable credence among the natives, being to the effect that three aeroplanes had landed in The Valley, and gone off to some destination unknown with loads of treasure. To overtake these rumours as far as possible, we decided on two things—first, to invite Lord Allenby and the various heads of the departments concerned to come and pay a visit to the tomb, and secondly, to send an authoritative account of the discovery to *The Times*. On the 29th, accordingly, we had an official opening of the tomb. . . .

On December 3rd, after closing up the entrance doorway with heavy timber, the tomb was filled to surface level. Lord Carnarvon and Lady Evelyn left on the 4th, on their way to England, to conclude various arrangements there, preparatory to returning later in the season; and on the 6th, leaving Callender to watch over the tomb in my absence, I followed them to Cairo to make my purchases. My first care was the steel gate, and I ordered it the morning I arrived, under promise that it should be delivered within six days. The other purchases I took more leisurely, and a miscellaneous collection they were, including photographic material, chemicals, a motor-car, packing-boxes of every kind, with thirty-two bales of calico, more than a mile of wadding, and as much again of surgical bandages. Of these last two important items I was determined not to run short. . . .

By December 13th the steel gate was finished and I had completed my purchases. I returned to Luxor, and on the 15th everything arrived safely in The Valley, delivery of the packages having been greatly expedited by the courtesy of the Egyptian State Railway officials, who permitted them to travel by express instead of on the slow freight train. On the 16th we opened up the tomb once more, and on the 17th the steel gate was set up in the door of the chamber and we were ready to begin work. On the 18th work was actually begun. . . .

Clearing the objects from the Antechamber was like playing a gigantic game of spillikins. So crowded were they that it was a matter of extreme difficulty to move one without running serious risk of damaging others, and in some cases they were so inextricably tangled that an elaborate system of props and supports had to be devised to hold one object or group of objects in place while another was being removed. At such times life was a nightmare. One was afraid to move lest one should kick against a prop and bring the whole thing crashing down. Nor, in many cases, could one tell without experiment whether a particular object was strong enough to bear its own weight. Certain of the things were in beautiful condition, as strong as when they first were made, but others were in a most precarious state, and the problem constantly arose whether it would be better to apply preservative treatment to an object *in situ,* or to wait until it could be dealt with in more convenient surroundings in the laboratory. The latter course was adopted whenever possible, but there were cases in which the removal of an object without treatment would have meant almost certain destruction.

There were sandals, for instance, of patterned bead-work, of which the threading had entirely rotted away. As they lay on the floor of the chamber they looked in perfectly sound condition, but, try to pick one up, and it crumbled at the touch, and all you had for your pains was a handful of loose, meaningless beads. This was a clear case for treatment on the spot—a spirit stove, some paraffin wax, an hour or two to harden, and the sandal could be removed intact, and handled with the utmost freedom. The funerary bouquets again: without treatment as they stood they would have ceased to exist; subjected to three or four sprayings of celluloid solution they bore removal well, and were subsequently packed with scarcely any injury. Occasionally, particularly with the larger objects, it was found better to apply local treatment in the tomb, just sufficient to ensure a safe removal to the laboratory, where more drastic measures were possible. Each object presented a separate problem, and, as I said before, there were cases in which only experiment could show what the proper treatment was to be.

It was slow work, painfully slow, and nerve-racking at that, for one felt all the time a heavy weight of responsibility. Every excavator must, if he have any archæological conscience at all. The things he finds are not his own property, to treat as he pleases, or neglect as he chooses. They are a direct legacy from the past to the present age, he but the privileged intermediary through whose hands they come; and if, by carelessness, slackness, or ignorance, he lessens the sum of knowledge that might have been obtained from them, he knows himself to be guilty of an archæological crime of the first magnitude. Destruction of evidence is so painfully easy, and yet so hopelessly irreparable. Tired or pressed for time, you shirk a tedious piece of cleaning, or do it in a half-hearted, perfunctory sort of way, and you will perhaps have thrown away the one chance that will ever occur of gaining some important piece of knowledge.

Too many people—unfortunately there are so-called archæologists among them—are apparently under the impression that the object bought from a dealer's shop is just as valuable as one which has been found in actual excavation, and that until the object in question has been cleaned, entered in the books, marked with an accession number, and placed in a tidy museum case, it is not a proper subject for study at all. There was never a greater mistake. Field-work is all-important, and it is a sure and certain fact that if every excavation had been properly, systematically, and conscientiously carried out, our knowledge of Egyptian archæology would be at least 50 per cent greater than it is. There are numberless derelict objects in the storerooms of our museums which would give us valuable information could they but tell us whence they came, and box after box full of fragments which a few notes at the time of finding would have rendered capable of reconstruction.

Granting, then, that a heavy weight of responsibility must at all times rest upon the excavator, our own feelings on this occasion will easily be realized. It had been our privilege to find the most important collection of Egyptian antiquities that had ever seen the light, and it was for us to show that we were worthy of the trust. So many things there were that might go wrong. Danger of theft, for instance, was an ever-present anxiety. The whole countryside was agog with excitement about the tomb; all sorts of extravagant tales were current about the gold and jewels it contained; and, as past experience had shown, it was only too possible that there might be a serious attempt to raid the tomb by night. This possibility of robbery on a large scale was negatived, so far as was humanly possible, by a complicated system of guarding, there being present in The Valley, day and night, three independent groups of watchmen, each answerable to a different authority —the Government Antiquities Guards, a squad of soldiers supplied by the Mudir of Kena, and a selected group of the most trustworthy of our own staff. In addition, we had a heavy wooden grille at the entrance to the passage, and a massive steel gate at the inner doorway, each secured by four padlocked chains; and, that there might never be any mistake about these latter, the keys were in the permanent charge of one particular member of the European staff, who never parted with them for a moment, even to lend them to a colleague. Petty or casual theft we guarded against by doing all the handling of the objects ourselves.

Another and perhaps an even greater cause for anxiety was the condition of many of the objects. It was manifest with some of them that their very existence depended on careful manipulation and correct preservative treatment, and there were moments when our hearts were in our mouths. There were other worries, too—visitors, for instance, but I shall have quite a little to say about them later—and I fear that by the time the Antechamber was finished our nerves, to say nothing of our tempers, were in an extremely ragged state. But here am I talking about finishing before we have even begun. We must make a fresh start. It is not time to lose our tempers yet.

Obviously, our first and greatest need was photography. Before anything else was done, or anything moved, we must have a series of preliminary views, taken in panorama, to show the general appearance of the chamber. For lighting we had available two movable electric standards, giving 3,000 candlepower, and it was with these that all the photographic work in the tomb was done. Exposures were naturally rather slow, but the light was beautifully even, much more so than would have been afforded by flashlight—a dangerous process in such a crowded chamber—or reflected sunlight, which were the two possible alternatives. Fortunately for us, there was an uninscribed and empty tomb close by—the Davis cache tomb of Akh·en·Aten. This we got permission from the Government [for the photographer] to use as a dark room. . . . It was not too convenient in some ways, but it was worth while putting up with a little inconvenience to have a dark room so close, for in the case of experimental exposures he could slip across and develop without moving his camera out of position. Moreover, these periodic dashes of his from tomb to tomb must have been a godsend to the crowd of curious visitors who kept vigil above the tomb, for there were many days during the winter in which it was the only excitement they had.

Our next step, after these preliminary photographs had been taken, was to devise an efficient method of registering the contents of the chamber, for it would be absolutely essential, later on, that we should have a ready means of ascertaining the exact part of the tomb from which any particular object might have come. Naturally, each object, or closely allied group of objects, would be given its own catalogue number, and would have that number securely attached to it when it was moved away from the chamber, but that was not enough, for the number might not indicate position. So far as possible, the numbers were to follow a definite order, beginning at the entrance doorway and working systematically round the chamber, but it was very certain that many objects now hidden would be found in the course of clearing, and have to be numbered out of turn. We got over the difficulty by placing printed numbers on every object and photographing them in small groups. Every number showed in at least one of the photographs, so that, by duplicating prints, we were able to place with the notes of every single object in our filing cabinets a print which showed at a glance its actual position in the tomb.

So far, so good, as far as the internal work in the tomb was concerned. Outside it, we had a still more difficult problem to solve, that of finding adequate working and storage space for the objects as they were removed. Three things were absolutely essential. In the first place we must have plenty of room. There would be boxes to unpack, notes and measurements to be taken, repairs to be carried out, experiments with various preservative materials to be made, and obviously we should require considerable table accommodation as well as ordinary storage space. Then, secondly, we must have a place that we could render thief-proof, for, as things were moved, the laboratory would come to be almost as great a source of danger as the tomb itself. Lastly, we must have seclusion. This may seem a less obvious need than the others, but we foresaw, and the winter's happenings proved us to be right, that unless we were out of sight of visitors' ordinary haunts we should be treated as a side-show, and should be unable to get any work done at all. Eventually we solved the problem by getting permission from the Government to take over the tomb of Seti II (No. 15 in The Valley catalogue). This certainly fulfilled the third of our requirements. It is not a tomb ordinarily visited by tourists, and its position, tucked away in a corner at the extreme end of The Valley, was exactly suitable to our purpose. No other tomb lay beyond it, so, without causing inconvenience to anyone, we could close to ordinary traffic the path that led to it, and thus secure complete privacy for ourselves.

It had other advantages, too. For one thing, it was so well sheltered by overhanging cliffs that at no time of day did the sun ever penetrate its doors, thus remaining comparatively cool even in the hottest of summer weather. There was also a considerable amount of open space in front of it, and this we utilized later as an open-air photographic studio and a carpenter's shop. We were somewhat restricted as to space, for the tomb was so long and narrow that all our work had to be done at the upper end of it, the lower part being useless except for storage purposes. It had also the disadvantage of being rather a long way from the scene of operations. These, however, were but minor drawbacks compared with the positive advantages which the tomb offered. We had a reasonable amount of room, we had privacy, and safety we ensured by putting up a many-padlocked steel gate, one and a half tons in weight.

One other point with regard to the laboratory work the reader should bear in mind. We were five hundred miles from anywhere, and, if we ran short of preservative materials, there might be considerable delay before we could secure a fresh supply. The Cairo shops furnished most of our needs, but there were certain chemicals of which we exhausted the entire

Cairo stock before the winter was over, and other things which, in the first instance, could only be procured in England. Constant care and forethought were therefore necessary to prevent shortage and the consequent holding up of the work.

By December 27th all our preparations were made, and we were ready to make a start on the actual removal of the objects. We worked on a regular system of division of labour. Burton came first with his photographs of the numbered groups of objects; Hall and Hauser followed with their scale plan of the chamber, every object being drawn on the plan in projection; Callender and I did the preliminary noting and clearing, and superintended the removal of the objects to the laboratory; and there Mace and Lucas received them, and were responsible for the detail-noting, mending, and preservation.

The first object to be removed was the painted wooden casket. Then, working from north to south, and thus putting off the evil day when we should have to tackle the complicated tangle of chariots, we gradually disencumbered the great animal couches of the objects which surrounded them. Each object as it was removed was placed upon a padded wooden stretcher and securely fastened to it with bandages. Enormous numbers of these stretchers were required, for, to avoid double handling, they were in almost every case left permanently with the object, and not re-used. From time to time, when a sufficient number of stretchers had been filled—about once a day, on an average—a convoy was made up and dispatched under guard to the laboratory. This was the moment for which the crowd of watchers above the tomb were waiting. Out came the reporters' note-books, *click, click, click* went the cameras in every direction, and a lane had to be cleared for the procession to pass through. I suppose more films were wasted in The Valley last winter than in any other corresponding period of time since cameras were first invented. We in the laboratory had occasion once for a piece of old mummy cloth for experimental purposes; it was sent up to us in a stretcher, and it was photographed eight times before it got to us!

The removal and transport of the smaller objects was a

comparatively simple matter, but it was quite otherwise when it came to the animal couches and the chariots. Each of the former was constructed in four pieces—the two animal sides, the bed proper, and the base to which the animals' feet were socketed. They were manifestly much too large to negotiate the narrow entrance passage, and must have been brought into the tomb in sections and assembled there. Indeed, strips of newer gold round the joints show where the damage they had incurred in handling had been made good after deposition. It was obvious that to get the couches out of the tomb we must take them apart again; no easy matter, for after three thousand years the bronze hooks had naturally set tight in the staples, and would not budge. We got them apart eventually, and with scarcely any damage, but it took no fewer than five of us to do it. Two supported the central part of the couch, two were responsible for the well-being of the animals, while the fifth, working from underneath, eased up the hooks, one after the other, with a lever.

Even when taken apart there was none too much room to get the side animals through the passage, and they needed very careful handling. However, we got them all out without accident, and packed them straight into boxes we had in readiness for them just outside the entrance to the tomb.

Most difficult of all to move were the chariots, which had suffered considerably from the treatment to which they had been subjected. It had not been possible to get them into the tomb whole in the first instance, for they were too wide for the entrance passage, and the wheels had had to be removed and the axles sawn off at one end. They had evidently been moved out of position and turned upside down by the plunderers, and in the subsequent tidying up the parts had been loosely stacked one upon another. Egyptian chariots are of very light construction, and the rough usage which they had undergone made these extremely difficult to handle. There was another complication, in that the parts of the harness were made of undressed leather. Now this, if exposed to humidity, speedily resolves itself into glue, and that was what had happened here—the black glutinous mass which represented the trappings having run down over everything and dropped, not only on the other parts of the chariots themselves, but upon other objects which had nothing to do with them. Thus the leather has almost entirely perished, but, fortunately, as I have already stated, we have for reconstructional purposes the gold ornamentation with which it was covered.

Seven weeks in all it took us to clear the Antechamber, and thankful indeed were we when it was finished, and that without any kind of disaster befalling us. One scare we had. For two or three days the sky was very black, and it looked as though we were in for one of the heavy storms that occasionally visit Thebes. On such occasions rain comes down in torrents, and if the storm persists for any length of time the whole bed of The Valley becomes a raging flood. No power on earth could have kept our tomb from being flooded under these conditions, but, fortunately, though there must have been heavy rain somewhere in the district, we escaped with but a few drops. Certain correspondents indulged in some highly imaginative writing on the subject of this threatened storm. As a result of this and other distorted news we received a somewhat cryptic cable, sent presumably by a zealous student of the occult. It ran: "In the case of further trouble, pour milk, wine and honey on the threshold." Unfortunately, we had neither wine nor honey with us, so were unable to carry out the directions. In spite of our negligence, however, we escaped the further trouble. Perhaps we were given absent treatment.

In the course of our clearing we naturally accumulated a good deal of evidence with regard to the activities of the original tomb-plunderers, and this will be as good a place as any to give a statement of the conclusions at which we arrived.

In the first place, we know from the sealings on the outer doorway that all the plundering was done within a very few years of the king's burial. We also know that the plunderers entered the tomb at least twice. There were broken scattered objects on the floor of the entrance passage and staircase, proving that at the time of the first attempt the passage-way

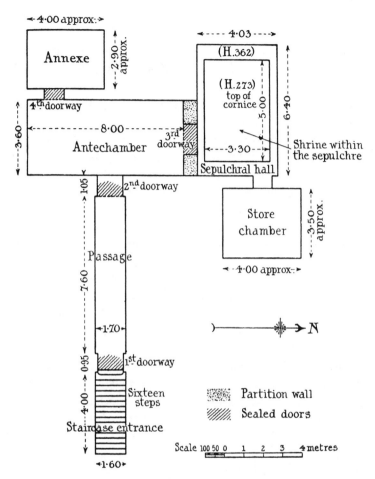

Sketch-Plan of the Tomb of Tut-ankh-Amen

between the inner and the outer sealed doors was empty. It is, I suppose, just possible that this preliminary plundering was done immediately after the funeral ceremonies. Thereafter the passage was entirely filled with stones and rubbish, and it was through a tunnel excavated in the upper left-hand corner of this filling that the subsequent attempts were made. At this final attempt the thieves had penetrated into all the chambers of the tomb, but their tunnel was only a narrow one, and clearly they could not have got away with any except the smaller objects.

Now as to internal evidence of the damage they had been able to effect. To begin with, there was a strange difference between the respective states in which the Antechamber and the Annexe had been left. In the latter, as we have described in the preceding chapter, everything was in confusion, and there was not a vacant inch of floor-space. It was quite evident that the plunderers had turned everything topsy-turvy, and that the present state of the chamber was precisely that in which they had left it. The Antechamber was quite different. There was a certain amount of confusion, it was true, but it was orderly confusion, and had it not been for the evidence of plundering afforded by the tunnel and the re-sealed doorways, one might have imagined at first view that there never had been any plundering, and that the confusion was due to Oriental carelessness at the time of the funeral.

However, when we commenced clearing, it quickly became manifest that this comparative orderliness was due to a process of hasty tidying-up, and that the plunderers had been just as busy here as they had in the Annexe. Parts of the same object were found in different quarters of the chamber; objects that should have been in boxes were lying on the floor or upon the couches; on the lid of one of the boxes there was a collar, intact but crumpled; behind the chariots, in an entirely inaccessible place, there was a box-lid, the box to which it belonged being far away, near the innermost door. Quite clearly the plunderers had scattered things here just as they had done in the Annexe, and someone had come after them and rearranged the chamber.

Later, when we came to unpack the boxes, we found still more circumstantial evidence. One, the long white box at the north end of the chamber, was half full of sticks, bows and arrows, and above, stuffed tightly in upon them, there was a mixed collection of the king's under-linen. Yet the metal points had been broken from all the arrows, and a few were found dropped upon the floor. Other sticks and bows that obviously belonged to this box were likewise scattered in the chamber. In another box there were a number of decorated robes, bundled together and thrust in anyhow, and mixed with them several pairs of sandals. So tightly had the contents of the box been stuffed, that the metal toe-thong of one of the sandals had pierced right through its own leather sole and penetrated that of another which lay beneath it. In still another box, jewellery and tiny statuettes had been packed on top of faience libation vases. Others, again, were half empty, or contained a mere jumble of odds and ends of cloth.

There was, moreover, certain evidence that this confusion was due to hasty repacking, and had nothing to do with the original arrangement of the boxes, for on the lids of several there were neat little dockets stating clearly what the contents should have been, and in only one case did the docket bear any sort of relation to the contents as they actually were. This particular docket called for "17 (unknown objects) of lapis lazuli colour." Within the box there were sixteen libation vases of dark blue faience, and a seventeenth was on the floor of the chamber some distance away. Eventually, in our final study of the material these dockets will be of great value. We shall be able, in a great many cases, to apportion out the objects to the boxes which originally contained them, and shall know exactly what is missing.

The best evidence of all was supplied by a very elaborate garment of faience, gold and inlay, comprising in one piece corslet, collar and pectoral. The largest portion of it was found in the box which contained the faience vases just mentioned; the pectoral and most of the collar were tucked away in the small gold shrine; and isolated pieces of it turned up in several other boxes, and were scattered all over the floor. There is nothing at present to show which of the boxes it originally belonged to, or even that it actually belonged to any of them. It is quite possible that the plunderers brought it from the innermost chamber to the better light of the Antechamber, and there deliberately pulled it to pieces.

From the facts at our disposal we can now reconstruct the whole sequence of events. A breach was first made in the upper left-hand corner of the first sealed door, just large enough to admit a man, and then the tunnelling began, the excavators working in a chain, passing the stones and baskets of earth back from one to another. Seven or eight hours' work might suffice to bring them to the second sealed door; a hole in this, and they were through. Then in the semi-darkness began a mad scramble for loot. Gold was their natural quarry, but it had to be in portable form, and it must have maddened them to see it glinting all around them, on plated objects which they could not move, and had not time to strip. Nor, in the dim light in which they were working, could they always distinguish between the real and the false, and many an object which they took for solid gold was found on closer examination to be but gilded wood, and was contemptuously thrown aside. The boxes were treated in very drastic fashion. Without exception they were dragged out into the centre of the room and ransacked, their contents being strewn about all over the floor. What valuables they found in them and made away with we may never know, but their search can have been but hurried and superficial, for many objects of solid gold were overlooked. One very valuable thing we know they did secure. Within the small gold shrine there was a pedestal of gilded wood, made for a statuette, with the imprint of the statuette's feet still marked upon it. The statuette itself was gone, and there can be very little doubt that it was a solid gold one, probably very similar to the gold statuette of Thothmes III, in the image of Amen, in the Carnarvon collection.

Next, the Antechamber having been thoroughly worked over, the thieves turned their attention to the Annexe, knocking a hole in its doorway just big enough to let them through, and overturning and ransacking its contents quite as thoroughly as they had done those of the outer chamber.

Then, and apparently not until then, they directed themselves towards the burial chamber, and made a very small hole in the sealed doorway which screened it from the Antechamber. How much damage they did there we shall know in due time, but, so far as we can tell at present, it was less than in the outer chambers. They may, indeed, have been disturbed at this particular stage in the proceedings, and there is a very interesting little piece of evidence that seems to bear the theory out.

It may be remembered that in our description of the objects in the Antechamber we mentioned that one of the boxes contained a handful of solid gold rings tied up in a fold of cloth. They were just the things to attract a thief, for their intrinsic value was considerable, and yet they could very easily be hidden away. Now, every visitor to Egypt will remember that if you give money to a *fellah* his ordinary proceeding will be to undo a portion of his head-shawl, put the coins in a fold of it, twist it round two or three times to hold the coins tight in place, and make it finally secure by looping the bag thus formed into a knot. These rings had been secured in exactly the same way—the same loose fold in the cloth, the same twisting round to form the bag, and the same loose knot. This, unquestionably, was the work of one of the thieves. It was not his head-shawl that he had used—the *fellah* of the period wore no such garment—but one of the king's scarves which he had picked up in the tomb, and he had fastened them thus for convenience in carrying. How comes it then that the precious bundle of rings was left in the tomb, and not carried off? It was the very last thing that a thief would be likely to forget, and, in case of sudden alarm, it was not heavy enough to impede his flight, however hurried that might be. We are almost forced to the conclusion that the thieves were either trapped within the tomb, or overtaken in their flight—traced, in any case, with some of the plunder still upon them. If this be so, it explains the presence of certain other pieces of jewellery and gold-work too valuable to leave and too big to overlook.

In any case, the fact that a robbery had been committed

got to the ears of the officials concerned, and they came to the tomb to investigate and make the damage good. For some reason they seem to have been in almost as great a hurry as the thieves, and their work of reparation was sadly scamped. The Annexe they left severely alone, not even taking the trouble to fill up the hole in the doorway. In the Antechamber the smaller objects with which the floor was covered were swept up, bundled together, and jammed—there is no other word—back into the boxes, no attempt being made to sort the material, or to put the objects into the boxes which had been originally intended for them. Some of the boxes were packed tight, others were left almost empty, and on one of the couches there were deposited two large bundles of cloth in which a miscellaneous collection of material had been wrapped. Nor even was all the small material gathered up. The sticks, bows and arrows were left in scattered groups; on the lid of a box were thrown a crumpled collar of pendants, and a pad of faience rings; and on the floor, one on one side of the chamber and one on the other, there was a pair of fragile bead-work sandals. The larger objects were pushed carelessly back against the walls, or stacked one upon another. Certainly no respect was shown, either to the objects themselves, or to the king whose property they were, and one wonders why, if they tidied up so badly, they took the trouble to tidy up at all. One thing we must credit them with. They did not do any pilfering, as they might easily have done, on their own account. We can be reasonably sure of that from the valuable objects, small and easily concealed, which they repacked into the boxes.

The Antechamber finished—so far, at least, as they intended to finish it—the hole in the innermost doorway was refilled, plastered, and stamped with the royal necropolis seal. Then, retracing their steps, they closed and sealed the Antechamber door, filled up the plunderers' tunnel through the passage-blocking, and made good the outer doorway. What further steps they took to prevent repetition of the crime we do not know, but probably they buried the whole entrance to the tomb deep out of sight. Better political conditions in the country might have prevented it for a time, but in the long run nothing but ignorance of its whereabouts could have saved it from further attempts at plundering; and very certain it is that. between the time of this re-closing and that of our discovery. no hand had touched the seals upon the door.

PART TWO.

*The*

*Land*

*of*

*Two*

*Rivers*

A Winged Being and the Arms-Bearer
of the King, Nimroud—Alabaster

# 4. LAYARD:

# *The Man Who Found Nineveh*

> *Far-call'd our navies melt away—*
> *On dune and headland sinks the fire—*
> *Lo, all our pomp of yesterday*
> *Is one with Nineveh and Tyre!*
> *Judge of the Nations, spare us yet,*
> *Lest we forget, lest we forget!*
>
> — KIPLING, *Recessional*

3. Behold, the Assyrian was a cedar in Lebanon with fair branches, and with a shadowing shroud, and of an high stature; and his top was among the thick boughs.

4. The waters made him great, the deep set him up on high with her rivers running round about his plants, and sent out her little rivers unto all the trees of the field. . . .

7. Thus was he fair in his greatness, in the length of his branches: for his root was by great waters. . . .

10. Therefore thus saith the Lord GOD: Because thou hast lifted up thyself in height, and he hath shot up his top among the thick boughs, and his heart is lifted up in his height;

11. I have therefore delivered him into the hand of the mighty one of the heathen; he shall surely deal with him: I have driven him out for his wickedness.

12. And strangers, the terrible of the nations, have cut him off, and have left him: upon the mountains and in all the valleys his branches are fallen, and his boughs are broken by all the rivers of the land, and all the people of the earth are gone down from his shadow, and have left him.

— EZEKIEL, 31

While the people of the Nile Valley were creating their great civilization, an even older culture was flourishing a thousand miles to the east, in the land the Hebrews called *Aram-naharaim* and the Greeks called *Mestopotamia.*

Both names meant the same thing: "The Land Between the Two Rivers." The rivers were the Tigris and the Euphrates, by whose fertile banks sprang up great cities and splendid temples.

A people called the Sumerians were the first to build there. They came out of mountainous country somewhere to the north, and entered Mesopotamia in waves, some time about 3500 B.C., displacing an even earlier and primitive people whose name has been lost. The Sumerians settled in southern Mesopotamia, built canals and reservoirs to irrigate their land, extended their territory by filling in the sea, and erected the famed cities of Ur, Nippur, Uruk, Lagash, and many another. They were a cultivated and sophisticated people, these Sumerians, but in time they were buried under a swarm of invaders.

A race from the west, speaking a language of the family we call Semitic, marched into Sumer about 2400 B.C. Under Sargon I, the invaders established the empire of Akkad, and for the first time unified all of Mesopotamia under one rule.

Sargon's empire lasted only three generations, and for a brief while afterward the Sumerians were able to gain control of their land once again. Then more Semitic-speaking invaders arrived, and the power of Sumer was broken forever. New kings arose—and, about 1750 B.C., one of these Semite rulers, Hammurabi, King of Babylon, was able to unite all Mesopotamia once again under a single authority.

While Babylonia flourished and then decayed, a new power was rising in the north, along the Tigris. This was Assyria, an old kingdom but not an important one until about 1200 B.C. The Assyrians were cousins of the Babylonians; they spoke a dialect of the same Semitic language, they used roughly the same cuneiform writing. Beginning a policy of imperialistic expansion toward the end of the Second Millennium B.C., the Assyrians achieved complete dominion over Mesopotamia by the ninth century B.C.

They were not a pleasant race. Military conquest was their great joy. Their art, their culture, their language—all this they borrowed from Babylonia. Only in the techniques of war were they original, and in war they were supreme.

Each king of Assyria built his own capital to celebrate his importance. Assurnasirpal, who ruled from 885 to 859 B.C., established his palace at the city of Calah; Sargon II, who arrogantly named himself after the great unifier of two millennia earlier, saw Dur-Sharrukin ("The City of Sargon") rise during his reign, 721-705 B.C. Other Assyrian rulers had their capitals at Assur, further to the south along the Tigris, and at the great city of Nineveh.

Under Tiglath-Pileser III (745-727 B.C.) Assyria's domain stretched from the Mediterranean to the Persian Gulf. Persia and Armenia sent tributes to the Assyrian king. Ancient Babylonia was incorporated into the Assyrian Empire. Sargon II extended the empire to the peak of its greatness. But under his successor, the madman Sennacherib, parts of the far-flung empire broke away. Sennacherib inflicted terrible punishment on the rebellious city of Babylon, but could not maintain the whole empire, and finally was murdered by his own brothers, who in turn were overthrown by Sennacherib's son Esarhaddon. This king briefly added Egypt to the Assyrian Empire.

Under Esarhaddon's son, Ashurbanipal, first Egypt, then Babylonia broke away; out of the mountains of the east came the armies of the Medes and the Persians, and in 612 Nineveh, Ashurbanipal's capital, fell to the invaders. The Assyrians at last toppled from their position of command. Their empire was divided between the Babylonians and the Persians; the great cities of Assyria were put to the torch.

Nineveh, Assur, Dur-Sharrukin, Calah—they became shapeless mounds in the desert. Nomads settled about them. Their ancient glories, even their names, were forgotten. Nineveh came to be called "Kuyunjik;" Assur, "Qalah Shergat;" Dur-Sharrukin, "Khorsabad," Calah, "Nimroud."

The years lengthened into centuries and millennia. European travellers stared at the great mounds baking under the Mesopotamian sun. They picked baked bricks out of the mounds, bricks stamped with odd wedge-shaped characters. Were these mounds the cities of Assyria? the travellers wondered.

One who did more than wonder was Paul Emile Botta, French Consul in the town of Mosul, on the upper Tigris. In 1842, Botta began to collect antiquities: old pots, vases, bricks with cuneiform inscriptions. He heard that antiquities could be found in the mounds near the city; he picked one at random and began to dig. It was Kuyunjik, which had been Nineveh, but Botta had little luck there. He moved on to Khorsabad, 14 miles away, and proceeded to unearth the palace of Sargon II. He could not identify the palace, of course, but he was struck with the sculptured reliefs, the imposing limestone walls. He shipped boatloads of treasure back to France, and published a lavishly illustrated book.

An Englishman named Austen Henry Layard was one of the first to be inflamed by Botta's finds. Born in 1817 in Paris, Layard had first travelled through the Near East when he was 22, living with savage tribes, examining the remnants of ancient cities. In 1842, Layard visited Mosul and met Botta. Three years later, his enthusiasm afire, Layard returned, cajoled £60 out of Sir Stratford Canning, the British Ambassador in Mosul, and began to dig. His first site was Nimroud —Assurnasirpal's city of Calah—and, after great success there, Layard turned to Kuyunjik (Nineveh) with equally encouraging results.

Layard returned to London in 1847. He wrote a two-volume account of his activities, *Nineveh and Its Remains*, which the firm of John Murray brought out in 1849. It was an immediate popular success; a letter of Layard's notes that the book was selling at a rate of 8000 copies a year, "which will place it side by side with *Mrs. Rundell's Cookery.*" A popular abridgement sold many thousands more. A large portfolio of plates, *The Monuments of Nineveh*, priced at a lofty ten guineas, sold out.

Layard returned to the Near East as a minor diplomatic official, and resumed his digging. From 1849 to 1851 he blazed through Mesopotamia, excavating not only at Kuyunjik and Nimroud, but at Qalah Shergat (Assur) and at Khorsabad (Dur-Sharrukin) as well. He also found time to venture south to dig into the mound of Babil near Baghdad, reputed to be the site of ancient Babylon, but his results were scanty there, as they likewise were at another southern mound that later was learned to be the Sumerian city of Nippur.

Again and again, Layard applied to Parliament for a grant to finance his work. The funds were refused, despite the public furore Layard's discoveries were causing, and in April, 1851, he concluded his Assyrian diggings forever. On his return to London, he wrote a second best-selling book, *Discoveries in the Ruins of Nineveh and Babylon* (1853), and produced a second portfolio of *Monuments of Nineveh*. Then he entered upon a political career. He served in Parliament, held cabinet posts, and in 1869 was named Ambassador to Spain. From 1877 to 1880, he represented Great Britain at the court of the Sultan in Constantinople, and was in a position to intercede for the new group of younger archaeologists working in Turkish domains. In his later years, Layard's chief interest was in

Venetian paintings, and he published numerous monographs on that subject.

As an archaeologist, Layard was more of the Belzoni school than a forerunner of Flinders Petrie. His chief aim was to uncover works of art, and in that he succeeded magnificently, while doing great structural damage to the mounds in which he burrowed. To his credit, though, he was no mere plunderer, but a serious student of history, and his two books are rich with fascinating speculation on the nature of Assyrian culture. That most of his conjectures proved incorrect does not detract from their interest. Layard began his work at a time when cuneiform writing had not been deciphered, and in his first book he could only refer to the builder of Dur-Sharrukin as "The Khorsabad King." (Before *Nineveh and Babylon* appeared, though, Major Henry Rawlinson had broken the secret of cuneiform, and Layard could safely identify "The Khorsabad King" as Sargon.)

Layard emerges from his two lengthy books as a genial and attractive person, and his works are undeniable classics of travel literature. For hundreds of pages at a time, Layard drops his account of the excavations for long narratives of his wanderings among the Kurdish and Nestorian tribesmen of what is now Iraq, and the color and detail excite admiration in any reader. The sections chosen here are from his first book, and deal chiefly with his excavations at Nimroud. Layard was under the impression that Nimroud, Qalah Shergat, Kuyunjik, and Khorsabad were all parts of one gigantic city of Nineveh, covering hundreds of square miles. Only later was it shown that these were four separate cities of the Assyrian Empire. Layard died in 1894, having lived to see Assyriology become a systematic science.

# THE MAN WHO FOUND NINEVEH

Kalah Sherghat, no less than Nimroud, was an Assyrian ruin: a vast, shapeless mass, now covered with grass, and showing scarcely any traces of the work of man except where the winter rains had formed ravines down its almost perpendicular sides, and had thus laid open its contents. A few fragments of pottery and inscribed bricks, discovered after a careful search among the rubbish which had accumulated round the base of the great mound, served to prove that it owed its construction to the people who had founded the city of which Nimroud is the remains. There was a tradition current amongst the Arabs, that strange figures carved in black stone still existed amongst the ruins; but we searched for them in vain. . . .

In the middle of April I left Mosul for Baghdad. As I descended the Tigris on a raft, I again saw the ruins of Nimroud, and had a better opportunity of examining them. It was evening as we approached the spot. The spring rains had clothed the mound with the richest verdure, and the fertile meadows, which stretched around it, were covered with flowers of every hue. Amidst this luxuriant vegetation were partly concealed a few fragments of bricks, pottery, and alabaster, upon which might be traced the well-defined wedges of the cuneiform character. Did not these remains mark the nature of the ruin, it might have been confounded with a natural eminence. A long line of consecutive narrow mounds, still retaining the appearance of walls or ramparts, stretched from its base, and formed a vast quadrangle. The river flowed at some distance from them; its waters, swollen by the melting of the snows on the Armenian hills, were broken into a thousand foaming whirlpools by an artificial barrier, built across the stream. On the eastern bank the soil had been washed away by the current; but a solid mass of masonry still withstood its impetuosity. . . .

From *Nineveh and Its Remains* (London: John Murray, 1849) by Austen Henry Layard.

My curiosity had been greatly excited, and from that time I formed the design of thoroughly examining, whenever it might be in my power, these singular ruins.

[In 1842 Layard passed through Mosul again and learned that the French Consul, M. Botta, had begun excavations in another mound on the opposite side of the river. His findings were significant but spotty, and Layard, financially unable to undertake the project, suggested that Botta try Nimroud. Botta declined, saying that Nimroud was inconveniently situated, and turned his attention to Khorsabad, where he made important finds. In 1845, Layard obtained a backer, Sir Stratford Canning, who agreed to underwrite limited digging at Nimroud. He returned to Mosul to begin.]

My first step on reaching Mosul was to present my letters of introduction to the governor of the province. Mohammed Pasha, being a native of Candia, was usually known as Keritli Oglu (the son of the Cretan) to distinguish him from his celebrated predecessor of the same name. . . . The appearance of his Excellency was not prepossessing, but it matched his temper and conduct. Nature had placed hypocrisy beyond his reach. He had one eye and one ear; he was short and fat, deeply marked by the smallpox, uncouth in gestures and harsh in voice. His fame had reached the seat of his government before him. On the road he had revived many good old customs and impositions, which the reforming spirit of the age had suffered to fall into decay. He particularly insisted on *dish-parassi* (literally, "tooth-money"); or a compensation in money, levied upon all villages in which a man of such rank is entertained, for the wear and tear of his teeth in masticating the food he condescends to receive from the inhabitants. On entering Mosul, he had induced several of the principal Aghas who had fled from the town on his approach, to return to their homes; and having made a formal display of oaths and protestations, cut their throats to show how much his word could be depended upon. At the time of my arrival, the population was in a state of terror and despair. . . .

Such was the Pasha to whom I was introduced two days

Lowering the Great Winged Bull, Nimroud

after my arrival by the British Vice-Consul, Mr. Rassam. He read the letters which I presented to him, and received me with that civility which a traveller generally expects from a Turkish functionary of high rank. His anxiety to know the object of my journey was evident, but his curiosity was not gratified for the moment.

There were many reasons which rendered it necessary that my plans should be concealed, until I was ready to put them into execution. Although I had always experienced from M. Botta the most friendly assistance, there were others who did not share his sentiments; from the authorities and the people of the town I could only expect the most decided opposition. On the 8th of November, having secretly procured a few tools, and engaged a mason at the moment of my departure, and carrying with me a variety of guns, spears, and other formidable weapons, I declared that I was going to hunt wild boars in a neighboring village, and floated down the Tigris on a small raft constructed for my journey. . . .

At this time of the year more than five hours are required to descend the Tigris, from Mosul to Nimroud. It was sunset before we reached the Awai, or dam across the river. We landed and walked to the village of Naifa. No light appeared as we approached, nor were we even saluted by the dogs, which usually abound in an Arab village. We had entered a heap of ruins. I was about to return to the raft, upon which we had made up our minds to pass the night, when a glare of fire lighted up the entrance to a miserable hovel. Through a crevice in the wall, I saw an Arab family crouching round a heap of half-extinguished embers. The dress of the man, the ample cloak and white turban, showed that he belonged to one of the Arab tribes, which cultivate a little land on the borders of the desert, and are distinguished, by their more settled habits, from the Bedouins. Near him were three women, lean and haggard, their heads almost concealed in black handkerchiefs, and the rest of their persons enveloped in the striped aba. Some children, nearly naked, and one or two mangy greyhounds completed the group.

As we entered all the party rose, and showed some alarm at this sudden appearance of strangers. The man, however, seeing that we were Europeans, bid us welcome, and spreading some cornsacks on the ground, invited us to be seated. The women and children retreated into a corner of the hut. Our host, whose name was Awad or Abd-Allah, was a sheikh of the Jehesh. His tribe had been plundered by the Pasha, and was now scattered in different parts of the country; he had taken refuge in the ruined village. He told us that owing to the extortions and perfidy of Keritli Oglu, the villages in the neighborhood had been deserted, and that the Arab tribe of Abou Salman had moved from the plain of Nimroud, which they usually inhabited, to the South of the Zab, and had joined with the Tai in their marauding excursions into the country on this side of the river. The neighborhood, he said, was consequently insecure, and the roads to Mosul almost closed.

Awad had learnt a little Turkish, and was intelligent and active. Seeing, at once, that he would be useful, I acquainted him with the object of my journey; offering him the prospect of regular employment in the event of the experiment proving successful, and assigning him regular wages as superintendent of the workmen. He had long been acquainted with the ruins, and entertained me with traditions connected with them. "The palace," he said, "was built by Athur, the Kiayah, or lieutenant of Nimrod. Here the holy Abraham, peace be with him! cast down and brake in pieces the idols which were worshipped by the unbelievers. The impious Nimrod, enraged at the destruction of his gods, sought to slay Abraham, and waged war against him. But the prophet prayed to God, and said, 'Deliver me, O God, from this man, who worships stones, and boasts himself to be the lord of all beings,' and God said to him, 'How shall I punish him?' And the prophet answered, 'To Thee armies are as nothing, and the strength and power of men likewise. Before the smallest of Thy creatures will they perish.' And God was pleased at the faith of the prophet, and he sent a gnat, which vexed Nimrod night and day, so that he built himself a room of glass in yonder palace, that he might dwell therein, and shut out the insect. But the gnat entered also, and passed by his ear into his brain, upon which it fed, and increased in size day by day, so that the servants of Nimrod beat his head with a hammer continually, that he might have some ease from his pain; but he died after suffering these torments for four hundred years."

Such are the tales to this day repeated by the Arabs who wander round the remains of a great city; which, by their traditions, they unwittingly help to identify.

Awad volunteered to walk, in the middle of the night, to Selamiyah, a village three miles distant, and to some Arab tents in the neighborhood, to procure men to assist in the excavations.

I had slept little during the night. The hovel in which we had taken shelter, and its inmates, did not invite slumber; but such scenes and companions were not new to me; they could have been forgotten, had my brain been less excited. Hopes, long cherished, were now to be realized, or were to end in disappointment. Visions of palaces underground, of gigantic monsters, of sculptured figures, and endless inscriptions, floated before me. After forming plan after plan for removing the earth, and extricating these treasures, I fancied myself wandering in a maze of chambers from which I could find no outlet. Then again, all was reburied, and I was standing on the grass-covered mound. Exhausted, I was at length sinking into sleep, when hearing the voice of Awad, I rose from my carpet, and joined him outside the hovel. The day already dawned; he had returned with six Arabs, who agreed for a small sum to work under my direction.

The lofty cone and broad mound of Nimroud broke like a distant mountain on the morning sky. But how changed was the scene since my former visit! The ruins were no longer clothed with verdure and many-colored flowers; no signs of habitation, not even the black tent of the Arab, were seen upon the plain. The eye wandered over a parched and barren waste, across which occasionally swept the whirlwind, dragging with it a cloud of sand. About a mile from us was the small village of Nimroud, like Naifa, a heap of ruins.

Twenty minutes' walk brought us to the principal mound. The absence of all vegetation enabled me to examine the remains with which it was covered. Broken pottery and fragments of bricks, both inscribed with the cuneiform character, were strewed on all sides. The Arabs watched my motions as I wandered to and fro, and observed with surprise the objects I had collected. They joined, however, in the search, and brought me handfuls of rubbish, amongst which I found with joy the fragment of a bas-relief. The material on which it was carved had been exposed to fire, and resembled, in every respect, the burnt gypsum of Khorsabad.

Convinced from this discovery that sculptured remains must

still exist in some part of the mound, I sought for a place where excavation might be commenced with a prospect of success. Awad led me to a piece of alabaster which appeared above the soil. We could not remove it, and on digging downward, it proved to be the upper part of a large slab. I ordered all the men to work around it, and they shortly uncovered a second slab to which it had been united. Continuing in the same line, we came upon a third; and in the course of the morning, laid bare ten more, the whole forming a square, with one stone missing at the N.W. corner. It was evident that the top of a chamber had been discovered, and that the gap was its entrance. I now dug down the face of the stones, and an inscription in the cuneiform character was soon exposed to view. Similar inscriptions occupied the centre of all the slabs, which were in the best preservation; but plain, with the exception of the writing. Leaving half the workmen to uncover as much of the chamber as possible, I led the rest to the S.W. corner of the mound, where I had observed many fragments of calcined alabaster.

I dug at once into the side of the mound, which was here very steep, and thus avoided the necessity of removing much earth. We came almost immediately to a wall, bearing inscriptions in the same character as those already described; but the slabs had evidently been exposed to intense heat, were cracked in every part, and, reduced to lime, threatened to fall to pieces as soon as uncovered.

Night interrupted our labors. I returned to the village well satisfied with their result. It was now evident that buildings of considerable extent existed in the mound; and that although some had been destroyed by fire, others had escaped the conflagration. As there were inscriptions, and as the fragment of a bas-relief had been found, it was natural to conclude that sculptures were still buried under the soil. I determined to follow the search at the N.W. corner, and to empty the chamber partly uncovered during the day. . . .

Next morning my workmen were increased by five Turcomans from Selamiyah, who had been attracted by the prospect of regular wages. I employed half of them in emptying the chamber partly uncovered on the previous day, and the rest in following the wall at the S.W. corner of the mound. Before evening, the work of the first was completed, and I found myself in a room built of slabs about eight feet high, and varying from six to four feet in breadth, placed upright and closely fitted together. One of the slabs had fallen backwards from its place, and was supported, in a slanting position, by the soil behind. Upon it was rudely inscribed, in Arabic characters, the name of Ahmed Pasha, one of the former hereditary governors of Mosul. A native of Selamiyah remembered that some Christians were employed to dig into the mound about thirty years before, in search of stone for the repair of the tomb of Sultan Abd-Allah, a Mussulman saint, buried on the left bank of the Tigris. . . . They uncovered this slab; but being unable to move it, they cut upon it the name of their employer, the Pasha. My informant further stated that, in another part of the mound, he had forgotten the precise spot, they had found sculptured figures, which they broke in pieces, the fragments being used in the reparation of the tomb.

The bottom of the chamber was paved with smaller slabs than those employed in the construction of the walls. They were covered with inscriptions on both sides, and on removing one of them, I found that it had been placed upon a layer of bitumen which must have been used in a liquid state, for it had retained, with remarkable distinctness and accuracy, an impression of the characters carved upon the stone. The inscriptions on the face of the upright slabs were about twenty lines in length, and all were precisely similar. . . .

In the rubbish near the bottom of the chamber, I found several ivory ornaments, upon which were traces of gilding; amongst them was the figure of a man in long robes, carrying in one hand the Egyptian crux ansata, part of a crouching sphinx, and flowers designed with great taste and elegance. Awad, who had his own suspicions of the object of my search, which he could scarcely persuade himself was limited to mere stones, carefully collected all the scattered fragments of gold leaf he could find in the rubbish; and, calling me aside in a mysterious and confidential fashion, produced them wrapped up in a piece of dingy paper.

"Oh, Bey," said he, "Wallah! your books are right, and the Franks know that which is hid from the true believer. Here is the gold, sure enough, and, please God, we shall find it all in a few days. Only don't say anything about it to those Arabs, for they are asses and cannot hold their tongues. The matter will come to the ears of the Pasha." The Sheikh was much surprised, and equally disappointed, when I generously presented him with the treasures he had collected, and all such as he might hereafter discover. He left me, muttering "Yia Rubbi!" and other pious ejaculations, and lost in conjectures as to the meaning of these strange proceedings.

On reaching the foot of the slabs in the S.W. corner, we found a great accumulation of charcoal, which was further evidence of the cause of the destruction of one of the buildings discovered. I dug also in several directions at this part of the mound, and in many places came upon walls branching out at different angles.

On the third day, I opened a trench in the high conical mound, and found nothing but fragments of inscribed bricks. I also dug at the back of the north end of the chamber first explored, in the expectation of discovering other walls beyond, but unsuccessfully. As my chief aim was to prove the existence, as soon as possible, of sculptures, all my workmen were moved to the S.W. corner, where the many ramifications of the building already identified, promised speedier success. I continued the excavations in this part of the mound until the 13th, still uncovering inscriptions, but finding no sculptures.

Some days having elapsed since my departure from Mosul, and the experiment now having been sufficiently tried, it was time to return to the town and acquaint the Pasha, who had, no doubt, already heard of my proceedings, with the object of my researches. I started, therefore, early in the morning of the 14th, and galloped to Mosul in about three hours. . . .

I called on the Pasha. . . . He pretended at first to be

ignorant of the excavations at Nimroud; but subsequently thinking that he would convict me of prevarication in my answers to his questions as to the amount of treasure discovered, pulled out of his writing-tray a scrap of paper, as dingy as that produced by Awad, in which was also preserved an almost invisible particle of gold-leaf. This, he said, had been brought to him by the commander of the irregular troops stationed at Selamiyah, who had been watching my proceedings. I suggested that he should name an agent to be present as long as I worked at Nimroud, to take charge of all the precious metals that might be discovered. He promised to write on the subject to the chief of the irregulars; but offered no objection to the continuation of my researches.

Reports of the wealth extracted from the ruins had already reached Mosul, and had excited the cupidity and jealousy of the Cadi and principal inhabitants of the place. Others, who well knew my object, and might have spared me any additional interruption without a sacrifice of their national character, were not backward in throwing obstacles in my way, and in fanning the prejudices of the authorities and natives of the town. It was evident that I should have to contend against a formidable opposition; but as the Pasha had not yet openly objected to my proceedings, I hired several Nestorian Chaldeans, who had left their mountains for the winter to seek employment in Mosul, and sent them to Nimroud. . . .

Whilst at Mosul, Mormous, an Arab of the tribe of Haddedeen, informed me that figures had been accidentally uncovered in a mound near the village of Tel Kef. As he offered to take me to the place, we rode out together; but he only pointed out the site of an old quarry, with a few rudely-hewn stones. Such disappointments were daily occurring; and I wearied myself in scouring the country to see remains which had been most minutely described to me as groups of sculptures, and slabs covered with writing, and which generally proved to be the ruin of some modern building, or an early tombstone inscribed with Arabic characters. . . .

Having finished my arrangements in Mosul, I returned

to Nimroud on the 19th. During my absence, the workmen, under the direction of my Cawass, had carried the excavations along the back of the wall and had discovered the entrance. Being anxious to make as much progress as possible, I increased my party to thirty men, and distributed them in three sets over the S.W. corner of the mound. . . . Neither the plan nor the nature of the edifice could be determined until the heap of rubbish and earth under which it was buried had been removed. The excavations were now carried on but slowly. The soil, mixed with sun-dried and kiln-burnt bricks, pottery, and fragments of alabaster, offered considerable resistance to the tools of the workmen; and when loosened, had to be removed in baskets and thrown over the edge of the mound. The Chaldeans from the mountains, strong and hardy men, could alone wield the pick; the Arabs were employed in carrying away the earth. The spade could not be used, and there were no other means, than those I had adopted, to clear away the ruins. A person standing on the mound would see no remains of building until he approached the edge of the trenches, into which the workmen descended by steps. Parts of the walls were now exposed to view; but it was impossible to conjecture which course they took, or whether the slabs were facing the inside, or formed the back of the chamber which had probably been discovered.

The Abou Salman and Tai Arabs continuing their depredations in the plains of Nimroud and surrounding country, I deemed it prudent to remove from Naifa, where I had hitherto resided, to Selamiyah. The latter village is built on a rising ground near the Tigris, and was formerly a place of some importance, being mentioned at a very early period as a market town by the Arab geographers, who generally connect it with the ruins of Athur or Nimroud. . . .

[Layard takes up residence in an abandoned and decayed mud hut.] The roofs not being constructed to exclude the winter rains now setting in, it required some exercise of ingenuity to escape the torrent which descended into my apartment. I usually passed the night on these occasions

Winged Human-Headed Lion, Northwest Palace, Nimroud

crouched up in a corner, or under a rude table which I had constructed. The latter, having been surrounded by trenches, to carry off the accumulating waters, generally afforded the best shelter. My Cawass, who was a Constantinopolitan, complained bitterly of the hardships he was compelled to endure, and I had some difficulty in prevailing upon my servants to remain with me. . . .

I had now to ride three miles every morning to the mound; and my workmen, who were afraid, on account of the Arabs, to live at Naifa, returned after the day's labor, to Selamiyah. The excavations were still carried on as actively as the means at my disposal would permit . . . But still no sculptures had been discovered; nor could any idea be yet formed of the relative position of the walls. I ordered a trench to be opened obliquely from the entrance into the interior of the mound, presuming that we would ultimately find the opposite side of the chamber, to which, it appeared probable, we had found the passage. After removing a large accumulation of earth mixed with charcoal, charred wood, and broken bricks, we reached the top of wall *f*, on the afternoon of the 28th November. In order to ascertain whether we were in the inside of a chamber, the workmen were directed to clear away the earth from both sides of the slabs. The south face was unsculptured, but the first stroke of the pick on the opposite side disclosed the top of a bas-relief. The Arabs were no less excited than myself by the discovery; and notwithstanding a violent shower of rain, working until dark, they completely exposed to view two slabs.

On each slab were two bas-reliefs, separated from one another by a band of inscriptions. The subject on the upper part of No. 1 was a battle scene. Two chariots, drawn by horses richly caparisoned, were each occupied by a group of three warriors; the principal person in both groups was beardless, and evidently an eunuch. He was clothed in a complete suit of mail, and wore a pointed helmet on his head, from the sides of which fell lappets covering the ears, the lower part of the face, and the neck. The left hand, the arm being extended, grasped a bow at full stretch; whilst the right, drawing the string to the ear, held an arrow ready to be discharged. A second warrior urged, with reins and whip to the utmost of their speed, three horses, who were galloping over the plain. A third, without helmet, and with flowing hair and beard, held a shield for the defence of the principal figure. Under the horses' feet, and scattered about the relief, were the conquered, wounded by the arrows of the conquerors.

I observed with surprise the elegance and richness of the ornaments, the faithful and delicate delineation of the limbs and muscles, both in the men and horses, and the knowledge of art displayed in the grouping of the figures, and the general composition. In all these respects, as well as in costume, this sculpture appeared to me not only to differ, but to surpass the bas-reliefs of Khorsabad. I traced also in the character used in the inscription a marked difference from that found on the monuments discovered by M. Botta. Unfortunately, the slab had been exposed to fire, and was so much injured that its removal was hopeless. The edges had, moreover, been cut away, to the injury of some of the figures and of the inscription; and as the next slab was reversed, it was evident that both had been brought from another building. This fact rendered any conjecture, as to the origin and form of the edifice we were exploring, still more difficult.

The lower bas-relief on No. 1, represented the siege of a castle or a walled city. To the left were two warriors, each holding a circular shield in one hand, and a short sword in the other. A tunic, confined at the waist by a girdle, and ornamented with a fringe of tassels, descended to the knee; a quiver was suspended at the back, and the left arm was passed through the bow, which was thus kept by the side, ready for use. They wore the pointed helmets before described. The foremost warrior was ascending a ladder placed against the castle. Three turrets, with angular battlements, rose above walls similarly ornamented. In the first turret were two warriors, the one in the act of discharging an arrow, the other raising a shield and casting a stone at the assailants, from whom the besieged were distinguished by their head-dress—a simple fillet binding the hair above the temples. Their beards, at the same time, were less carefully arranged. The second turret was occupied by a slinger preparing his sling. In the interval between this turret and the third, and over an arched gateway, was a female figure, known by her long hair descending upon the shoulders in curls. Her right hand was elevated as if in the act of asking for mercy. In the third turret were two more of the besieged, the first discharging an arrow, the second elevating his shield and endeavoring with a torch to burn an instrument resembling a catapult, which had been brought up to the wall by an inclined plane built on a heap of boughs and rubbish. These figures were out of all proportion when compared with the size of the building. A warrior with a pointed helmet, bending on one knee, and holding a torch in his right hand, was setting fire to the gate of the castle, whilst another in full armor was forcing the stones from the foundation with an instrument, probably of iron, resembling a blunt spear. Between them was a wounded man falling headlong from the walls.

No. 2 was a corner stone very much injured, the greater part of the relief having been cut away to reduce it to convenient dimensions. The upper part, being reversed, was occupied by two warriors; the foremost in a pointed helmet, riding on one horse and leading a second; the other, without helmet, standing in a chariot, and holding the reins loosely in his hands. The horses had been destroyed, and the marks of the chisel were visible on many parts of the slab, the sculptures having been in some places carefully defaced. The lower bas-relief represented a singular subject. On the walls of the castle, two stories high, and defended by many towers, stood a woman tearing her hair to show her grief. Beneath and by the side of a stream, figured by numerous undulating lines, crouched a fisherman drawing from the water a fish he had caught. This slab had been exposed to fire like that adjoining, and had sustained too much injury to be removed.

As I was meditating in the evening over my discovery, Daoud Agha entered, and seating himself near me, delivered a long speech, to the effect, that he was a servant of the Pasha, who was again the slave of the Sultan; and that servants were bound to obey the commands of their master, however disagreeable and unjust they might be. I saw at once to what this exordium was about to lead, and was prepared for the announcement, that he had received orders from Mosul to stop the excavations by threatening those who were inclined to work for me.

On the following morning, therefore, I rode to the town, and waited upon his Excellency. He pretended to be taken by surprise, disclaimed having given such orders, and directed his secretary to write at once to the commander of the irregular troops, who was to give me every assistance rather than throw impediments in my way. He promised to let me have the letter in the afternoon before I returned to Selamiyah; but an officer came to me soon after, and stated that as the Pasha was unwilling to detain me he would forward it in the night. I rode back to the village, and acquainted Daoud Agha with the result of my visit. About midnight, however, he returned to me, and declared that a horseman had just brought him more stringent orders than any he had yet received, and that on no account was he to permit me to carry on the work.

Surprised at this inconsistency, I returned to Mosul early next day, and again called upon the Pasha. "It was with deep regret," said he, "I learnt, after your departure yesterday, that the mound in which you are digging had been used as a burying-ground by Mussulmans, and was covered with their graves; now you are aware that by the law it is forbidden to disturb a tomb, and the Cadi and Mufti have already made representations to me on the subject." [Layard insists that no graves are being disturbed, but the Pasha insists that he is correct, and adds craftily:] "No, I cannot allow you to proceed; you are my dearest and most intimate friend; if anything happens to you, what grief should I not suffer! Your life is more valuable than old stones: besides, the responsibility would fall upon my head." Finding that the Pasha had resolved to interrupt my proceedings, I pretended to acquiesce in his answer, and requested that a Cawass of his own might be sent with me to Nimroud, as I wished to draw the sculptures and copy the inscriptions which had already been uncovered. To this he consented, and ordered an officer to accompany me. . . .

On my return to Selamiyah there was little difficulty in inducing the Pasha's Cawass to countenance the employment of a few workmen to *guard* the sculptures during the day; and as Daoud Agha considered that this functionary's presence relieved him from any further responsibility, he no longer interfered with any experiment I might think proper to make.

Wishing to ascertain the existence of the graves, and also to draw one of the bas-reliefs, which had been uncovered, though not to continue the excavations for a day or two, I rode to the ruins on the following morning. . . . [Daoud Agha confessed to me on our way that he had received orders to make graves on the mound, and that his troops had been employed for two nights in bringing stones from distant villages for that purpose.] "We have destroyed more real tombs of the true Believers," said he, "in making sham ones, than you could have defiled between the Zab and Selamiyah. We have killed our horses and ourselves in carrying those accursed stones." A steady rain setting in, I left the horsemen and returned to the village. . . .

I continued to employ a few men to open trenches by way of experiment, and was not long in discovering other sculptures. Near the western edge we came upon the lower part of several gigantic figures, uninjured by fire. It was from this place that in the time of Ahmed Pasha, materials were taken for rebuilding the tomb of Sultan Abd-allah, and the slabs had been sawn in half, and otherwise injured. At the foot of the S.E. corner was found a crouching lion, rudely carved in basalt, which appeared to have fallen from the building above, and to have been exposed for centuries to the atmosphere. In the centre of the mound we uncovered part of a pair of gigantic winged bulls, the head and half the wings of which had been destroyed. On the back of the enormous slabs, the length of which was fourteen feet, while the height must have been originally the same, on which these animals had been carved in high relief, were inscriptions in large and well-cut characters. A pair of small winged lions, the heads and upper part destroyed, were also discovered. They appeared to form an entrance into a chamber, were admirably designed and very carefully executed. Finally, a human figure, nine feet high, the right hand elevated, and carrying in the left a branch with three flowers, resembling the poppy, was found in wall *k*. I uncovered only the upper part of these sculptures, satisfied with proving their existence, without exposing them to the risk of injury, should my labors be at any time interrupted.

Still no conjecture could be formed as to the contents of the mound, or as to the nature of the buildings I was exploring. Only detached and unconnected walls had been discovered, and it could not even be determined which side of them had been laid bare.

The experiment had been fairly tried; there was no longer any doubt of the existence not only of sculptures and inscriptions, but even of vast edifices in the interior of the mound of Nimroud, as all parts of it that had yet been examined, furnished remains of buildings and carved slabs. I lost no time, therefore, in acquainting Sir Stratford Canning with my discovery, and urging the necessity of a Firman, or order from the Porte [Sultan], which would prevent any further interference on the part of the authorities, or the inhabitants of the country.

It was now nearly Christmas, and as it was desirable to remove all the tombs, which had been made by the Pasha's orders, on the mound, and others more genuine, which had since been found, I came to an understanding on the subject with Daoud Agha. I covered over the sculptures brought to light, and withdrew altogether from Nimroud, leaving an agent at Selamiyah.

On entering Mosul on the morning of the 18th, I found the whole population in a ferment of joy. A Tartar had that morning brought from Constantinople the welcome news that the Porte, at length alive to the wretched condition of the province, and to the misery of the inhabitants, had disgraced the governor, and named Ismail Pasha, a young Major-General of the new school, to carry on affairs until Hafiz Pasha, who had been appointed to succeed Keritl Oglu, could reach his government. Only ten days previously the inhabitants had been well-nigh driven to despair by the arrival of a Firman, confirming Mohammed Pasha for another year; but this only proved a trick on the part of the secretaries of the Porte to obtain the presents which are usually given on these occasions, and which the Pasha, on receipt of the document, hastened to remit to Constantinople. His Excellency was consequently doubly aggrieved by the loss of his Pashalic and of his money.

Ismail Pasha, who had been for some time in command of the troops at Diarbekir, had gained a great reputation for justice amongst the Mussulmans, and for tolerance among the Christians. Consequently his appointment had given much satisfaction to the people of Mosul, who were prepared to receive him with a demonstration. However, his Excellency slipped into the town during the night, some time before he had been expected. On the following morning a change had taken place at the Serai, and Mohammed Pasha, with his followers, were reduced to extremities. The dragoman of the Consulate, who had business to transact with him, found the late Governor sitting in a dilapidated chamber, through which the rain penetrated without hindrance. "Thus it is," said he, "with God's creatures. Yesterday all those dogs were kissing my feet; today every one, and every thing, falls upon me, even the rain!"

During these events the state of the country rendered the continuation of my researches at Nimroud almost impossible. I determined, therefore, to proceed to Baghdad, to make arrangements for the removal of the sculptures at a future period, and to consult generally with Major Rawlinson, from whose experience and knowledge I could derive the most valuable assistance. A raft having been constructed, I started with Mr. Hector, a gentleman from Baghdad, who had visited me at Nimroud, and reached that city on the 24th of December.

[Returning to Mosul in January, Layard resumes excavating.]

Security had been restored, and Nimroud offered a more convenient and more agreeable residence than Selamiyah. Hiring, therefore, from the owners three huts, which had been hastily built in the outskirts of the village, I removed to my new dwelling-place. A few rude chairs, a table, and a wooden bedstead, formed the whole of my furniture. . . .

As there was a ravine running far into the mound, apparently formed by the winter rains, I determined to open a trench in the center of it. In two days the workmen reached the top of a slab, which appeared to be both well preserved, and to be still standing in its original position. On the south side I discovered, to my great satisfaction, two human figures, considerably above the natural size, sculptured in low relief, and still exhibiting all the freshness of a recent work. . . . In a few hours the earth and rubbish had been completely removed from the face of the slab, no part of which had been injured. The ornaments delicately graven on the robes, the tassels and fringes, the bracelets and armlets, the elaborate curls of the hair and beard, were all entire. The figures were back to back, and furnished with wings. They appeared to represent divinities, presiding over the seasons, or over particular religious ceremonies. The one, whose face was turned to the East, carried a fallow deer on his right arm, and in his left hand a branch bearing five flowers. Around his temples was a fillet, adorned in front with a rosette. The other held a square vessel, or basket, in the left hand, and an object resembling a fir cone in the right. On his head he wore a rounded cap, at the base of which was a horn. The garments of both, consisting of a stole falling from the shoulders to the ankles, and a short tunic underneath, descending to the knee, were richly and tastefully decorated with embroideries and fringes, whilst the hair and beard were arranged with study and art. Although the relief was lower, yet the outline was perhaps more careful, and true, than that of the Assyrian sculptures of Khorsabad. The limbs were delineated with peculiar accuracy, and the muscles and bones faithfully, though somewhat too strongly, marked. An inscription ran across the sculpture.

To the west of this slab, and fitting to it, was a cornerstone ornamented with flowers and scroll-work, tastefully arranged, and resembling in detail those graven on the injured tablet, near entrance *d* of the S.W. building. I recognized at once from whence many of the sculptures, employed in the construction of that edifice, had been brought; and it was evident that I had at length discovered the earliest palace of Nimroud.

The corner-stone led me to a figure of singular form. A human body, clothed in robes similar to those of the winged

men on the previous slab, was surmounted by the head of an
eagle or of a vulture. The curved beak, of considerable length,
was half open, and displayed a narrow pointed tongue, which
was still covered with red paint. On the shoulders fell the
usual curled and bushy hair of the Assyrian images, and a
comb of feathers rose on the top of the head. Two wings
sprang from the back, and in either hand was the square vessel and fir cone.

On all these figures paint could be faintly distinguished,
particularly on the hair, beard, eyes, and sandals. The slabs
on which they were sculptured had sustained no injury, and
could be without difficulty packed and moved to any distance.
There could no longer be any doubt that they formed part of
a chamber, and that, to explore it completely, I had only to
continue along the wall, now partly uncovered.

On the morning following these discoveries, I rode to the
encampment of Sheikh Abd-ur-rahman, and was returning to
the mound, when I saw two Arabs of his tribe urging their
mares to the top of their speed. On approaching me they
stopped. "Hasten, O Bey," exclaimed one of them—"hasten to
the diggers, for they have found Nimrod himself. Wallah, it
is wonderful, but it is true! we have seen him with our eyes.
There is no God but God;" and both joining in this pious
exclamation, they galloped off, without further words, in
the direction of their tents.

On reaching the ruins I descended into the new trench, and
found the workmen, who had already seen me, as I approached, standing near a heap of baskets and cloaks. Whilst
Awad advanced, and asked for a present to celebrate the occasion, the Arabs withdrew the screen they had hastily constructed, and disclosed an enormous human head sculptured
in full out of the alabaster of the country. They had uncovered
the upper part of the figure, the remainder of which was still
buried in the earth. I saw at once that the head must belong
to a winged lion or bull, similar to those of Khorsabad and
Persepolis. It was in admirable preservation. The expression
was calm, yet majestic, and the outline of the features showed

a freedom and knowledge of art, scarcely to be looked for in the works of so remote a period. The cap had three horns, and, unlike that of the human-headed bulls hitherto found in Assyria, was rounded and without ornament at the top.

I was not surprised that the Arabs had been amazed and terrified at this apparition. It requires no stretch of imagination to conjure up the most strange fancies. This gigantic head, blanched with age, thus rising from the bowels of the earth, might well have belonged to one of those fearful beings which are pictured in the traditions of the country, as appearing to mortals, slowly ascending from the regions below. One of the workmen, on catching the first glimpse of the monster, had thrown down his basket and run off towards Mosul as fast as his legs could carry him. I learnt this with regret, as I anticipated the consequences.

Whilst I was supervising the removal of the earth, which still clung to the sculpture, and giving directions for the continuation of the work, a noise of horsemen was heard, and presently Abd-ur-rahman, followed by half his tribe, appeared on the edge of the trench. As soon as the two Arabs had reached the tents, and published the wonders they had seen, every one mounted his mare and rode to the mound, to satisfy himself of the truth of these inconceivable reports. When they beheld the head they all cried out together, "There is no God but God, and Mohammed is his Prophet!" It was some time before the Sheikh could be prevailed upon to descend into the pit, and convince himself that the image he saw was of stone. "This is not the work of men's hands," exclaimed he, "but of those infidel giants of whom the Prophet, peace be with him! has said, that they were higher than the tallest date tree; this is one of the idols which Noah, peace be with him! cursed before the flood." In this opinion, the result of a careful examination, all the bystanders concurred.

I now ordered a trench to be dug due south from the head, in the expectation of finding a corresponding figure, and before nightfall reached the object of my search about twelve feet distant. Engaging two or three men to sleep near the

Winged Lion, the Palace of Ashurnasirpal, Nimroud

sculptures, I returned to the village and celebrated the day's discovery by a slaughter of sheep, of which all the Arabs near partook. As some wandering musicians chanced to be at Selamiyah, I sent for them, and dances were kept up during the greater part of the night. On the following morning Arabs from the other side of the Tigris, and the inhabitants of the surrounding villages congregated on the mound. Even the women could not repress their curiosity, and came in crowds, with their children, from afar. My Cawass was stationed during the day in the trench, into which I would not allow the multitude to descend.

As I had expected, the report of the discovery of the gigantic head, carried by the terrified Arab to Mosul, had thrown the town into commotion. He had scarcely checked his speed before reaching the bridge. Entering breathless into the bazaars, he announced to everyone he met that Nimrod had appeared. The news soon got to the ears of the Cadi, who, anxious for a fresh opportunity to annoy me, called the Mufti and the Ulema together, to consult upon this unexpected occurrence. Their deliberations ended in a procession to the Governor, and a formal protest, on the part of the Mussulmans of the town, against proceedings so directly contrary to the laws of the Koran. The Cadi had no distinct idea whether the bones of the mighty hunter had been uncovered, or only his image; nor did Ismail Pasha very clearly remember whether Nimrod was a true-believing prophet, or an Infidel. I consequently received a somewhat unintelligible message from his Excellency, to the effect that the remains should be treated with respect, and be by no means further disturbed, and that he wished the excavations to be stopped at once, and desired to confer with me on the subject.

I called upon him accordingly, and had some difficulty in making him understand the nature of my discovery. As he requested me to discontinue my operations until the sensation in the town had somewhat subsided, I returned to Nimroud and dismissed the workmen, retaining only two men to dig leisurely along the walls without giving cause for further interference. I ascertained by the end of March the existence of a second pair of winged human-headed lions, differing from those previously discovered in form, the human shape being continued to the waist and furnished with arms. In one hand each figure carried a goat or stag, and in the other, which hung down by the side, a branch with three flowers. They formed a northern entrance into the chamber of which the lions previously described were the southern portal. I completely uncovered the latter, and found them to be entire. They were about twelve feet in height, and the same number in length. The body and limbs were admirably portrayed; the muscles and bones, although strongly developed to display the strength of the animal, showed at the same time a correct knowledge of its anatomy and form. Expanded wings sprung from the shoulder and spread over the back; a knotted girdle, ending in tassels, encircled the loins. These sculptures, forming an entrance, were partly in full and partly in relief. The head and fore-part, facing the chamber, were in full; but only one side of the rest of the slab was sculptured, the back being placed against the wall of sun-dried bricks. That the spectator might have both a perfect front and side view of the figures, they were furnished with five legs; two were carved on the end of the slab to face the chamber, and three on the side. The relief of the body and three limbs was high and bold, and the slab was covered, in all parts not occupied by the image, with inscriptions in the cuneiform character. These magnificent specimens of Assyrian art were in perfect preservation; the most minute lines in the details of the wings and in the ornaments had been retained with their original freshness. Not a character was wanting in the inscriptions. . . .

[The coming of summer forces Layard to suspend work. He travels into the highlands, returning to his excavations in the autumn. Work continues until the spring rains approach.]

Although early in the spring, the Shammar and other formidable tribes had not yet encamped in the vicinity of Mosul; still, casual plundering parties had made their appearances among the villages, and it was predicted that as soon as their tents were pitched nearer the town the country without the walls would not only be very unsafe, but almost uninhabitable.

These circumstances induced me to undertake the removal of the larger sculptures as early as possible. The dry season had enabled me to carry on the excavations without interruption. As no rain fell to loosen the earth above the trenches there was no occasion to prop up the sides of the trenches, or to cover the sculptures: considerable expense was thus saved. Had there been the usual violent storms, not only would the soil have continually fallen in and reburied the building, but the bas-reliefs would have been exposed to injury. A marsh would also have been formed round the base of the mound, completely cutting me off from the river, and impassable to any cart carrying the larger sculptures. My first plan, when anticipating the usual wet weather, was to wait, before moving the bas-reliefs, until the rain had completely ceased, and the low ground under the mound had been dried up. I could not, in that case, commence operations before the month of May, when the Tigris would still be swollen by the melting of the snows in the Armenian hills. The stream would be sufficiently rapid to carry to Baghdad a heavily laden raft, without the fear of obstruction from shallows and sandbanks. This year, however, there was no marsh round the ruins, nor had any snow fallen in the mountains to promise a considerable rise in the river. I determined, therefore, to send the sculptures to Busrah in the month of March or April, foreseeing that as soon as the Bedouins had moved northwards from Babylonia, and had commenced their plundering expeditions in the vicinity of Mosul, I should be compelled to leave Nimroud.

The Trustees of the British Museum had not contemplated the removal of either a winged bull or lion, and I had at first believed that, with the means at my disposal, it would have been useless to attempt it. They wisely determined that these sculptures should not be sawn into pieces, to be put together again in Europe, as the pair of bulls from Khorsabad. They were to remain, where discovered, until some favorable opportunity of moving them entire might occur; and I was directed to heap earth over them, after the excavations had been brought to an end. Being loath, however, to leave all these fine specimens of Assyrian sculpture behind me, I resolved upon attempting the removal, and embarkation of two of the smallest and best preserved. . . .

I formed various plans for lowering the smaller lion and bull, for dragging them to the river, and for placing them upon rafts. Each step had its difficulties, and a variety of original suggestions and ideas were supplied by my workmen, and by the good people of Mosul, At last I resolved upon constructing a cart, sufficiently strong to bear any of the masses to be moved. As no wood but poplar could be procured in town, a carpenter was sent to the mountains with directions to fell the largest mulberry tree, or any tree of equally compact grain, he could find; and to bring beams of it, and thick slices from the trunk, to Mosul.

By the month of March this wood was ready. I purchased from the dragoman of the French Consulate a pair of strong iron axles, formerly used by M. Botta in bringing sculptures from Khorsabad. Each wheel was formed of three solid pieces, nearly a foot thick, from the trunk of a mulberry tree, bound together by iron hoops. Across the axles were laid three beams, and above them several cross-beams, all of the same wood. A pole was fixed to one axle, to which were also attached iron rings for ropes, to enable men, as well as buffaloes, to draw the cart. The wheels were provided with movable hooks for the same purpose.

Simple as this cart was, it became an object of wonder in the town. Crowds came to look at it, as it stood in the yard of the vice-consul's khan; and the Pasha's tepjis, or artillerymen, who, from their acquaintance with the mysteries of gun carriages, were looked up to as authorities on such matters, daily declaimed on the properties and use of this vehicle, and of carts in general, to a large circle of curious and attentive listeners. As long as the cart was in Mosul, it was ex-

Discovery of the Gigantic Head, Nimroud

amined by every stranger who visited the town. But when the news spread that it was about to leave the gates, and to be drawn over the bridge, the business of the place was completely suspended. The secretaries and scribes from the palace left their divans; the guards their posts; the bazaars were deserted; and half the population assembled on the banks of the river to witness the maneuvres of the cart. A pair of buffaloes, with the assistance of a crowd of Chaldeans and shouting Arabs, forced the ponderous wheels over the rotten bridge of boats. The multitude seemed to be fully satisfied with the spectacle. The cart was the topic of general conversation in Mosul. . . .

To lessen the weight of the lion and bull, without in any way interfering with the sculpture, I reduced the thickness of the slabs, by cutting away as much as possible from the back. Their bulk was thus considerably diminished; and as the back of the slab was never meant to be seen, being placed against the wall of sun-dried bricks, no part of the sculpture was sacrificed. As in order to move these figures at all, I had to choose between this plan and that of sawing them into several pieces, I did not hesitate to adopt it.

To enable me to move the bull from the ruins, and to place it on the cart in the plain below, it was necessary to cut a trench nearly two hundred feet long, about fifteen feet wide, and, in some places, twenty feet deep. A road was thus constructed from the entrance, in which stood the bull, to the edge of the mound. There being no means at my disposal to raise the sculpture out of the trenches, like the smaller bas-reliefs, this road was necessary. It was a tedious undertaking, as a very large accumulation of earth had to be removed. About fifty Arabs and Nestorians were employed in the work. . . .

As the bull was to be lowered on its back, the unsculptured side of the slab having to be placed on rollers, I removed the walls behind it as far as the entrance *a*. An open space was thus formed, large enough to admit of the sculpture when prostrate, and leaving room for the workmen to pass on all sides of it. The principal difficulty was of course to lower the mass; when once on the ground, or on rollers, it could be dragged forwards by the united force of a number of men; but, during its descent, it could only be sustained by ropes. If not strong enough to bear the weight, they chanced to break, the sculpture would be precipitated to the ground, and would, probably, be broken in the fall. The few ropes I possessed had been expressly sent to me, across the desert, from Aleppo; but they were small. From Baghdad, I had obtained a thick hawser, made of the fibres of the palm. In addition I had been furnished with two pairs of blocks, and a pair of jack-screws belonging to the steamers of the Euphrates expedition. These were all the means at my command for moving the bull and lion. The sculptures were wrapped in mats and felts, to preserve them, as far as possible, from injury in case of a fall; and to prevent the ropes chipping or rubbing the alabaster.

The bull was ready to be moved by the 18th of March. The earth had been taken from under it, and it was now only supported by beams resting against the opposite wall. Amongst the wood obtained from the mountains were several thick rollers. These were placed upon sleepers, or half beams, formed out of the trunks of poplar trees, well greased and laid on the ground parallel to the sculpture. The bull was to be lowered upon these rollers. A deep trench had been cut behind the second bull, completely across the wall, and, consequently, extending from chamber to chamber. A bundle of ropes coiled round this isolated mass of earth, served to hold two blocks, two others being attached to ropes wound round the bull to be moved. The ropes, by which the sculpture was to be lowered, were passed through these blocks; the ends or falls of the tackle, as they are technically called, being led from the blocks above the second bull, and held by the Arabs. The cable having been first passed through the trench, and then round the sculpture, the ends were given to two bodies of men. Several of the strongest Chaldeans placed thick beams against the back of the bull, and were directed to withdraw them gradually, supporting the weight of the slab, and checking it in its descent, in case the ropes should give way.

My own people were reinforced by a large number of the Abou Salman. I had invited Sheikh Abd-ur-rahman to be present, and he came attended by a body of horsemen. The inhabitants of Naifa and Nimroud having volunteered to assist on the occasion, were distributed amongst my Arabs. The workmen, except the Chaldeans who supported the beams, were divided into four parties, two of which were stationed in front of the bull, and held the ropes passed through the blocks. The rest clung to the ends of the cable, and were directed to slack off gradually as the sculpture descended.

The men being ready, and all my preparations complete,

I stationed myself on the top of the high bank of earth over the second bull, and ordered the wedges to be struck out from under the sculpture to be moved. Still, however, it remained firmly in its place. A rope having been passed round it, six or seven men easily tilted it over. The thick, ill-made cable stretched with the strain, and almost buried itself in the earth round which it was coiled. The ropes held well. The mass descended gradually, the Chaldeans propping it up firmly with the beams. It was a moment of great anxiety. The drums, and shrill pipes of the Kurdish musicians, increased the din and confusion caused by the war-cry of the Arabs, who were half frantic with excitement. They had thrown off nearly all their garments; their long hair floated in the wind; and they indulged in the wildest postures and gesticulations as they clung to the ropes. The women had congregated on the sides of the trenches, and by their incessant screams, and by the ear-piercing tahlehl, added to the enthusiasm of the men. The bull once in motion, it was no longer possible to obtain a hearing. The loudest cries I could produce were buried in the heap of discordant sounds. Neither the hippopotamus hide whips of the Cawasses, nor the bricks and clods of earth with which I endeavored to draw attention from some of the most noisy of the group, were of any avail. Away went the bull, steady enough as long as supported by the props behind; but as it came nearer to the rollers, the beams could no longer be used. The cable and ropes stretched more and more. Dry from the climate, as they felt the strain, they creaked and threw out dust. Water was thrown over them, but in vain, for they all broke together when the sculpture was within four or five feet of the rollers. The bull was precipitated to the ground. Those who held the ropes, thus suddenly released, followed its example, and were rolling one over the other, in the dust. A sudden silence succeeded to the clamor. I rushed into the trenches, prepared to find the bull in many pieces. It would be difficult to describe my satisfaction, when I saw it lying precisely where I had wished to place it, and uninjured! The Arabs no sooner got on their legs again, than seeing the result of the accident, they darted out of the trenches, and seizing by the hands the women who were looking on, formed a large circle, and yelling their war-cry with redoubled energy, commenced a most mad dance. The musicians exerted themselves to the utmost; but their music was drowned by the cries of the dancers. Even Abd-ur-rahman shared in the excitement, and throwing his cloak to one of his attendants, insisted upon leading off. . . .

I now prepared . . . to move the bull into the long trench which led to the edge of the mound. The rollers were in good order; and as soon as the excitement of the Arabs had sufficiently abated to enable them to resume work, the sculpture was dragged out of its place by ropes.

Sleepers were laid to the end of the trench, and fresh rollers were placed under the bull as it was pulled forwards by cables, to which were fixed the tackles held by logs buried in the earth, on the edge of the mound. The sun was going down as these preparations were completed. I deferred any further labor to the morrow. The Arabs dressed themselves; and placing the musicians at their head, marched towards the village, singing their war-songs. . . .

I rode back with Abd-ur-rahman. . . . The Sheikh, his enthusiasm once cooled down, gave way to moral reflections. "Wonderful! Wonderful! There is surely no God but God, and Mohammed is his Prophet," exclaimed he, after a long pause. "In the name of the Most High, tell me, O Bey, what you are going to do with those stones. So many thousands of purses spent upon such things! Can it be, as you say, that your people learn wisdom from them; or is it, as his reverence the Cadi declares, that they are to go to the palace of your Queen, who, with the rest of the unbelievers, worships these idols? . . . . But God is great! God is great! Here are stones which have been buried ever since the time of the holy Noah, —peace be with him! Perhaps they were under ground before the deluge. I have lived on these lands for years. My father, and the father of my father, pitched their tents here before me; but they never heard of these figures. For twelve hundred years have the true believers . . . been settled in this country, and none of them ever heard of a palace under ground. . . . But lo! here comes a Frank from many days' journey off, and he walks up to the very place, and he takes a stick . . . and makes a line here, and makes a line there. Here, says he, is the palace; there, says he, is the gate; and he shows us what has been all our lives beneath our feet, without our having known anything about it. Wonderful! Wonderful! Is it by books, is it by magic, is it by your prophets, that you have learnt these things? Speak, O Bey; tell me the secret of wisdom." . . .

Everything had been prepared on the previous day for moving the bull, and the men had now only to haul on the ropes. As the sculpture advanced, the rollers left behind were removed to the front, and thus in a short time it reached the end of the trench. There was little difficulty in dragging it down the precipitous side of the mound. When it arrived within three or four feet of the bottom, sufficient earth was removed from beneath it to admit the cart, upon which the bull itself was then lowered by still further digging away the soil. It was soon ready to be dragged to the river. Buffaloes were first harnessed to the yoke; but, although the men pulled with ropes fastened to the rings attached to the wheels, and to other parts of the cart, the animals, feeling the weight behind them, refused to move. We were compelled, therefore, to take them out; and the Tiyari, in parties of eight, lifted by turns the pole, whilst the Arabs, assisted by the people of Naifa and Nimroud, dragged the cart. The procession was thus formed. I rode first . . . to point out the road. Then came the musicians, with their drums and fifes, drumming and fifing with might and main. The cart followed, dragged by about three hundred men, all screeching at the top of their voices, and urged on by the Cawasses and superintendents. The procession was closed by the women, who kept up the enthusiasm of the Arabs by their shrill cries. Abd-ur-rahman's horsemen performed divers feats round the group, dashing backwards and forwards, and charging with their spears.

We advanced well enough, although the ground was very heavy, until we reached the ruins of the former village of Nimroud. It is the custom, in this part of Turkey, for the villagers to dig deep pits to store their corn, barley, and straw for the autumn and winter. These pits generally surround the villages. Being only covered by a light framework of boughs and stakes, plastered over with mud, they become, particularly when half empty, a snare and a trap to the horseman; who, unless guided by someone acquainted with the localities, is pretty certain to find the hind legs of his horse on a level with its ears, and himself suddenly sprawling in front. The corn-pits around Nimroud had long since been emptied of their supplies, and had been concealed by the light sand and dust, which, blown over the plain during summer, soon fill up every hole and crevice. Although I had carefully examined the ground before starting, one of these holes had escaped my notice, and into it two wheels of the cart completely sank. The Arabs pulled and yelled in vain. The ropes broke, but the wheels refused to move. We tried every means to release them, but unsuccessfully. After working until dusk, we were obliged to give up the attempt. I left a party of Arabs to guard the cart and its contents, suspecting that some adventurous Bedouins, attracted by the ropes, mats, and felts, with which the sculpture was enveloped, might turn their steps towards the spot during the night. My suspicions did not prove unfounded; for I had scarcely got into bed before the whole village was thrown into commotion by the reports of firearms, and the war-cry of the Jebour. Hastening to the scene of action, I found that a party of Arabs had fallen upon my workmen. They were beaten off, leaving behind them, however, their mark; for a ball, passing through the matting and felt, struck and indented the side of the bull. I was anxious to learn who the authors of this wanton attack were, and had organized a scheme for taking summary vengeance. But they were discovered too late; for, anticipating punishment, they had struck their tents, and had moved off into the desert.

Next morning we succeeded in clearing away the earth,

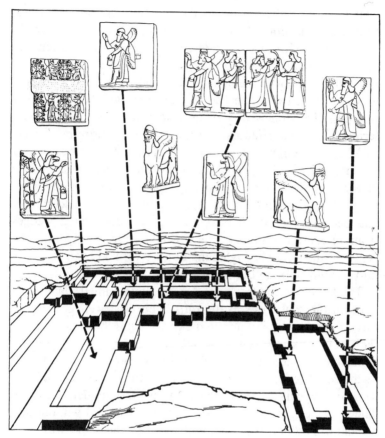

Perspective Drawing: Inner Court, Palace of
Ashurnasirpal II

and in placing thick planks beneath the buried wheels. After
a few efforts the cart moved forwards amidst the shouts of
the Arabs; who, as was invariably their custom on such occasions, indulged, whilst pulling at the ropes, in the most
outrageous antics. The procession was formed as on the
previous day, and we dragged the bull triumphantly down
to within a few hundred yards of the river. Here the wheels

buried themselves in the sand, and it was night before we contrived, with the aid of planks and by increased exertions, to place the sculpture on the platform prepared to receive it, and from which it was to slide down on the raft. The tents of the Arabs, who encamped near the river, were pitched round the bull, until its companion, the lion, should be brought down; and the two embarked together for Baghdad. The night was passed in renewed rejoicings, to celebrate the successful termination of our labors. On the following morning, I rode to Mosul, to enjoy a few days' rest after my exertions. . . .

On the 20th of April, there being fortunately a slight rise in the river, and the rafts being ready, I determined to attempt the embarkation of the lion and bull. The two sculptures had been so placed on beams that, by withdrawing wedges from under the sculpture, they would slide nearly into the center of the raft. The high bank of the river had been cut away into a rapid slope to the water's edge. . . .

The beams of poplar wood, forming an inclined plane from beneath the sculptures to the rafts, were first well greased. A raft, supported by six hundred skins, having been brought to the river bank, opposite the bull, the wedges were removed from under that sculpture, which immediately slid down into its place. The only difficulty was to prevent its descending too rapidly, and bursting the skins by the sudden pressure. The Arabs checked it by ropes, and it was placed without any accident. The lion was then embarked in the same way, and with equal success, upon a second raft of the same size as the first; in a few hours the two sculptures were properly secured, and before night they were ready to float down the river to Busrah.

Many slabs, including the large bas-reliefs of the king on his throne, between the eunuchs and winged fingers, which formed the end of chamber *g,* the altar-piece in chamber *b,* and above thirty cases containing small objects discovered in the ruins, were placed on the rafts with the lion and the bull.

After the labors of the day were over, sheep were slaughtered for the entertainment of Abd-ur-rahman's Arabs, and for those who had helped in the embarkation of the sculptures. The Abou Salman returned to their tents after dark. Abd-ur-rahman took leave of me, and we did not meet again. . . .

On the morning of the 22nd, all the sculptures having been embarked, I gave two sheep to the raftmen to be slain on the bank of the river, as a sacrifice to insure the success of the undertaking. The carcasses were distributed, as is proper on such occasions, amongst the poor. A third sheep was reserved for a propitiatory offering, to be immolated at the tomb of Sultan Abd-Allah. This saint still appears to interfere considerably with the navigation of the river, and closed the further ascent of the Tigris against the Frank steamer, because they neglected to make the customary sacrifice. All ceremonies having been duly performed, Mullah Ali kissed my hand, placed himself on one of the rafts, and slowly floated, with the cargo under his charge, down the stream.

I watched the rafts until they disappeared behind a projecting bank forming a distant reach of the river. I could not forbear musing upon the strange destiny of their burdens; which, after adorning the palaces of the Assyrian kings, the objects of the wonder, and may be the worship, of thousands, had been buried unknown for centuries beneath a soil trodden by Persians under Cyrus, by Greeks under Alexander, and by Arabs under the first descendants of their prophet. They were now to visit India, to cross the most distant seas of the southern hemisphere, and to be finally placed in a British Museum. Who can venture to foretell how their strange career will end?

A View of the Ancient City of Nippur, Showing the
Eighty-Foot Wall Enclosing the Castle Excavated
by American Archaeologists

# 5. HILPRECHT:

# *Disaster at Nippur*

The narrative that follows is the account of perhaps the
most badly bungled archaeological expedition ever attempted.
It ended in chaos, disaster, and confusion. Yet it was notable
on two accounts that merit its inclusion here: it was the first
American venture into archaeology in the Near East, and it
produced a rich yield of material despite the overall mismanagement of the expedition.

The city of Nippur, where these excavations were conducted,

was one of the most ancient in the ancient land of Sumer. It was not, however, a commercial or politically-minded city. Rather, it seems to have been founded as a religious shrine, a center for the worship of the god Enlil, and it remained aloof from the dynastic struggles that engaged the energies of Ur, Kish, Lagash, and the other Sumerian city-states in the period between 3000 and 1700 B.C.

When Layard visited the mound of Niffar (Nuffar) in January, 1851, the very existence of Sumer had been forgotten. A Biblical reference to "the land of Shinar" was unexplained; Sumer itself was an unknown name. Layard spent a month at Niffar, a vast mound fifty feet high along the banks of the Euphrates, far to the south of the ancient cities of Assyria. The surface of the mound was covered with the fragments of brick, glazed and unglazed pottery, glass, and mud, that marked the other sites of southern Mesopotamia.

But Layard was searching for sculpture, not bricks and the remains of walls, and of museum pieces he found few at Niffar. Rumors of a "great black stone" existing somewhere in the mounds led him on in vain. There was little but rubbish at Niffar, Layard thought. He unearthed nearly a hundred slipper-shaped clay coffins, and found a few small cups and vases and bones—but no gold, no silver, no limestone reliefs, no statuary. "On the whole I am much inclined to question whether extensive excavations carried on at Niffar would produce any very important or interesting results," Layard noted, and returned to the more productive mounds of Assyria.

The decades that followed saw the rediscovery of Sumer. In 1869 a French archaeologist, Jules Oppert, discovered cuneiform inscriptions in southern Mesopotamia that referred to an early ruler who styled himself "King of Sumer and Akkad." Oppert suggested the existence of a people he called the "Sumerians," who had ruled in Mesopotamia long before the rise of the Semitic kingdoms of Babylonia and Assyria.

Other excavators soon were turning up cuneiform inscriptions which seemed to be in a language totally unlike Akkadian, the language of Assyria and Babylonia. The controversy over the existence of a pre-Semitic race of Sumerians became a heated one, the so-called "Sumerian Question," raging through the latter part of the 19th century. Ultimately the Sumerian hypothesis was accepted by nearly all archaeologists. Today it is more than a hypothesis: it is an established fact. Bilingual inscriptions, whole dictionaries of Sumerian and Akkadian, unlocked the Sumerian records. We know now that Sumer flourished long before the Semites entered Mesopotamia, and that the Sumerians were absorbed into the ranks of the invaders. Though Sumer disappeared as a political entity, the Sumerian language remained alive as a priestly tongue, holding much the same relationship to the religious devotions of the Assyrians and Babylonians as Latin does to those of Roman Catholics today.

Late in the 19th century, many of the Sumerian cities came under the excavator's spade. Among them was Nippur, where an American-sponsored expedition commenced work. The main figures in this party were John P. Peters, an expert on Hebrew philology; H.V. Hilprecht, an authority on the Assyrian language; and J. H. Haynes, an explorer and excavator. They were all strong-willed men, and, as will be seen presently, they were unable to agree on the policies of their expedition virtually from the start.

Peters and Haynes were of the opinion that the main purpose of the expedition was to obtain specimens for the museum of the University of Pennsylvania, one of the sponsors of the expedition. Peters, the Hebrew philologist, was particularly eager to bring back large numbers of the cuneiform tablets in which Nippur abounded. Hilprecht, though himself a philologist, preferred to see a careful architectural study of the city carried out. There was also disagreement about who should head the expedition.

All this might not have harmed the work seriously, but for the poor relations established with the natives. Peters in particular took a high-handed attitude toward them, refusing to deal directly with them and declining to hand out the small bribes that the natives expected. Deprived of their *bakshish,* the Arabs preyed on the archaeologists, matters deteriorated swiftly, and the first season at Nippur culminated in a disastrous fire.

A second campaign three years later, in 1890, was somewhat more successful, but was marred by dissension among the archaeologists. Haynes and Peters still preferred to intimidate the natives rather than to bribe them and this caused problems.

There was a third Nippur campaign in 1893-1896, again under Haynes. Finally, in 1899, the University of Pennsylvania sponsored a fourth campaign under the long-suffering Hilprecht, who had disagreed with practically everything Haynes and Peters had done. This fourth campaign was highly successful. Hilprecht explored the *ziggurat,* or step-tower, of Nippur, and came upon the temple library, containing some 20,000 cuneiform tablets. So rich has been the yield from Nippur that tablets found by Hilprecht more than sixty years ago still await translation; it has been impossible to deal with them all. The tablets of Nippur have provided an unequalled sampling of Sumerian literature, religious writing, and commercial documents—30,000 tablets in all, covering a span of a thousand years. This great mass of material will offer fresh revelations about Sumer for years to come.

Peters published his account of his work at Nippur in 1897: *Nippur or Explorations and Adventures on the Euphrates.* But his book skirted over much of the mismanagement of the early years of the Nippur work. It remained for Hilprecht to tell the full story.

The German-born Hilprecht (1859-1925) was not an adventurer in the Layard-Belzoni tradition. He was of the new species of scholarly archaeologists that established the fabric of the science in the late 19th century. As Clark Research Professor of Assyriology at the University of Pennsylvania, he was probably the foremost authority on ancient Mesopotamia in the United States at the turn of the century.

He told the story of the Nippur expeditions in the massive 800-page *Explorations in Bible Lands During the 19th Cen-*

*tury,* published in 1903. The book is a survey of all archaeological work done in the Near East through 1900, but the heart of the book, nearly 300 pages, deals with the Nippur work alone. The book is perhaps the most detailed relation of the archaeology of Mesopotamia in the 19th century ever written, and is still a valuable reference work today.

Hilprecht makes an attempt at impartiality; there is no concealing his animus for Haynes, however. His account of the campaigns at Nippur not only brings to life this episode in archaeological history, but provides a revealing glimpse into the behind-the-scenes "politics" that frequently afflicts any form of scientific research.

# DISASTER AT NIPPUR

F*irst Campaign, 1888-89.* The meeting at which Dr. Peters submitted his plans to the public was held at the house of Provost Pepper on November 30, 1887. About thirty persons were present, including Dr. Ward, the previous leader of the Wolfe Expedition, and Professor Hilprecht, as the official representative of Assyriology in the University of Pennsylvania. Both had been invited by the chairman to express their respective views with regard to the contemplated undertaking. In the course of the discussion it became more and more apparent that the enthusiastic originator of the new scheme and the present writer differed essentially from each other on fundamental questions. On the basis of Dr. Ward's recommendation, the former declared in favor of a large promising site, like Anbâr, Nuffar, El-Birs, etc., as most suitable for the Philadelphia excavations. He proposed that the staff of the expedition should consist of four persons, a director, a well-known Assyriologist, formerly connected with the British

From *Explorations in Bible Lands During the 19th Century* (Philadelphia: A. J. Holman & Co., 1903) by H. V. Hilprecht et al.

Museum, and the photographer and the interpreter of the Wolfe Expedition; and he estimated the total expense for a campaign of three consecutive years, as previously stated by him, at $15,000. The present writer, on the other side, pointed out that while he fully agreed with Dr. Peters as to the importance of either of the proposed mounds for archæological research, especially of Nuffar, so frequently and prominently mentioned in the earliest cuneiform inscriptions, he nevertheless felt it his duty to affirm that none of these extensive mounds could be excavated in the least adequately within the period stated, and that, moreover, according to his own calculations, even a small expedition of only four members and a corresponding number of servants and workmen would necessarily cost more in the first year than the whole sum required for three years. He furthermore called attention to the fact that the national honor and the scientific character of this first great American enterprise in Babylonia would seem to require the addition of an American Assyriologist and architect, and, if possible, even of a surveyor and a naturalist, to the proposed staff of the expedition. If, however, in view of a very natural desire on the part of the director and his financial supporters, the principal stress was to be laid on the rapid acquisition of important museum objects and inscribed tablets rather than on the methodical and complete examination of an entire large ruin, it would be by far wiser to select from among the different sites visited by Dr. Ward one which was somewhat smaller in size and considerably less superimposed with the remains and rubbish of the post-Babylonian period than any of the ruins submitted for consideration. The results showed only too plainly that the view maintained by the present writer was correct, and that his objections, raised for the sole purpose of preventing unpleasant complications and later disappointments with regard to "the white elephant," as the expedition was soon to be styled, were based upon a careful discrimination between uncertain hopes and sober facts.

The same evening "The Babylonian Exploration Fund" was called into existence, about half of the sum requested

($15,000) subscribed, and an expedition with Dr. Peters as director recommended. . . . Dr. Peters was confirmed as director, but the general plan previously outlined by him was somewhat modified in accordance with the writer's suggestions. Upon the director's recommendation, Dr. Robert Francis Harper, then instructor in Yale University, was appointed Assyriologist, Mr. Perez Hastings Field, of New York, architect and surveyor, Mr. Haynes photographer and business manager, and Mr. Noorian interpreter and director of the workmen, while Mr. J. D. Prince, just graduating from Columbia College and offering to accompany the expedition at his own expense, was attached as the director's secretary. But having fallen seriously ill on the way down the Euphrates valley, he left the expedition at Baghdad, and returned to America by way of India and China.

On April 4, I received an urgent note from Provost Pepper requesting me to see him at once and stating that it was his especial desire that I should serve on this expedition as the University of Pennsylvania's Assyriologist, all the necessary expenses to be paid by himself and Rev. Dr. H. Clay Trumbull, editor of "The Sunday School Times." I consented to go without a salary. . . . In the course of the summer the members of the expedition left at intervals for the East, finally meeting at Aleppo on December 10. Peters and Prince had spent three months in Constantinople to obtain a firmân for successive excavations at El-Birs and Nuffar; Harper, Field, and Haynes had visited the Hittite districts of Senjirli, Mar'ash and Jerâbîs (Carchemish); while the present writer had worked on the cuneiform inscriptions of the Nahr el-Kelb and Wâdi Berîsa, at the same time searching the whole Lebanon region for new material. After an uneventful trip down "the great river" and a fortnight's stay at Baghdad, largely devoted to the examination and purchase of antiquities, the party proceeded by way of Hilla to Nuffar, the scene of its future activity. For after a visit to the high-towering mound of El-Birs and the adjoining site of Tell Ibrâhîm el-Khalîl, which together constitute the remains of ancient Borsippa, it had been decided unanimously not to commence operations here, but to move further on to the second place granted by the firmân, which practically represented an entirely fresh site only superficially scratched before by Layard.

The next military station from Nuffar is Dîwânîye, situated on both sides of the Euphrates and (according to the season and the extent of the inundations) about six to nine hours to the southwest of it. At the time of our first campaign it was a miserable and fast decreasing town consisting chiefly of mud houses, and governed by a *qâimmagâm,* under whose immediate jurisdiction we were to be. But since the water supply of the lower Euphrates has been regulated through the construction of the Hindîye dam above Babylon, it has rapidly changed its aspect and become a neat and flourishing town. At the expense of Hilla it has been raised to the seat of a *mutesarrif* and received a considerable increase of soldiers, including even artillery, in order to check the predatory incursions of the roaming Bedouins of the desert, and to control the refractory 'Afej tribes around Nuffar, which until recently acknowledged only a nominal allegiance to the Ottoman government, regarding themselves as perfectly safe in the midst of their swamps and mud castles, the so-called *meftûls.* Peters, Harper, and Bedry Bey, our Turkish commissioner, took this circuitous route by way of Dîwânîye, to pay their respects to the local governor there and to make the necessary arrangements for the prompt despatch and receipt of our mail.

The rest of us, accompanied by thirty-two trained workmen from Jumjuma and another village near El-Birs, a crowd of women and children attached to them, and a large number of animals carrying our whole outfit, provisions, and the implements for excavations, struck directly for Nuffar. The frequent rumors which we had heard at Baghdad and Hilla concerning the unsettled and unsafe condition of this section of the country, inhabited as it was said to be by the most unruly and turbulent tribes of the whole vilayet, were in an entire accord with Layard's reports, and only too soon to be confirmed by our own experience. The 'Afej and the powerful

Shammar, who sometimes descend as far down as the Shatt el-Haï, were fighting for the pasture lands, driving each other's camels and sheep away, and two of the principal subdivisions of the 'Afej had a blood-feud with each other. On the second day of our march, while temporarily separated from our caravan, we were suddenly surprised by a *ghazu* (razzia) and with difficulty escaped the hands of the marauding Arabs. The nearer we came to the goal of our journey, the more disturbed was the population. Finally on the third morning Bint el-Amîr, majestically towering above the wide stretched mounds of Nuffar, rose clear on the horizon. More than 2000 years ago the huge terraces and walls of the most renowned Babylonian sanctuary had crumbled to a formless mass. But even in their utter desolation they still seemed to testify to the lofty aspirations of a bygone race, and to reëcho the ancient hymn once chanted in their shadow:—

"*O great mountain of Bêl, Imgarsag,*
   *Whose summit rivals the heavens,*
*Whose foundations are laid in the bright abysmal sea,*
   *Resting in the land as a mighty steer,*
 *Whose horns are gleaming like the radiant sun,*
   *As the stars of heaven are filled with lustre.*"

Even at a distance I began to realize that not twenty, not fifty years would suffice to excavate this important site thoroughly. What would our committee at home have said at the sight of this enormous ruin, resembling more a picturesque mountain range than the last impressive remains of human constructions! But there was not much time for these and similar reflections; our attention was fully absorbed by the exciting scenes around us. The progress of the motley crowd along the edge of the cheerless swamps was slow enough. The marshy ground which we had to traverse was cut up by numerous old canals, and offered endless difficulties to the advance of our stumbling beasts. Besides, the whole neighborhood was inflamed by war. Gesticulating groups of armed men watched our approach with fear and suspicion. Whenever we passed a village, the signal of alarm was given. A piece of black cloth fluttered in an instant from the *meftûl*, dogs began to bark savagely, shepherds ran their flocks into shelter, and the cries of terrified women and children sounded shrill over the flat and treeless plain. Greeted by the wild dance and the rhythmical yells of some fifty 'Afej warriors, who had followed our movements from a peak of the weather-torn ruins, we took possession of the inheritance of Bêl.

Immediately after our arrival we began to pitch our tents on the highest point of the southwestern half of the ruins, where we could enjoy an unlimited view over the swamps and the desert, and which at the same time seemed best protected against malaria and possible attacks from the Arabs. With the aid of Berdi, shaikh of the Warish (a subdivision of the Hamza), who was ready to assist us, a number of native huts, so-called *sarîfas*, made of bunches of reed arched together and covered with palm-leaf mats, were placed in a square around us. They served for stables, store-rooms, servants' quarters, workshop, dining-room, kitchen and other purposes, and also protected us against the sand storms and the thievish inclinations of the children of the desert. Before this primitive camp was established, Field began surveying the mounds, as a preliminary map had to be submitted to the wâli of Baghdad, in order to secure his formal approval of our excavations. In the mean while the director and the two Assyriologists used every spare moment to acquaint themselves with the topography of the ruins and to search for indications on the surface which might enable them to ascertain the probable character and contents of the more prominent single mounds.

In connection with repeated walks over the whole field I prepared a rough sketch of the principal ruins for my own use, gathered numerous pieces of bricks, stone and pottery, and immediately reached the following general conclusions: 1. Certain portions of the ruins are remarkably free from blue and green enamelled pottery, always characteristic of late settlements on Babylonian sites, and show no trace of an extensive use of glass on the part of its inhabitants. As the latter is never mentioned with certainty in the cuneiform inscriptions (then at our disposal), and as the Assyrian excavations at Khorsabâd, Nebî Yûnus, and Nimrûd had yielded but a few glass vessels, these parts of ancient Nippur must have been destroyed and abandoned at a comparatively early date. 2. In accordance with such personal observations and inferences and in view of Layard's discoveries in the upper strata of Nuffar, it became evident that the southwest half of the ruins, which on an average is also considerably higher than the corresponding other one, was much longer inhabited and to a larger extent used as a graveyard in the post-Christian period than the northeast section. 3. As Bint el-Amîr, the most conspicuous mound of the whole ruins, no doubt represents the ancient *ziggurrat* or stage-tower, as generally asserted, it follows as a matter of course, that the temple of Bêl, of which it formed part, must also have been situated in the northeast section, and therefore is hidden under the mounds immediately adjoining it towards the east. 4. The question arose, what buildings are covered by the two remaining groups of mounds to the northwest and southeast of the temple complex. The important rôle which from the earliest times the cult of Bêl must have played in the life and history of the Babylonian people, as testified by the enormous mass of ruins and numerous passages in the cuneiform literature, pointed unmistakably to the employment of a large number of priests and temple officers, and to the existence of a flourishing school and a well equipped temple library in the ancient city of Nippur. Which of the two mounds under consideration most probably represented the residences of the priests with their administrative offices and educational quarters? 5. The large open court to the northwest of the temple, enclosed as it was on two sides by the visible remains of ancient walls, on the third by the *ziggurrat,* and on the fourth by the Shatt en-Nîl, suggested at once that the undetermined northwest group flanking this court served more practical purposes and contained out-houses, stables, store-rooms, magazines, sheds, servants' quarters, etc., which were not required in the immediate neighborhood and in front of the temple. 6. It was therefore extremely probable that the houses of the priests, their offices, school, and library must be looked for in the large triangular southeast mound, separated by a branch of the Shatt en-Nîl from the temple proper. Situated on the bank of two canals, in close proximity to the sanctuary of Bêl, open on all sides to the fresh breezes in the summer, and yet well protected against the rough north winds, which swept down from the snow-capped mountains of Persia during the winter, this section of the ruins seemed to fulfill all the conditions required, and from the very beginning was therefore pointed out by the present writer as the most important mound for our work next to the temple ruin proper.

It will always remain a source of deep regret that Dr. Peters did not rely more upon the judgment and scientific advice of his Assyriologists in deciding strictly technical questions, but that in his anxious but useless efforts to arrange all the essential details of this first expedition in person, he allowed himself frequently to be led by accidents and secondary considerations rather than by a clearly definite plan of methodical operations. The first trenches were opened on February 6 by the thirty-two workmen hired in Hilla. The circumstance that some of the Arabs, while gathering bricks for certain constructions in our camp, had accidentally struck a large tomb in a small gully near us influenced the director to begin the excavations at this point, which soon led to the discovery of a construction of columns made of baked bricks and of such a mass of slipper-shaped coffins, funeral urns, bones, ashes, and other remains of the dead, that at first we were inclined to regard the whole southwestern half of Nuffar as a vast graveyard or a regular "city of the dead," similar to those explored by Moritz and Koldewey at Surghul and El-Hibba. The next point attacked by him was an extremely insignificant out-of-the-way mound at the northwestern end of the Shatt en-Nîl, selected chiefly because it was small enough to be excavated completely within a few weeks. Several days later, when a sufficient number of workmen had been obtained from the neighboring tribes, the systematic exploration of Bint el-Amîr was undertaken in accordance with a plan prepared by the Assyriologists and the architect. The first task which we had set for ourselves was to determine the corners and walls of the stage-tower, and to search for barrel cylinders and other documents which might have been deposited in this ancient structure by the different monarchs who restored it. If ever they existed,—and certain discoveries made later in the rubbish around its base proved that they actually did,—these building records must have been destroyed at the time of the Parthian invasion, when the whole temple complex was remodelled for military purposes.

Apart from a stray cuneiform tablet of the period of Sargon I.—the first of its kind ever discovered,—three small fragments of inscribed stone picked up by the Arabs, a few Hebrew bowls, and a number of bricks bearing short legends of the kings Ur-Gur, Bur-Sin I., Ur-Ninib, and Ishme-Dagan, all of the third pre-Christian millennium, no inscribed documents had been unearthed during the first ten days of our stay at Nuffar. No wonder that Dr. Peters, who began to realize that his funds of $15,000 were nearly exhausted, grew uneasy as to the tangible results of the expedition, the future of which depended largely upon quick and important discoveries. I seized this opportunity to submit once more for his consideration my views, given above, concerning the topography of the northeast half of the ruins, pointing out that in all probability tablets would be found in that large isolated hill, which I believed to contain the residences of the priests and the temple library, and requested him to let me have about twenty men for a few days to furnish the inscribed material so eagerly sought after. This was a somewhat daring proposition, which scarcely would have been made with this self-imposed restriction of time had I not been convinced of the general correctness of my theory. After some hesitation the director was generous enough to place two gangs of workmen at my disposal for a whole week in order to enable me to furnish the necessary proof for my subjective conviction. On February 11 two trenches were opened at the western edge of IV on a level with the present beds of the ancient canal. Before noon the first six cuneiform tablets were in our possession, and at the close of the same day more than twenty tablets and fragments had been recovered. Thus far the beginning was very encouraging, and far surpassed my boldest expectations. But it remained to be seen whether we had struck only one of those small nests of clay tablets as they occasionally occur in all Babylonian ruins, or whether they would continue to come forth in the same manner during the following weeks and even increase gradually in number. At the end of February several hundred tablets and fragments had been obtained from the same source, and six weeks later, when our first campaign was brought to a sudden end, mound IV had yielded more than two thousand cuneiform inscriptions from its seemingly inexhaustible mines. For the greater part they were unbaked, broken, and otherwise damaged. With regard to their age, two periods could be clearly distinguished. The large mass was written in old Babylonian characters not later than the first dynasty of Babylon (about 2000 B.C.), but less than one hundred tablets gathered in the upper strata were so-called neo-Babylonian contracts generally well preserved and dated in the reigns of Ashurbânapal, Nabopolassar, Nebuchadnezzar, Evil-Merodach (2 Kgs. 25:27; Jer. 52:31), Nabonidos, Cyrus, Cambyses, Darius, and Xerxes. Three of them were of unusual historical interest. Being dated in the second and fourth year of Ashuretililâni, "king of Assyria," they proved conclusively that Nabopolassar's rebellion against the Assyrian supremacy (626 B.C.) was originally confined to the capital and its immediate environment, and that, contrary to the prevalent view, long after Babylon itself had regained and maintained its independence, important cities and whole districts of the Southern empire still paid homage to Ashurbânapal's successor on the throne of Assyria.

But the earlier inscriptions, though as a rule very fragmentary, were of even greater significance. None of them was evidently found *in situ,* except ten large tablets in a most excellent state of preservation taken from a kiln, where they had

been in the process of baking when one of the terrible catas-
trophes by which the city was repeatedly visited overtook
ancient Nippur. They consisted of business documents referring to the registry of tithes and to the administration of the
temple property, and of tablets of a decided literary character,
comprising some very fine syllabaries and lists of synonyms,
letters, mathematical, astronomical, medical and religious
texts, besides a few specimens of drawing and a considerable
number of mostly round tablets which must be classified as
school exercises. Those which were dated bore the names of
Hammurabi, Samsuiluna, Abeshum, Ammisatana, and Am-
misadugga. As about four-fifths of all the tablets were literary,
there could no longer be any doubt that we were not far from
the famous temple library, unless indeed we already were
working in its very ruins. In order to arrive at more definite
results, it would have been necessary to continue the two
large trenches which I had started, through the center to the
eastern edge of the mound. In the course of the second half
of March five extra gangs were put on "the tablet hill," as it
was henceforth styled, to carry out this plan. But time and
money were soon lacking, and circumstances arose which
forced us to excavate Nuffar before many weeks were over.
Otherwise we could not have failed to discover, in 1889, those
tablet-filled rooms which were unearthed eleven years later,
when the present writer personally was held responsible for
the preparation of the plans and the scientific management of
the expedition.

The work at the temple complex, where finally more than
one hundred men were employed, proceeded but slowly,
owing to the enormous amount of rubbish accumulated here
and to the tenacity of the unbaked bricks which had to be
cut through. Small and graceful terra-cotta cones similar to
those discovered by Loftus at Warkâ, but generally broken,
were excavated in large number along the base of the north-
west wall of the *ziggurrat*. Evidently they had fallen from
the top of the tower, and once belonged to a shrine contem-
poraneous with the inscribed bricks of Ashurbânapal, the

last known restorer of the temple of Bêl, near whose material they were lying. The remains of the lowest story of the huge building began to rise gradually out of the midst of the encumbering ruins. But they offered problems so complicated in themselves and with regard to other constructions discovered all around the *ziggurrat* at a much higher level, that it was well-nigh impossible to form a satisfactory idea of the character and extent of the temple, before the whole neighborhood had been subjected to a critical examination. For very apparent reasons there were only a few and very late tombs unearthed in this part of the city, while again they occurred more frequently in the lower mounds to the southwest of the temple. Among the various antiquities which came from the trenches of the sanctuary itself may be mentioned especially about a dozen vase fragments inscribed with very archaic characters, two of them exhibiting the name of Lugalzaggisi, an otherwise unknown king of Erech whose precise period could then not be determined; a well preserved brick stamp of Narâm-Sin (about 3750 B.C.), the first document of this half-mythical monarch which reached the shores of Europe; a fine marble tablet containing a list of garments presented to the temple; and a door-socket of the Cassite ruler Kurigalzu.

In the course of time our workmen had been gradually increased to about 250, so that experimental trenches could also be cut in the extreme western and southern wings of the ruins. A number of contract tablets of the time of the Chaldean and Persian dynasties were excavated in the upper strata of the last mentioned section. The fragment of a barrel cylinder of Sargon, king of Assyria, which came from the same neighborhood, indicated that a large public building must have occupied this site previously, a supposition subsequently strengthened by the discovery of two more fragments which belonged to duplicates of the same cylinder. Stray cuneiform tablets and seal cylinders; a considerable number of terra-cotta figurines, mostly bearded gods with weapons and other instruments in their hands, or naked goddesses holding their breasts or suckling a babe; and a few clay reliefs, among which an exquisitely modelled lioness excited our admiration, were discovered in various other parts of the ruins. They belonged to the Babylonian period, in which naturally our interest centered. But, as was to be expected, most of the trenches yielded antiquities which illustrated the life and customs of the early post-Christian inhabitants of the country rather than those of the ancient Babylonians. Especially in the ruins of the Parthian building, with its interesting brick columns, which in the first week the Arabs had disclosed to the east of our camp, we uncovered hundreds of slipper-shaped coffins and funeral urns, numerous vases and dishes, and small peculiar tripods, so-called stilts, which were used in connection with the burning of pottery in exactly the same way as they are employed in china-manufactories to-day. Terra-cotta toys, such as horses, riders, elephants, rams, monkeys, dogs, birds, eggs, marbles, and baby rattles in the shape of chickens, dolls and drums, spear-heads and daggers, metal instruments and polishing stones, Parthian coins, weights and whorls, jewelry in gold, silver, copper, bone, and stone, especially necklaces, bracelets, ear and finger rings, fibulae and hair-pins, together with about thirty bowls, inscribed with Hebrew, Mandean and Arabic legends, and frequently also covered with horrible demons supposed to molest the human habitations and to disturb the peace of the dead, completed our collections.

Soon after we had reached Nuffar, Dr. Peters had made us acquainted with the low ebb in the finances of the expedition. It was, therefore, decided to close the excavations of the first campaign at the beginning of May. But the working season was brought to a conclusion more quickly than could have been anticipated. The trouble started with the Arabs. The methodical exploration of the ruins had proceeded satisfactorily for about nine weeks till the middle of April, tablets being found abundantly, and the topography of ancient Nippur becoming more lucid every day. Notwithstanding those countless difficulties which, more or less, every expedition working in the interior of Babylonia far away from civilization has to meet at nearly every turn, we began to enjoy the life in the desert and to get accustomed to the manners of the fickle Arabs, whose principal "virtues" seemed to consist in lying, stealing, murdering, and lasciviousness. And the 'Afej, on the other hand, had gradually abandoned their original distrust, after they had satisfied themselves that the Americans had no intention of erecting a new military station out of the bricks of the old walls for the purpose of collecting arrears of government taxes. But there existed certain conditions in our camp and around us which, sooner or later, had to lead to serious complications. Hajji Tarfâ, the supreme shaikh of all the 'Afej tribes, a man of great diplomatic skill, liberal views and far-reaching influence, was unfortunately absent in the Shamîye when we commenced operations at Nuffar. His eldest son, Mukota, who meanwhile took the place of his father, was a sneaking Arab of the lowest type, little respected by his followers, begging for everything that came under his eyes, turbulent, treacherous, and a coward, and brooding mischief all the while. Two of the principal 'Afej tribes, the Hamza and the Behahtha, both of which laid claim to the mounds we had occupied, and insisted on furnishing workmen for our excavations, were at war with each other. At the slightest provocation and frequently without any apparent reason they threw their scrapers and baskets away and commenced the war-dance, brandishing their spears or guns in the air and chanting some defiant sentence especially made up for the occasion, as, *e.g.*, "We are the slaves of Berdi," "The last day has come," "Down with the Christians," "Matches in his beard who contradicts us," etc. The Turkish commissioner and the *zabtîye* (irregular soldiers),—whose number had been considerably increased by the *qâimmaqâm* of Dîwânîye, much against our own will,—picked frequent quarrels with the natives and irritated them by their overbearing manners. The Arabs, on the other hand, were not slow in showing their absolute independence by wandering unmolested around the camp, entering our private tents and examining our goods, like a crowd of naughty boys; or by squatting with their guns and clubs near the trenches and hurling taunting and offensive expressions at the Ottoman government.

It was also a mistake that we had pitched our tents on the top of the ruins. For as the mounds of Nuffar had no recognized owner and yet were claimed by the Turks, the Bedouins, and the Ma'dân tribes at the same time, we were practically under nobody's protection, while by our very conspicuous position we not only suffered exceedingly from hot winds and suffocating sand storms, but invited plundering by every loiterer and marauder in the neighborhood. Moreover, unacquainted as we all were then with the peculiar customs of Central Babylonia, we had not provided a *mudhîf* or lodging-house, a spacious and airy *sarîfa*, which in every large village of the country is set apart for the reception of travellers and guests. What wonder that the simple-minded children of the desert and the half-naked peasants of the marshes, who noticed our strange mode of living and saw so many unknown things with us for which they had no need themselves, shook their heads in amazement. On the one hand they observed how we spent large sums of money for uncovering old walls and gathering broken pottery, and on the other they found us eating the wild boar of the jungles, ignoring Arab etiquette, and violating the sacred and universal law of hospitality in the most flagrant way,—reasons enough to regard us either as pitiable idiots whom they could easily fleece or as unclean and uncouth barbarians to whom a pious Shiite was infinitely the superior.

Repeated threats to burn us out had been heard, and various attempts had been made to get at our rifles and guns. One night our bread-oven was destroyed, and a hole was cut in the reed-hut which served as our stable. Soon afterwards four sheep belonging to some of our workmen were stolen. The thief, a young lad from the Sa'îd, a small tribe of bad repute, half Bedouin and half Ma'dân, encouraged by his previous success, began to boast, as Berdi told me later, that he would steal even the horses of the Franks without being detected. Though he might have suspected us to be on the alert, he and a few comrades undertook to execute the long-cherished plan in the night of the fourteenth of April. Our sentinels, who had previously been ordered to occupy the approaches to the camp night and day, frustrated the attempt and opened fire at the intruders. In an instant the whole camp was aroused, and one of the thieves was shot through the heart. This was a most unfortunate occurrence, and sure to result in further trouble. No time was therefore lost to inform the 'Afej chiefs, to despatch a messenger to the next military station, and to prepare ourselves for any case of emergency. Then followed a period of anxious suspense. Soon the death wail sounded from a village close beneath us, indicating that the body of the dead Arab had been carried off to the nearest encampment. Then a signal fire was kindled. This was answered by another and another, until the whole plain was clothed with little lights, while through the still night came the sounds of bustle and preparation for the attack. On the next morning we decided to avoid the consequences of the severe laws of Arab blood revenge by paying an adequate indemnity to the family of the fallen man. But our offer was proudly rejected by the hostile tribe, and an old Sa'îd work-man, employed as a go-between, returned with torn garments and other evidences of a beating. The American party was equally prompt in refusing to give up the "murderer." The days and nights which followed were full of exciting scenes. Mukota, Berdi, and other 'Afej shaikhs, who professed to come to our assistance, had occupied the spurs around us. Thirty irregular soldiers, with six hundred rounds of cartridges, were sent from Dîwânîye and Hilla, and others were expected to arrive in the near future. There were constant alarms of an attack by the Sa'îd. The 'Afej, not concealing their dis-pleasure at seeing so large a number of *zabtîye* in their terri-tory, were evidently at heart in sympathy with the enemy. Besieged as we practically were, we were finally forced to withdraw our laborers from the trenches and make arrangements for quitting Nuffar altogether. On Thursday, April 18, long before the sun rose, the whole expedition was in readiness to vacate the mounds and to force their way to Hilla, when upon the treacherous order of Mukota, an Arab secretly set fire to our huts of reeds and mats and laid the whole camp in ashes in the short space of five minutes. For a while the utmost confusion prevailed, the *zabtîye* got demoralized, and occupied a neighboring hill; and while we were trying to save our effects, many of the Arabs commenced plundering. Half the horses perished in the flames, firearms and saddle-bags and $1000 in gold fell into the hands of the marauders, but all the antiquities were saved. Under the war-dance and yells of the frantic Arabs the expedition finally withdrew in two divisions, one on horseback, past Sûq el-'Afej and Dîwânîye, the other on two boats across the swamps to Daghâra, and back to Hilla, where soon afterwards the governor-general of the province arrived, anxious about our welfare and determined, if necessary, to come to our rescue with a military force.

On the way to Baghdad Harper handed in his resignation, Field gave his own a day later, Haynes, who, on the recommendation of the Philadelphia Committee, had been appointed United States Consul at Baghdad, prepared to settle in the city of Hârûn ar-Rashîd, and with Noorian to await further developments, Peters was recalled by cable to America, and the present writer was requested to remain in charge of the expedition in Mesopotamia. But circumstances beyond his control made it impossible for him to accept this trust at once, and necessitated his immediate return to Europe. Our first year at Babylonia had ended in a serious disaster. Dr. Peters, to quote his own words, "had failed to win the confidence of his comrades," and more than $20,000 had been expended merely to scratch the surface of one of the most enormous ancient sites in all Western Asia. How would the Ottoman government view the unexpected turn in our work among the turbulent Arabs? Would they allow the expedition to return in the fall? And if no obstacle was raised in Constantinople, would the Philadelphia Committee, after so many disappointments, be willing to resume the exploration of Nuffar, which had proved to be a task by far more expensive and wearisome than most of the contributors could have expected?

*Second Campaign, 1889–1890.*  It is to the great credit of the small number of enthusiastic gentlemen who had previously furnished the funds, that far from being discouraged by what had occurred, they were rather "favorably impressed with the results accomplished by the first year's campaign," and decided to continue the excavations at Nuffar for another year under Dr. Peters, provided that the Turkish authorities at Constantinople would approve of their plan. The wâli of Baghdad, who was principally held responsible for the safety of the party in a section of his province over which he had little control, most naturally opposed the return of the expedition with all his power. But thanks to the lively interest and the energetic support of Hamdy Bey, the Grand Vizier viewed the whole matter very calmly and in a different light from what it had been represented to him by the local officials. Accordingly he authorized the University of Pennsylvania's expedition to resume its interrupted labors in Babylonia in the same year. On October 10, Dr. Peters was able to leave the Turkish capital for Beirût, and from there, by way of Damascus and Palmyra, to travel to Baghdad, which he reached about the middle of December.

Important changes had meanwhile taken place in 'Irâq el-'Arabî. Soon after our departure, in May, 1889, a fearful cholera epidemic had broken out in lower Babylonia, and, following the courses of the two rivers, had spread rapidly to the northern districts. With the exception of Hît, Nejef, and some other remarkably favored places, it had devastated the entire country, with special fury raging in the marshy districts between Nuffar and the Shatt el-Haï, where our old enemy, Mukota, was carried off as one of its first victims, and in certain notoriously unclean and densely populated quarters of Baghdad, which for several weeks in the summer were almost completely deserted by the frightened population. In view of the lingering presence of the dreaded scourge in the

valleys of the Euphrates and the Tigris, and the possibility of
a renewed outbreak of the same plague in the spring, the
director deemed it necessary to engage the services of a native
physician of Syria, Dr. Selim Aftimus, who at the same time
was expected to make those botanical and zoölogical collections for which the present writer had earnestly pleaded,
before the first expedition was organized. Haynes and Noorian
were again induced to associate themselves with the practical management of the undertaking on the road and in the
field, and to serve in the same capacities in which they had
been employed the previous year. But, at the special desire
of Dr. Peters, this time an American scientific staff was entirely
dispensed with, though Field and Hilprecht would have been
willing to accompany the expedition again, without a salary
but with increased responsibility. This was a most unfortunate
decision on the part of the director. It is true, a solid scientific
basis of operations had been established in the first campaign,
and consequently there was no immediate need of an architect
and Assyriologist at the beginning of the new excavations;
and yet it was impossible to excavate properly for any length
of time without the constant advice of either of them. If,
nevertheless, this expedition, sent out to investigate the history of one of the largest, most ancient, and, at the same time,
most ruined and complicated sites in the country, attempted
to solve its difficult problem without the trained eyes and
scientific knowledge of technically prepared men, it necessarily
had to be at the expense of a strictly methodical exploration
and at the sacrifice of half of the possible results, of which
it deprived itself in consequence of its inability to follow up
every indication on the ground, and to determine most of the
perplexing archæological questions in the trenches.

But while in the interest of scientific research we cannot
approve of Dr. Peters' fatal course, to a certain degree we
can explain it. He was anxious to save expenses in connection with an undertaking the original estimate of which
he had considerably underrated; and not fully aware of the
fact that he damaged his own cause, for which he was work-

ing with such an admirable patience, energy, and courage, he desired a greater freedom in his movements and decisions from the influence of specialists, who formerly had caused him great trouble, as they frequently differed with him in regard to the most fundamental questions. His mind being firmly fixed upon tangible results which by their mere number and character would appeal to the public, he naturally took great pains to obtain them at the least possible outlay of time and money, according to the manner of Rassam and other earlier explorers, rather than to examine these immense ruins systematically according to the principles laid down by the modern school of archæologists. We must bear this circumstance in mind, in order to understand and judge his work leniently and to appreciate his results, which, though one-sided and largely misunderstood by him, proved ultimately to be of great importance for our knowledge of the Cassite and Parthian periods of Babylonian history, and furnished welcome material for our restoration of the chronology of the second millennium.

On the last day of 1889 the caravan left Baghdad. After repeated unsuccessful attempts by the local governors of Hilla and Dîwânîye at preventing the expedition's return to the ruins, the excavations were resumed on January 14, with about two hundred workmen from Hilla, who, in consequence of the ravages of cholera, lack of rain, and failing crops, had been reduced to the utmost poverty, and now looked eagerly for employment in the trenches of Nuffar. They continued this time for nearly four months, and terminated peacefully on May 3, 1890. In accordance with the advice of the natives, and profiting from our last year's experience, Dr. Peters and his comrades pitched their somewhat improved camp in the plain to the south of the western half of the ruins, and placed themselves under the protection of but a single chief, Hamid el-Birjûd, shaikh of the Nozair, one of the six tribes which constitute the Hamza, a subdivision of the 'Afej.

There could be little doubt that the Arabs of the whole neighborhood were glad to see the expedition once more

established among them. All the preceding troubles seemed
to be forgotten entirely. The Sa'îd themselves had conducted
Haynes and his workmen to the mounds in the natural expectation of receiving some kind of recognition for their friendly
attitude, doubly remarkable, as the old blood-feud existing
between them and the expedition had not yet been settled.
An excellent opportunity was thus given to remove the only
cause for much annoyance and anxiety on the part of the
Americans, and to make friends and valuable supporters out
of deadly enemies, by recognizing the general law of the desert
and paying a small sum of money to the family of the man
who had been killed in the act of robbery. Only ten
Turkish liras ($44) were demanded. But unfortunately,
Dr. Peters, who otherwise entered into the life and feelings
of the people most successfully, mistook the acknowledgment
and prompt arrangement of the whole affair for a sign of weak-
ness, and refused to listen to any proposal, thereby creating a
feeling of constant uneasiness and unsafety on the part of
Haynes, which was not at all unreasonable, and as a matter
of course at times interfered seriously with the work of the
expedition.

Like the Sa'îd, who vainly endeavored to obtain a certain
share in our work, the 'Afej could not always be trusted.
They all wanted to guard the rare "goose that laid the golden
egg," and soon became jealous of the Nozair chief, who had
pledged himself for the security of the party. "Fabulous stories
of our immense wealth were in circulation. Everything was
supposed to contain money, even our boxes of provisions."
"The Arabs believed that we were digging out great treasures,
and it was confidently asserted that we had secured the golden
boat, or *turrâda,* which from time immemorial had been supposed to be contained in these mounds." [Hilprecht is quot-
ing from Peters' report.] The mere sight of a gold crown
on one of Peters' teeth, which was eagerly pointed out by
those who had discovered it to every friend and new-comer,
seemed to strengthen their conviction and excite their lust.
The comparative ease with which in the previous year so

much spoil had been carried off through Mukota's treacherous behavior, aroused the cupidity of all the Arabs and their ardent desire to repeat his example. The presence of two hundred workmen from Hilla and Jumjuma, who could not always be managed to keep peace with one another, was regarded by the 'Afej shaikhs as an affront intended to diminish their personal income, since they were entitled to one sixth of the wages received by their own tribesmen. Besides, murderers and other desperadoes, who had fled from various parts of the country to the safer districts of the Khôr el-'Afej, were never lacking, and were always ready to join in a conspiracy which would lead to stealing and burning, and thus raise their importance in the eyes of the people. In spite of the friendly assurances from the Arabs, there prevailed a general sense of insecurity all the while around Nuffar, which, indeed, is the atmosphere more or less characteristic of all modern Babylonia.

Fortunately, however, there was one circumstance which proved of priceless value to the members of the expedition. The notion was spread among the 'Afej and their neighboring tribes that the foreigners were armed with great magical power, and that, in punishment of the firing and plundering of their camp, they had brought upon their enemies the cholera, which was not quite extinct even in the year following. Several successful treatments of light ailments, and exceedingly bitter concoctions wisely administered to various healthy chiefs, who were curious to see and to taste the truth of all that was constantly reported, served only to assure and confirm this belief; and Peters, on his part, seized every opportunity to encourage and to develop such sentiment among the credulous 'Afej. He intimated to them that nothing was hidden from his knowledge, and that the accursed money which had been stolen would find its way back to him; he made mysterious threats of sore affliction and loss by death which would cause consternation among them; and to demonstrate his superior power and to indicate some of the terrible things which might happen at any moment, he finally gave them a drastic exhibition of his cunning art, which had a tremendous effect upon all who saw it. We will quote the story in his own language: "Just before sunset, when the men were all in camp and at leisure, so that I was sure they would notice what we did, Noorian and I ascended a high point of the mound near by, he solemnly bearing a compass before me on an improvised black cushion. There, by the side of an old trench, we went through a complicated hocus-pocus with the compass, a Turkish dictionary, a spring tape-measure, and a pair of field glasses, the whole camp watching us in puzzled wonder. Immediately after our dinner, while most of the men were still busy eating, we stole up the hill, having left to Haynes the duty of preventing any one from leaving the camp. Our fireworks were somewhat primitive and slightly dangerous, so that the trench which we had chosen for our operations proved rather close quarters. The first rocket had scarcely gone off when we could hear a buzz of excited voices below us. When the second and third followed, the cry arose that we were making the stars fall from heaven. The women screamed and hid themselves in the huts, and the more timid among the men followed suit. As Roman candles and Bengal lights followed, the excitement grew more intense. At last we came to our *pièce de résistance,* the tomato-can firework. At first this fizzled and bade fair to ruin our whole performance. Then, just as we despaired of success, it exploded with a great noise, knocking us over backward in the trench, behind a wall in which we were hidden, and filling the air with fiery serpents hissing and sputtering in every direction. The effect was indescribably diabolical, and every man, woman, and child, guards included, fled screaming, to seek for hiding-places, overcome with terror."

Great as the immediate impression of the fearful spectacle was upon the minds of the naïve children of the desert, who firmly believed in the uncanny powers of demons or *jinna,* this successful coup did not stop future quarrels, pilfering, and murderous attempts altogether, nor did it secure for the camp a much needed immunity from illness and the embarrassing consequences of the great drought which at the outset was upon the waters of Babylon, or of the subsequent deluge, which turned the whole country into one huge puddle and the semi-subterranean storehouses, kitchens, and stables of the camp into as many cisterns. Poor Dr. Aftimus, on whose technical knowledge the fondest hopes had been built, was himself taken down with typhoid fever the very day the party arrived at Nuffar. Without having treated a single Arab he had to be sent back to Baghdad while in a state of delirium, but fortunately he recovered slowly in the course of the winter. After this rather discouraging first experience of medical assistance in connection with our archæological explorations, we have never had courage to repeat the experiment. With a simple diet, some personal care, and a strict observation of the ordinary sanitary laws, the expedition as a whole escaped or overcame the peculiar dangers of the Babylonian climate during the following campaigns.

In spite of all the disappointments and hardships, which were scarcely less in the second year than they had been in the first, the great purpose of the expedition was not for a moment lost sight of. Our past excavations had been scattered over the entire surface of the mounds. Trial trenches had been cut in many places, to ascertain the general character and contents of the ruins, until work finally concentrated at three conspicuous points,—the temple, the so-called tablet hill, and the more recent building with its fine court of columns near our old camp and the long ridge to the southeast of it. By means of written documents, the first expedition had adduced conclusive evidence that the ruins of Nuffar contained monuments of the time of Narâm-Sin (about 3750 B.C.) and even of a period considerably antedating it. It had discovered numerous remains of the third pre-Christian millennium, and clearly demonstrated that thousands of tablets and fragments of the ancient temple library still existed in the large triangular mound to the south of the temple complex, thereby almost determining the very site of this famous library. It furthermore had traced the history of Nippur by a few inscriptions through the second millennium down to the time of the Persian kings, and lastly shown, in connection with Parthian coins and constructions, Sassanian seals, Hebrew and Mandean bowls, Kûfic coins of the 'Abbâside caliphs, and other antiquities, that parts of the ruined city were inhabited as late as the ninth century of our own era. In other words, it had submitted material enough to prove that at least five thousand years of ancient history were represented by this enormous site. It remained for the second and the following expeditions to fill this vast period with the necessary details, and, if possible, even to extend its limits by concentrated methodical excavations at the principal elevations.

Among the various mounds and ridges which constitute the ruins of Nuffar, there was none more important than the conical hill of Bint el-Amîr with its irregular plateau of *débris,* containing the stage-tower and temple of Bêl. "This great mass of earth covered a surface of more than eight acres," the careful examination of which was an ambitious problem in itself, especially as none of the large Babylonian temples had yet been excavated completely. At the outset the expedition had therefore decided to investigate this complex methodically, to determine its characteristic architectural features, and to trace its development through all the periods of Babylonian history down to its final decay. But owing to the large accumulations of rubbish and the very limited time in the first year at our disposal, we had not been able to do much more than to fix the corners of the ancient *ziggurrat* and to run trenches along its peculiar lateral additions. As the latter were constructed of large crude bricks and surrounded by extensive remains of rooms built of the same material, and as numerous antiquities of the Hellenistic period and coins of the Arsacide kings (about 250 B.C.–226 A.D.) were unearthed in connection with them, I had "reached the conclusion that the ruins we had found were those of a Parthian fortress built on the site of the ancient temple; and the majority of the members of the expedition inclined to this opinion." But soon afterwards Peters changed his conviction and put forth his own theory, according to which we "had found the ancient temple of Bêl" itself. For the following years it was impossible for me to test his statements by a personal examination of the trenches; and as Haynes simply adopted his predecessor's theory and failed to throw any new light on this fundamental question, there remained nothing but either to acquiesce in Peters' view, which, however, ignored essential facts brought to light by the previous excavations, and was contrary to certain established laws of Babylonian architecture, or to regard the famous sanctuary of Bêl as a hopeless mass of crumbling walls, fragmentary platforms, broken drains, and numerous wells, reported by Haynes to exist at widely separated levels, often in very strange places and without any apparent connection with each other.

What were the new features developed at this "perplexing mound" in the course of the second campaign? By engaging a maximum force of four hundred Arab laborers, half from Hilla and Jumjuma, half from the 'Afej tribes around Nuffar, and by placing the greater part of his men at the temple mounds, the director was able to attack the problem more vigorously and to remove such an enormous mass of rubbish that at the end of his work he could boast "that in cubic feet of earth excavated, and size and depth of trenches," his excavations "far surpassed any others ever undertaken in Babylonia," and that De Sarzec's work of several seasons at Tellô "was probably not even the tenth part as large as our work of as many months." But this difference was due to various causes, and not the least to the difference of methods pursued by the two explorers, quite aside from the fact that the amount of rubbish extracted from a ruin can never be used as a standard by which the success or failure of an archæological mission is to be judged. Peters himself characterizes his manner of excavating as follows: "We sank small well-shafts or deep narrow trenches, in many cases to the depth of fifty feet or more, and pierced innumerable small tunnels (one of them 120 feet in length) after the native method." In other words, he examined the mounds pretty much as the Arab peasants did at Babylon, El-Birs, and other places, only on a larger scale, —either by deep perpendicular holes or by "innumerable" horizontal mines, instead of peeling off the single layers successively and carefully. Was this scientific research? The results, as indicated above, were naturally commensurate with the method employed. Peters did not procure a satisfactory plan nor the necessary details of the originally well-preserved vast complex of buildings which occupied the site of the temple of Bêl "at the time of its last great construction;" he failed to ascertain its character and purpose, and to define its precise relation to the *ziggurrat;* he was unable to determine its age, or even to fix the two extreme limits of the three successive periods of its occupation; and he did not recognize that the line of booths situated outside of the southeast fortified enclosure and yielding him a fine collection of inscribed Cassite monuments belonged to the same general epoch as the mass of crude brickwork covering the temple. As far as possible, his assertions have either been verified or corrected by the present writer's later investigations on the ruins. But, unfortunately, much of the precious material had been removed in the course of the second and third campaigns, or was subsequently destroyed by rain and other causes, so that it could no longer be used for the study and reconstruction of the history of the venerable sanctuary of Nippur.

The following is Peters' own view in a nutshell: There are about sixteen feet of ruins below a surface layer of three feet, which represent the last important restoration of the ancient temple by a monarch "not far removed from Nebuchadrezzar in time," and living about 500 B.C. This ruler consequently can have been only one of the Persian kings, notably Darius I, or perhaps Xerxes. The sacred precincts were no longer "consecrated to the worship of Bêl," but stood in the service of "a new religion." The old form of the *ziggurrat* was changed by "huge buttress-like wings added on each of the four sides," which gave the structure "a cruciform shape unlike that of any other *ziggurrat* yet discovered." The sanctuary continued to exist in the new form for about three hundred to three hundred and fifty years, until after the Seleucidan period, somewhere about or before 150 B.C., when men ceased to make additions or repairs, and the ancient temple of Bêl fell gradually into ruins.

It is unnecessary to disprove this fantastic theory in detail. Peters' own excavations and our previous and later discoveries make it entirely impossible. But while we cannot accept his inferences, which are contrary to all the evidence produced, we recognize that he brought to light a number of facts and antiquities, which enable us to establish at least some of the more general features of this latest reconstruction. He showed that a considerable area around the *ziggurrat* was enclosed by two gigantic walls protected by towers. He ascertained their dimensions, followed their courses, and described the extraordinary size of their bricks. He excavated fourteen chambers on the top of one of the outer walls, and found the entire space between the inner wall and the *ziggurrat* occupied completely by similar rooms. He arrived at the conclusion that the various constructions belonged together and formed an organic whole. A long, narrow street, however, which ran parallel with the southeastern line of fortifications, divided the houses in the interior into two distinct sections. Several of the chambers in the southern part were filled with "great masses of water-jars piled together." They doubtless had served as storerooms; others were kitchens, as indicated "by the fireplaces and other arrangements;" while in some of the rooms "were curious closets with thin clay partitions." The rubbish of most of the chambers yielded numerous fragments of pottery of the Hellenistic and Roman periods, remarkable among them a fine brown enamelled lamp (head of Medusa), and many terracotta figurines, especially heads of women frequently wearing a peculiar high head-dress, children, and groups of lovers. It is a characteristic feature of these late Babylonian terracottas that they are generally hollow in the interior, while their outside is often covered with a chalk paste by which the artist endeavored to work out the delicate facial lines, the curled hair, the graceful foldings of the garments, and other details, with greater accuracy, and thus to produce a better effect of the whole figure, which sometimes also was colored. Teeth of wild boars repeatedly found in this stratum indicate that the occupants of those later constructions were fond of hunting the characteristic animal of the swamps around Nippur.

From the extraordinary amount of dirt and débris accumulated during the period of occupancy of the rooms, and from the different styles of art exhibited by the antiquities discovered in them, it became evident that these latest constructions must have been inhabited for several hundred years. A similar result was obtained by an examination of the stage-tower. It was observed that the *ziggurrat* of the cruciform shape above referred to, which consisted only of two stages, had two or three distinct additions, and that the unbaked material employed in them was identical with that found in the rooms around it.

In his endeavor to reach the older remains before the more recent strata had been investigated in the least adequately, Peters broke through the outer casing of the *ziggurrat* built of "immense blocks of adobe," in a cavity of which he discovered a well-preserved goose egg, and perceived that there was an older stage-tower of quite a different form and much smaller dimensions enclosed within the other. By means of a diagonal trench cut through its centre, he ascertained its height and characteristic features down to the level of Ur-Gur, and came to the conclusion (which, however, did not prove correct) that the *ziggurrat* of this ancient monarch was the earliest erected at Nippur. "Wells and similar shafts were sunk at other points of the temple," especially at the northern and western corners, where he reached original constructions of Ashur-bânapal (668–626 B.C.) and Ur-Gur (about 2700 B.C.), and discovered scattered bricks with the names of Esarhaddon (681–668 B.C.), Rammanshumusur (about 1100 B.C.), Ka-dashman-Turgu (about 1250 B.C.), Kurigalzu (about 1300 B.C.), Bur-Sin of Nisin (about 2500 B.C.), in addition to those previously found, "showing that many kings of many ages had honored the temple of Bêl at Nippur." At a place near the western corner of the *ziggurrat,* on the northwestern side, he descended through a tunnel some six feet below the plain level, striking a terra-cotta drain with a platform at its mouth and a wall of plano-convex bricks similar to those preceding the time of Ur-Ninâ at Tellô, in which he unearthed also a beautiful, highly polished jade axe-head and an inscribed pre-Sargonic clay tablet.

Immediately in front of the southeastern face of the stage-tower, Peters conducted a larger trench with a view of ascertaining the successive strata of the whole temple plateau. Below the level of the Parthian castle he disclosed "a mass of rubble and débris containing no walls, but great quantities of bricks, some of them with green glazed surfaces, and many bearing inscriptions of Ashurbânapal." In penetrating a few feet farther, he came upon fragments of pavements and soon afterwards upon the crude brick terrace of Ur-Gur. As he saw that the walls and towers of the Parthian fortress, which required a more solid foundation, descended to this deep level, he unhesitatingly pronounced them to have been in existence 2500 years before they were built, and "thought it not impossible" that at that ancient time two of these formidable fortification towers "were columns of the same general significance as the Jachin and Boaz which stood before the Temple of Yahweh [Jehovah] at Jerusalem"! While excavating in the stratum immediately above Ur-Gur's platform, he came accidentally upon the first three door-sockets and a brick stamp of Shargâni-shar-âli, soon afterwards identified by me as Sargon I, the famous king of Agade, who according to Nabonidos lived about 3800 B.C., but who until then had been regarded generally as a half-mythical person. In the same layer there were found about eighty fragments of stone vases and other antiquities inscribed with the names of Manishtusu and Uru-mush (Âlusharshid), two kings of Kish little known, who lived about the same time; Lugalzaggisi and Lukalkigubnidudu, two even earlier rulers of Erech, and Entemena, *patesi* of Lagash, familiar to us from De Sarzec's excavations. In spite of Haynes' very emphatic statement to the contrary, Peters

claims to have reached the real level of Sargon and his predecessors at two points within the court of the *ziggurrat,* in one
case descending almost sixteen feet below the present plain.
Be this as it may, the building remains, which he had hitherto
disclosed, were examined by him far too poorly and unsys-
tematically to convey to us even a tolerably clear idea of the
revered sanctuary of Bêl; and the inscriptions gathered were so
small or fragmentary that they furnished us little more than
the names and titles of ancient kings and *patesis.* But the material obtained sufficed to show that there were considerable
ancient Babylonian ruins, and numerous though generally
broken cuneiform inscriptions, including even antiquities con-
temporaneous with the earliest monuments of Tellô, contained
in the temple hill of Nuffar.

It is characteristic of Peters' work in the second year that
it was not carried on with the purpose of excavating one or
two layers at one or more of the principal mounds of the
enormous site methodically, but with the intention of "sounding" as many places as possible, and of discovering inscribed
objects. Consequently he dug a little here and a little there and
disturbed many strata at the same time. No wonder that he
opened trenches also in the southern and southeastern ridges
of the *ziggurrat.* Nothing of importance came to light in the
former, but his labors were crowned with a remarkable success in the latter. . . . The temple mound is separated from
mound IV, which I regard as the probable site of the library,
by a deep depression doubtless representing an old branch of
the Shatt en-Nîl. On the northeastern edge of this gully there
is a low wall-like elevation, which rises only about thirteen
feet above the plain. It was in this narrow ridge that Peters
excavated more than twenty rooms resting on a terrace of
earth and built of precisely the same material—"unbaked
bricks of large, almost square blocks," as characterizes the
late construction on the top of the temple of Bêl. Under
ordinary circumstances he probably would have drawn the
obvious inference that both belong to the same period. But
the discovery in one of these rooms of a large number of Cas-

site votive objects—the first great collection of antiquities of this dynasty ever found—induced him to ascribe this whole row of booths to a time a thousand years earlier than it actually was. He formulated a new fantastic theory, according to which these cameos of agate and thin round tablets of lapis lazuli, with their brief votive inscriptions, were sold as charms to pilgrims, some of them being "a sort of masses said for the repose of the soul of such and such a king." The true facts are the following. All these interesting Cassite relics in agate, magnesite, feldspar, ivory, turquoise, malachite, lapis lazuli, and an imitation of the last-mentioned three stones in glass, "together with gold, amethyst, porphyry and other material not yet worked," were originally contained in a wooden box, traces of which (carbonized fragments and copper nails) were lying around them. Most, if not indeed the whole, of this unique collection had been presented by a number of Cassite kings to various shrines of the temple of Bêl somewhere between 1400 and 1200 B.C. A thousand years later, when the temple was in ruins, an inhabitant of Nippur, and himself a dealer in precious stones, searched in the neighborhood of his booth for raw material, and discovered them, or purchased them from other diggers. He was about to manufacture beads for necklaces and bracelets, rings, charms, and the like out of them, when another catastrophe befell Nippur. Several other "jeweller's shops" of the Parthian period excavated by our expedition at different sections of the ruins established the correctness of this interpretation beyond any doubt. And when in May, 1900, I spent a few days with the expedition at Babylon, Koldewey had found a similar shop in the mound of 'O(A)mrân ibn 'Alî, which, besides purely Parthian antiquities, contained several more ancient objects from various Babylonian ruins, and for this reason proved particularly instructive. No sooner had the German explorer submitted the inscribed objects of this shop to me for examination, than I recognized and pointed out to him a number of Cassite objects, which, according to their material, forms, and inscriptions belonged originally to the temple at Nippur, illustrating in an excellent way how the trade in "useful" antiquities flourished in Babylonia even two thousand years before our own time. . . .

To the east of our first camp we had previously discovered the remains of tapering brick columns, symmetrically arranged around an open square court. It was natural to suppose that this peculiar structure belonged to a more pretentious building with interesting architectural features, as the mere presence of columns indicated sufficiently. Though the present writer had assigned it without hesitation to the Seleucido-Parthian period (about 250 B.C.), it was desirable and necessary to excavate it completely, before the more important Babylonian strata beneath it should be examined. In order to execute this task, Peters began to remove the Jewish and early Arabic houses representing the latest traces of human settlements everywhere in the precincts of ancient Nippur, and the numerous Parthian and Sassanian coffins, sepulchral urns, and pottery drains immediately below them. The former were characterized by Kûfic coins, Hebrew, Arabic, and Mandean incantation bowls, and other articles of domestic use, which were generally found in low and narrow rooms made of mud-bricks. We had frequently noticed the outlines of their walls in the preceding year, as we walked over the hills in the early morning, when the rapidly evaporating humidity of the ground drew the salt-petre contained in the clay to the surface. The tombs, on the other hand, occurred in an indescribable confusion in all possible positions and at nearly every depth in the layer of rubbish which filled the space between the uppermost settlement and the floor of the building just mentioned to the height of six to ten feet. In no instance, however, were they discovered below the level of the court of columns, while repeatedly the burial-shafts were cut through the walls of the rooms grouped around it. Hence it follows that these interments must have taken place at a time when the imposing building was already in ruins,— in other words, at a period commencing shortly before our own era, and terminating about the sixth or seventh century A.D., if the palace in question was really of Seleucido-Parthian origin. This, however, was contested by Peters, who believed to have found evidence that the structure was a thousand years earlier. His work in and around this building may be sketched briefly as follows:—

The open court flanked by columns having been excavated completely in 1889, Peters undertook next to search for the rooms to which it probably gave light and access. As, in consequence of the slope of the hill, a considerable part of the ancient building had been washed away in the northeast and southeast directions, he concentrated his efforts upon an examination of the highest section of the mound, exploring especially the ruined mass southwest of the colonnade. He was soon able to show that, contrary to our previous theory, certain pieces of charred wood and small heaps of ashes discovered along the edge of the court did not belong to subsequent burials, but were remains of palm beams which originally rested on the columns and stretched across a narrow space to the walls of chambers surrounding the former on all four sides. We should expect that Peters, once having established this interesting fact, would have spared no pains to examine a building systematically, which, as late as 1897, he described as "the most interesting and ambitious structure excavated at Nippur next to the temple." But judging, as he did, the success of his expedition mainly "by the discovery of inscribed objects or failure to discover them," and nervously endeavoring to secure them at all hazards, he unfortunately adopted the injurious and antiquated methods of Layard and Rassam, which I have characterized above, also for the exploration of the west section of the ruins. Instead of removing layer after layer of all the superincumbent rubbish, he excavated only portions of seven rooms with their adjoining corridors by digging along their walls and leaving the central mass untouched. And when even this process proved too slow and tedious, he drove tunnels into the mound above and below the floor of the building, which afterwards caved in, ruined part of the construction, and caused infinite trouble to himself and his successors. At the same time the excavated earth was not carried to a previously explored place at a safe distance, but was dumped on the same mound, and in part on an un-explored section of the very ruins which he was desirous to examine, and whence the present writer had to remove it ten years later. . . .

The exploration of the large and important building remains grouped around the *ziggurrat* and "the court of columns" had formed one of Peters' principal tasks during his second campaign. But his hope of discovering many inscribed Babylonian tablets while excavating these ruins was not to be realized. To find these eagerly-sought treasures somewhere in the vast mounds he had conducted extensive excavations from the beginning in several other parts of the ruins. Above all, he most naturally had directed his attention to the triangular mound (IV) to the south of the temple, which had yielded almost all the tablets obtained by the first expedition. He now "riddled it with trenches everywhere" and without difficulty secured about 2000 tablets more of the same general type as those discovered previously—business documents, school exercises, and numerous tablets of a strictly scientific or literary character, especially astronomical, mathematical, and medical. As, however, Peters did not possess the necessary Assyriological knowledge to determine their age and contents, and as, moreover, these tablets were never deposited in any large number together, but "seemed to lie loose in the earth" or "con-fused among buildings with which they did not belong," he came to the conclusion that this hill with its two principal strata, which I had declared to be the probable site of the temple library, was "the home of well-to-do citizens, rather than the site of the great public building of the city," and abandoned it towards the middle of March, "because he had ceased to find tablets in paying quantities."

It was about the same time that the southeastern wing of the mounds on the other side of the canal (VI, and the ridge immediately to the northwest of it) began to yield tablets "in an extraordinary manner." The prospect of a more rapid in-crease of the coveted inscriptions being thus given, all the "tablet diggers" were transferred at once to this new promising locality. Before many weeks had elapsed, more than 5,000 tablets and fragments had been gathered, so that with regard to the mere number of clay documents recovered, Peters might well be pleased with the success which he had scored. Without troubling himself about the methodical examination and removal of the highest strata, which in the previous year had yielded contracts of the late Babylonian and Persian periods, he cut "sounding-trenches at various points in the interior, where the water had washed out deep gullies." In every instance he came upon rooms of mud brick containing "quantities of tablets," mixed with earth and grotesque clay figures of Bêl and his consort. There was in particular one chamber, thirty-two feet long by sixteen feet wide, which was literally filled with them. So numerous were the tablets there "that it took thirty or forty men four days to dig them out and bring them into camp." For the most part they were unbaked, and lay in fragments on the floor. But as the ashes observed in connection with them clearly indicated, they originally "had been placed around the walls of the room on wooden shelves," which broke or were burned, when the house was destroyed and the roof fell in. All the tablets discovered in these rooms and in this ridge in general are so-called private contracts and official records, such as receipts, tax-lists, statements of income and expense written in behalf of the government and of the temple, and, as a rule, are dated according to the reigns of the last kings of Ur (about 2600 B.C.), the first dynasty of Babylon (about 2300–2000 B.C.), Rîm-Sin of Larsa (a contemporary of Hammurabi), and especially several kings of the Cassite dynasty (about 1400–1200 B.C.). The older documents are valuable chiefly for their closing lines containing brief references to the principal historical events, after which the single years of the monarchs were called and counted. The tax-lists from the latter half of the second millennium are of importance because of their bearing upon the chronology of the Cassite kings, and because they give us a first insight into the civil administration of Central Babylonia under those foreign conquerors of whom previously we knew little more than their names, and these often enough only very imperfectly.

Peters confesses frankly: "My trenches here were dug principally for tablets." Little attention, therefore, could be paid to the fundamental question, whether at the different periods of its occupation this ridge was covered with "ordinary houses" only, or whether the single rooms formed an organic whole, an annex of the temple, a large government building with registering offices, a kind of bazaar, or both, as seems to result with great probability from a study of the tablets and from later discoveries made in this neighborhood by the present writer. Indeed, it was a dark day when Peters decided to excavate the ruins of Nuffar without the aid of a specialist, whether Assyriologist or architect. Fortunately Pognon, then French consul at Baghdad, occasionally lent a helping hand in determining the age and contents of some of the better preserved inscriptions from squeezes and photographs submitted to him, and Peters could congratulate himself that at the time of his greatest need a Hungarian engineer, in the employ of the Ottoman government, Coleman d'Emey, appeared suddenly in the camp to hunt in the Babylonian swamps. He was easily induced to devote part of his time to a renewed survey of the principal ruins and to the preparation of plans of the excavated walls and rooms of the two Parthian palaces. It is true, according to the director's own statement, the real merits of his drawings are to be judged leniently, but in connection with Peters' scanty notes they enabled us at least to form a general idea of the character and disposition of the latest constructions on the temple mound.

On the third day of May the excavations of the second campaign came to a more peaceful ending than those in the previous year. Before the trenches were abandoned, Peters very wisely decided to send part of his material out of the country, "to insure the preservation of something in case of disaster." For in consequence of his stubborn refusal to pay the often demanded blood-money to the Sa'îd, the disappointed tribe very naturally sought to indemnify itself in another way. A first

boat-load of antiquities had left Nuffar safely towards the end
of April. At the same time Haynes, who not without reason
feared being waylaid and plundered by a *ghazu*, "stole away
in the night," and "pressed through to Hilla in hot haste." To
prevent an attack planned by the enemy upon his camp for the
night preceding the final departure of the expedition, Peters
"resorted once more to stratagem, and gave a second exhibition
of fireworks," which again had the desired effect. The Sa'îd
then hoped to intercept him as he left the territory of the 'Afej,
and try to extort blackmail. But the American slipped out of
their hands before they realized that he had gone. As soon as
all the workmen from Jumjuma had been sent in detachments
through the marshes and everything was packed upon the last
boats, including the Turkish commissioner and the *zabtîye*,
Peters and Noorian, accompanied by some trusted Arab laborers and a personal servant, turned to the village of Hajji
Tarfâ to examine the more prominent mounds in the south.
With a door-socket of Gimil-Sin of Ur (about 2550 B.C.)
picked up at Muqayyar, and with another of the same monarch
and a whole box of fine tablets, through a fortunate accident
discovered at Jôkha after a little scratching of the surface, they
returned to the north by way of Samâwa, Nejef, and Kerbelâ,
reaching Baghdad on the 7th of June, 1890. About a week
later Peters was on his way to the Mediterranean coast, returning to America in November, while Haynes and Noorian
left the country separately by different routes and at different
times in the course of the same year.

# 6. KOLDEWEY:

# *The Rediscovery of Babylon*

19. And Babylon, the glory of kingdoms, the beauty of the Chaldees' excellency, shall be as when God overthrew Sodom and Gomorrah.

20. It shall never be inhabited, neither shall it be dwelt in from generation to generation: neither shall the Arabian pitch tent there; neither shall the shepherds make their fold there.

21. But wild beasts of the desert shall lie there; and their houses shall be full of doleful creatures; and owls shall dwell there, and satyrs shall dance there.

22. And the wild beasts of the islands cry in their desolate houses, and dragons in their pleasant places: and her time is near to come, and her days shall not be prolonged.

— ISAIAH, 13

The Ruins of the Temple of Esagila, Babylon

Of all the cities of Mesopotamia, none is more celebrated in literature, none more widely known, than Babylon. The name echoes through the Old Testament, synonymous with fleshly pleasures, with rampant hedonism. "Babylon" conjures images of magnificence beyond compare, of oriental splendor unexampled.

Small wonder, then, that Babylon was deemed the great prize by the archaeologists of the 19th century. It eluded excavation, however, until techniques were devised to meet the special problems the city presented.

Babylon was not an ancient city by Mesopotamian standards. During the great days of Sumer, it seems to have been no more than an obscure village. Not until Hammurabi the Law-Giver came to rule in Babylon, in the 18th century before Christ, did the name of Babylon begin to resound through the ancient world.

Hammurabi made Babylon the capital of a vast Mesopotamian empire embracing much of what once had been Sumer, and gave the name of his city to the new political entity of Babylonia. Though after Hammurabi's day the Babylonian Empire never again attained such widespread dominion, the name Babylonia continued to stand for the area in Mesopotamia south of Assyria.

Babylon had periods of greatness and periods of decline in the millennium after Hammurabi, but its power waned permanently in time, and it became one of the many cities of the new Assyrian Empire. Assyrian rule did not sit lightly on Babylon, and revolts were frequent—until, in 689 B.C., the Assyrian tyrant Sennacherib resolved the thorny Babylonian problem in his own way, by destroying the city.

Sennacherib's own account of the sack of Babylon is typical of the annals of the Assyrian kings:

"The city and its houses, foundations and walls, I destroyed, I burned with fire. The wall and the outerwall, temples and gods, temple-towers of bricks and earth, as many as there were, I razed and dumped them into the Arahtu canal. Through the midst of that city I dug canals, I flooded its site with water, and the very foundations thereof I destroyed. I made its destruction more complete than by a flood. That in days to come, the site of that city, and its temples and gods, might not be remembered, I completely blotted it out with floods of water and made it like a meadow. . . . After I had destroyed Babylon, had smashed the gods thereof, and had struck down its people with the sword . . . that the ground of that city might be carried off, I removed its ground and had it carried to the Euphrates and on to the sea."

Sennacherib fell, and his son Esarhaddon came to power. He ordered Babylon rebuilt, placing one of his own sons on the city's throne. But in 625, the new city of Babylon regained its independence under Nabopolassar, a Babylonian who called himself "of low rank, of no birth." Nabopolassar and his son Nebuchadnezzar made Babylon the most celebrated city of its time. The carnage wreaked by Sennacherib was forgotten. A towering *ziggurat* rose, an imposing new temple, a massive wall of stupefying size, a splendid palace, and the "Hanging Gardens" that were one of the wonders of the ancient world.

This resurgence of Babylon was short-lived. In 539 B.C., traitors within the city surrendered it to the Persians under Cyrus, and it never again regained its independence. Rebelling again under the rule of Xerxes, the city was destroyed a second time, and this time there was no rebuilding. It ceased to be inhabited, even by peasant tribes, after the sixth century A.D. Desert sand and silt gradually buried Babylon.

Its location was never really lost. The inhabitants of nearby Baghdad called the mound *Babil,* and told travellers of its great antiquity. In 1811, a young Englishman named Claudius Rich visited Babil, found inscriptions in cuneiform on brick, and explored the mound. He told of his findings in an important book, *Memoir on the Ruins of Babylon.*

Layard was the first to make a serious attempt at excavation. He visited Babil in 1851, found some bricks inscribed with the name of Nebuchadnezzar, some pottery, a few skeletons. "The discoveries," he wrote, "were far less numerous and important than I could have anticipated, nor did they tend to prove that there were remains beneath the heaps of earth and rubbish which would reward more extensive excavations. . . . There will be nothing to be hoped for from the site of Babylon."

Layard was mistaken, as he was about Nippur. But the archaeological problem in Babylonia was substantially different from that of Assyria. The palaces of Assyria were built of limestone, and excavation was relatively simple. Southern Mesopotamia, however, is alluvial land. There is no available stone for building. The cities of Sumer and Babylonia were built from mud brick. Certain buildings were fashioned of baked brick, which is relatively sturdy, but most Sumerian-Babylonian architecture utilized sun-dried mud. It was impossible for Layard to distinguish the mud of the walls from the mud of debris. He slashed through walls and rubbish indiscriminately.

It took half a century before archaeology had developed techniques equal to the task of excavating cities of mud. The prize of Babylon fell to a German team, led by Robert Koldewey, who in 18 years of brilliant work laid bare Nebuchadnezzar's city. Nothing was left, of course, of the city of Hammurabi, so thoroughly destroyed by the vengeful Sennacherib. But Nebuchadnezzar's great city, with its huge wall, its tower (prototype of the Biblical Tower of Babel), its Hanging Gardens—all this emerged as the careful Germans proceeded in their methodical way.

Koldewey, born in 1855, was a veteran archaeologist by the time he tackled Babylon. He had worked in the Greek islands, in Syria, in Italy, in Sicily, and on several minor sites in Babylonia. When he was 40, he found it necessary to retire temporarily from archaeology to take a teaching post, but after three years of chafing inactivity he carried off the assignment to excavate Babylon.

His appointment disturbed some of his contemporaries. Koldewey did not seem to have the necessary seriousness for the task. He was a light-hearted, prankish man, much given to practical jokes and to composing bits of doggerel like this one, his New Year's greeting in 1907:

> *Darksome wind the ways of fate,*
> *Uncertain stars the future keep,*
> *I like to drink a cognac straight,*
> *Before I lay me down to sleep!*

Lacking though he was in the requisite Teutonic heaviness, Koldewey still got the job. The Royal Museum of Berlin sponsored the expedition which commenced operations at Babil in March, 1899. The results were immediate and gratifying. The Babylon of Nebuchadnezzar lay within easy reach. The work was taxing, of course—debris had to be removed virtually a spoonful at a time so that no damage would be done to the ancient buildings—but the rewards were exceptionally great.

Koldewey's excavations at Babylon continued until war halted them in 1917. The work has never been resumed. Only one of Koldewey's books on Babylon has been translated into English: *The Excavations at Babylon,* from which we quote here. It was first published in 1913 in German, and the English translation, by Agnes S. Johns, appeared a year later.

## THE REDISCOVERY OF BABYLON

In the time of Nebuchadnezzar the traveller who approached the capital of Babylonia from the north would find himself where the Nil Canal flows today, face to face with the colossal wall that surrounded mighty Babylon. Part of this wall still exists and is recognizable at the present time in the guise of a low earthen ridge about 4 to 5 kilometers in length. Up to

From *The Excavations at Babylon* (London: Macmillan, 1914) by Robert Koldewey, translated from the German by Agnes S. John. Copyright 1914 by Macmillan & Co., Ltd., and reprinted by permission of the publishers.

the present we have only excavated a small part, so that it is only possible to give a detailed description of the most noteworthy features of these fortifications, that were rendered so famous by Greek authors.

There was a massive wall of crude brick 7 meters thick, in front of which, at an interval of about 12 meters, stood another wall of burnt brick 7.8 meters thick, with the strong wall of the fosse at its foot, also of burnt brick and 3.3 meters thick. The fosse must have been in front of this, but so far we have not searched closely for it, and therefore the counterscarp has not yet been found.

Astride on the mud wall were towers 8.37 meters (about 24 bricks) wide, that projected beyond the wall on both its faces. Measured from center to center these towers were 52.5 meters apart. Thus there was a tower at intervals of about 100 ells, for the Babylonian ell measured roughly half a meter.

Owing to the unfinished state of the excavations it is not yet possible to say how the towers on the outer wall were constructed. The space between the two walls was filled in with rubble, at least to the height at which the ruins are preserved and presumably to the crown of the outer wall. Thus on the top of the wall there was a road that afforded space for a team of four horses abreast, and even for two such teams to pass each other. Upon this crown of the wall the upper compartments of the towers faced each other like small houses.

This broad roadway on the summit of the wall, which was of world-renown owing to the descriptions of it given by classical writers, was of the greatest importance for the protection of the great city. It rendered possible the rapid shifting of defensive forces at any time to that part of the wall which was specially pressed by attack. The line of defence was very long; the north-east front, which can still be measured, is 4400 meters long, and on the south-east the ruined wall can be traced without excavation for a length of 2 kilometers. These two flanks of the wall certainly extended as far as the Euphrates as it flowed from north to south. With the Euphrates they enclosed that part of Babylon of which the ruins exist at the present time, but according to Herodotus and others they were supplemented on the other side of the Euphrates by two other walls, so that the town site consisted of a quadrangle through which the Euphrates flowed diagonally. Of the western walls nothing is now to be seen. Whether the traces of a line of wall to the south near the village of Sindjar will prove to have formed part of them has yet to be ascertained.

The excavations carried on up to the present time have yielded no surrounding walls beyond this fortification. The circuit extended for about 18 kilometers. Instead of this, Herodotus gives about 86 kilometers and Ctesias about 65 kilometers. There must be some error underlying this discrepancy. The 65 kilometers of Ctesias approximate so closely to four times the correct measurement that it may well be suspected that he mistook the figures representing the whole circumference for the measure of one side of the square. We shall later turn more in detail from the testimony of the ancient writers to the evidence of the ruins themselves. Generally speaking, the measurements given are not in accordance with those actually preserved, while the general description, on the contrary, is usually accurate. Herodotus describes the wall of Babylon as built of burnt brick. To an observer from without it would no doubt appear as much, as only the top of the inner mud wall could be seen from outside. The escarp of the fosse was formed of the square bricks that are so extraordinarily numerous in Babylon, that measure 33 centimeters and bear the usual stamp of Nebuchadnezzar. Those of the brick wall are somewhat smaller (32 centimeters) and unstamped. These smaller unstamped bricks are common previous to the time of Nebuchadnezzar, but nevertheless they may very well date from the early years of his reign, as we shall see farther on. To what period the mud-brick wall may be assigned we do not yet know; it is certainly older. It apparently possessed an escarp, of which there are some scanty remains within the great brick wall. It appears to have been cut through on the outside by the latter.

Up to the present we have found about 15 of the towers

A      The mound Amran.
ADK    Ancient ruined village of Kweiresh.
AE     Ancient Euphrates bed.
AK     Ancient ruined canal.
AN     Ancient Nil canal.
AS     Outer city wall.
B      The mound Babil.
DA     The village of Ananeh.
DD     The village of Djumdjumma.
DK     The village of Kweiresh.
DS     The village of Sindjar.
E      Euphrates.

EM     E-Mach, the temple of Ninmach.
EP     E-Patutila, the temple of Ninib.
ES     E-Sagila, the temple of Marduk.
ET     E-Temenanki, the tower of Babylon.
F      Fields.
FK     Farm of Karabet.
G      Tomb of Amran Ibn Ali.
GM     Garden wall.
H      The mound Homera.
IA     Ishin aswad.
IS     Inner city wall.
K      The mound Kasr.

M      Merkes.
MR     Remains of walls.
N      The Nil canal.
NB     The Nil bridge.
NK     New canal.
P      Palms.
S      Sachn.
T      The Greek theatre.
TI     Temple of Ishtar of Agade.
W      Road.
WBH    Road from Bagdad to Hilleh.
Z      Temple Z of some unknown divinity.

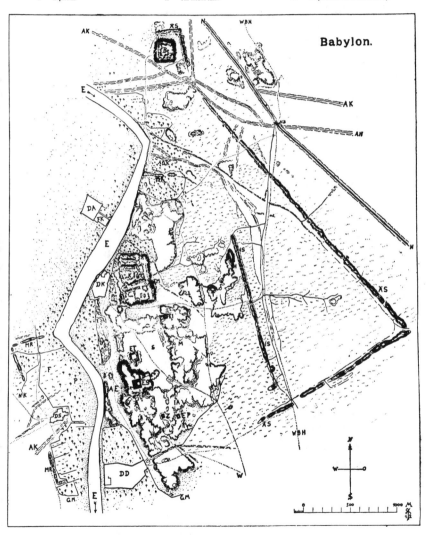

Plan of the Ruins of the City of Babylon

on the mud wall only. They are the so-called Cavalier towers, and project both at the front and the back, thus placed astride on the wall. They were, of course, higher than the walls, but we can get no clue from the ruins as to the height of walls or towers, as only the lower parts remain. The towers are 8.36 meters wide and are placed 44 meters apart. Thus on the entire front there were about 90, and on the whole circumference—provided the town formed a square—there must have been 360 towers. How many there were on the outer wall we do not know. Ctesias gives the number as 250. No gateway has yet been found, which is not surprising, considering the limited extent of the excavations. . . .

While the foundations of the brick wall are below the present water-level, the mud wall stands on an artificial embankment. As a general rule mud walls were not provided with deep foundations. The mortar employed for the mud wall was clay, and for the brick wall bitumen was used. The same method of construction can be recognized in other parts of the city, where it is better preserved and can be more satisfactorily studied.

At the northern end of our line of wall, which encloses the mound of ruins, called "Babil," with a hook-like curve, the inner wall was also built of brick. This appears, at least, from the two deep trenches left by plunderers which occur here, but it must be inferred pending excavation. The digging for the valuable bricks which occurred in recent times has left deep traces in the otherwise smooth surface of the ground which we do not find in the attempted demolitions of more ancient times.

For this reason, with the exception of the portion near Babil there is nothing to be seen of the burnt-brick wall without excavating, while the mud wall, which has merely suffered from the ravages of time, has left behind a clearly marked line of ruins of some height. The town wall of Seleucia on the Tigris, likewise a mud wall, stands out similarly above its mounds of debris to a considerable height. It cannot therefore be said that a burnt-brick wall of 480 stadia, the gigantic dimensions recorded by Herodotus, must necessarily have left considerable and unmistakable traces, and it is not this consideration that leads us to doubt the existence of an encircling wall of such dimensions, which has been accepted as an established fact since Oppert's excavations in Babylon. Neither does the immense size of itself demand dismissal as fantastic. The great wall of China, 11 meters high and 7.5 meters broad, with its length of 2450 kilometers, is just 29 times as long as that of Herodotus. . . . In any case the city, even in circumference, was the greatest of any in the ancient East, Nineveh itself not excepted, which in other respects rivalled Babylon. But the period in which the fame of Babylon's vast size spread over the world was the time of Herodotus, and then Nineveh had already ceased to exist.

A comparison with modern cities can scarcely be made without further consideration. It must always be remembered that an ancient city was primarily a fortress of which the inhabited part was surrounded and protected by the encircling girdle of the walls. Our great modern cities are of an entirely different character, they are inhabited spaces, open on all sides. A reasonable comparison can, therefore, only be made between Babylon and other walled cities, and when compared with them Babylon takes the first place, both for ancient and modern times, as regards the extent of its enclosed and inhabited area.

Nebuchadnezzar frequently mentions this great work in his inscriptions. The most important passage occurs in his great [East India House] inscription, col. 7 1. 22-55: "That no assault should reach Imgur-Bel, the wall of Babylon; I did, what no earlier king had done, for 4000 ells of land on the side of Babylon, at a distance so that it (the assault) did not come nigh, I caused a mighty wall to be built on the east side of Babylon. I dug out its moat, and I built a scarp with bitumen and bricks. A mighty wall I built on its edge, mountain high. Its broad gateways I set within it and fixed in them double doors of cedar wood overlaid with copper. In order that the enemy who devised (?) evil should not press on the flanks of Babylon, I surrounded it with mighty floods, as is the land with the wave-tossed sea. Its coming was like the coming of the great sea, the salt water. In order that no breach should be made in it, I piled up an earthen embankment by it, and encompassed it with quay walls of burnt brick. The bulwark I fortified cunningly and made the city of Babylon into a fortress. . . ." It can hardly be expected that we can yet reach absolute certainty as to the meaning of all the details here given. That can best be afforded by a complete excavation, which is urgently to be desired.

Following the ridge of the ruined city wall from the excavated portion farther to the north-west, one reaches a gap in the wall where it was ruthlessly broken down by later canals, now themselves dried up. They were forerunners of the present Nil Canal. The Arabic word *nil* denotes the blue color which is generally produced by indigo, and has given its name to various watercourses on Arab soil; the name of the Egyptian Nile is probably connected with it. The Nil Canal runs today a few hundred meters to the north-east along the city wall and roughly parallel with it. The embankments of these canals, which in places are of immense height, intersect the plain with a sharp line. The contrast with the plain is most striking when they are seen on the horizon, where the mirage comes to their aid and makes them look like hills of some importance. At first sight, also, they appear to be entirely out of proportion with the small amount of water that flows so slowly through the canal. That, however, is only the case where the canal has been in use for some long time. When the canal is first constructed each embankment, under normal circumstances, consists of no more than half of the earth which is dug out, as these irrigation works, wherever the lie of the ground permits, are so arranged that the surface of the water may be higher than the surrounding plain. Only in this way would it be possible with comparatively small expenditure, and without special machinery for raising water, to provide the field with a gentle supply of the fructifying moisture. But the Euphrates at the period of high water, when the irrigation takes place, bears a quantity of material in suspension that is specially valuable for agriculture. If the water stands quiet for long, as it does in a lake, it becomes clear as glass, and is no longer suitable for irrigation, it is "dead," as the Arabs say. As the water flows slowly through these canals it deposits this precious material in the canal-beds, and especially sand and mud in great quantities. Thus it is necessary every year to clear out the canals, and the material thrown out on to the embankments continually raises them in height. Obviously there must come a moment in the history of each canal when it is more expensive to clear it out than to construct a new one, and thus every canal bears within it the germ of its own destruction. The sanding up of the canal-bed is naturally more insistent in portions nearest the river, and hence it is that this canal displacement occurs so frequently in the neighborhood of the river-course. On the way from Bagdad to Hilleh in the neighborhood of the Euphrates, one crosses extraordinarily numerous groups of abandoned canals, most of which are nothing else than the older courses of the same irrigation system that is in use today.

This explanation must be borne in mind when bewildered by the first sight of these ruined canals, either in reality or on a plan. As one approaches the mound Babil from the north or the east—the mound, by the way, which alone has preserved its ancient name to the present day—one encounters the annoyance of this ruthless disturbance of the ground; it is hardly possible to see the mound till one has climbed the embankment nearest to it, but the impression is then all the more striking.

The mound rises with a steep slope to the height of 22 meters above the plain. Its area forms a square of about 250 meters, and this hill, consisting of broken brick or clayey earth, is pierced by deep ravines and tunnels, while on the north and south-west remains of walls of very considerable height are still standing, with courses of mud brick held together by layers of well-preserved reed stems. They date from a later period, and may have belonged to a fort which was

(The Bettman Archive)

Wall and Hanging Gardens of Babylon

erected in Sassanid or Arabic times on the already ruined Babylonian building.

The astoundingly deep pits and galleries that occur in places owe their origin to the quarrying for brick that has been carried on extensively during the last decades. The buildings of ancient Babylon, with their excellent kiln bricks, served even in antiquity, perhaps in Roman times, certainly in Parthian days, as a quarry for common use. Later centuries appear to have done less to destroy the ruins, but in modern times the quarrying for bricks has assumed far more important dimensions. About twenty years ago, when the Euphrates first began to pour its life-giving waters into the Hindiyeh, a side branch somewhat farther above Babylon, near Musseyib, an attempt was made to head back the river into its old bed by building up a dam, the *Sedde,* which with us has a somewhat evil reputation. Building was carried on year after year without interference at this dam, as long as the height of the water permitted, and that with bricks from Babylon. Quite recently this outrage has been checked by the powerful influence of Halil Bey, Director-General of the Ottoman museums, and of Bedri Bey, the Turkish Commissioner on the excavations; so now there is a well-grounded hope that the ruins of the most celebrated city of the East, or perhaps of the world, shall go down to posterity without further injury. Soon after the commencement of the excavations I had interested myself in checking this spoliation, but that was possible only for the Kasr, at Babil it still went on. Even at the Kasr I had to drive these workers out of their pits, and we set the people to work in our diggings, as the Arab is entirely indifferent to the method by which he earns his scanty wage. The only objectors were the contractors, through whom the materials for the Sedde building were sold. Very recently the latter also made an attack on the tower of Borsippa, but their barbarous attempt was promptly stopped by the action of the Turkish Government.

The robbers carried away the walls layer after layer, carefully leaving the adjoining earth untouched, as the trench grew daily deeper, since a downfall would render it inaccessible. This enables us to make some instructive observations in the interior even before beginning our excavations at this place.

It was a building consisting of many courts and chambers, both small and large, a palace upon a substructure about 18 meters in height. The latter is so constructed that the building walls throughout are continuous and of the same thickness above and below, while the intermediate spaces are filled up to the height of the palace floor with earth and a packing of fragments of brick. As on part of the Kasr, the floor consists of sandstone flags on the edge of which is inscribed, "Palace of Nebuchadnezzar, King of Babylon, son of Nabopolassar, King of Babylon." There are also many portions of a limestone pavement that consists of a thick rough under stratum, and a fine upper stratum half a centimeter thick, and colored a fine red or yellow. This pavement is similar to those of the best Greek period, and it may be considered to be an addition of the time of the Persian kings, or of Alexander the Great and his successors. All the bricks stamped with the name of Nebuchadnezzar, of which we learn more when we turn to the Kasr, were laid either in asphalt or in a gray lime mortar, both of which also occur at the Kasr.

All these things considered, it is impossible to doubt that Babil was a palace of Nebuchadnezzar's. The parallel passage in his great inscription very probably refers to it. . . . "On the brick wall toward the north my heart inspired me to build a palace for the protecting of Babylon. I built there a palace like the palace of Babylon of brick and bitumen. For 60 ells I built an *appa danna* towards Sippar; I made a *nabalu,* and laid its foundation on the bosom of the underworld, on the surface of the (ground) water in brick and bitumen. I raised its summit and connected it with the palace, with brick and bitumen I made it high as a mountain. Mighty cedar trunks I laid on it for roof. Double doors of cedar wood overlaid with copper, thresholds and hinges made of bronze did I set up in its doorways. That building I named 'May Nebuchadnezzar live, may he grow old as restorer of Esagila' " (translated by H. Winckler).

Various expressions remain extremely obscure, and their explanation awaits the excavation of the building. Especially should we like to know what was meant by the *appa danna.* These words in Babylonian mean a "strong nose," which taken absolutely literally is nonsense. In this connection, however, as the appendage of a palace they recall so strongly the *apadana* with which the Persian kings in Persepolis denoted their palaces that one can hardly be mistaken in thinking there must be some esoteric connection. . . . It would be very interesting and of the highest importance in the history of architecture to discover what a building of Nebuchadnezzar's in Babylon looked like. . . . It is only excavation that can give the long-delayed answer to that question.

The heights of Babil afford a fine view over the entire city, especially toward evening when the long purple shadows cast on the plain throw up the golden yellow outlines of the ruins in high relief. No human habitation is in sight. The villages on the left bank of the Euphrates—Kweiresh, where our house is, and Djumdjumma farther south—are so buried among the green date palms that one can scarcely catch a glimpse of even a wall. On the other bank are Sindjar and Ananeh also concealed in the same way, although the latter village with the farm of Karabet stands forward somewhat more clearly. The Euphrates is fringed with palms which cluster more thickly near the water. To the south above their ornamental crowns the minaret of Hilleh gleams, and in the blue distance can be seen a somewhat pointed hill surmounted by a jagged wall, the ruin of E-ur-imin-an-ki, the tower of Borsippa. Due east is the mound of Oheimir, where are the ruins of the ancient Babylonian Kish (?), towards the north the palms of Khan Mhauil are to be seen, and, when the weather is favorable, Tell Ibrahim, the ancient Kutha. With these exceptions all that is visible is the somber dun-colored desert. The cultivated stretches are diminishing in extent and are only noticeable for those few weeks in the year when they are clothed with green.

To those accustomed to Greece and its remains it is a constant surprise to have these mounds pointed out as ruins. Here are no blocks of stone, no columns: even in the excavations there is only brickwork, while before work commenced only a few brick projections stood out on the Kasr. Here in Babylonia mounds form the modern representatives of ancient glories, there are no columns to bear witness to vanished magnificence.

The great mound, the Kasr or castle, forms the center of the city. It is the great castle of Nebuchadnezzar that he built for a palace, completing the work of his father, Nabopolassar. The modern name Kasr thus expresses the purpose for which it was built. By Greek historians it was called the Acropolis, by Romans the Arx. In area it is three or four times as large as Babil, but it is not so high, and when observed from that hill the greater part is hidden by palms. . . .

The Kasr presents so many different aspects that it is not easy to give a clear representation of it. We will first traverse the whole of it and try to give some account of what is to be seen there, before classing together the buildings of different periods. Almost all that is visible at a first glance is of the time of Nebuchadnezzar, who throughout his reign of 43 years must have been unremitting in the work of building and extending his castle.

The ascent was from the north in the north-east corner. All uncertainty on this point has been removed by our recent excavations. Here we had to uncover walls of great extent and deeply buried, and discover their connection with each other. To do this, almost the whole of our men were set to work on the site. We regularly employ from 200 to 250 men, divided into gangs. The leader breaks up the ground with a pickaxe, and 16 men carry away the earth in baskets which are filled by three men with broad axes. This is the usual method, which is necessarily varied according to circumstances. The leader receives 5 piastres daily, the basket-fillers 4, and the carriers 3, as wages. At the diggings we adopt various methods according to the nature of the site and the object aimed at.

Here the workmen descend abreast in a broad line down a slanting incline to the prescribed verge. Having reached it, they draw back to a distance of 5 meters and recommence work. In this way sloping layers of earth are successively peeled off and the walls gradually emerge. By means of a field railway the earth is removed some distance to a site which provisionally we decide to be unimportant. When one of these slopes reaches the lowest level, which is generally the water-level, the workmen face in the opposite direction and remove the remainder in a similar fashion, only leaving a portion of the slope on the edge of each excavation available for transport.

At this point the ends of two parallel walls came to light running south, which we shall describe later with the fortification walls. Between them is a broad street or roadway, which leads direct to the Ishtar Gate, made by Nebuchadnezzar as a processional road for the God Marduk, to whose temple of Esagila it eventually leads. It still possesses the brick pavement covered with asphalt which formed a substratum for the immense flagged pavement. The central part was laid with mighty flags of limestone measuring 1.05 meters each way, and the slides with slabs of red breccia veined with white, 66 centimeters square. The bevelled edges of the joints were filled in with asphalt. On the edges of each slab, which, of course, were not visible, was an inscription, "Nebuchadnezzar, King of Babylon, son of Nabopolassar, King of Babylon, am I. The Babel Street I paved with blocks of shadu stone for the procession of the great Lord Marduk. Marduk, Lord, grant eternal life." On the flags of breccia the word *Turminabanda,* breccia, has been substituted for *Shadu,* mountain. The fine hard limestone may have been brought from the neighborhood of Hit or Anah, where a similar stone is quarried, and transport by river would present little difficulty; of the provenance of the turminabanda I have not been able to acquire any knowledge. The great white paving-stones give the impression of being intended for wheeled traffic, but those that are still *in situ* do not show the slightest traces of being used for any such purpose, they are merely polished and slippery with use.

The Kasr roadway lies high, 12.5 meters above zero, and slopes gently upwards from the north to the Ishtar Gateway. A later restoration, possibly of the Persian (?) period in brick, rendered it horizontal. Before the time of Nebuchadnezzar it was considerably lower, but as he placed the entire palace on

Reconstruction of the Peribolos, with the Tower of Babylon,
the Temple Esagila, the Quay Wall of Nabonidus, and the
Euphrates Bridge. The Tower is Shown Incomplete.

a level higher than that of its predecessor, he was forced also
to raise the roadway. In consequence of this we can today
enjoy the glorious view over the whole city as far as the outer
walls. It is clearly of this work of his that Nebuchadnezzar
speaks in his great [East India House] inscription: "From Dul-
azag, the place of the decider of fates, the Chamber of Fate, as
far as Aibur-shabu, the road of Babylon, opposite the gateway
of Beltis, he (Nabopolassar) had adorned the way of the
procession of the great lord Marduk with turminabanda stones.
Aibur-shabu, the roadway of Babylon, I filled up with a high
filling for the procession of the great lord Marduk, and with
turminabanda stone and with shadu stone I made Airbur-
shabu, from the Illu Gate to the Ishtar-sakipat-tebisha, fit for
the procession of his godhead. I connected it together with the
portions that my father had built and made the road glorious.
. . ." Ishtar-sakipat-tebisha is the Ishtar Gate, and from this
we find that the inscription does not refer to the whole of
the Kasr Street, but only to part of it, either that which ad-
joined the Ishtar Gate on the north or on the south.

The fine view now obtainable from the street of Kasr was
certainly not visible in antiquity, for the roadway was bordered
on both sides with high defensive walls. They were 7 meters
thick and formed the junction between the northern advanced
outworks and the earlier defences, of which the Ishtar Gateway
is part. They guarded the approach to the gate. Manned by
the defenders, the road was a real pathway of death to the foe
who should attempt it. The impression of peril and horror was
heightened for the enemy, and also for peaceful travellers, by
the impressive decoration of long rows of lions advancing one
behind the other with which the walls were adorned in low
relief and with brilliant enamels.

The discovery of these enamelled bricks formed one of the
motives for choosing Babylon as a site for excavation. As
early as June 1887 I came across brightly colored fragments
lying on the ground on the east side of the Kasr. In December
1897 I collected some of these and brought them to Berlin,
where the then Director of the Royal Museums, Richard

Schöne, recognized their significance. The digging commenced on March 26, 1899, with a transverse cut through the east front of the Kasr. The finely colored fragments made their appearance in great numbers, soon followed by the discovery of the eastern of the two parallel walls, the pavement of the processional roadway, and the western wall, which supplied us with the necessary orientation for further excavations.

The tiles represented lions advancing to right or to left according to whether they were on the eastern or the western wall. Some of them were white with yellow manes, and others yellow with red manes, of which the red has now changed to green owing to decomposition. The ground is either light or dark blue, the faces, whether seen from the left or the right, are all alike as they have been cast in a mould. None have been found *in situ*. The walls were plundered for brick, but they were not so completely destroyed as to prevent our observing that they were provided with towers that projected slightly and were obviously placed at distances apart equal to their breadth. Black and white lines in flat enamel on the edges of the towers divided the face of the two walls into panels, defining the divisions made by the towers in the two long friezes of 180 meters, the plinth was decorated with rows of broad-leaved rosettes. As the lions are about 2 meters long, it is possible that each division contained two lions. That would give 60 lions at each side, a total of 120 that agrees well with the number of fragments found.

We must now consider the reliefs and their coloring. For the reliefs a working model must first have been obtained of which the several parts could be used for making the mould. The most natural method would be to build a temporary wall the size of one of these lions with bricks of a plastic clay, and with a strong mortar compounded with sand, on which the relief could be modelled. The jointing was carefully considered, for it is so arranged as not to cut through the figures too obviously, and each brick bears a considerable share of the relief. The joints serve an actual purpose in regulating the proportions, and take the place of the squaring lines with which Egyptian artists prepared their work.

With the help of these models, moulds could be made for each separate brick. They were probably of burnt pottery similar to the moulds made for the abundant terra-cottas of Babylonia. The mould would form one side of the frame in which the brick was struck, and, according to the regular method of bonding, a course of whole bricks (33 x 33 centimeters) would be followed by a course of half bricks (33 x 16½). Thus the ground of the reliefs and the wall surface were actually identical, and there is not even a projecting base on which the paws of the great beasts might appear to rest, as would be the case with stone reliefs. This is art in clay, a specialized art, distinguished from all other kinds of relief. . . .

The brick when moulded and before it was enamelled was burnt like any ordinary brick; the contours were then drawn on it with black lines of a readily fusible vitreous composition, leaving clearly marked fields. These were filled with liquid colored enamels, the whole dried and then fused, this time apparently in a gentler fire. As the black lines had the same fusing-point as the colored portions they often mixed with the colors themselves, thus giving the work that marvellous and harmonious brilliancy and life which we admire today. . . .

The bricks had then to be arranged according to the design. In order to facilitate this and to ensure an accurate distribution of them on the building site, the bricks were marked on the upper side in rough glaze with a series of simple signs and numerals. The sign on the side of a brick and on that which was to be placed next to it are identical. . . .

A complete study of these details could not be made in Babylon as we were cramped for space and could not spread out the pieces. The chemical preservation of them was carried out in Berlin with great care under the able direction of Professor Rathgen. The antiquities from the ruin sites, more especially the pottery, were completely permeated with salts, saltpeter and the like. These materials, owing to long exposure to air, had formed hard crystals on the surface, which had to be removed by long-continued soaking. Here in Babylon also we numbered each piece so that we could be certain at what part of the Processional Street each fragment had been found. . . .

The street pavement extended through the Ishtar Gate, and in the southern gateway court the older pavement is still in place. Here there are three layers of brick set in asphalt, which curve upward near the walls, forming a shallow trough. Its purpose must have been to prevent the collected water soaking into the joints of the walls. Similar curves in other places are the result of the unequal settling of the lighter material of the filling below the pavement and of the unyielding walls of baked brick, while a curve in the opposite sense can often be remarked on the flooring of buildings of crude brick, because the closely compressed mud wall settled with greater force than the slightly compressed filling under the pavement.

On leaving the Ishtar Gate we cross the substructure of the threshold, which rested on many layers of brick and must itself have been of stone. On the south of the gate some later insignificant buildings, perhaps Parthian, have clustered round it. These leave the entrance free, and Nebuchadnezzar's great paving-blocks of the upper roadway, over which Nebuchadnezzar, Daniel, and Darius must frequently have passed, are still in position. Farther on only the lower pavement remains. It extends parallel with the east front of the Southern Citadel as far as the end of the mound, where it surrounds an altar (?) of mud brick.

A branch of the street leads to the principal entrance of the Southern Citadel. A great number of limestone and turminabanda paving stones found in the southern portion originally formed part of the destroyed upper pavement. It appears that during the Greek or Parthian periods balls for projectiles were made out of this limestone, as many have been found here. . . .

South of the Citadel the street crosses a watercourse, which

The Procession Street, Babylon—Colored Ceramic

apparently varied at different periods both in width and in name. In the time of Nebuchadnezzar it was perhaps the canal "Libil-higalla," while in Persian and Greek times it was the Euphrates itself that flowed here. We dug a ditch here that extended from the mound to the recommencement of the street, and which clearly showed the stratum to have been formed by the deposit of water. The strata contain no ruins with the exception of a canal, which in places is barely 3 meters broad. This canal is constructed in later fashion with the ancient bricks of Nebuchadnezzar, the best outside, the fragments inside, and all laid in mud. To the east it soon comes to an end and disappears in the banked-up watercourse. To the west it first widens out into a basin of three times its breadth, where narrow steps lead down the embankments to the level of the water, and then once more narrows to its ordinary width. Farther to the west we know nothing of it. At the narrow portions, at about the height of the ancient water-level, courses of squared limestone of considerable size were laid. In the western part the northern bank contained a square opening many brick courses deep. The whole conveys the impression of a kind of sluice, which perhaps served to connect a watercourse in the east, of high water-level, with another in the west of lower level. The construction may date from the time of Neriglissar, when throwing a bridge across the canal to carry the Procession Street presented no difficulty. In earlier times the street appears to have been carried on a dam with walled embankments, which latter still exist below the walls of the canal.

The eastern canal, Libil-higalla, was restored by Nebuchadnezzar, according to [his inscription]: "Lib:l-higalla, the eastern canal of Babylon, which a long time previously had been choked (?) with downfallen earth (?) and filled with rubbish, I sought out its place, and I laid its bed with baked bricks and bitumen from the banks of the Euphrates up to Ai-ibur-sabu. At Ai-ibur-sabu, the street of Babylon, I added a canal bridge and made the way broad for the procession of the great lord Marduk. . . ." Neriglissar also says of himself. . . . "The eastern arm, which an earlier king (indeed) dug, but had not constructed its bed, (this) arm I dug (again) and constructed its bed with bricks and kiln bricks; beneficient, inexhaustible water I led to the land."

To the north of the Citadel there is a similar canal constructed after the same fashion, of which the vaulting still exists. My opinion is that this canal conveyed to the east the water of the Euphrates, which was probably still called "Arachtu" there, and that possibly it flowed round the Kasr in somewhat irregular fashion, even in the Neo-Babylonian period. This easterly body of water would then return to the Euphrates by means of the canal just described. At the southwest corner of the Kasr buildings, where they joined the wall of Nabonidus, the openings through which the water escaped are still preserved in this wall.

To the south of our water-channel the street appears once more, but at a much lower level. It is paved with brick, plastered with asphalt, and is of the same breadth as the southern Kasr Street. It passes between the houses of Merkes and the sacred peribolos of Etemenanki, keeping close to the latter, but at a sufficient distance from the secular dwellings of the Babylonians. The first part of the street, as far as the great gate of Etemenanki, had a flooring of kiln bricks overlaid with paving-stones of turminabanda, which still lie undisturbed on the branch leading to the gate. They bear the same dedicatory inscription as that on the Kasr: some of them, however, have in addition on the underside the name of Sennacherib, the bloodthirsty Assyrian who while still well disposed to the city often beautified it, only at last to destroy it utterly, as he emphatically states in his Bavian inscription.

Nebuchadnezzar makes no reference to this work of one of his predecessors, he only refers to that of his father Nabopolassar. . . .: "From Du-azag, the place of the deciding of fates, the chamber of fate, to Aibursabu, the street of Babylon, opposite the 'Lady' Gate, he (Nabopolassar) had paved the Procession Street of the great lord Marduk splendidly with paving-stones of breccia" (trans. by Delitzsch). Of these paving-stones of Nabopolassar there are certainly no remains that can be identified with certainty. Just as Nebuchadnezzar made use of the blocks of Sennacherib for his new building, so doubtless he would appropriate those of his father.

In addition to digging out the street on the east side of the peribolos we also excavated a portion of it on the south side.

Inscription from the Procession Street, Babylon

Here we could trace it between the peribolos and Esagila as far as the (Urash?) gate in the Nabonidus wall and the Euphrates bridge there. In this whole length, several superimposed pavements of baked brick, separated from each other by shallow layers of earth, occurred rather frequently; all the upper ones bear the stamp of Nebuchadnezzar, the bricks of the lowest pavement are unstamped and smaller (32 centimeters): these may date from Nabopolassar, but not necessarily. North of the Ishtar Gate we only find Nebuchadnezzar's brick stamps. Consequently the above-quoted passage seems to refer to the section of the street between Esagila and the Kasr. If so, the "Lady" Gate (bâb bilti) must be sought on the eastern front of the Kasr, and Du-azag either in Esagila or in the peribolos of Etemenanki. The Procession Street on the Kasr was called Aiburshabu. To this latter section only the above-quoted passage applies. . . .

We found a brick, although not *in situ,* with an inscription that refers to the construction of the street by Nebuchadnezzar, with a number of fragments of similar content: "Nebuchadnezzar, King of Babylon, he who made Esagila and Ezida glorious, son of Nabopolassar, King of Babylon. The streets of Babylon, the Procession Streets of Nabû and Marduk my lords, which Nabopolassar, King of Babylon, the father who begat me, had made a road glistening with asphalt and burnt bricks: I, the wise suppliant who fears their lordship, placed above the bitumen and burnt bricks a mighty superstructure of shining dust, made them strong within with bitumen and burnt bricks as a high-lying road. Nabû and Marduk, when you traverse these streets in joy, may benefits for me rest upon your lips; life for distant days and well-being for the body. Before you will I advance (?) upon them (?). May I attain eternal age" (trans. by Weissbach).

Here and there on the street, and also below the procession pavement, are Babylonian graves. The adults are in large jars, the children in shallow elliptical bowls of pottery. We have observed no traces of monuments above ground, nor could we expect to find any in such a position on the street, nor yet in the other usual places of burial—the streets and squares of the city, on the fortification walls, and in the ruins of fallen houses.

The route from the south-west corner of the Kasr to Amran leads first to a small mound which we have named the south-west building. It consists largely of mud-brick masonry that belongs to the later Parthian (?) period. So far we have done little excavation here. We next pass the long low-lying stretch that now represents a water-channel that once lay here. We then ascend a range of mounds that also extends from east to west. A cross-cut has shown that it consists of the ruins of Babylonian houses of crude brick, lying one above another. . . . This was the town site of the common people.

On the other side of this range of mounds a somewhat considerable plain of remarkable uniformity stretches away to the hill of Amran Ibn Ali, cut through diagonally by the road that leads from our village of Kweiresh to Hilleh. It is called Sachn, literally "the pan," a term which in modern days is applied to the open space enclosed by arcades that surround the great pilgrimage mosques, such as those of Kerbela or Nedjef. Our Sachn, however, is no other than the modern representation of the ancient sacred precinct in which stood the zikurrat Etemenanki, "the foundation stone of heaven and earth," the tower of Babylon, surrounded by an enclosing wall against which lay all manner of buildings connected with the cult.

This enclosing wall forms almost a square, divided by cross walls into separate parts. . . . All the buildings consisted largely of crude brick, and only, as an exception, the very considerable crude-brick core of the tower in the south-west corner was enclosed in a thick wall of burnt brick, which has been removed deep down by brick robbers. Now only their deep and broad trenches are to be seen, but these enable us to recognize the site of a great open stairway which led up to the tower from the south. The ruin is not yet excavated.

Many additions and restorations were carried out in connection with these buildings, and they can clearly be distinguished, especially in the enclosing wall itself. The east end of the northern front is very instructive in this respect. We can distinguish the original building and a strengthening wall, the kisu, in front of it. Here it is of crude brick, but on the west front . . . it is of burnt brick. On the original building three periods lie superposed, as also on the kisu. Of each of these building periods slightly projecting towers are placed on the walls close together, and differently distributed, which considerably aids us in distinguishing the periods, as the mud-brick courses are frequently placed immediately over each other. Inside the lowest kisu, somewhat farther to the west, there is a vertical gutter. . . . In this were inscribed bricks of Esarhaddon, with the statement that he built the zikurrat of Etemenanki. The two upper portions of the kisu must therefore belong to a later period, and the lower part of the main building to an earlier period, than that of Esarhaddon. The other excavations have produced in addition 12 stamped bricks of Sardanapalus and 4 inscribed bricks of Nebuchadnezzar, all of which refer to the building of Etemenanki. Even if these bricks were not intended for the peribolos, but for the tower itself, their occasional use for the former is in no way surprising. All that we have been able to excavate so far is connected with the original building, of which the later repairing and rebuilding carefully follow the ancient line of the wall. We need not therefore lay too much stress on the various periods.

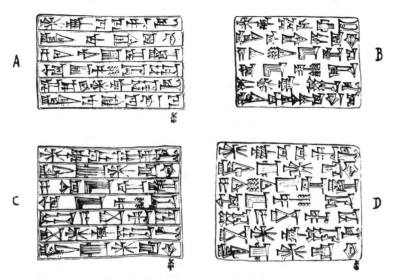

Brick Stamps of Nebuchadnezzar

The surrounding wall is for the greater part a double wall, in which uniform broad chambers are constructed by means of cross walls. The ornamental towers on the inner walls are always placed between two doors of these chambers, while on the outside, where the two ornamental grooves that used to decorate both the towers and the intermediate spaces still exist in places, both towers and spaces are of the same breadth.

There are buildings at other points of the encircling walls always joined to the outer wall. Large as they are, they have none of the characteristics of temples. Two large buildings lay on the east side, each with a large court surrounded by deep chambers uniform in size. In the corner there is a dwelling grouped round a courtyard, and on the south side there are four similar ones, which, although smaller, are very large and dignified mansions. At the east of the northern part the usual small private houses form an independent line of street.

Two doors in the north and ten elaborate gateways with an

inner court and towered facade afforded access to the interior. The two eastern of these and the four at the south are placed at the end of deep recesses formed by the outer wall being carried back, thus forming roomy forecourts. . . .

Very little remains of the south-east corner. Near the south-west corner a chambered wall projects to the north, and with the outer wall forms a long narrow court in which there were no other chambers than those formed in the wall. . . .

We thus have three divisions inside the peribolos: the northern court with the small houses, the long, narrow western court, and the principal court, which contained the zikurrat of Etemenanki and all the other monumental buildings.

Low down on the north, close to the zikurrat, there were ancient buildings orientated in an entirely different direction, and on the east front, also at a great depth, there lay a large ancient building, over which the main building of the peribolos was carried. Neither of these had anything to do with the sanctuary as such.

We can only hazard a guess as to the purpose of all those buildings. The wall chambers are adapted by their simplicity to house a number of pilgrims, who could dwell there and have direct access to the great courts. The buildings in the south I take to have been priests' dwellings. Under no circumstances can they have been temples, as all the necessary features are absent, such as the towered facade and the postament niche. The priests of Etemenanki must have occupied very distinguished positions as representatives of the god who bestowed the kingship of Babylon, and the immense private houses to the south of our peribolos agree very well with the supposition in regard to this Vatican of Babylon, that the principal administrative apparatus would be housed there. The numerous chambers of the two great buildings in the east will be recognized by all as store-rooms where the property of the sanctuary and the things needed for processions, etc., could be stored. In one of these chambers, which for the most part are not yet cleared, we found a great stone weight in the form of a duck, the usual form of such weights. It weighs 29.68 kilograms and, according to the chiselled inscription on it, was called a "correct talent." All the buildings are much ruined, often as low down as beneath the ancient pavement. In the north-east corner of the peribolos a stela with emblems of the gods was found.

The main approach lay between the two store-houses just mentioned, where from the existence of a specially deep and wide recess we can surmise a specially large gateway, which, though it exists no longer, admits of easy reconstruction. The turminabanda pavement of the Procession Street reaches as far as this, and continues in the recess where the paving-blocks still lie that bear the inscription of Nebuchadnezzar on their edge. Some of these have the name and title of Sennacherib on the under side.

In the Ripley-cylinder of Neriglissar . . . the peribolos is called "lânu ma-hir-tim." According to Muss-Arnolt's dictionary the words mean "enclosure" and "storehouse". With the exception of these two words I give Bezold's translation, which otherwise only requires correction in slight details: "The peribolos of the storehouses of Esagila to the north, wherein the consecrated temple treasury of Esagila rests (trans. by Delitzsch, 'wherein the priests of Esagila dwell') whose foundations an earlier king laid but did not build the summit, (this building) had sunk in its foundations, its walls were fallen down, its joints were loosened, and its base had become weak. Then my lord the great Marduk inspired me to raise up the building, entrusted me (?) with the splendor (?) and the regulation of the temple tribute. In order to incur no Shiddim and no offences, I dug up the ancient foundation stone and read it (its records). On its ancient foundation stone I based it (the building), its summit I raised like a mountain, I made firm its threshold and fixed the doors in its doorway. The firm Kisu I built of asphalt and burnt brick (?)." According to this the Kisu of burnt brick which was found in the excavations on the west side was of Neriglissar.

The original of the second Babylonian text that refers to the enclosure has disappeared. We possess only an epitome of it

The Bull of the Ishtar Gate, Babylon

given by Smith. . . . But the statements can only be reconciled with the existing remains with great difficulty, and then only in general. The measurements given for the three courts should agree with the ruins, at least as regards the relations of length to breadth, but this is not so whether we take the measurement of the walls outside or of the open space within the courts. The only possible solution appears to me to be that we take the measures given as those of the "great court" to be meant for the south-east portion, including the buildings surrounding it, that we take the "court of Ishtar and Zamana" to mean what we call the north court, and the third to mean the inner open space of our great court. But even so there are difficulties. Under these circumstances we need not attach any great importance to the measurements given for the alleged 7 stages of the tower. Those uncertainties are caused by the fact that the original inscription is not at hand, we do not know the object for which these statements were made.

Herodotus (i. 181) names the group of buildings "the brazen-doored sanctuary of Zeus Belus." The zikurrat inside the sanctuary he describes as a massive tower on which stood a second, third, up to an eighth tower, above which was a "great temple." This is the sole ground for our conception of the "terraced towers" of Mesopotamia. In Khorsabad there was the ruin of a tower, where the excavators suspected similar retreating stages to have existed, but Place clearly formed his conclusion under the long-accepted suggestion drawn from the description given by Herodotus, and the ruins themselves no longer exist. In the words of Herodotus himself, however, there is nothing whatever about stepped terraces. He speaks of 8 towers standing one above another, but he does not say that each was smaller than the one below it. I myself desired to accept the general conception of stepped towers, but I know of no safe ground for such a conception. The only remedy I can see for this difficulty is to excavate the best-preserved zikurrat we possess, that of Borsippa.

From the ruins as they now exist before excavation, we must assume that a colossal stairway led up from the south to the top of the immense mass of building. Steps in antiquity were always extremely steep, as we have found them here, and the height and breadth were usually the same, so according to the measurements of the length of the foundation of the steps we may take their height to have been 50 meters.

We do not know the complete height of the tower. Nabopolassar, however, lays great stress on it . . . and so does Nebuchadnezzar . . . in his cylinder-inscription of Etemenanki. Nabopolassar says: "At this time Marduk commanded me . . .; the tower of Babylon, which in the time before me had become weak, and had been brought to ruin, to lay its foundation firm on the bosom of the underworld, while its top should stretch heavenwards. . . ." Nebuchadnezzar says: "To raise up the top of Etemenanki that it may rival heaven, I laid to my hand." In both inscriptions mud brick, burnt brick, asphalt, mud, and mighty cedars of Lebanon are mentioned as the materials employed. The latter could scarcely have been employed otherwise than to roof in the temple on the top of the tower.

In distinction to this upper temple Herodotus calls Esagila lying before it to the south the . . . lower temple. In the upper temple, according to Herodotus, there was only a golden table . . . , and according to Ctesias three gold figures of Zeus, Hera, and Rhea. My opinion is that the designation of the zikurrat as bearing a temple is confirmed by this. The Babylonian term only expresses height, and nothing that can suggest stages. It is obvious that the roof of so lofty a temple would be welcomed by the Babylonian astronomers as a platform for their observations. It would be necessary for them to be raised above the thick atmosphere of the plain. Owing to excessive dryness, the air is almost opaque at a distance, and the horizon up to a height of 10 or 20 grades is a dusky circle of dust, through which the sun and moon often assume torn and distorted forms, if their setting can be seen at all.

It is true that during the summer we have no clouds, with the exception of the *Bachura,* a type of weather that occurs at the beginning of August, but we have sandstorms, through which the sun appears like a blood-red disk. The greatly-renowned clearness of the Babylonian sky is largely a fiction of European travellers, who are rarely accustomed to observe the night sky of Europe without the intervention of city lights.

The original complete height of the tower of Babylon we do not know. The east side of the peribolos, which is almost similar to the north side, measures 409 meters in round numbers. For the entire sacred enclosure Herodotus gives a measure of 2 square stadia, and 1 stadion as the side length of the area of the zikurrat; the ruins themselves show 90 meters.

But what is all this written information in comparison with

the clearness of the evidence we gain from the buildings themselves, ruined though they are. The colossal mass of the tower,
which the Jews of the Old Testament regarded as the essence
of human presumption, amidst the proud palaces of the priests,
the spacious treasuries, the innumerable lodgings for strangers
—white walls, bronze doors, mighty fortification walls set
round with lofty portals and a forest of 1000 towers,—the
whole must have conveyed an overwhelming sense of greatness, power, and wealth, such as could rarely have been found
elsewhere in the great Babylonian kingdom.

I once beheld the great silver standing statue of the Virgin,
over life-size, laden with votive offerings, rings, precious stones,
gold and silver, borne on a litter by forty men, appear in
the portal of the dome of Syracuse, high above the heads of
the assembled crowds, to be brought out in festival procession
with inspiring music and among the fervent prayers of the
people into the garden of the Latomia. After the same fashion
I picture to myself a procession of the god Marduk as he issued
forth from Esagila, perhaps through the peribolos, to proceed
on his triumphant way through the Procession Street of
Babylon.

Herodotus must have seen the enclosure in a comparatively
good state of preservation. Under Alexander it needed repairs,
and 600,000 days' wages were spent on clearing out the precincts and removing the rubbish (Strabo, xvi. 1). During the
eleven years of our work we have expended about 800,000
daily wages for the great clearance of Babylon. . . .

The ancient celebrated temple, Esagila, according to Jastrow
"the lofty house" . . . , the temple of Marduk, lies beneath
the hill of Amran Ibn Ali, buried to a depth of 21 meters
below the upper level of the hill. We have already excavated
some part of it, and by means of deep shafts and galleries we
have established the ground-plan and the different divisions.
There are two buildings adjacent to each other; the principal
one on the east is very regularly and magnificently planned,
of the Western Annex we have only recovered the outer circuit.

We will first survey the principal building.

The temple is almost square, with its northern front of 79.3 meters and its western front of 85.8 meters long. Inside it is a court 31.3 meters broad and 37.6 meters long. On the west of this court, as we learn from the mighty-towered facade, there was the principal cella, that of Marduk. The chambers are not yet excavated. On the south side towards the east there is a smaller cella, which can be recognized as such by the niche in the wall. The cella lies on the east side of a square, which on the west side has a door leading to a small chamber which may also be the remains of a cella.

A third cella has been excavated on the north side of the court. It is apparently the sanctuary of the god Ea, who in Greek times was identified with Serapis. It was here that the generals of Alexander sought counsel of the god with regard to his illness, whether the king should permit himself to be transported hither in search of healing. Doors lead north to two chambers behind the cella, an arrangement that is not found in any other cella. If my expressed opinion is correct these chambers may have been the dormitories in which oracular dreams could be secured. In the cella, which also had a side chamber at the east end, the postament for the statue still stands in front of the niche. Imprinted on the asphalt covering of its flat top we found traces of a wooden throne, which, during the conflagration, had become charred and broken up. Of the richly carved work some fragments could still be recognized, the figures that supported the throne, holding the water vase with which Ea, god of the abyss of waters, was usually represented, a fine head of a dragon, a fish, and so forth.

The paved floor with its wash of asphalt is slightly dominated by the postament, which has in front of it a shallow step flanked by two small balustrades.

The pavement was repeatedly raised, and with it the mighty door sockets and the postaments. Of the six pavements the two upper ones are Nebuchadnezzar's, and the two middle ones are of Sardanapalus, who states on the stamps of his brick, 33 x 33 centimeters, that he made the "bricks of Esagila and Etemenanki." In this pavement there was one, 40 x 40 centimeters, brick of Esarhaddon, which, according to the stamp, belonged to "the pavement of Esagila." The name of the temple is therefore fully established by inscription as Esagila. On bricks found by us in the vicinity, Esagila is often mentioned in conjunction with Etemenanki or with Babylon. The two lower pavements have no stamps. The walls of the court at this lower and more ancient level are adorned with moldings, while the walls above are plain.

At the doors, and in front of the wall piers, we again found the brick caskets; in one of these lay a clay figure of a bearded man with bull's feet, and holding a palm or something of the kind.

The upper pavement lies on an average 4.5 meters above zero. The enclosing walls, which, including the 2-meters-thick kisu, are 6 meters thick, consist, like the entire building, of mud brick, and the kisu of 32 x 32-centimeter unstamped burnt brick; it must therefore be older than the time of Nebuchadnezzar, who does not appear to have carried out any vigorous restoration here.

The treatment of the walls is similar to that of Emach in an intensified form. Here every tower is placed between two flanking towers, thus forming a unit of three towers. This also occurs in the great temple of Nebo in Borsippa. Exactly in the middle of each side there is a great gateway elaborated with massive projecting towers. Paved ramps, with side balustrades, lead up to the three gateways on the north, west, and south. All is on a larger scale than in other temples. The symmetrical planning which in other temples leaves much to be desired, is here remarkably accurate, and here alone is an entrance to be found on each side.

Although from the outside these gateways all appear to be alike, the east gate must have been the principal entrance, as it has a passage through a magnificent vestibule that leads direct to the court, while the entrance through the north and south doors leads first into a small vestibule and then through a corridor that runs by the side of it. On the walls of the court also doorways and towers are symmetrically alternated.

A considerable similarity exists between our temple and the description of the "temples" that lay near the zikurrat given in Smith's summary of an inscription. . . . Smith was not then aware of the difference between Esagila and the Bel sanctuary of Herodotus. His "temples" have measurements and proportions which, on account of their disproportionate length, are entirely impossible as such. For enclosed chambers they are far too widely spanned. They can therefore only be measurements of the area of separate parts of the temples, including the adjacent walls. If all of these are added together we find that they amount almost exactly to the occupied area of Esagila. Furthermore, these areas can with ease be arranged so as to fill in the ground plan of Esagila with very few discrepancies.

Then again the principal cellae are here, that of Marduk and of Zarpanit in the west, and that of Ea in the north, while that of Anu and Bel may at least find its counterpart in the double cella in the south of Esagila. Thus the measurements of Smith's "temples" must have been taken either directly from Esagila or perhaps from the temple on the top of the zikurrat, which must then have had much the same dimensions and arrangements as Esagila. It is to be expected that the further excavations of Esagila will throw light on these most interesting questions.

Allusions to Esagila, and information regarding its rebuilding and endowment, are, of course, very frequent in Babylonian inscriptions, especially in those of Nebuchadnezzar, who calls himself the "fosterer of Esagila" on every one of his millions of bricks. In the [East India House] inscription he says . . . : "Silver, gold, costly precious stones, bronze, mismakannu, and cedar wood, all conceivable valuables, great (?) superabundance, the product of the mountains, the wealth of the sea, a heavy burden, a sumptuous gift, I brought to my city of Babil before him, and deposited in Esagila, the palace of his lordship, a gigantic abundance. Ekua, the chamber of Marduk, lord of the gods, I made to gleam like the sun. Its walls I clothed with solid (?) gold instead of clay (?) or chalk (?), with lapis and alabaster the temple area. Kahilisir, or the 'door of state,' as also the Ezida gate of Esagila, I caused to be made bright as the sun—Du-azag, the place of the naming of destiny, that is Ub-su-ukkenna, the chamber of destiny, in which at Zakmuk or the New Year, on the 8th and 11th day, the 'King of the gods of heaven and earth,' the lord of the gods takes up his abode, while the gods of heaven and of earth, reverentially awaiting him, bow before him, at the place where he allotteth the destiny of eternal duration as the lot of my life:—the same chamber, the chamber of majesty, the chamber of the lordship of the wise one among the gods, the exalted Marduk, that an earlier king had furnished with silver, I clothed with shining gold, a magnificent adornment. The outfit of the temple of Esagila I beautified with solid (?) gold, the Kua-ship with sarir and stones like unto the stars of heaven. The temples of Babil I caused to be re-established and I took care of them. I covered the top of Etemenanki with blue glazed burnt brick. My heart impels me to build Esagila, I keep it perpetually before mine eyes. The best of my cedars, that I brought from Lebanon, the noble forest, I sought out for the roofing over of Ekua, the chamber of his lordship, with deliberate care, the mightiest cedars I covered with gleaming gold for the roofing of Ekua. The sibi below the roofing cedars I decorated with gold and precious stones. For the restoration of Esagila I make supplication every morning to the king of gods, the lord of lords". . . .

[According to Herodotus] there was a great seated statue of Zeus, that like the throne, the footstool, and table was formed of gold of the weight of 800 talents.

Small objects found on the pavement showed that this must have remained open as late as the Seleucid period. Thus the building existed long unroofed, and crumbled into an accumulation of rubbish amounting to 4 or 5 meters high. Then the mud walls fell down flat, and in this position we found them, and over them rubbish of all sorts was accumulated for a long period, which, during our excavations, appeared in most unpleasant guise as a horrible, black, powdery mass. At a height of 14 meters above zero mud-brick houses begin once more, which become poorer in the higher parts of the midden, until at last they almost entirely disappear. The upper layer certainly contains traces of habitation, and among them many Arabic glazed sherds, but scarcely walls, and the Babylon of that period, whose inhabited area was confined to this mound, must have presented a somewhat miserable aspect. As Hilleh was founded in the eleventh century A.D., we may assume that Babylon ceased to be inhabited at that time. . . .

# 7. WOOLLEY:

# *The City of Abraham*

27. Now these are the generations of Terah: Terah begat Abram, Nahor, and Haran; and Haran begat Lot.

28. And Haran died before his father Terah in the land of his nativity, in Ur of the Chaldees.

— GENESIS, 11

*O City, a bitter lament set up as thy lament;*
*Thy lament which is bitter—O city, set up thy lament.*
*His righteous city which has been destroyed—bitter is its lament.*
*His Ur which has been destroyed—bitter is its lament.*

*Its walls were breached; the people groan.*
*In its lofty gates, where they were wont to promenade, dead*
*    bodies were lying about;*
*In its boulevards, where the feasts were celebrated, scattered*
*    they lay.*

— *Lamentation over the Destruction of Ur*
(c. 2000 B.C. Translation by Samuel Noah Kramer)

245

18. Bull's Head from the King's Grave at Ur

Ur "of the Chaldees" was the best known of the cities of Sumer long after Sumer itself had been forgotten. The Old Testament had enshrined Ur's name by mentioning it as the birthplace of the Hebrew patriarch Abraham.

By the time Oppert, in 1869, had put forth his Sumerian theory, Ur had already been rediscovered. In 1854 J. E. Taylor, the British Consul at Basra, had conducted excavations in southern Mesopotamia at a mound called Tell al Muqayyar, "The Mound of Pitch." Taylor turned up cylinders of baked clay which bore inscriptions of Nabonidus, the archaeologically-minded king of Babylon. About 550 B.C., Nabonidus had visited the then-ancient city of Ur and had carried out temple repairs.

These cylinders were inscribed in the Akkadian language. Rawlinson, who had recently learned to read Akkadian, was able to decipher the inscriptions and identify Tell al Muqayyar as the ruin of Ur. Nothing more was done on the site until 1918 when R. Campbell Thompson of the British Museum drove some trial trenches. The following February, a British Museum expedition under H. R. Hall began work at Ur, but lack of funds soon forced a halt.

The Ur excavations were resumed in 1922 under the joint sponsorship of the British Museum and the University of Pennsylvania Museum. Under the leadership of Leonard Woolley, work continued for twelve years, with results that stand as a model of archaeological accomplishment.

Sir Leonard Woolley was born in 1880, at London, the son of a clergyman. After studies at New College, Oxford, he was for two years the assistant keeper of the Ashmolean Museum there, and then went into field archaeology—first in Britain and Italy, then in the Near East. His earliest outstanding work was performed at the ancient Hittite city of Carchemish, in Turkey, where his collaborator was T. E. Lawrence, "Lawrence of Arabia."

Woolley's work at Carchemish was interrupted by World War I. He served as a British intelligence officer, fell into Turkish hands, and spent most of the war a prisoner. After the war, Woolley returned to Carchemish and worked there until receiving the assignment to lead the Ur expedition.

The twelve years at Ur by no means concluded Woolley's brilliant archaeological career. He moved on in 1935—the year of his knighthood—to conduct important excavations in Turkey, at Tel Atchana (the ancient Alalakh, a Hittite city). From 1943 to 1946 Woolley served his country again, as archaeological adviser to the British War Office. He was instrumental in having ancient monuments spared from military attack. He died in 1960.

Woolley was perhaps the foremost archaeologist of the 20th century. His work was marked by precision and efficiency, and his ability to interpret what he uncovered was matchless. The quiet clarity of Woolley's literary style is a good token of the caliber of his archaeological work; the one shared with the other his overriding characteristics of sobriety, perceptivity, and superb organizational sense.

Woolley's many popular books made him famous as a public interpreter to the layman of the archaeology of the Near East. His *The Sumerians* (1928) told the story of that then little-known people as well as it has ever been told. *Ur of the Chaldees,* which appeared in 1929, went through seven printings by 1931 and a second edition in 1950. Our selection is from that book, which is the account of Woolley's first seven years at Ur. In 1954, Woolley rewrote and recast *Ur of the Chaldees* in the light of the discoveries of his final five years at Ur, and republished it as *Excavations at Ur.* Another of his most successful books is *Digging up the Past* (1930), a slim but admirable general discussion of the science of archaeology.

Ur, Woolley found, was a city of great antiquity. His excavations took him down to a pre-Sumerian period which he named "the al-'Ubaid period" after a mound near Ur. His work in the Sumerian strata yielded wonderful art treasures, many of which are to be seen at the University Museum in Philadelphia, and also data on two dramatic episodes in the history of Ur: the Great Deluge and the Royal Burial.

Driving his shaft deep into the mound of Ur, Woolley came

upon a layer of water-deposited sediments—with al-'Ubaid pottery beneath! It was a clear sign of a great flood. "No other agency could possibly account for it," he wrote. "Inundations are of normal occurrence in Lower Mesopotamia, but no ordinary rising of the rivers would leave behind it anything approaching the bulk of this clay bank: 8 feet of sediment imply a very great depth of water, and the flood which deposited it must have been of a magnitude unparalleled in local history." Woolley went on to speculate that this flood was the Deluge of Noah, and the evidence he adduces is impressive.

The second of Woolley's best-publicized discoveries was a royal tomb which attracted nearly as much attention as that of Tutankhamen. In 1928, the spades of the diggers uncovered, deep in the bowels of the mound, what could only have been royal graves. They were a chilling sight, these 5000-year-old graves, for the king and queen had been buried along with their entire retinue. "Clearly, when a royal person died," Woolley wrote, "he or she was accompanied to the grave by all the members of the court: the king had at least three people with him in his chamber and sixty-two in the death-pit; the queen was content with some twenty-five in all."

Selecting a single chapter on Woolley's excavations at Ur was a difficult task. The one chosen here is perhaps less dramatic than the account of the royal graves, but gives a clear picture of Woolley's deductive methods. The full story of the work at Ur is being told in voluminous technical reports. Of the five volumes that have appeared thus far, four are wholly or largely by Woolley: I: *Al 'Ubaid* (1927); II: *The Royal Cemetery* (1934); IV: *The Early Periods* (1955); V: *The Ziggurat and Its Surroundings* (1939).

The history of Ur is told in various chronicle-tablets found in Mesopotamia, and Woolley's excavations confirmed most of what the tablets told. The earliest reliable dates in Mesopotamian history are about 2500 B.C. when writing seems to have been developed, and it is from that time that the history of Ur dates. The king-lists of Sumer name a group of mythological kings of antediluvian days, and then the dynasties that ruled after the flood. Of these, the third to rule was the First Dynasty of Ur, which Woolley originally dated at about 3100 B.C., but which is now thought to have come to power six centuries later.

The First Dynasty of Ur ruled Sumer for some hundred fifty years. Then the dynasty came to a violent end, and sovereignty passed to other cities—now Lagash, now Kish, now Erech. Then came the non-Sumerian Sargon of Akkad, who conquered the warring city-states about 2350 B.C.

The breakup of Sargon's empire a century and a half later ushered in a time of chaos, out of which emerged a dominant Sumerian dynasty for the last time: the Third Dynasty of Ur, the final flourish of Sumer's greatness. (Nothing is known of the Second Dynasty of Ur.) Woolley's account of this Third Dynasty, which follows, places it too far in the past, as he himself later recognized. Current archaeological thinking is that the Third Dynasty held sway during the years 2123–2016 B.C.


## THE CITY OF ABRAHAM


At no time in its long history was the city of Ur so important as in the days of the Third Dynasty, about 2300 B.C. to 2180 B.C., when it was the capital of the Sumerian empire. The founder of the dynasty was Ur-Nammu (or Ur-Engur, as the name used to be written), and he founded a royal house of which four generations after him were to sit upon the throne; he was a great conqueror and a great ruler, famous for his justice and his good works, whose dominions extended from the Persian Gulf to the Mediterranean, and his monuments were broadcast throughout the cities of Mesopotamia. It is a curious fact that no literary texts of his reign or of the

From *Ur of the Chaldees* (London: Ernest Benn, 1929) by C. Leonard Woolley. Copyright 1929 by Ernest Benn, Ltd., and reprinted by permission of the publishers.

Rough Map Showing the Position of Ur in Sumer

reigns of his posterity survive, and that what we know of him has to be pieced together from scattered references and from the ruins of his buildings.

Two fragmentary inscriptions on stone found in the temple of the Moon-goddess throw some light on the beginnings of his kingdom. Each of them records the founding by Ur-Nammu of a temple or shrine, but whereas nearly all Ur-Nammu's other dedications are made to Nannar, the god of the city of Ur, here the deities he honours are the patron gods of the city of Erech, and he prays for the life of Utun-khegal the king of Erech, calling himself only by the title of 'governor.' Now, Erech was the seat of the dynasty which in the king-lists precedes that of Ur, and it is clear that when these temples were built Ur-Nammu was a vassal of Utu-khegal; it was by rebellion against his master that he made himself overlord of the empire.

When once he had established his position as independent king Ur-Nammu showed himself an indefatigable builder, but especially was he determined to make his own city worthy of its rank as capital. Probably during the long period of subjection to foreign kings and the comparative poverty which had resulted from that subjection the temples of the gods had fallen into disrepair; in any case, they were old and out of date; the programme of the new ruler provided for a virtual rebuilding of the whole central part of the city.

What strikes one most about the extant work of Ur-Nammu is its amazing solidity; he seemed to build for all time and shrank from no amount of labour to that end, and it is no wonder that his reign of eighteen years did not suffice for the completion of all he planned. Last winter we carried out some experimental work on the city walls and discovered the substructure of the defences with which Ur-Nammu encircled his capital. Rising 26 feet or more above the plain and acting as retaining-wall to the platform on which the town buildings were raised, there was a rampart constructed of unbaked brick throughout which at its base was no less than 77 feet thick! The wall proper, built of baked brick, which ran along the top of the rampart, has disappeared at the point where our trial excavations were made, but, judging from the unusually large size of the bricks employed for it, it must have been a very solid structure; but even apart from that, few kings would lightly embark on the task of putting up a wall 77 feet thick around a space which must measure some three-quarters of a mile in length and nearly half a mile in width, yet this was not the only work of Ur-Nammu and scarcely even the greatest.

About seventy-five years ago Mr. J. E. Taylor, then British Consul at Basra, was engaged by the British Museum to investigate some of the ancient sites of southern Mesopotamia, and amongst others he visited Ur, in those days a place difficult and dangerous of access. Struck by the obvious importance of one mound, which from its height, overshadowing all the other ruins, he rightly judged to be the Ziggurat, he attacked it from above, cutting down into the brickwork of the four corners. The science of field archaeology had not then been devised and the excavator's object was to find things that might

Copper Figure of a Sumerian Ruler Carrying a Basket

enrich the cases of a museum, while the preservation of buildings on the spot was little considered. To the greatest monument of Ur Taylor did damage which we cannot but deplore to-day, but he succeeded in his purpose and at least made clear the importance of the site whose later excavation has so well repaid us. Hidden in the brickwork of the top stage of the tower he found, at each angle of it, cylinders of baked clay on which were long inscriptions giving the history of the building. The texts date from about 550 B.C., from the time of Nabonidus, the last of the kings of Babylon, and state that the tower, founded by Ur-Nammu and his son Dungi, but left unfinished by them and not completed by any later king, he had restored and finished. These inscriptions not only gave us the first information obtained about the Ziggurat itself, but identified the site, called by the Arabs al Mughair, the Mound of Pitch, as Ur 'of the Chaldees,' the biblical home of Abraham.

Taylor's excavations did not go very far. Those were the days when Rawlinson was unearthing in the north of Mesopotamia the colossal human-headed bulls and pictured wall-slabs which now enrich the British Museum, and dazzled by such discoveries people could not realise the value of the odds and ends which alone rewarded the explorer in the south: the site was deserted, and the upper stage of the Ziggurat which Taylor had exposed was left to the mercies of the weather and of Arab builders in search of cheap ready-made bricks, and when British troops advanced to Mughair in 1915 only a few bits of ragged brick showed at the corners of a mound up which a man could ride on horseback. In 1918 part of one end was cleared by Dr. Hall, and it was found that lower down the casing was wonderfully well preserved. In 1922-3 the excavation of the tower was seriously taken in hand and for two seasons employed a large number of our men, while work on the surrounding buildings was continued until 1929.

The amount of rubbish which had to be removed before the ruins of the tower stood free was very great, running into thousands of tons, and in all this mass we found scarcely any objects of interest. Near the surface of the lower part of the slope there were quantities of bricks covered with a bright blue glaze, wreckage from the little shrine with which Nabonidus had crowned the ancient monument; flung down in a gateway at the back of the tower we found the mutilated statue of Enteremena to which reference has already been made, and in front of the tower fragments of an inscription on black stone, of late date, recording the buying-up of various blocks of house property for the enlargement of a temple; but otherwise we had to be content with the tower itself as the result of our prolonged toil. And it was a result well worth having. The top part, as we knew beforehand, was the work of Nabonidus, but the bulk of the construction was original, and on its bricks could be read the name and title of the first founder.

The Ziggurat is a peculiar feature of Sumerian architecture and as such calls for explanation. I have already said that we do not quite know who the Sumerians are; tradition would make them come from the East; the study of their bones and skulls shows that they were a branch of the Indo-European stock of the human race resembling what is called Caucasian man, a people who in stature and in appearance might pass as modern Europeans rather than as Orientals. Geographically, it is likely that their original homeland was in hilly country, and this is made more likely by certain facts such as that their gods are often represented standing upon mountains and the animals pictured in their art are often of a mountain type, while the evidence that their temple architecture was really a translation into brick of an original timber structure would indicate that they had first learnt to build in a wooded and therefore in a high-lying country. People living in a mountainous land nearly always associate their religion with the outstanding natural features of that land and worship their gods on 'high places,' and this would seem to have been true of the Sumerians. When they moved down into the alluvial plain of the Euphrates they found themselves in a country where there were no hills meet for the service of god, a country

Restoration of a House of the Time of Abraham in Ur

so flat that even a private house, if it was to be safe from the periodic inundations, had to be raised on an artificial platform. The latter fact supplied a hint as to how the former difficulty could be solved: the platform had only to be built high enough, and there, made by man, was the high place which nature had failed to provide; and so the Sumerians set to work to build —using 'bricks instead of stone, and slime (bitumen) had

they for mortar'—a 'ziggurat' whose name might be called
'the Hill of Heaven' or 'the Mountain of God.' In every important city there was at least one such tower crowned by a
sanctuary, the tower itself forming part of a larger temple
complex; of them all the biggest and the most famous was
the Ziggurat of Babylon, which in Hebrew tradition became
the Tower of Babel, now entirely destroyed, but its ground-
plan shows that it was but a repetition on a larger scale of
the Ziggurat at Ur, the best-preserved of all these monuments.

The Ziggurat stands at the back of the temple of Nannar
the Moon-god, of which it is the main feature. The outer court
of the temple was a terrace raised 10 feet or more above the
level in front of it, and behind the court rose a second and
higher terrace on which stood the sanctuary and the tower.
The tower measures a little more than 200 feet in length by
150 feet in width, and its original height was about 70 feet;
the whole thing is one solid mass of brickwork, the core being
of unbaked brick and the face a skin of baked brick set in
bitumen, about 8 feet thick. The walls, relieved by shallow
buttresses, are battered, or built with a pronounced inward
slope, and stand some 50 feet high; this forms the lowest stage.
Above this point the tower is taken up in steps or stages each
smaller than the one below, leaving narrow passages along the
main sides and wider terraces at either end; but the stages are
curiously unsymmetrical, so that there are three storeys at
the north-west end of the building and four at the south-east
end, all communicating by flights of brick stairs; on the top-
most storey, which was virtually a square, stood the little
shrine of the god.

On three sides the walls rose sheer to the level of the first
terrace, but on the north-east face fronting the Nannar temple
was the approach to the shrine. Three brick stairways, each of
a hundred steps, led upwards, one projecting out at right
angles from the building, two leaning against its wall, and all
converging in a great gateway on the level of the second terrace; from this gate a single flight of stairs ran straight up to

the door of the shrine, while lateral passages with smaller flights of stairs gave access to the terraces at either end of the tower; the angles formed by the three main stairways were filled in with solid flat-topped buttress-towers.

When first we started the work of drawing out the plan and elevations of the Ziggurat we were puzzled to find that the different measurements never seemed to agree; then it was discovered that in the whole building there is not a single straight line, and that what we had assumed to be such were in fact carefully calculated curves. The walls not only slope inwards, but the line from top to bottom is slightly convex; on the ground plan the wall line from corner to corner of the building has a distinct outward bend, so that sighting along it one can only see as far as the centre; the architect has aimed at an optical illusion which the Greek builders of the Parthenon at Athens were to achieve many centuries afterwards, the curves being so slight as not to be apparent, yet enough to give to the eye an appearance of strength where a straight line might by contrast with the mass behind it have seemed incurved and weak. The employment of such a device does great credit to the builders of the twenty-third century before Christ.

Indeed, the whole design of the building is a masterpiece. It would have been so easy to pile rectangle of brickwork above rectangle, and the effect would have been soulless and ugly; as it is, the heights of the different stages are skillfully calculated, the slope of the walls leads the eye upwards and inwards to the centre, the sharper slope of the triple staircase accentuates that of the walls and fixes the attention on the shrine above, which was the religious focus of the whole structure, while across these converging lines cut the horizontal planes of the terraces, the division of the building which they effect being emphasised by zones of colour. At least in the latter period the lower stages were painted black, the uppermost was red, and the shrine, as we have seen, was covered with blue-glazed tiles, and it is probable that the shrine roof took the form of a dome of gilded metal: these colours had their mystical significance and stood for the various divisions

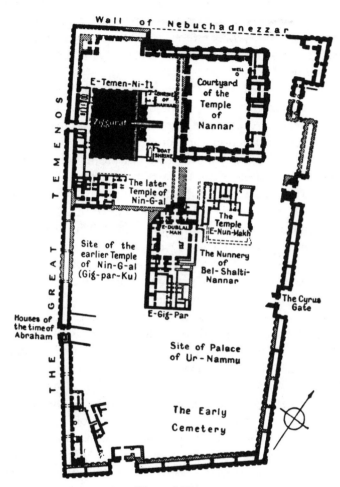

Plan of Ur

of the universe, the dark underworld, the habitable earth, the heavens, and the sun.

No one looking at the Ziggurat can fail to notice the tall and narrow slits which at regular intervals and in rows one above another pierce the brickwork of the walls; they run clean through the burnt-brick casing and deep into the mud brick of the core, where they are loosely filled with broken pottery. These are 'weeper-holes' intended to drain the interior, a necessary precaution, for with damp the mud brick would swell and make the outer walls bulge if it did not burst them altogether.

This is the obvious and correct explanation and for a long time it satisfied us; but then the difficulty arose, how was the damp likely to get into the core? There was no real danger at the time of construction, for though there would then be plenty of water in the mud mortar used for the crude bricks, this would dry—indeed, with so vast an area to build over, one course would be virtually dry before the next was laid above it—and the tendency of the core would be to shrink rather than to expand. It is true that torrential rains fall in Mesopotamia, but in the days of the Third Dynasty it was usual to lay pavements of burnt brick two, three, or even five courses thick set in bitumen mortar, and no surface water could penetrate this and do harm below. If there had been such a pavement, the precaution was needless; and if there was not such, why not? And further, at each end of the tower there is in one of the buttresses a deep recess in the brickwork running from the edge of the first terrace to the ground, and at the bottom of this there is what engineers call an "apron,' a mass of brick waterproofed with bitumen and built with its top at a slant calculated to carry off smoothly and without splash water falling from above: evidently there was water on the terrace.

In the doorway of a room of late date lying against the brick wall of the tower we found the great diorite hinge-stone bearing an inscription of Nabonidus in which he refers to his repairs of the building and states that he cleared the 'Gig-par-ku' of fallen branches. As the excavations progressed we were able to establish that the Gig-par-ku was a part of the temple complex dedicated to the Moon-goddess, and that it lay close under the south-east end of the Ziggurat; somehow the site of this building had become encumbered with branches of trees. There may have been trees in the Gig-par-ku itself, but as most of it was roofed in, this is not very likely; and the only other place from which the branches could have fallen into it was the Ziggurat itself.

This explains the weeper-holes. The terraces of Ur-Nammu's staged tower were not paved with brick but were covered with soil, and in this trees were planted; the long recesses in the buttresses may have carried off the waters of a violent storm, but they may equally have served as water-hoists for the irrigation of the terrace; and what made possible the swelling of the core of the tower and therefore necessitated the weeper-holes in its facing was just this irrigation—the water poured at the roots of the trees would percolate through the top soil into the crude brick, and if it had no outlet would really endanger the building.

Thus we have to imagine trees clothing every terrace with greenery, hanging gardens which brought more vividly to mind the original conception of the Ziggurat as the Mountain of God, and we shall recognise how much better the sloping outer walls harmonise with this conception, rising as they do like the abrupt bare sides of some pine-topped crag, than if they had been uncompromisingly vertical, the walls of a house of man's building.

With the destruction of the upper storey there is nothing left to show the character of the shrine as built by Ur-Nammu, but from what does remain we can see how splendid a monument his Ziggurat was and how well adapted for the use of those processions which formed a part of Sumerian religious ritual; the priests in robes of state bearing the statue and emblem of Nannar up and down the triple staircase against the background of coloured brick and trees must have made a magnificent spectacle, and it is easy to think that some tradition of these great feast-days was at the bottom of the vision which showed to Jacob ladders set up to Heaven and the angels ascending and descending on them. Yet the tower was only one part of the Temple of Nannar. Against one side of it lay the sanctuary of that temple, and in front of it, at a lower level, stretched the great court, a paved space some ninety yards across surrounded with chambers and storerooms and en-

Spouted Gold Libation Cup, Fluted Gold Tumbler
and Fluted Gold Bowl from the Royal Cemetery at Ur

tered by a triple gate passing under a high gate tower. The
excavation of this has taken us a long time, and the temple had
been so often altered and repaired that not much of the original
founder's work survives, but its plan and a good deal of its
history have come to light.

The walls which we first found when we came to dig deep

along the confines of the temple were not those of the Third Dynasty at all; we got down to the foundations of the terrace and yet no sign of them appeared, and it looked as if they had been completely destroyed. Then it was found that a king reigning about three hundred years after Ur-Nammu had enlarged the terrace on which the court of the temple stands and had built a new retaining wall outside the old and, filling up the space between them with rubbish, had erected his new flanking chambers along the edge of the wider platform: we had to dig through the floors of these chambers to find the buried remains of the old terrace wall.

When it was found, a fresh problem arose: the lower section of the wall which supported the terrace was of mud bricks whose size proved them to be of Third Dynasty date, but they bore no stamp of authorship; such of the superstructure as was left, the walls of the range of rooms built along the terrace edge and enclosing the courtyard, were of burnt bricks stamped with the name not of Ur-Nammu but of his son Dungi. The bricks of the Ziggurat bear Ur-Nammu's name exclusively, the Ziggurat is part of the temple, and until the lower terrace of the courtyard was built the construction of the Ziggurat terrace and of the Ziggurat itself could not have been begun; therefore the mud-brick wall upholding the courtyard terrace must have been the work of Ur-Nammu. The inscribed cylinders of Nabonidus found by Taylor in the upper brickwork of the tower state that it was built by Ur-Nammu and his son Dungi; in the Ziggurat itself we have found no trace of Dungi's work, but since tower and temple are essentially one we can apply the statement to the whole building and see how well it harmonises with discovered facts.

Ur-Nammu started, as he was bound to do, with the sub-structures, the lower terrace which was to be the courtyard area, the higher terrace which was to be the platform for the temple sanctuary and the Ziggurat. As soon as that was done, he concentrated all his efforts on the sanctuary (where we find his brick-stamps commonly) and on the great tower, and so far as the evidence of the ruins goes he finished both these;

then, before the walls of the outer court had risen above
ground-level, the king died. Probably the early part of his
reign of eighteen years had been spent in war, and during
most of it he may have been absent from his capital and not
so firmly established that he could afford to spend much time
and money on bricks and mortar; certainly his building activity
seems to have been confined rather to his later years and had
been deferred too long; the temple of Nannar is not the only
case at Ur where we have found the father's work completed
by the son. In this case it was the outer court which Dungi
had to build, and the fact of the divided authorship enables
us to date the building with unusual precision—the scanty
relics of burnt-brick construction which define the outlines
of the court chambers belong to the very first years of the
reign of the new king.

Very little of his work is preserved, and it would have been
impossible to make out even its groundplan but for the pious
conservativism which Mesopotamian rulers observed in most
of their dealings with temples; however thorough might be
the repairs required, even though they amounted to the complete reconstruction of the fabric, the restorers were nearly
always at pains to reproduce as nearly as might be the general
lay-out of the old building. Very often they would raze the
old walls but leave in position one course of bricks to serve
as a guide to the new builders, and when such reconstruction
has been repeated more than once we may find in the lowest
four or five courses of the standing walls bricks stamped with
the names of three or four kings of different dates, giving with
each course a fresh chapter in the life-history of the temple.
Here Dungi's walls had not been used as a substructure for
the new building, but were buried uselessly beneath its floors,
hacked away and cut across in every direction by the labourers
who dug the trenches for the foundations of the larger temple,
but just enough was preserved to prove that the new work did
reproduce, though on a larger scale and in a more ornate form,
the Third Dynasty model, and we could with full confidence
complete on paper a plan which in the field was represented

only by fragments of brickwork, shapeless and at first sight without meaning.

When we were clearing the ruins of the sanctuary lying under the shadow of the Ziggurat on its northwest side we found, re-used as hinge-sockets in a later doorway, two fragments of limestone carved in relief; in the courtyard of the temple Dublal-makh, some hundred and fifty yards away to the south-east, more carved fragments were discovered which actually fitted on to the first two, and another piece apparently belonging to the same monument turned up in the ruins of yet another temple, E-Nun-makh.

The fragments found thus widely scattered made up a considerable part of a limestone stela which originally measured 5 feet across and may have been as much as 15 feet high. It was sculptured on both sides and recorded in pictorial and in written form the achievements of Ur-Nammu. One scene at least commemorated the king's exploits in war, for we have him seated on his throne while prisoners with bound hands are led before him; two scenes show sacrifice to the gods; two panels, practically identical, are of a more unusual sort—the king is represented standing in the attitude of prayer, while an angel flying down from above pours water on to the ground from a vase held between his hands. An inscription giving a list of the canals in the neighbourhood of Ur dug by orders of the king explains the scene: Ur-Nammu has been responsible for the actual earth-work of the canals, but he assigns to the gods credit for the blessed gift of water which brings fertility to the land. It is a pleasing instance of modesty in a great king, and the earliest representation of an angel in art.

But there was another act of which Ur-Nammu seems to have been particularly proud, seeing that to it were devoted no less than three distinct panels of the relief, and that is the construction of the Ziggurat. In one scene the ruler is shown twice over making libations, on the one side to Nannar and on the other side to his wife the goddess Nin-Gal, and Nannar holds out to him the measuring-rod and coiled line of the architect, thereby symbolising his wish that Ur-Nammu should

Silver Harp from the Royal Cemetery at Ur

build him a house. In the next scene, sadly incomplete, the king obediently presents himself before the god bearing on his shoulder the tools of the architect and of the builder, compasses, mortar-basket, pick and trowel; in a third, yet more fragmentary, the workmen are seen carrying hods of mortar up ladders and laying the bricks of the tower. It is an extraordinary chance which has given us together with the best preserved of all the ziggurats of Mesopotamia the contemporary record of its building, and scarcely less extraordinary was the chance which brought together fragments deliberately smashed and so widely scattered. The monument is still very far from complete, but at any moment we may discover fresh bits of what is undoubtedly the most important sculpture known from Ur.

The Ziggurat was itself so solidly built that we need not be surprised if it stood almost unaltered and unrepaired for seventeen hundred and fifty years, but the Nannar Temple underwent in that time many changes. In the courtyard we can trace various modifications some of which date from very little later than the time of Dungi its joint founder: new altars were erected; at one end there was built what seems to have been a miniature ziggurat with a secret chamber hidden in the heart of its brickwork; and then came the enlargement which has already been described. One feature of the new temple deserves special mention, for it was peculiar in itself and was to be copied by future restorers: the outer façade and the wall dividing the court from the sanctuary were decorated with brick half-columns, down the centre of which ran double grooves or recesses; this scheme of ornament, which belonged to the temple standing in Abraham's time, is in striking contrast to the normal Sumerian tradition of rectangles and heavy masses almost unrelieved and must have given to the building a grace quite new to the architects of Ur.

About six hundred years after this reconstruction the temple of Nannar had become so ruinous that the king who then reigned at Babylon and was overlord of the south country also razed its walls to the ground and built them afresh; for the outer façade he preferred a simpler style, plainly rectangular, but perhaps not less impressive; square buttresses with complicated re-entrant angles were set regularly along the front of the building with a deeper projection towards the centre, where there stood out boldly a huge gate-tower higher and more massive than that of former days; only inside the court the front wall of the sanctuary imitated with its rows of half-columns the work of six centuries before.

In about 650 B.C. fresh reconstruction was called for. During the preceding age various kings had carried out minor repairs, and we find new pavements of burnt brick laid down, the bricks stamped with the king's name, and old pavements patched with bricks nameless or borrowed from some other work; but now the governor who ruled Ur in the name of the king of Assyria was obliged by the state of the chief temple of the city to embark on a more thorough-going restoration. It is eloquent of the low estate on which Ur had fallen in these latter days that the Assyrian's work should have been of so shoddy a character; where he employed burnt bricks for wall foundations they were old material collected from the ruins, mere house-breakers' rubbish, and all his new buildings were in mud brick disguised by plaster and whitewash, while his floors were but of beaten mud.

When we started digging out the temple, the very first wall encountered was that of the Assyrian period dividing the court from the sanctuary, and at first it puzzled us not a little. Close below the modern surface a mud-brick wall was found and the pickman was ordered to follow it along; it ran straight for perhaps a yard, then took four right-angled turns in the length of a foot, then swelled out in a bold curve which after 2 feet or so was broken by the eight angles of a double recess and continued in a fresh curve back to the original line, only to curve out again as before. The workman, hard put to it to distinguish the crumbling brick at all, was further bewildered by these seemingly inconsequential meanderings of what ought to have been a straight face, and reported that the wall was mad. Mistrusting his work, for it is only too easy for a man armed with a pick to carve the soft mud brick into a shape quite other than that which the builder gave it, I ordered him to retrace his steps and dig deeper to a level at which the bricks might be better preserved; he did so, and at a depth to which the rain-water did not penetrate to rot the brickwork found the wall with its coating of mud plaster and whitewash, pitted indeed by the ravages of the white ant, but almost intact.

It was the wall built by Sin-balatsu-ikbi the Assyrian more than 2,500 years ago, with its row of half-columns and recesses copied from a model nearly 1,500 years older still, and the

The Ziggurat of Ur-Nammu. Restored Sketch; the Temple
Buildings in the Angles of the Stairs are Omitted from
this Reconstruction

whitewash was no worse than one might see on any modern
house in the nearest market-town of Iraq; it was crumbly, and
a touch would flake it off, but it was the pride of our Arab
pickmen to use their tools so delicately that the columns freed
from the earth glistened white, and though the rains of one
winter washed away virtually every trace of whitewash and
mortar and reduced the sharp angles and curves of the brickwork to a shapeless wavy line, yet we have photographs in
which the lower part of the wall at least looks as it did when
the Assyrians were masters of Ur.

One good reason for the wonderful preservation of the whitewash was that the walls had not stood very long above ground. Within fifty years of their being built, the lower part of them had been protected by a solid casing of earth. Nebuchadnezzar, who was king of Babylon about 600 B.C., once more repaired the Nannar temple, and part of his scheme was to bring the forecourt and the sanctuary to one level by raising the former; masses of soil were heaped over Sin-balatsu-ikbi's mud floor and a new brick pavement was laid down over this. Using the buried footing of the old walls as a foundation, he built new walls in mud brick with doorways at the new level, sank a well at one end of the court so as to have a handy supply of water for the temple rites, and then remodelled the sanctuary also, adding to it another wing on the south-east side of the Ziggurat and putting here a shrine which, judging from the long narrow brick base occupying the greater part of the chamber, was a 'boat shrine' containing the model of the ship in which the Moon-god crossed the sky—that high-prowed and high-sterned ship which is so like the moon's crescent.

This was the last transformation which the ancient temple was to undergo; no other royal builder interested himself in it, and before very long, when the Persian conquerors of Mesopotamia changed their religion and adopted Zoroastrianism with its worship of unembodied fire, Nannar's great house, like all the old temples, was doomed to destruction. Of Nebuchadnezzar's work very little survives today, only a few patches of brick pavement almost flush with the modern surface, a few bricks of the walls and, deeper underground, the brick boxes which shelter the hinge-stones of the doors and prove by their position against the jambs of the buried doors of the Assyrian that Nebuchadnezzar's temple followed the lines of its predecessor: very little, but just enough to complete the life history of the most famous of the temples of Ur.

From the sixth century B.C. back to the twenty-third we have traced the evidence of reconstruction and repair and have laid bare what remains of the great building which Ur-

Nammu planned and did not live to finish; but underneath that there is still made soil and in it enough to prove that the Third Dynasty temple was not the first to occupy the site, though of what went before it we shall never know much. In the courtyard we found only a few bricks of that 'plano-convex' type which goes back to the fourth millennium before Christ; but when we were following up the back wall of the temple enceinte which runs along the edge of the platform behind the Ziggurat, we came on more decisive evidence.

Inside Ur-Nammu's wall and parallel with it there ran underground, buried in the filling of the platform, a wall of mudbricks, slightly round-topped, though not quite of the type of those of the First Dynasty of Ur, which were laid not flat but on edge and slantwise, herringbone fashion. Experience shows that this peculiar style of building belongs to a period between the First and the Third dynasties, and provisionally we may assign it to that Second Dynasty of Ur about which in fact we know nothing at all. The herringbone wall not only is parallel to the later but shows traces of cross-walls belonging to a range of chambers exactly like the chambers in the double platform-wall of Ur-Nammu and his successors; it is an earlier version of the same thing and it must have had the same purpose, i.e. it enclosed a terrace on which stood a ziggurat and a temple of Nannar.

That there should have been a ziggurat at Ur before the days of Ur-Nammu is a foregone conclusion, for so important a city as Ur could not have but possessed, from the earliest time, one of those staged towers which were typical of Sumerian architecture; now we know precisely where it stood. Underneath the vast bulk of the Ziggurat which we see to-day there lies whatever may remain of an older and a smaller tower: built probably as early as the reign of Mes-anni-pad-da and repaired, as can be assumed from the existence of the mud-brick wall, by some nameless king of the Second Dynasty, the old ziggurat was used by Ur-Nammu as a foundation for his more ambitious building and either buried beneath the level of his new terrace or, more probably, embedded in the core of his tower. It would be a crime on our part to destroy one of the principal monuments of Iraq merely to prove the existence of what we know must have existed, and the chance is slight that we should find any such treasures as enriched the platform of the temple at al-'Ubaid, which in like fashion was buried beneath a new platform built by king Dungi: here theory must suffice, for we shall never see the older Ziggurat of Ur.

In describing the temple I have more than once had occasion to mention the hinge-sockets of the doors, and the phrase calls for explanation. The Sumerian door consisted of a wooden leaf fixed to a pole rather higher than itself; the top end of the pole was held by a metal ring projecting from the corner of the door lintel and revolved in it; the lower end was shod with metal and went down through a hole in the pavement to rest and turn on the hinge-stone. This was a boulder of imported hard stone, limestone or diorite, in which a cup-shaped hollow had been cut to take the pole-shoe, and generally one part of it (when the door was that of a temple) had been smoothed and inscribed with the name of the king who dedicated the building and of the god in whose honour he built it.

Door-sockets are thus invaluable evidence for the date and nature of the buildings we unearth; they have to be used with caution, because imported stones were valuable and an old socket would often be taken away and re-used for some other building than that for which it was first intended and the old inscription may no longer apply, but even so the text may yield new facts, and where the stone is certainly in its original position the information it gives may be invaluable. Without such inscriptions it would have been impossible to identify the sanctuary of the Nannar temple and so to complete its groundplan; we had not suspected its position and had no notion of the form it might assume, and the walls of the Ur-Nammu building were so terribly ruined, seldom standing at all above floor level, that at first little could be made of them. The door-sockets lying below floor-level and therefore undis-

"Ram in the Thicket" from Ur

turbed bore the inscription 'the House of Nannar,' and from their position on the wall-line we could fix the whereabouts of the chamber doors, thus giving sense to the plan.

One furnished us with a new experience. The wall had vanished and only part of the bitumen-covered brick pavement was left, but in it was a square hole filled with earth; going down into this we found not only the block of diorite with Ur-Nammu's inscription but, still standing upright in the worn cup-like hollow in which it had once revolved, the copper shoe of the hinge-pole with a duplicate inscription on its side. The contrast between the complete destruction of the building above ground and the preservation of the hinge which had not even lost its balance on the stone could not but impress one.

At the far end of what we call the Sacred Area, the enclosure which contained the various buildings dedicated to the Moon-god or to the minor deities associated with him, there is another building of king Ur-Nammu. Part of this was excavated seventy years ago by Taylor, and where he dug very little of the structure survives to-day; another part was excavated by Dr. Hall, and the final clearing was done by the Joint Expedition. Dr. Hall found that the paved floors were of bricks stamped with the name of Dungi and giving the name of the building as 'the House of the Mountain,' apparently a palace. When we dug here we found that the bricks of the actual walls were stamped with Ur-Nammu's name and the title of the building was merely 'the House of Nannar,' which might apply to almost any section of the Sacred Area.

Here there was a contradiction which had to be straightened out, so we searched the corners of the building for a 'foundation-deposit' and duly found what we had hoped for: built into the wall foundations at each corner there was a box of burnt bricks lined with matting and waterproofed with bitumen, and in each box there stood a copper object of which the upper half was a human figure from the waist upwards and the lower half more like a nail or cone; the figure was that of the royal founder presented in the guise of a temple servant or labourer bearing on his head a basket of mortar: in front of the figure there lay a small stone cut into the shape of a brick, the foundation-stone of the building. It was the regular custom at this period in Sumerian history to bury such statuettes and stones in the foundation-boxes, and the king's name and the name of the temple were recorded on the front of the figure and on the polished surface of the stone. What was, then, our dismay when, having looked to these very objects to solve all our difficulties, we found them absolutely blank! There was nothing to show whether the statuette represented Dungi or Ur-Nammu, whether the building were a palace or a temple. Then we had recourse to the doorways, and at every one we found a socket-stone in place, and not one bore a sign of inscription.

As the clearing of the building progressed its resemblance to the normal temple became more and more clear. At one end there was an entrance leading into a wide but shallow court from which a double gateway flanked by what seemed to be purification-chambers gave access to the main or inner court; on the far side of this two doors led through little antechambers into a long room which corresponded exactly with the sanctuary or Holy of Holies in other temples close by. A heavy wall running right through the building separated the 'temple' part from a complex of chambers clearly of a more domestic nature and divided into two apparently residential units each consisting of rooms grouped about an open central court; one of the groups was reached directly by a doorway from the inner court of the 'temple,' the other only by a winding passage and double doors from the 'sanctuary.' Most temples contained residential quarters for the priests, and therefore everything in the arrangement of this building agreed with its identification as a temple. But as against this there was the ambiguity of the texts on the bricks of the floor and the walls respectively, the uncompromising blankness of the foundation-figures, which ought to have been inscribed, and the equal blankness of the door-sockets—and we have never yet found a temple in which none of the door-stones bore an inscription. It was an archæological problem to which perhaps no final solution can be given, but one which the archæologist ought to do his best to solve so far as the evidence allows.

The contradiction in the question of authorship presents no great difficulty. The walls of a building must be put up before the floors are laid, and the two operations need not be the work of one person. Ur-Nammu built the walls and then died, leaving the building unfinished as he had left unfinished the Temple of Nannar, and his son Dungi put the final touches to it. Ur-Nammu calls it the 'House of Nannar,' which need mean no more than that it formed part of the group of religious foundations under the patronage of the god; Dungi may possibly have used for the floors bricks manufactured for another building whose site we have not yet discovered, but there is no need to assume this, and his name 'the House of the Mountain' may quite well be the particular name of the building more vaguely described by his father. Copper foundation-figures such as we found in the corner boxes were, so far as we know, only used for religious buildings, but then they are generally inscribed, and the fact that here they are not is against the building being really a temple, and the same is true of the door-sockets. The answer may be given by the ground-plan, which is so like that of a temple that it almost proves the building to be something else.

We know that according to Sumerian beliefs a king was the vice-gerent of god upon earth—'tenant-farmer,' they called him—and that the god was the real ruler of the land. The god then being the king, his court exactly reproduced that of his human representative. Attached to the principal temple there would be ministers of War and Justice, of Communications, of Agriculture, of Finance, of the Harem, and so on; and as with the personnel, so it was with the house in which the visible statue of him was lodged: in the sanctuary he received the adoration of those who might approach him, but he also had his bed-chamber, his place for dining, and necessarily, too, rooms and offices in which the business of his temple and estates could be carried on. It is most probable that in the details of its arrangements a great temple, which was the

House of God, afforded a close parallel to the palace which was the house of the king. We have many examples of temples and none hitherto of palaces, but because Ur-Nammu's building is so like a temple I think that we may accept Dungi's name for it and take it to be the palace of the kings of Ur.

If that be so, we might hazard an explanation of the copper statuettes. The Sumerian kings claimed divine powers and were deified in their lifetimes, so that the royal palace would fittingly be placed within the Sacred Area under Nannar's protection and its founding might well be marked by the same ritual as that of a temple; but where the building was in the king's own honour there would be a difficulty about the inscription on his statuette, and it might be omitted. We have never found an inscribed door-socket in a private house, and here the blank stone may mean that in Dungi's mind, as his brick inscriptions show, the idea of the palace of the earthly king overshadowed that of the house of god's vice-gerent himself deified.

Certainly in this light we can interpret the building satisfactorily. The temple-like section comprises the public reception rooms where the ruler, seated on his throne in the long back room, just like the god on his pedestal in the sanctuary, gave audience to his subjects gathered in the inner court; the two groups of residential quarters were for the king and his women-folk respectively, and the difference between them agrees well with this, one being easy of access, while the harem-rooms are hidden away and hard to come to.

I have gone at length into this subject because the interpretation of evidence is not the least important part of the field-worker's task, and I have chosen a problem to which the answer is not certain because it illustrates better the kind of difficulty which one encounters nearly every day and generally forgets as soon as it is solved. If the identification of the building which I have suggested is correct, it adds much to its interest, for it is no small thing to possess the ruins of the actual house of the greatest of the kings of Ur.

PART THREE.

——————

*The*

*City*

*of*

*Priam*

# 8. SCHLIEMANN:

# *The Excavation of Troy*

*The day shall come, the great avenging day,*
*Which Troy's proud glories in the dust shall lay*
*When Priam's powers and Priam's self shall fall,*
*And one prodigious ruin swallow all.*

—*The Iliad*
(Translated by Alexander Pope)

Is there an archaeologist more familiar to the general public than Heinrich Schliemann? Is there an epic greater than Homer's tale of the taking of Troy? I think not. Schliemann has become a legendary character in his own right, fit to match the great story that inspired his career.

Homer has always been read. But, until the 19th century —until the coming of a monomaniac named Schliemann, in fact—no one regarded the *Iliad* and the *Odyssey* as anything

more than colorful tale-spinning. The city of Troy? A myth.
Agamemnon, Priam, Odysseus, Achilles? The inventions of a
fertile bard. The ten years' siege, the sack of Troy? A grand
fantasy, no more.

Then came Schliemann, with his *idée fixe* that Homer had
been no tale-spinner but a war correspondent. Born in 1822 in
Ankhershagen, Germany, Schliemann grew up hearing the
tales of Homer until he knew them from memory, and the
exploits of Ajax and Hector became more real to him than his
own drab childhood. When he was 7, his father gave him a
book that showed Troy ablaze and as he stared at the gaudy
illustration, it struck the boy that walls so massive as those of
Troy could not simply have vanished from the earth. That
those walls might never have existed did not occur to him.

Troy obsessed him. A drunken miller's helper began one
night to recite the verses of Homer, and young Schliemann
bribed him with brandy to declaim them thrice over, though
he could not understand a word. It was Greek, it was the
story of Troy, and that was enough to satisfy Schliemann.

At 19, Schliemann went to sea as a cabin-boy. Shipwrecked
off the Netherlands, he settled in Amsterdam, found a clerical
job, and began an impressive self-education in modern languages with the hope of improving his position. He mastered
English in six months, French in six months more, and went
on to Dutch, Spanish, Italian, and Portuguese without great
effort. "It did not take me more than six weeks to write each
of these languages and to speak them fluently," he tells us in
the autobiographical foreword to *Troy and Its Remains*.

Russian was the next language Schliemann conquered, and
in 1846 his employers sent him off to St. Petersburg as their
representative. He broke away, and at the age of 25 founded
his own mercantile house in Russia. Commerce kept him too
busy to learn new languages over the next seven years and,
he notes, "it was not until the year 1854 that I found it possible
to acquire the Swedish and Polish languages."

All this time Schliemann never lost his obsessive interest in
Homer. But the job of earning his fortune came first, which

is why he postponed the study of classical Greek until 1856 while learning more useful tongues. Six weeks with modern Greek gave him a mastery of it, and then he turned to Homer's language.

During these years, Schliemann had been growing wealthy and had travelled widely. He turned up in California just in time for the gold rush of 1849, opened a bank there, and reaped a new fortune. (He also became an American citizen while he was there.) In 1858, Schliemann travelled through the Near East, from Cairo to Jerusalem—he acquired a knowledge of Arabic en route—and the following year was about to visit Odysseus' Ithaca when illness compelled him to return to St. Petersburg.

In 1863, at 41, Schliemann retired from commerce, "in order to devote myself exclusively to the studies which have the greatest fascination for me." A projected trip to the Homeric lands in 1864 was cancelled when "I allowed myself to be persuaded to visit India, China, and Japan, and to travel round the world." He spent two years on this journey, then settled in Paris for a period of study, and it was not until 1868, at 46, that he finally set foot in the land of Homer.

Schliemann knew that the best scholarship of his day proclaimed the stories of Homer pure myth. He brushed these notions aside. He visited Ithaca first, sitting in the village square and reading Homer to the descendants of Odysseus. "I forgot heat and thirst," he wrote. "Now I was investigating the neighborhood, reading in the *Odyssey* the stirring scenes enacted there, now admiring the splendid panorama."

He dug in Ithaca and published his results, which were of no great significance. But his real interest was excavating the site of Troy, and there he turned in 1869.

It was agreed that if Troy had existed at all, its location had been in Asia Minor, along the coast of Asian Turkey. A village called Bunarbashi was the traditional site. Schliemann went there, accompanied by his second wife, the beautiful, 17-year-old Sophia whom he had married the year before. *Iliad* in hand, he prowled the muddy village of Bunarbashi,

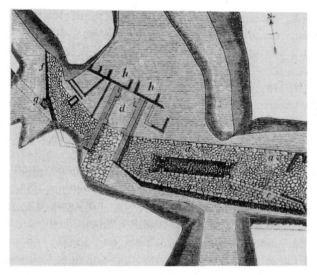

Schliemann's Map of the Tower and Scæan Gate

comparing its topography to that described by Homer, and soon concluded that the resemblance between Bunarbashi and Homer's Troy was slight and fortuitous. Pondering his text—which he regarded as an historical document—Schliemann surveyed the area and fastened upon the village of Hissarlik as the site of Troy.

The rest of the story is an often-told one. Schliemann began digging in April, 1870 and was rewarded with layer after layer of ancient settlements. One of these he identified as Priam's Troy. He was mistaken in this, as work by the American archaeologist Carl William Blegen showed in 1939. But Schliemann *had* found Troy—it was one of the other cities on the mound at Hissarlik.

In his early work at Hissarlik, Schliemann worked hastily

and destructively, cutting a huge trench through the mound and doing incalculable damage to the many strata, creating the kind of confusion that Flinders Petrie, in another context, called "ghastly charnel houses of murdered evidences." But Schliemann's archaeological technique improved after he added to his staff a young German, Wilhelm Dörpfeld, who impressed upon him the importance of slow, cautious work and diligent record-keeping. Schliemann's later work at Troy—and other sites at Mycenae and Tiryns—was outstanding for its time, so far as understanding of stratigraphy went. Still, there was a certain barbarism in the way he hewed through "unimportant" cities high up in the mound in order to reach the city of Priam, and later archaeologists at Hissarlik have had reason to bemoan Schliemann's lack of subtlety.

Regrettable as Schliemann's methods sometimes were, there is no denying the towering nature of his achievement. He found Troy and confounded the musty scholars who called the *Iliad* mythology. His later work at Mycenae, the city of Agamemnon, revealed the pre-Homeric Aegean culture that has been the subject of much 20th-century excavation and speculation. Most important, the stream of books that came from Schliemann's busy pen captivated the world and no doubt served as recruiting literature for the new generation of archaeologists, just as Layard's books had done thirty years earlier.

Schliemann was a great pioneer. He opened the entire field of Aegean archaeology, and served as publicity agent supreme for the archaeological science. The work he set in motion is still going on with startling new accomplishments all the time. And his bulky volumes, lavishly illustrated with photographs and stratigraphic data, were the first archaeological field reports with any pretense to scientific organization.

The one great failure of Schliemann's career came on the island of Crete. Late in his life, he went to Crete to search for the fabled palace of King Minos. But he spent three years in negotiations for the right to dig and, unable to come to terms with the owner of the mound where Minos' palace lay, Schliemann had to leave Crete in 1889 with nothing accomplished. A year later, he was dead. It remained for an Englishman, Arthur Evans, to find the palace of Minos a decade later.

Three of Schliemann's books deal with his work at Troy—all of them published in English by the house of John Murray. The best known of the three is *Ilios*, published in 1881, an 800-page account of his experiences at Troy. It was followed in 1884 by *Troja*, which tells of Schliemann's later work at Troy.

The selection which follows, however, comes from *Troy and Its Remains* (1875), which is Schliemann's day-by-day diary of the Hissarlik excavations, and which has an immediacy and a spontaneity not to be found in the later works. For all Schliemann's mastery of languages, he did not attempt to translate *Troy and Its Remains* himself; the task was performed by Philip Smith.

## THE EXCAVATION OF TROY

In my work 'Ithaca, the Peloponnesus, and Troy,' published in 1869, I endeavoured to prove, both by the result of my own excavations and by the statements of the Iliad, that the Homeric Troy cannot possibly have been situated on the heights of Bunarbashi, to which place most archæologists assign it. At the same time I endeavoured to explain that the site of Troy must necessarily be identical with the site of that town which, throughout all antiquity and down to its complete destruction at the end of the eighth or the beginning of the ninth century A.D., was called Ilium, and not until 1000 years after its disappearance—that is 1788 A.D.—was christened Ilium Novum by Lechevalier, who, as his work proves, can never have visited his *Ilium Novum;* for in his map he places it on the other side of the Scamander, close to *Kum-*

From *Troy and Its Remains* (London: John Murray, 1875) by Heinrich Schliemann, translated from the German by Philip Smith.

*kaleh,* and therefore 4 miles from its true position.

The site of Ilium is upon a plateau lying on an average about 80 feet above the Plain, and descending very abruptly on the north side. Its north-western corner is formed by a hill about 26 feet higher still, which is about 705 feet in breadth and 984 in length, and from its imposing situation and natural fortifications this hill of *Hissarlik* seems specially suited to be the Acropolis of the town. Ever since my first visit, I never doubted that I should find the Pergamus of Priam in the depths of this hill. In an excavation which I made on its north-western corner in April 1870, I found among other things, at a depth of 16 feet, walls about 6½ feet thick, which, as has now been proved, belong to a bastion of the time of Lysimachus. Unfortunately I could not continue those excavations at the time, because the proprietors of the field, two Turks in Kum-Kaleh, who had their sheepfolds on the site, would only grant me permission to dig further on condition that I would at once pay them 12,000 piasters for damages, and in addition they wished to bind me, after the conclusion of my excavations, to put the field in order again. As this did not suit my convenience, and the two proprietors would not sell me the field at any price, I applied to his Excellency Safvet Pacha, the Minister of Public Instruction, who at my request, and in the interest of science, managed that Achmed Pacha, the Governor of the Dardanelles and the Archipelago, should receive orders from the Ministry of the Interior to have the field valued by competent persons, and to force the proprietors to sell it to the Government at the price at which it had been valued: it was thus obtained for 3000 piasters.

In trying to obtain the necessary firman for continuing my excavations, I met with new and great difficulties, for the Turkish Government are collecting ancient works of art for their recently established Museum in Constantinople, in consequence of which the Sultan no longer grants permission for making excavations. But what I could not obtain in spite of three journeys to Constantinople, I got at last through the intercession of my valued friend, the temporary *chargé d'af-*

*faires* of the United States to the Sublime Porte—Mr. John P. Brown, the author of the excellent work 'Ancient and Modern Constantinople' (London, 1868).

So on the 27th of September I arrived at the Dardanelles with my firman. But here again I met with difficulties, this time on the part of the before named Achmed Pacha, who imagined that the position of the field which I was to excavate was not accurately enough indicated in the document, and therefore would not give me his permission for the excavations until he should receive a more definite explanation from the Grand Vizier. Owing to the change of ministry which had occurred, a long time would no doubt have elapsed before the matter was settled, had it not occurred to Mr. Brown to apply to his Excellency Kiamil-Pacha, the new Minister of Public Instruction, who takes a lively interest in science, and at whose intercession the Grand Vizier immediately gave Achmed Pacha the desired explanation. This, however, again occupied 13 days, and it was only on the evening of the 10th of October that I started with my wife from the Dardanelles for the Plain of Troy, a journey of eight hours. As, according to the firman, I was to be watched by a Turkish official, whose salary I have to pay during the time of my excavations, Achmed Pacha assigned to me the second secretary of his chancellary of justice, an Armenian, by name Georgios Sarkis, whom I pay 23 piasters daily.

At last, on Wednesday, the 11th of this month, I again commenced my excavations with 8 workmen, but on the following morning I was enabled to increase their number to 35, and on the 13th to 74, each of whom receives 9 piasters daily (1 franc 80 centimes). As, unfortunately, I only brought 8 wheelbarrows from France, and they cannot be obtained here, and cannot even be made in all the country round, I have to use 52 baskets for carrying away the rubbish. This work, however, proceeds but slowly and is very tiring, as the rubbish has to be carried a long way off. I therefore employ also four carts drawn by oxen, each of which again costs me 20 piasters a day. I work with great energy and spare no cost, in order, if possible, to reach the native soil before the winter rains set in, which may happen at any moment. Thus I hope finally to solve the great problem as to whether the hill of Hissarlik is—as I firmly believe—the citadel of Troy.

As it is an established fact that hills which consist of pure earth and are brought under the plough gradually disappear—that for instance, the Wartsberg, near the village of Ankershagen in Mecklenburg, which I once, as a child, considered to be the highest mountain in the world, has quite vanished in 40 years —so it is equally a fact, that hills on which, in the course of thousands of years, new buildings have been continually erected upon the ruins of former buildings, gain very considerably in circumference and height. The hill of Hissarlik furnishes the most striking proof of this. As already mentioned, it lies at the north-western end of the site of Ilium, which is distinctly indicated by the surrounding walls built by Lysimachus. In addition to the imposing situation of this hill within the circuit of the town, its present Turkish name of *Hissarlik*, "fortress" or "acropolis . . ."—seems also to prove that this is the Pergamus of Ilium; that here Xerxes (in 480 B.C.) offered up 1000 oxen to the Ilian Athena; that here Alexander the Great hung up his armour in the temple of the goddess, and took away in its stead some of the weapons dedicated therein belonging to the time of the Trojan war, and likewise sacrificed to the Ilian Athena. I conjectured that this temple, the pride of the Ilians, must have stood on the highest point of the hill, and I therefore decided to excavate this locality down to the native soil. But in order, at the same time, to bring to light the most ancient of the fortifying walls of the Pergamus, and to decide accurately how much the hill had increased in breadth by the *débris* which had been thrown down since the erection of those walls, I made an immense cutting on the face of the steep northern slope, about 66 feet from my last year's work. This cutting was made in a direction due south, and extended across the highest plateau, and was so broad that it embraced the whole building, the foundations of which, consisting of large hewn stones, I had already

Terra-cotta Vase, "Palace of Priam," Troy

laid open last year to a depth of from only 1 to 3 feet below
the surface. According to an exact measurement, this building,
which appears to belong to the first century after Christ, is
about 59 feet in length, and 43 feet in breadth. I have of course
had all these foundations removed as, being within my excavation, they were of no use and would only have been in the
way.

The difficulty of making excavations in a wilderness like
this, where everything is wanting, are immense and they increase day by day; for, on account of the steep slope of the hill,
the cutting becomes longer the deeper I dig, and so the difficulty of removing the rubbish is always increasing. This, moreover, cannot be thrown directly down the slope, for it would
of course only have to be carried away again; so it has to be
thrown down on the steep side of the hill at some distance to
the right and left of the mouth of the cutting. The numbers

of immense blocks of stone also, which we continually come upon, cause great trouble and have to be got out and removed, which takes up a great deal of time, for at the moment when a large block of this kind is rolled to the edge of the slope, all of my workmen leave their own work and hurry off to see the enormous weight roll down its steep path with a thundering noise and settle itself at some distance in the Plain. It is, moreover, an absolute impossibility for me, who am the only one to preside over all, to give each workman his right occupation, and to watch that each does his duty. Then, for the purpose of carrying away the rubbish, the side passages have to be kept in order, which likewise runs away with a great deal of time, for their inclinations have to be considerably modified at each step that we go further down.

Notwithstanding all these difficulties the work advances rapidly, and if I could only work on uninterruptedly for a month, I should certainly reach a depth of more than 32 feet, in spite of the immense breadth of the cutting. . . .

My dear wife, an Athenian lady, who is an enthusiastic admirer of Homer, and knows almost the whole of the 'Iliad' by heart, is present at the excavations from morning to night. I will not say anything about our mode of life in this solitude, where everything is wanting, and where we have to take four grains of quinine every morning as a precaution against the pestilential malaria. All of my workmen are Greeks, from the neighbouring village of Renkoï; only on Sunday, a day on which the Greeks do not work, I employ Turks. My servant, Nikolaos Zaphyros, from Renkoï, whom I pay 30 piasters a day, is invaluable to me in paying the daily wages of the workmen, for he knows every one of them, and is honest. Unfortunately, however, he gives me no assistance in the works, as he neither possesses the gift of commanding, nor has he the slightest knowledge of what I am seeking.

I naturally have no leisure here, and I have only been able to write the above because it is raining heavily, and therefore no work can be done. On the next rainy day I shall report further on the progress of my excavations.

Since my report of the 4th of this month I have continued the excavations with the utmost energy, but I am now compelled to stop the works this evening, for my three foremen and my servant, who is also my cashier, have been seized by the malignant marsh-fever, and my wife and I are so unwell that we are quite unable to undertake the sole direction throughout the day in the terrible heat of the sun. We shall therefore leave our two wooden houses and all our machines and implements in charge of a watchman, and to-morrow we shall return to Athens.

The admirers of Homer, on visiting the Pergamus of Troy, will find that I have not only laid bare the Tower on the south side, along the whole breadth of my trench, down to the rock upon which it stands, at a depth of 14 meters or 46½ feet, but that by my excavations on the east and west I have uncovered it considerably further, without having found its end. On the contrary, upon the east side, where it is 40 feet broad, and seems even to be broader still, I found the ruins of a second storey, of which, however, as far as I can at present judge, four broad steps have been preserved. On the western side it is only 9 meters or 30 feet in breadth, and on this side there extends to the north an enormous wall, the thickness of which I have not been able to ascertain. The fact of my not having been able to carry these new excavations down to the primary soil, but only to a depth of 11 meters (36½ feet) is owing to the brittle nature of the walls of rubbish and ruins round about the Tower, which, as anyone may convince himself, consist of red ashes and of stones calcined by the heat, and which threatened at any moment to fall in and bury my workmen. . . .

After having had no rain here for four months, to-day, curiously enough, just after stopping the works, we have had a thunderstorm accompanied by a tremendous downpour of rain, and I regret extremely not to have been able to make a channel for leading off the rain-water from the Tower as far as the western declivity of the hill. But such a channel would need to be 50 feet deep and as many broad, otherwise its walls, consisting of calcined ruins and loose red ashes, would fall in. I should therefore have to remove 5000 cubic meters (6000 cubic yards) of *débris,* and such a gigantic piece of work I cannot now undertake.

In stopping the excavations for this year, and in looking back upon the fearful dangers to which we have continually been exposed since the 1st of April, between the gigantic layers of ruins, I cannot but fervently thank God for His great mercy, that not only has no life been lost, but that none of us has even been seriously hurt.

Now, as regards the results of my excavations, everyone must admit that I have solved a great historical problem, and that I have solved it by the discovery of a high civilization and immense buildings upon the primary soil, in the depths of an ancient town, which throughout antiquity was called Ilium and declared itself to be the successor of Troy, the site of which was regarded as identical with the site of the Homeric Ilium by the whole civilized world of that time. The situation of this town not only corresponds perfectly with all the statements of the Iliad, but also with all the traditions handed down to us by later authors; and, moreover, neither in the Plain of Troy, nor in its vicinity, is there any other place which could in the slightest degree be made to correspond with them. To regard the heights of Bunarbashi as the site of Troy, contradicts, in every respect, all the statements of Homer and of tradition. My excavations of Bunarbashi, as well as the form of the rocks, prove that those heights, as far as the three sepulchral mounds, can never have been inhabited by men. As I have already said, behind those tumuli there are the ruins of a very small town, the area of which, surrounded on two sides by the ruins of an enclosing wall, and on the other side by precipices, is so insignificant, that at most it can have only possessed 2000 inhabitants. The enclosing wall of its small Acropolis is scarcely a foot thick, and the gate scarcely 3¼ feet wide. The accumulation of *débris* is not worth mentioning, for in many places the naked flat rocks are seen on the ground of the Acropolis. Here in Ilium, however, the proportions are very different. The area of the Greek city, which is indicated by the surrounding wall built by Lysimachus, is large enough for a population of more than 100,000 souls; and that the number of the inhabitants was actually as large is proved by the stage of the theatre, which is 200 feet in breadth. Here the surrounding wall of Lysimachus is 6½ feet thick, whereas the wall which runs out from the Tower at a great depth below the other seems to be five times as thick, and Homer assuredly ascribed the erection of the walls of Troy to Poseidon and Apollo on account of their enormous proportions. Then, as regards the accumulation of *débris,* here in the Pergamus there is no place where it amounts to less than 14 meters, or 46½ feet, and in many places it is even much more considerable. Thus, for instance, on my great platform, I only reached the primary soil at a depth of 16 meters, or 53 1/3 feet, and in the depths of the temple, on the adjacent field, belonging to Mr. Frank Calvert, I have not yet reached it at a depth of 15½ meters, or 51 2/3 feet. Such an accumulation of ruins has never as yet been discovered in any other part of the world, except occasionally in the rocky valleys of Jerusalem; where, however, it has only begun to accumulate since the destruction of the city by Titus, and hence is scarcely more than 1800 years old. Here in Troy the remains of the Greek period cease entirely at a depth of ½, 1, or 2 meters, and thence, down to the primary soil, we find in regular succession the mighty layers of ruins belonging to four very ancient nations.

In like manner, as regards the more than a hundred thousand objects which I have brought to light, and which were used by those very ancient tribes, I venture to say that I have revealed a new world to archæology; for, in order to give but one instance, I have here found many thousands of those wheels, volcanoes, or tops (*carrousels*) of terra-cotta with the most various Aryan religious symbols.

If, as it seems, neither the Trojans nor any of the three succeeding peoples possessed a written language, we must, as far as possible, replace it by the *"monuments figurés"* which I have discovered. As already said, I make a drawing in my diary each evening of every one of the objects which have been found during the day, and more especially of the pictorial symbols, with the greatest exactness. By comparing the innumerable symbols I have succeeded in deciphering some of them, and I hope that my learned colleagues will succeed in explaining the rest. Archæology shall on no account lose any one of my discoveries; every article which can have any interest for the learned world shall be photographed, or copied by a skilful draughtsman, and published in the Appendix to this work; and by the side of every article I shall state the depth in which I discovered it.

I wrote my last memoir on the 14th of last month, and on the 10th of this month, accompanied by my wife and Sisilas the land-surveyor, I returned to Troy in order to make a new plan of the Pergamus, which contains the most exact picture of my excavations, as well as of the depth in which the remains of immortal fame were discovered by me. I also took the photographer Siebrecht from the Dardanelles with me, in order to have photographs taken of my excavations, of two of the four springs situated on the north side of Ilium, of Ilium's Great Tower and the Plain of Troy, as well as of the Hellespont as seen from this monument.

To my horror, upon arriving there, I found that the watchman whom I had left in charge had been faithless, and that an immense number of large hewn stones dug out of my excavations, with which I had erected walls in several places in order to prevent the winter rains from washing away the *débris* which we had pulled down, had been carried off. The man excused himself by saying that the stones had been used for a good purpose, namely for the construction of a belfry in the Christian village of Yenishehr, and for building houses in the Turkish village of Chiplak. I, of course, packed him off directly, and engaged in his place a watchman whom I armed with a musket. He had the reputation of being honest, and his physical strength will inspire the pilferers of the stones with respect. What vexed me most was, that these thieves had even laid their hands upon the splendid bastion of the time of Lysimachus, which I had uncovered on the south side of the hill; they had made off with two large stones from it, and the bastion would assuredly have vanished entirely had I been away a week longer.

I also regret to see that the downpour of rain on the 14th of August has filled the great cutting, which I made on the south side of the Tower, in order to bring the Tower to light down as far as the rock upon which it is built, with *débris* to a height of 2 meters (6½ feet). So, immediately upon my arrival, I engaged 20 workmen, 10 of whom are busy clearing the south side of the Tower as far as the primary soil, in wheeling away the *débris,* and in building in front of the cutting a wall of large blocks of stone, through which the rain-water can escape, but not the *débris* that may be washed down.

I have now had an opportunity of convincing myself that the rain does not harm the Tower, for it disappears directly to the right and left of it in the loose *débris.* Of the other ten workmen, six are occupied in repairing the walls which have been destroyed or injured by wanton hands, while the other four are working in order to lay bare as far as possible an exceedingly remarkable wall, which rises at an angle of 40 degrees at the depth of 15½ meters (50½ feet) and at 43½ yards from the edge of the hill, on the site of the temple, exactly 6½ feet *below* the Trojan wall which I there brought to light. . . . As I have before remarked, the strata of *débris,* which run obliquely to the north below that Trojan wall, prove that it was built upon the steep slope of the hill, and this is an additional and infallible proof that the buttress, which is erected 6½ feet below it, can have served no other purpose than for consolidating and strengthening the ground of the declivity so effectually that buildings of an enormous weight might be erected upon the summit without danger. Now as I have never hitherto found buttresses of this kind for consolidating the declivity of the hill among the strata of the pre-Hellenic period, although there was no lack of grand buildings in the Pergamus of Troy (as is proved by the colossal masses of hewn and unhewn stones from 16½ to 20 feet high, mixed with charred *débris*, with which I had to struggle upon my great platform), I positively believe that the above-mentioned buttress was erected to support the site of a temple of great sanctity. I believe this all the more, as the buttress here forms a curve and appears to protect the whole of the north-eastern corner of the hill, which was the extreme end of the Pergamus and perfectly corresponds with Homer's statement about the position of the temple of Athena, "on the summit of the city" (ἐν πόλει ἄκρῃ: *Iliad*, VI. 297). I have no doubt that in ascending from this buttress I shall find the ruins of that ancient temple at a distance of less than 10 meters (33 feet). But in order to penetrate further, I must first of all pull down the Trojan wall, 10 feet high and 6½ feet thick, which I have already frequently mentioned, and remove the enormous masses of *débris;* this work must be deferred till the 1st of February, for I am now too ill and tired to attempt it. The discovery of the very ancient temple of Athena at the north-eastern corner would, moreover solve the great problem— whence arises the colossal accumulation of *débris*, which here covers the declivity with a crust as hard as stone, 131 feet in thickness, and which caused me so much trouble, not only in this excavation, but also at the eastern end of my platform, along an extent of more than 80 feet. It will be found that this enormous crust has arisen solely from the remains of the sacrifices offered to the Ilian Athena.

I had not noticed this buttress at the time of my departure on the 15th of August, and I have now only discovered it because the rain has laid bare two of its stones. It is built of blocks of shelly limestone (*Muschelkalk*), from about a foot to 2 feet 2 inches long and broad, joined with earth, and it probably covered the whole north-eastern corner of the hill from the bottom to the top. I presume that the drain of green sandstone, nearly 8 inches broad and about 7 inches high, which I spoke of in my report of the 25th of April, belongs to the very ancient temple of Athena; it will be remembered that I found it at about 11½ feet above my great platform, and at a distance of 46 feet from the edge of the declivity.

The block of triglyphs with the Sun-god and the four horses, which I found here, proves that the temple which it adorned was built in the Doric style; and, as the Doric is confessedly the oldest style of architecture, the ancient temple of the Ilian Athena was doubtless in that style. We know, however, from the Iliad that there was also a temple of Apollo in the Pergamus. It probably stood at the south-eastern corner of the hill, for at the foot of it may be seen, in a small excavation, a wall composed of splendid Corinthian pillars joined by means of cement. It is probable that these pillars belong to a temple of Apollo of the time of Lysimachus. In excavating the Tower further to the east, I hope to find the site of this temple, and in its depths the ruins of the very ancient temple of Apollo.

If the Trojans possessed an alphabetical language, I shall probably find inscriptions in the ruins of the two temples. I am, however, no longer sanguine in regard to this, as I have hitherto found no trace of writing in the colossal strata of the four tribes which preceded the Greek colony.

Since my report of the 16th of last month I have had many interruptions, for the Greek Easter festival lasts six days, then the feast of Saint George and its after celebrations again took away several days, so that during all this time I have had only four days of actual work; however, on these days, with on an average of 150 men, I have continued the works with great energy.

As we have had continual fine weather since the beginning of April, my men no longer go to the neighbouring villages for the night as they have hitherto done; but they sleep in the open air and even in the excavations, which is very convenient for me, as I now have them always at hand. Besides this, the long days are of great advantage to me, for I can continue work from a quarter to five till a quarter past seven in the evening.

On the top of the tumulus, which is half an hour distant from the Pergamus, and which, according to the Iliad (II. 811–815), was called by men the tomb of Batiea, and by the gods

the tomb of Myrina, I have had a shaft sunk, 10¾ feet broad
and 17½ feet long; and I find that the layer of soil there is
scarcely more than ¾ of an inch thick, and then follows
brown earth as hard as stone, which alternates with strata
of calcareous earth. In the brown earth I found a mass of
fragments of brilliant black, green, and brown vases, of the
same description as those which I find here in the Pergamus
at a depth of from 8 to 10 meters (26 to 33 feet); also many
fragments of jars ($\pi\iota\theta o\iota$). Beyond these I discovered nothing
at all, and at a depth of 4½ meters (13¾ feet) I came upon
the white limestone rock. What is most surprising to me is that
I did not even find any charcoal, much less the bones of the
burnt corpse. That I should have missed the traces of the
funeral pile, if such really existed, is inconceivable to me,
when I consider the size of my cutting and of its perpendicular
walls.

Now, although I have failed in the actual object of this
excavation, still it has this important result for archæology,
that, by means of all the fragments of pottery discovered
there, it enables us to determine with some degree of certainty the date of the erection of this mound; for it evidently
belongs to a time when the surface of the Pergamus was from
26 to 33 feet lower than it is now. It is therefore of the same
date as the Tower-road already described, which is paved
with large flags of stone, and above which I have carried on
the excavations with the greatest industry. I finished these
excavations to-day. They have brought to light two large
buildings of different ages, the more recent of which is erected
upon the ruins of the more ancient one. Both have been destroyed by terrible fires, of which the walls bear distinct traces;
moreover all the rooms of both houses are filled with black,
red, and yellow wood-ashes and with charred remains. The
more recent house was erected when the ruins of the more
ancient house were perfectly covered with ashes and with
burnt *débris,* as is obvious from the fact that the more recent
walls run in all directions above the more ancient ones, never
standing directly upon them, and are frequently separated

from them by a layer of calcined *débris,* from 6½ to 10 feet high. The lower, as well as the upper house, is built of stones joined with earth, but the walls of the lower house are much thicker and much more solidly built than those of the upper one. The Tower-road can only have been used when the more ancient house was still inhabited, for it leads directly into it, and the more recent house was not built till the street was covered to a height of 10 feet by the ruins of the more ancient house.

I was firmly convinced that this splendid street, paved with large flags of stone, must proceed from the principal building of the Pergamus, and I therefore confidently carried on the excavation in order to bring that edifice to light. To accomplish this, I was most unfortunately compelled to break down three of the large walls of the more recent house. The result has, however, far surpassed my expectations, for I not only found two large gates, standing 20 feet apart, but also the two large copper bolts belonging to them. . . . The first gate is 12¼ feet broad, and is formed by two projections of the wall, one of which stands out 2½ feet, the other 2¾ feet; both are 3¼ feet high, and 3¾ feet broad. The street paved with the large flags of stone ends at the first gate, and the road from this to the second gate, which is situated a little more than 20 feet further to the north-east, is very roughly paved with large unhewn stones. The pavement has probably become uneven through the walls of the more ancient house having fallen upon it.

The second gate is likewise formed by two projections in the wall, which are 2 feet high, above 3 feet broad, and project about 2½ feet.

I have cleared the street as far as 5 feet to the north-east of the second gate, but I have not ventured to proceed further, as this could not be done without breaking down more of the walls of the second house, the preservation of which is of the greatest interest to archæology. For, although it must be of a much more recent date than the lower one upon the ruins of which it stands, yet, as is proved by the terra-cottas and

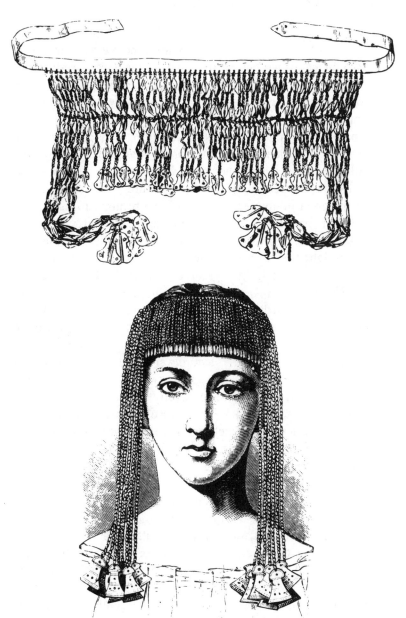

The Treasure of Priam, Worn by Schliemann's Wife Sophia

the idols with owls' heads, as well as by its position at a depth of from 6 to 7 meters (20 to 23 feet) below the surface, it was built centuries before the time of the Greek settlement, the ruins of which extend only to a depth of 6½ feet. This upper and later house is therefore certainly older than the Homeric poems.

In my last report I expressed the firm conviction that the Tower-road, which inclines abruptly towards the Plain to the south-west, must lead to the Scæan Gate, which I thought could at most be 492 feet distant. I now venture positively to assert that the great double gate which I have brought to light must necessarily be the SCAEAN GATE. For in the mound, which runs out far to the south-west from the foot of the Pergamus and in a straight line with the Tower-road—which mound I had supposed to contain the great city wall of Ilium and the Scæan Gate,—in this mound, close to the main hill, I have sunk a shaft, nearly 6 feet broad and 11 feet long. Here I found exclusively Greek fragments of pottery, and I came upon the rock at the small depth of 7½ feet; thus I convinced myself that ancient Troy can never have extended so far towards the Plain. A second excavation, 11¼ feet long and 6½ feet broad, which I made exactly 443 feet further to the east up the plateau, had a similar result, for I came upon the rock at a depth of 16½ feet, and here also I found exclusively fragments of Hellenic pottery (which in the Pergamus I meet with only at a depth of 6½ feet), and no trace of Trojan pottery.

This sufficiently proves that the ancient city cannot even have extended as far as this point, and its area must have been connected with the Pergamus still further eastwards. I am at present occupied in making fifteen other shafts in this direction, and I hope, in spite of the great depth I have to sink them, that I shall succeed, at least to some extent, in determining the topography of Troy. I shall leave all the shafts open, so that every visitor may convince himself about the truth of my statements.

Meanwhile the two shafts described above have gained this

much for archaeology, that the street which runs down abruptly at an angle of 65 degrees towards the Plain, in a south-western direction from the double gate and the Great Tower, cannot possibly have led to a second gate, so that the double gate which I have laid bare must necessarily have been the Scæan Gate; it is in an excellent state of preservation, not a stone of it is wanting.

Here, therefore, by the side of the double gate, upon Ilium's Great Tower, at the edge of the very abrupt western declivity of the Pergamus, sat Priam, the seven elders of the city, and Helen; and this is the scene of the most splendid passage in the *Iliad*.* From this spot the company surveyed the whole Plain, and saw at the foot of the Pergamus the Trojan and the Achæan armies face to face about to settle their agreement to let the war be decided by a single combat between Paris and Menelaus.

When Homer makes Hector descend from the Pergamus and rush through the city in order to arrive at the Scæan Gate, this can only have arisen from the fact that, after the destruction of Troy, the gate, as well as the street which led down from it to the Plain, were covered with a layer of *débris* 10 feet thick, so that the names only were known from tradition, and their actual site was unknown. . . .

This gate, as well as the large ancient building, stands upon the wall or buttress already mentioned as leaning on the north side of the Tower. At this place the buttress appears to be about 79 feet thick, and to be made of the *débris* which was broken off the primary soil when the Tower was erected. The site of this building, upon an artificial elevation directly above the gate, together with its solid structure, leave no doubt that

---

* *Iliad*, III. 146–244:—

      "Attending there on aged Priam, sat
      The Elders of the city;  .  .  .  .  .
      All these were gathered at the Scæan Gates.
     .  .  .  .  .  so on Ilion's Tower
      Sat the sage chiefs and councillors of Troy.
      Helen they saw, as to the Tower she came."

The Double Scæan Gate, "Palace of Priam," and Tower of Ilium

it was the grandest building in Troy; nay, that it must have been the PALACE OF PRIAM. I am having an accurate plan made, so far as I can, of the portion that has been laid bare; I cannot, however, bring to light the whole of it, for in order to do this I should have to pull down both my stone and my wooden house, beneath which it extends; and even if I did pull down my own houses, I should still be unable to make a complete plan of the house till I had removed the building which stands upon it, and this I cannot at once make up my mind to do.

Anyone may convince himself that the elevation, upon which stands the Palace of King Priam above the Scæan Gate, is in reality an artificial one, by examining my last year's great cutting, which pierces through a portion of this elevation. The walls of that cutting, from the shaft as far as the gate, show that the mound consists of the native earth which has been thrown up, mixed with fragments of rare pottery and shells.

Now, with regard to the objects found in these houses, I must first of all mention having discovered, at a depth of 26 feet, in the palace of Priam, a splendid and brilliant brown vase, 24¼ inches high, with a figure of the tutelar goddess of Troy, that is, with her owl's head, two breasts, a splendid necklace, indicated by an engraved pattern, a very broad and beautifully engraved girdle, and other very artistic decorations; there are no arms, nor are there any indications of them. Unfortunately this exquisite vase has suffered from the weight of stones which lay upon it, and although I myself cut it with a knife from among the stones and the stone-hard *débris* with the greatest care, I did not succeed in getting it out without breaking it to pieces. I have, however, carefully collected all the fragments and sent them to Athens to be put together, that I may give a drawing of it.

Among the very remarkable vases discovered in this palace, I must also mention one nearly a foot high, with two handles, and an encircling row of cuneiform engravings above which, on both sides, there is a very prominent decoration, in the form of spectacles, which is connected with a kind of necklace by an engraved tree. I must further draw special attention to an exceedingly remarkable vase, which was found in the same house, and upon which there are actual letters in a circle round it. One piece of the vase is wanting, and with it a portion of the inscription. I must also draw attention to a vase, upon which at first sight it seems as if there were a row of letters; at a closer examination, however, it appears not to be writing, but symbolical signs, as the cross is conspicuous in almost every figure.

In the same house I found three brilliant red vases, with two handles, a prominent decoration on either side in the form of spectacles, and two mighty wings, standing erect by the side of the neck;—half-a-dozen vases of various sizes, with uncommonly long tubes at the sides and with holes in the mouth for suspending them by strings!—a very large and brilliant black vase, with two handles and two ornaments in the form of large ears;—likewise a smaller vase, with large perforated ears for the string by which it was hung up;—a vase with three feet, rings for hanging it up, and beautiful engraved decorations, namely, two encircling stripes with zigzag lines, and five lines round the neck. Further, I found a vase rounded at the bottom, with perforated handles, and completely covered with dots;—also two covers with pretty owls' heads, one of which has remarkably large eyes;—also a fragment of the fore part of a vase with a sheep's head;—a curious small but very broad vase, with three feet and long tubes for hanging it up by strings;—a peculiar terra-cotta lamp, with a perforated handle in the form of a crescent, and two other projecting handles, with tubes for suspension;—a red jug with a handle, a neck completely bent back, a beak-shaped mouth, and two eyes;—a small vase, covered with dots and possessing two handles and two immense erect ears;—a jug, with two female breasts;—a vase, with the owl's face and the body of the Ilian Athena, and two upraised arms;—also the upper portion of another vase, upon which may be seen a mouth below the beak of the Trojan tutelary goddess; and a vase, with a large hollow foot, very long tubes at the sides for hanging it up, and two prominent decorations in the form of spectacles. . . .

I also discovered in the same house six beautifully-polished axes of diorite; also one of those round twice-perforated terra-cottas, arched on both sides and flattened on the edge of one side, the whole of this flat side being filled with a stamp bearing the impression of an eagle and a stag or an antelope; further, four of those frequently-described large red goblets, round below and with two large handles, which can only stand on the mouth. These four goblets are, unfortunately, all broken, and I shall not be able to have them repaired till I return to Athens.

I now venture positively to maintain that these goblets, which, from my former reports and drawings are known to be from 5 to nearly 16 inches high, must necessarily be the Homeric "δέπα ἀμφικύπελλα," and that the usual interpretation of these words by "*double cups, with a common bottom in the centre,*" is entirely erroneous. It really appears as if this wrong translation arose solely through Aristotle; for, as is clear from his *Hist. Anim.* (9, 40), there were in his time double cups with a common bottom in the centre; and, in fact, many years ago it is said that such a cup was discovered in Attica, and bought by the Museum in Copenhagen. But in the Homeric Troy there were no such cups, otherwise I should have found them. As already remarked in one of my previous reports, I found on the primary soil, at a depth of from 46 to 52½ feet, several fragments of brilliant black goblets, which I then considered to be fragments of double cups, because there was a hollow upon both sides of the bottom; but the one hollow was in all cases quite small in comparison with the other, and must, therefore, have been in the foot of the cup. If δέπας ἀμφικύπελλον means *double cup*, then ἀμφιφορεύς must mean *double urn,* which is not possible either in the Iliad (XIII. 92), the Odyssey (XXIV. 74), or elsewhere in Homer; moreover, it has never occurred to anyone to translate it otherwise than "urn with two handles;" consequently, δέπας ἀμφικύπελλον cannot be translated otherwise than by "cup with two handles." As an actual double cup can, of course, only be filled on one side at a time, Homer would certainly never have constantly described the filled cup as a double cup, for there would have been no sense in the name. By the term ἀμφικύπελλον, however, he wished to signify that the filled cup was presented by one handle and accepted by the other handle. Interpreted in this manner, there is a great deal of meaning in the name. . . .

As the excavation above the Scæan Gate is finished, I am now again vigorously at work on the great platform on the north side, which I have lately had worked whenever I had workmen to spare. We now come upon several houses there at a depth of from 33 to 20 feet; also, as it seems, upon a great wall of fortification in the lower strata.

As it is extremely important to know what were the fortifications on the west and north-west of the Pergamus at the time of the Trojan war, and as I see another wall, 11½ feet

thick, running in a north-western direction from the Scæan
Gate, which however it is impossible to follow from this side,
during the last eight days I have been making a cutting, 33
feet broad and 141 long, on the north-west side of the hill,
at the point where, in April 1870, I made the first cutting,
which therefore my men call ἡ μάμμη τῶν ἀνασκαφῶν ("the grand-
mother of the excavations"). I am having the *débris* removed
simultaneously by a small platform, made at a depth of 34¼
feet on the declivity of the hill, and by three galleries. The distance is not great, and the wheel-barrows proceed across level
ground, and moreover the *débris* here is very light, and only
requires to be thrown down the declivity; so the work advances
very rapidly. Upon the lower platform I came upon the surrounding wall built by Lysimachus, which is 13 feet high and
10 feet thick, and is composed of large hewn blocks of limestone laid upon one another without any kind of cement. I have
just finished breaking through this wall. Directly behind it
I came upon an older wall, 8¾ feet high and 6 feet thick,
which is composed of large hewn stones joined with earth,
and which of course I am also having broken through. This
second wall is immediately followed by that wall of large
hewn stones which I laid bare three years ago, and which I
have hitherto regarded as a bastion; it is, however, probable
that it will prove to be something else, and I shall describe it
in detail in my next report.

This part of the Pergamus was evidently much lower in
ancient times; as seems to be proved not only by the surrounding wall, which must at one time have risen to a considerable
height above the surface of the hill, whereas it is now covered
with 16½ feet of *débris,* but also by the remains of the Hellenic
period, which here extend down to a great depth. It appears,
in fact, as if the rubbish and refuse of habitations had been
thrown down here for centuries, in order to increase the
height of the place. This also explains how it is that I find
here a quantity of small but interesting objects from the Greek
period. Among others are 24 heads of terra-cotta figures, 17
of which are of great beauty; also a great number of other

fragments of statuettes of the same description, which display skilful workmanship; a terra-cotta slab 5½ inches in length, upon which is a representation of a woman; also eight small terra-cotta slabs, nearly ·2 inches in length, upon which I find very curious and to me utterly unknown objects in high relief. I also found here the fragments of some vessels of exquisite workmanship; two beautifully decorated lamps; and a leaden plate, 2¾ inches long and broad, with a pig's head in bas-relief, which, as I conjecture, may have been a coin. We also discovered here a vessel 28¾ inches long, of an extremely fanciful shape, with a long and very thin foot, a long thin neck, and two enormous handles. . . .

As I no longer require the surface of the Tower for removing the *débris,* I have had it quite cleared, and I find in the centre of it a depression, 45¼ feet long, from 8¼ to 14¾ feet broad, and barely 3 feet deep, which may have been used for the archers. It has now become evident to me that what I last year considered to be the ruins of a second storey of the Great Tower are only benches made of stones joined with earth, three of which may be seen rising behind one another like steps. From this, as well as from the walls of the Tower and those of the Scæan Gate, I perceive that the Tower never can have been higher than it now is.

The excavations of the north side of the field belonging to Mr. Calvert, which I opened to discover other sculptures, have been stopped for some time, as I can no longer come to terms with him. At present, I have only two foremen, for I was obliged to dismiss Georgios Photidas, three weeks ago, for urgent reasons.

In conclusion, I have to mention that, during the Greek Easter festival, accompanied by my esteemed friend, Judge Schells of Ratisbon, and my wife, I visited Bunarbashi and the neighbouring heights. In their presence, I made some small excavations, and I have proved that even in the village the accumulation of *débris* amounts only to 1¾ foot in the court-yards of the buildings, and that upon and beside the street there is nothing but the virgin earth; further, that upon the small site of Gergis, at the end of the heights, which was formerly regarded as identical with Troy, the naked rock projects everywhere; and besides, in the accumulation of *débris,* which nowhere amounts to 1¾ foot in the town itself, and to only a little more in the Acropolis, I found nothing but fragments of pottery from the Hellenic period, that is, from the third and fifth centuries B.C.

I must also add that I now positively retract my former opinion, that Ilium was inhabited up to the ninth century after Christ, and I must distinctly maintain that its site has been desolate and uninhabited since the end of the fourth century. I had allowed myself to be deceived by the statements of my esteemed friend, Mr. Frank Calvert, of the Dardanelles, who maintained that there were documents to prove that the place had been inhabited up to the thirteenth and fourteenth centuries after Christ. Such documents, if they really do exist, must necessarily refer to Alexandria Troas, which is always, as for instance in the New Testament, simply called Troas; for on its site quantities of Byzantine antiquities are found even on the surface, which seem to prove that the city was inhabited up to the fourteenth century, or still longer. Here in Ilium, on the other hand, there is no trace of Byzantine architecture, of Byzantine sculpture, of Byzantine pottery, or of Byzantine coins. Altogether I found only two copper medals of Byzantine monasteries, which may have been lost by shepherds. I found hundreds of coins belonging to the time of Constantine the Great, Constans II., but no medals whatever of the later emperors.

As hitherto it was in the Pergamus alone that I found no trace of the Byzantine period, I thought that it was only the fortress that was uninhabited during that period, but that the region of the city had been occupied. But my fifteen shafts, which I am having made on the most various points of the site of Ilium, as well as the two shafts made upon the primary soil, prove, as anyone may convince himself, that below the surface there is no trace of the Byzantine period, nay that, beyond a very thin layer of earth, which however only exists in some parts, the ruins of the Greek period extend up to the very surface, and that in several of the shafts I came upon the walls of Greek houses even on the surface.

It is impossible that a Byzantine town or a Byzantine village, nay, that even a single Byzantine house, can have stood upon this hilly and stone-hard ground, which covers the ruins of a primeval city, without leaving the most distinct traces of its existence, for here, where for nine or ten months of the year it never rains, except during rare thunderstorms, the productions of human industry do not become weather-beaten and destroyed, as in other countries where there is frequent rain. The very fragments of sculptures and inscriptions, which I find here in the Pergamus and in the other districts of the city, upon the surface, and which have lain exposed to the open air for at least 1500 years, are still almost as fresh as if they had been made yesterday. . . .

Since my report of the 10th of last month I have been especially anxious to hasten the great excavation on the northwest side of the hill, and for this purpose I have made a deep cutting on the west side also, in which, unfortunately, I came obliquely upon the enclosing wall of Lysimachus, which is 13 feet high and 10 feet thick. I was therefore compelled to break out from this wall a double quantity of stones in order to gain an entrance; but I again came upon the ruins of colossal buildings of the Hellenic and pre-Hellenic periods, so that this excavation can only proceed slowly. Here, at a distance of 69 feet from the declivity of the hill, at a depth of 20 feet, I met with an ancient enclosure 5 feet high, and with a projecting battlement. It is not connected with the wall which runs out from the Scæan Gate in a north-westerly direction, and, on account of its very different structure and small height, it must belong to a post-Trojan period. In any case, however, it is much older than the Greek colony, because it is built of stones and earth, and because I found by the side of it several marble idols of the tutelar goddess of Ilium. I am, unfortunately, obliged to break down a portion of this wall to a length of 17½ feet, in order to proceed further, but I have left standing nearly 8 feet of the part I have excavated, so that the wall may be examined. Behind it I found a level place paved partly with large flags of stone, partly with stones more or less hewn, and after this a wall of fortification 20 feet high and 5 feet thick, built of large stones and earth; it runs below my wooden house, but 6½ feet above the Trojan city wall which proceeds from the Scæan Gate.

In the new large excavation on the north-west side, which is connected with the one I have just been describing, I have convinced myself that the splendid wall of large hewn stones, which I uncovered in April 1870, belongs to a tower, the lower projecting part of which must have been built during the first period of the Greek colony, whereas its upper portion seems to belong to the time of Lysimachus. To this tower also belongs the wall that I mentioned in my last report as 9 feet high and 6 feet broad, and as continuous with the surrounding wall of Lysimachus; and so does the wall of the same dimensions, situated 49 feet from it, which I have likewise broken through. Behind the latter, at a depth of from 26 to 30 feet, I uncovered the Trojan city wall which runs out from the Scæan Gate.

In excavating this wall further and directly by the side of the palace of King Priam, I came upon a large copper article of the most remarkable form, which attracted my attention all the more as I thought I saw gold behind it. On the top of this copper article lay a stratum of red and calcined ruins, from 4¾ to 5¼ feet thick, as hard as stone, and above this again lay the above-mentioned wall of fortification (6 feet broad and 20 feet high) which was built of large stones and earth, and must have belonged to an early date after the destruction of Troy. In order to withdraw the Treasure from the greed of my workmen, and to save it for archæology, I had to be most expeditious, and although it was not yet time for breakfast, I immediately had *"païdos"* called. This is a word of uncertain derivation, which has passed over into Turkish, and is here employed in place of ἀνάπαυσις, or time for rest. While the men were eating and resting, I cut out the Treasure with a large knife, which it was impossible to do without the very greatest exertion and the most fearful risk of my life, for the great fortification-wall, beneath which I had to dig, threatened every moment to fall down upon me. But the sight of so many objects, every one of which is of inestimable value to archæology, made me foolhardy, and I never thought of any danger. It would, however, have been impossible for me to have removed the Treasure without the help of my dear wife, who stood by me ready to pack the things which I cut out in her shawl and to carry them away.

The first thing I found was a large copper shield (the ἀσπὶς ὀμφαλόεσσα of Homer) in the form of an oval salver, in the middle of which is a knob or boss encircled by a small furrow (αὖλαξ). This shield is a little less than 20 inches in length; it is quite flat, and surrounded by a rim (ἄντυξ) 1½ inch high; the boss (ὀμφαλεός) is 2⅓ inches high and 4⅓ inches in diameter; the furrow encircling it is 7 inches in diameter and ⅖ of an inch deep. *

The second object which I got out was a copper caldron with two horizontal handles, which certainly gives us an idea

---

\* This round shield of copper (or bronze?), with its central boss, and the furrow and rim so suitable for holding together a covering of ox-hides, reminds us irresistibly of the seven-fold shield of Ajax:—*Iliad,* VII. 219–223 (cf. 245–247):—

> "Ajax approached; before him, as a tower,
> His mighty shield he bore, seven-fold, brass-bound,
> The work of Tychius, best artificer
> That wrought in leather; he in Hyla dwelt.
> Of seven-fold hides the ponderous shield was wrought
> Of lusty bulls: the eighth was glittering brass."

It is equally striking to compare the shield of the Treasure with the description of Sarpedon's shield, with its round plate of hammered copper (or bronze), and its covering of ox-hides, fastened to the inner edge of the rim by gold wires or rivets (*Iliad,* XII. 294–297):—

> "His shield's broad *orb* before his breast he bore,
> Well wrought, *of beaten brass,* which the armourer's hand
> Had beaten out, and lined with stout bull's hide
> With golden rods, continuous all around."

of the Homeric λέβης; it is 16½ inches in diameter and 5½ inches high; the bottom is flat, and is nearly 8 inches in diameter.

The third object was a copper plate ⅖ of an inch thick, 6⅓ inches broad, and 17⅓ inches long; it has a rim about 1/12 of an inch high; at one end of it there are two immovable wheels with an axle-tree. This plate is very much bent in two places, but I believe that these curvatures have been produced by the heat to which the article was exposed in the conflagration; a silver vase 4¾ inches high and broad has been fused to it; I suppose, however, that this also happened by accident in the heat of the fire. The fourth article I brought out was a copper vase 5½ inches high and 4⅓ inches in diameter. Thereupon followed a globular bottle of the purest gold, weighing 403 grammes (6220 grains, or above 1 lb. troy); it is nearly 6 inches high and 5½ inches in diameter, and has the commencement of a zigzag decoration on the neck, which, however, is not continued all around. Then came a cup, likewise of the purest gold, weighing 226 grammes (7¼ oz. troy); it is 3½ inches high and 3 inches broad.

Next came another cup of the purest gold, weighing exactly 600 grammes (about 1 lb. 6 oz. troy); it is 3½ inches high, 7¼ inches long, and 7⅕ inches broad; it is in the form of a ship with two large handles; on one side there is a mouth, 1⅕ inch broad, for drinking out of, and another at the other side, which is 2¾ inches broad, and, as my esteemed friend Professor Stephanos Kumanudes, of Athens, remarks, the person who presented the filled cup may have first drunk from the small mouth, as a mark of respect, to let the guest drink from the larger mouth. This vessel has a foot which projects about 1/12 of an inch, and is 1⅓ inch long, and ⅘ of an inch broad. It is assuredly the Homeric δέπας ἀμφικύπελλον. But I adhere to my supposition that all of those tall and brilliant red goblets of terra-cotta, in the form of champagne-glasses with two enormous handles, are also δέπα ἀμφικύπελλα, and that this form probably existed in gold also. I must further make an observation which is very important for the history of art, that the above-mentioned gold δέπας ἀμφικύπελλον is of *cast gold,* and that the large handles, which are not solid, have been fused on to it. On the other hand the gold bottle and the gold cup mentioned above have been *wrought with the hammer.*

The Treasure further contained a small cup of gold alloyed with 20 per cent of silver, that is the mixed metal called *electrum.* It weighs 70 grammes (2¼ oz. troy), and is above 3 inches high, and above 2½ inches broad. Its foot is only ⅓ of an inch high and nearly an inch broad, and is moreover not quite straight, so that the cup appears to be meant only to stand upon its mouth.

I also found in the Treasure six pieces of the purest silver in the form of large knife-blades, having one end rounded, and the other cut into the form of a crescent; they have all been wrought with the hammer. The two larger blades are nearly 8½ inches long and 2 inches broad, and weigh respectively 190 and 183 grammes. The next two pieces are about 7¼ inches long and 1½ broad, and weigh respectively 174 and 173 grammes. The two other pieces are nearly 7 inches long and 1⅕ inch broad, and weigh respectively 173 and 171 grammes. It is extremely probable that these are the Homeric *talents* (τάλαντα), which could only have been small, as, for instance, when Achilles offers for the first prize a woman, for the second a horse, for the third a caldron, and for the fourth two gold talents.

I also found in the Treasure three great silver vases, the largest of which is above 8¼ inches high and nearly 8 inches in diameter, and has a handle 5½ inches in length and 3½ in breadth. The second vase is 6.9 inches high and nearly 6 inches in diameter; another silver vase is welded to the upper part of it, of which, however, only portions have been preserved. The third vase is above 7 inches high and above 6 inches in diameter; the foot of the vase has a great deal of copper fused onto it, which must have dripped from the copper objects contained in the Treasure during the conflagration. All of the three vases are perfectly round below, and therefore cannot stand upright without resting against something.

I found, further, a silver goblet above 3⅓ inches high, the mouth of which is nearly 4 inches in diameter; also a silver flat cup or dish (φιάλη) 5½ inches in diameter, and two beautiful small silver vases of most exquisite workmanship. The larger one, which has two rings on either side for hanging it up by strings, is nearly 8 inches high with its hat-shaped lid, and 3½ inches in diameter across the bulge. The smaller silver vase, with a ring on either side for suspension by a string, is about 6¾ inches high, with its lid, and above 3 inches broad.

Upon and beside the gold and silver articles, I found thirteen copper lances, from nearly 7 to above 12½ inches in length, and from above 1½ to 2⅓ inches broad at the broadest point; at the lower end of each is a hole, in which, in most cases, the nail or peg which fastened the lance to the wooden handle is still sticking. The pin-hole is clearly visible in a lance-head which the conflagration has welded to a battle-axe. The Trojan lances were therefore quite different from those of the Greeks and Romans, for the latter stuck the shaft into the lance-head, the former fastened the head into the shaft.

I also found fourteen of those copper weapons, which are frequently met with here, but which have never been discovered elsewhere; at one end they are pointed but blunt, and at the other they end in a broad edge. I formerly considered them to be a species of lance, but now after mature consideration I am convinced that they could have been used only as battle-axes. They are from above 6 to above 12 inches in length, from nearly ½ to above ¾ of an inch thick, and from above 1 to nearly 3 inches broad; the largest of them weighs 1365 grammes (about 3 lbs. avoirdupois). . . .

There were also seven large double-edged copper daggers, with a handle from about 2 to 2¾ inches long, the end of which is bent round at a right angle. These handles must at one time have been encased in wood, for if the cases had been made of bone they would still have been wholly or partially preserved. The pointed handle was inserted into a piece of wood, so that the end projected about half an inch beyond it, and this end was simply bent round. . . .

Of common one-edged knives I only found one in the Treasure; it is above 6 inches in length. I also found a piece of a sword which is 8⅔ inches long and nearly 2 inches broad: also a four-cornered copper bar ending in an edge; it is nearly 15 inches long, and also appears to have served as a weapon.

As I found all these articles together, forming a rectangular mass, or packed into one another, it seems to be certain that they were placed on the city wall in a wooden chest (φωριαμός), such as those mentioned by Homer as being in the palace of King Priam. This appears to be the more certain, as close by the side of these articles I found a copper key above 4 inches long, the head of which (about 2 inches long and broad) greatly resembles a large safe-key of a bank. Curiously enough this key has had a wooden handle; there can be no doubt of this from the fact that the end of the stalk of the key is bent round at a right angle, as in the case of the daggers.

It is probable that some member of the family of King Priam hurriedly packed the Treasure into the chest and carried it off without having time to pull out the key; that when he reached the wall, however, the hand of an enemy or the fire overtook him, and he was obliged to abandon the chest, which was immediately covered to a height of from 5 to 6 feet with the red ashes and the stones of the adjoining royal palace.

Perhaps the articles found a few days previously in a room of the royal palace, close to the place where the Treasure was discovered, belonged to this unfortunate person. These articles were a helmet, and a silver vase 7 inches high and 5½ inches broad, containing an elegant cup of electrum 4⅓ inches high and 3½ inches broad. The helmet was broken in being taken out, but I can have it mended, as I have all the pieces of it. The two upper portions, composing the crest (φάλος), are uninjured. Beside the helmet, as before, I found a curved copper pin, nearly 6 inches in length, which must have been in some way attached to it, and have served some purpose.

At 5 or 6 feet above the Treasure, the successors of the Trojans erected a fortification wall 20 feet high and 6 feet broad, composed of large hewn and unhewn stones and earth; this wall extends to within 3¼ feet of the surface of the hill.

That the Treasure was packed together at terrible risk of life, and in the greatest anxiety, is proved among other things also by the contents of the largest silver vase, at the bottom of which I found two splendid gold diadems (κρήδεμνα); a fillet, and four beautiful gold ear-rings of most exquisite workmanship: upon these lay 56 gold ear-rings of exceedingly curious form and 8750 small gold rings, perforated prisms and dice, gold buttons, and similar jewels, which obviously belonged to other ornaments; then followed six gold bracelets, and on the top of all the two small gold goblets.

The one diadem consists of a gold fillet, 21⅔ inches long and nearly ½ an inch broad, from which there hang on either side seven little chains to cover the temples, each of which has eleven square leaves with a groove; these chains are joined to one another by four little cross chains, at the end of which hangs a glittering golden idol of the tutelar goddess of Troy, nearly an inch long. The entire length of each of these chains, with the idols, amounts to 10¼ inches. Almost all these idols have something of the human form, but the owl's head with the two large eyes cannot be mistaken; their breadth at the lower end is about ⁹/₁₀ of an inch. Between these ornaments for the temples there are 47 little pendant chains adorned with square leaves; at the end of each little chain is an idol of the tutelary goddess of Ilium, about ¾ of an inch long; the length of these little chains with the idols is not quite 4 inches.

The other diadem is 20 inches long, and consists of a gold chain, from which are suspended on each side eight chains completely covered with small gold leaves, to hang down over the temples, and at the end of every one of the sixteen chains there hangs a golden idol 1¼ inch long, with the owl's head of the Ilian tutelary goddess. Between these ornaments for the temples there are likewise 74 little chains, about 4 inches long, covered with gold leaves, to hang down over the forehead; at the end of these chains there hangs a double leaf about ¾ of an inch long.

The fillet ἄμπυξ is above 18 inches long and ⅖ of an inch broad, and has three perforations at each end. Eight quadruple rows of dots divide it into nine compartments, in each of which there are two large dots; and an uninterrupted row of dots adorns the whole edge. Of the four ear-rings only two are exactly alike. From the upper part, which is almost in the shape of a basket, and is ornamented with two rows of decorations in the form of beads, there hang six small chains on which are three little cylinders; attached to the end of the chains are small idols of the tutelar goddess of Troy. The length of each ear-ring is 3½ inches. The upper part of the other two ear-rings is larger and thicker, but likewise almost in the shape of a basket, from it are suspended five little chains entirely covered with small round leaves, on which are likewise fastened small but more imposing idols of the Ilian tutelar divinity; the length of one of these pendants is 3½ inches, that of the other a little over 3 inches.

Of the six gold bracelets, two are quite simple and closed, and are about ⅕ of an inch thick; a third is likewise closed, but consists of an ornamented band $\frac{1}{25}$ of an inch thick, and ¼ of an inch broad. The other three are double, and the ends are turned round and furnished with a head. The princesses who wore these bracelets must have had unusually small hands, for they are so small that a girl of ten would have difficulty in putting them on.

The 56 other gold ear-rings are of various sizes, and three of them appear to have also been used by the princesses of the royal family as finger-rings. Not one of the ear-rings has any resemblance in form to the Hellenic, Roman, Egyptian, or Assyrian ear-rings; 20 of them end in four leaves, ten in three leaves, lying beside one another and soldered together, and they are thus extremely like those ear-rings of gold and electrum which I found last year at a depth of 9 and 13 meters (29½ and 42½ feet). Eighteen other ear-rings end in six leaves; at the commencement of these there are two small studs, in the centre two rows of five small studs each, and at the end three small studs. Two of the largest rings, which, owing to the thickness of the one end, certainly cannot have been used as ear-rings, and appear to have been finger-rings only, terminate in four leaves, and at the commencement of these there are two, in the middle three, and at the end again two small studs. Of the remaining ear-rings two have the form of three, and four the form of two, beautifully ornamented serpents lying beside one another.

Besides the ear-rings, a great number of other ornaments strung on threads, or fastened on leather, had been put into the same large silver vase; for above and below them, as already said, I found 8750 small objects; such as gold rings, only ⅛ of an inch in diameter; perforated dice, either smooth or in the form of little indented stars, about ⅙ of an inch in diameter; gold perforated prisms ¹⁄₁₀ of an inch high and ⅛ of an inch broad, decorated longitudinally with eight or sixteen incisions; small leaves about ⅕ of an inch long, and ⅙ of an inch broad, and pierced longitudinally with a hole for threading them; small gold pegs ⅓ of an inch long, with a button on one side, and a perforated hole on the other; perforated prisms about ⅕ of an inch long and ¹⁄₁₀ of an inch broad; double or triple gold rings soldered together and only ¼ of an inch in diameter, with holes on both sides for threading them; gold buttons or studs ⅕ of an inch high, in the cavity of which is a ring above ¹⁄₁₀ of an inch broad for sewing them on; gold double buttons, exactly like our shirt studs, ³⁄₁₀ of an inch long, which, however, are not soldered, but simply stuck together, for from the cavity of the one button there projects a tube (αὐλίσκος) nearly ¼ of an inch long, and from the other a pin (ἔμβολον) of the same length, and the pin is merely stuck into the tube to form the double stud. These double buttons or studs can only have been used, probably, as ornament upon leather articles, for instance upon the handlestraps (τελαμῶνες) of swords, shields, or knives. . . .

The person who endeavoured to save the Treasure had fortunately the presence of mind to stand the silver vase, containing the valuable articles described above, upright in the chest, so that not so much as a bead could fall out, and everything has been preserved uninjured.

My esteemed friend M. Landerer, of Athens, a chemist well known through his discoveries and writings, who has most carefully examined all the copper articles of the Treasure, and analysed the fragments, finds that all of them consist of pure copper without any admixture of tin or zinc, and that, in order to make them more durable, they have been wrought with the hammer (σφυρήλατον).

As I hoped to find other treasures here, and also wished to bring to light the wall that surrounded Troy, the erection of which Homer ascribes to Poseidon and Apollo, as far as the Scæan Gate, I have entirely cut away the upper wall, which rested partly upon the gate, to an extent of 56 feet. Visitors to the Troad can, however, still see part of it in the north-western earth-wall opposite the Scæan Gate. I have also broken down the enormous block of earth which separated my western and north-western cutting from the Great Tower; but in order to do this, I had to pull down the larger one of my wooden houses, and I had also to bridge over the Scæan Gate, so as to facilitate the removal of the *débris*. The result of this new excavation is very important to archæology; for I have been able to uncover several walls, and also a room of the Royal Palace, 20 feet in length and breadth, upon which no buildings of a later period rest.

Of the objects discovered there I have only to mention an excellently engraved inscription found upon a square piece of red slate, which has two holes not bored through it and an encircling incision, but neither can my learned friend Émile Burnouf nor can I tell in what language the inscription is written. Further, there were some interesting terra-cottas, among which is a vessel, quite the form of a modern cask, and with a tube in the centre for pouring in and drawing off the liquid. There were also found upon the wall of Troy, 1¾ feet below the place where the Treasure was discovered, three silver dishes (φιάλαι), two of which were broken to pieces in digging down the *débris;* they can, however, be repaired, as I have all the pieces. These dishes seem to have belonged to the Treasure, and the fact of the latter having otherwise escaped our pickaxes is due to the above-mentioned large copper vessels which projected, so that I could cut everything out of the hard *débris* by means of a knife.

I now perceive that the cutting which I made in April 1870 was exactly at the proper point, and that if I had only continued it, I should in a few weeks have uncovered the most remarkable buildings in Troy, namely, the Palace of King Priam, the Scæan Gate, the Great Surrounding Wall, and the Great Tower of Ilium; whereas, in consequence of abandoning this cutting, I had to make colossal excavations from east to west and from north to south through the entire hill in order to find those most interesting buildings.

In the upper strata of the north-western and western excavations we came upon another great quantity of heads of beautiful terra-cotta figures of the best Hellenic period, and at a depth of 23 feet upon some idols, as well as the upper portion of a vase with the owl's face and a lid in the form of a helmet. Lids of this kind, upon the edge of which female hair is indicated by incisions, are frequently found in all the strata between 4 and 10 meters (13 and 33 feet) deep, and as they belong to vases with owls' faces, the number of lids gives us an idea of the number of the vases with the figure of the owl-headed Athena, which existed here in Troy.

But Troy was not large. I have altogether made twenty borings down to the rock, on the west, south-west, south, south-east'and east of the Pergamus, directly at its foot or at some distance from it, on the plateau of the Ilium of the Greek colony. As I find in these borings no trace either of fragments of Trojan pottery or of Trojan house-walls, and nothing but fragments of Hellenic pottery and Hellenic house-walls, and as, moreover, the hill of the Pergamus has a very steep slope towards the north, the north-east, and the north-west, facing the Hellespont, and is also very steep towards the Plain, the city could not possibly have extended in any one of these directions. I now most emphatically declare that the city of Priam cannot have extended on any one side beyond the primeval plateau of this fortress, the circumference of which is indicated to the south and south-west by the Great Tower and the Scæan Gate, and to the north-west, north-east and east by the surrounding wall of Troy. The city was so strongly fortified by nature on the north side, that the wall there consisted only of those large blocks of stone, loosely piled one upon another in the form of a wall, which last year gave me such immense trouble to remove. This wall can be recognized at once, immediately to the right in the northern entrance of my large cutting, which runs through the entire hill.

I am extremely disappointed at being obliged to give so small a plan of Troy; nay, I had wished to be able to make it a thousand times larger, but I value truth above everything, and I rejoice that my three years' excavations have laid open the Homeric Troy, even though on a diminished scale, and that I have proved the Iliad to be based upon real facts.

Homer is an epic poet, and not an historian: so it is quite natural that he should have exaggerated everything with poetic licence. Moreover, the events which he describes are so marvellous, that many scholars have long doubted the very existence of Troy, and have considered the city to be a mere invention of the poet's fancy. I venture to hope that the civilized world will not only not be disappointed that the city of Priam has shown itself to be scarcely a twentieth part as large as was to be expected from the statements of the Iliad, but that, on the contrary, it will accept with delight and enthusiasm the certainty that Ilium did really exist, that a large portion of it has now been brought to light, and that Homer, even although he exaggerates, nevertheless sings of events that actually happened. Besides, it ought to be remembered that the area of Troy, now reduced to this small hill, is still as large as, or even larger than, the royal city of Athens, which was confined to the Acropolis, and did not extend beyond it, till the time when Theseus added the twelve villages, and the city was consequently named in the plural Ἀθῆναι. It is very likely that the same happened to the town of Mycenæ (Μυκῆναι), which

Homer describes as being rich in gold, and which is also spoken of in the singular, εὐρυάγνια Μυκήνη.

But this little Troy was immensely rich for the circumstances of those times, since I find here a treasure of gold and silver articles, such as is now scarcely to be found in an emperor's palace; and as the town was wealthy, so was it also powerful, and ruled over a large territory.

The houses of Troy were all very high and had several storeys, as is obvious from the thickness of the walls and the colossal heaps of *débris*. But even if we assume the houses to have been of three storeys, and standing close by the side of one another, the town can nevertheless not have contained more than 5000 inhabitants, and cannot have mustered more than 500 soldiers; but it could always raise a considerable army from among its subjects, and as it was rich and powerful, it could obtain mercenaries from all quarters.

As I do not find in my shafts (that is, beyond the hill itself) a trace of earthenware belonging to the successors of the Trojans up to the time of the Greek colony, it may with certainty be assumed that Troy had increased in size at Homer's time only to the small amount of what was added through the heaps of rubbish caused by the destruction of the city. Homer can *never* have seen Ilium's Great Tower, the surrounding wall of Poseidon and Apollo, the Scæan Gate or the Palace of King Priam, for all these monuments lay buried deep in heaps of rubbish, and he made no excavations to bring them to light. He knew of these monuments of immortal fame only from hearsay, for the tragic fate of ancient Troy was then still in fresh remembrance, and had already been for centuries in the mouth of all minstrels.

Homer rarely mentions temples, and, although he speaks of the temple of Athena, yet, considering the smallness of the city, it is very doubtful whether it actually existed. It is probable that the tutelar goddess at that time possessed only the sacrificial altar which I discovered, and the crescent form of which greatly resembles the upper portion of the ivory idol found in the lowest strata, as well as the one end of the six talents contained among the Treasure. . . .

The Scæan Gate gives us the age of the royal edifice in front of which it stands, and of the vessels of pottery which are found in that house. This earthenware is indeed better than what is generally found here at a depth of from 7 to 10 meters (23 to 33 feet), but it is exactly similar; and consequently all the strata of *débris* from these depths belong to the Trojan people. These strata are composed of red, yellow, and occasionally black wood-ashes, and every stone found there bears the marks of the fearful heat to which it has been exposed. In these strata we never meet with those brilliant black plates and dishes, with a long horizontal ring on either side, found at the depth of from 13 to 16 meters (42½ to 52½ feet), nor do we meet with the vases with two long tubes on either side. Besides the vessels in the lowest strata are entirely different in quality and in form from those found at a depth of from 23 to 33 feet, so that they certainly cannot have belonged to the same people. But they belong, at all events, to a kindred Aryan nation, as these too possessed in common with the Trojans the whorls ornamented with Aryan religious symbols, and also idols of the Ilian Athena. I formerly believed that the most ancient people who inhabited this site were the Trojans, because I fancied that among their ruins I had found the δέπας ἀμφικύπελλον, but I now perceive that Priam's people were the succeeding nation, because in their ruins I have discovered the actual δέπας ἀμφικύπελλον, made of gold and also of terra-cotta, and likewise the Scæan Gate.

Several geologists, who have visited me here, maintain that the stratum of scoriæ, which runs through the greater part of the hill, at an average depth of 9 meters (29½ feet), has been formed by melted lead and copper ore, quantities of which must have existed here at the time of the destruction of Troy; and this opinion is also shared by the engineer, Adolphe Laurent, who has returned to help me with my last works, and to make some new plans.

Strabo says, "No trace of the ancient city (Troy) has been preserved. This is very natural; for, as all the towns round about were desolated, yet not completely destroyed, while Troy was razed to the ground, so all the stones were carried off to renovate the others. Thus, at least, Archæanax of Mitylene is said to have built a wall round Sigeum with the stones." These statements of Strabo are, however, completely erroneous, and the tradition of antiquity, that Troy was razed to the ground, can only be explained by its having been buried deep beneath colossal masses of wood-ashes and stone, which were built over by a new town; the latter being again destroyed, and again surmounted by buildings which had a similar fate; till at last the mass of *débris* lying upon Troy reached a height of from 6 to 8 meters (20 to 26 feet), and upon this was established the Acropolis of the Ilium of the Greek colony.

In consequence of my former mistaken idea, that Troy was to be found on the primary soil or close above it, I unfortunately, in 1871 and 1872, destroyed a large portion of the city, for I at that time broke down all the house-walls in the higher strata which obstructed my way. This year, however, as soon as I had come by clear proofs to the firm conviction that Troy was not to be found upon the primary soil, but at a depth of from 23 to 33 feet, I ceased to break down any house-wall in these strata, so that in my excavations of this year a number of Trojan houses have been brought to light. They will still stand for centuries, and visitors to the Troad may convince themselves that the stones of the Trojan buildings can *never* have been used for building other towns, for the greater part of them are still *in situ*. Moreover, they are small, and millions of such stones are to be found upon all the fields of this district.

Valuable stones, such as those large flags which cover the road leading from the Scæan Gate to the Plain, as well as the stones of the enclosing wall and of the Great Tower, have been left untouched, and not a single stone of the Scæan Gate is wanting. Nay, with the exception of the houses which I myself destroyed, it would be quite possible to uncover the "carcasses" of all the houses, as in the case of Pompeii. The houses, as I have already said, must have been very high, and a great deal of wood must have been used in their construction, for otherwise the conflagration could not have produced such an enormous quantity of ashes and rubbish.

In my excavations of 1871 and 1872, at a depth of from 7 to 10 meters (23 to 33 feet), I found only house-walls composed of sun-dried bricks; and, as anyone may convince himself by examining the houses which I have uncovered, this style of building was almost exclusively met with during that year. It is only the buildings by the side of the Scæan Gate, and a few houses in the depths of the Temple of Athena, that are made of stones and earth.

As may be seen from my plan of the site of Troy, I have excavated two-thirds of the entire city; and, as I have brought to light the Great Tower, the Scæan Gate, the city wall of Troy, the royal palace, the sacrificial altar of the Ilian Athena, and so forth, I have uncovered the grandest buildings, and, in fact, the best part of the city. I have also made an exceedingly copious collection of all the articles of the domestic life and the religion of the Trojans; and therefore it is not to be expected that science would gain anything more by further excavations. If, however, my excavations should at any time be continued, I urgently entreat those who do so to throw the *débris* of their diggings from the declivity of the hill, and *not* to fill up the colossal cuttings which I have made with such infinite trouble and at such great expense, for they are of great value to archæology, inasmuch as in these cuttings all the strata of *débris,* from the primary soil up to the surface of the hill, can be examined with little trouble. . . .

# PART FOUR

# Old Cities in the New World

# 9. STEPHENS:

# *An Explorer Buys a City*

It is impossible to contemplate these mysterious monuments of a lost civilization, without a strong feeling of curiosity as to who were their architects, and what is their probable age. The data, on which to rest our conjectures of their age, are not very substantial; although some find in them a warrant for an antiquity of thousands of years, coeval with the architecture of Egypt and Hindostan. But the interpretation of hieroglyphics, and the apparent duration of trees, are vague and unsatisfactory. And how far can we derive an argument from the discoloration and dilapidated condition of the ruins, when we find so many structures of the Middle Ages dark and mouldering with decay, while the marbles of the Acropolis, and the grey stone of Paestum, still shine in their primitive splendor?

—PRESCOTT, *The Conquest of Mexico*

Limestone Figure: "Maize God" from Copan, Honduras

Before white men came to the New World, Indian civilizations of a high order of sophistication and complexity flourished in South and Central America. The Incas ruled in Peru; the Aztecs in upper Mexico; and in what is now Guatemala, Honduras, and the Yucatán Peninsula, the stone cities of the people we call the Mayas were built.

The Spanish invaders dealt with these civilizations as invaders will. Cortez smashed the Aztec culture; Pizarro, that of Peru. The conquest of the Mayas was less bloody, because the Mayas were not organized into a tightly bound empire, and so did not provide an effective resistance to the *conquistadores*. The process of subduing them was one of attrition rather than one of direct and grim destruction.

The Spaniards pursued a policy of shattering these cultures by executing the elite and destroying all historical and religious literatures. At a stroke, the Aztecs and Incas were left leaderless and cultureless, and the energetic *padres* filled the void with Christianity. Among the Mayas, too, the Spaniards worked their evil, but more slowly, so that it was not until 1697, a century and a half after the conquest, that the last isolated village of independent Mayas surrendered.

After that, the jungle was allowed to reclaim the Mayan cities. Mighty stone temples and pyramids a thousand years old disappeared beneath the green tide. The Mayas themselves forgot their great heritage. The Spaniards never cared to remember it. By the beginning of the 19th century, it was as though the great achievements of the Mayas had never been. The Mayan cities, in only three centuries, were lost to memory as thoroughly as those of Sumer, ten times as old.

Early in the 19th century, one Colonel Galindo of Mexico, otherwise unknown, had ventured into the wilds of Yucatán, and published a report on certain great cities he had found there. It was a vague, confused story of ancient monuments, perhaps of Egyptian origin. Few took the book seriously.

Among those few was an American traveller and explorer, John Lloyd Stephens. He resolved at once to see Yucatán for himself and verify Galindo's findings. The idea of discover-

ing monuments in the jungle appealed to him, for he had
seen the wonders of Syria and Egypt and thirsted for new
worlds to conquer.

Stephens was born in New Jersey in 1805, but grew up in
New York City. At 13, he entered Columbia College, after
schooling under an Irishman "wondrously good at drill and
flogging." He went on to take a law degree, and then set out
upon his life of travels.

Small, wiry and tense, Stephens roamed the world com-
pulsively, as though demon-driven. His first tour was of
the American West; he ventured into Shawnee country in a
Conestoga wagon, then floated down the Mississippi from
Pittsburgh to New Orleans in a flat-bottomed boat. He returned to New York red-bearded and travel-hardened, and
promptly entered local politics as a violently liberal-minded
follower of Andrew Jackson.

A strenuous career as a lawyer and political speaker, and
an addiction to long black cheroots, brought Stephens low in
1834 with an inflammation of the throat. He went to Paris
for treatment, and continued on to Rome, thence to war-
devastated Greece, where he eyed the ruins of Athens, sought
out the alleged tomb of Agamemnon, read Herodotus at the
battlefield of Marathon. Sailing on to the Near East, he wandered through the provinces of Turkey and did his first travel
writing: a series of letters to the *American Monthly Magazine*
under the general title, *Scenes of the Levant*.

In 1836, Stephens journeyed up the Nile and then, garbed
in a long red silk gown, a colorful turban, yellow slippers,
and a pair of huge Turkish pistols, he affixed himself to an
expedition bound for the Sinai Peninsula. They crossed the
Red Sea and trekked into the desert where a shortage of
water nearly brought the party to grief. (Some years later,
the young Herman Melville saw Stephens in church. Melville's
aunt whispered to him, "See what big eyes he has! They got
so big because when he was almost dead with famishing in
the desert, he all at once caught sight of a date-tree, with ripe
fruit hanging on it.")

Stephens' adventures abroad resulted in two books entitled *Incidents of Travel*—the first dealing with Egypt, Arabia Petraea, and the Holy Land, the second with Greece, Turkey, Russia, and Poland. The books met with immediate popularity, helped by a favorable review from Edgar Allan Poe, and went through half a dozen editions the first year.

Stephens' travels in the Holy Land had been guided by a map signed "F. Catherwood." On his way back to the United States, Stephens sought out Catherwood in London and the Englishman presently followed Stephens to the United States.

Frederick Catherwood, born in 1799, was an accomplished draftsman and an authority on architecture; he had, in fact, taught architecture at the University of Cairo. At their meeting in London, Catherwood showed Stephens Colonel Galindo's report on the ruined city of Palenque, in the Mexican jungles, and the two men promptly resolved to explore Yucatán, Catherwood to illustrate and Stephens to write a book of travel memoirs.

Back in the United States, Stephens took up politicking for Jackson's successor, Martin Van Buren, and soon was able to wangle a diplomatic appointment from Van Buren, to be Special Confidential Agent from the United States to Central America. With the United States Government underwriting his travel expenses—and providing him with a diplomatic passport in the bargain—Stephens set out in October, 1839, for Central America, accompanied by Catherwood.

Central America was in a state of political chaos. Guatemala, Salvador, Nicaragua, Honduras, and Costa Rica had broken free from Spain in 1823 and had formed a unified republic, but the confederation had collapsed and civil war raged. General Morazán of the Federal Party held Salvador; a young Indian named Carrera, of dictatorial tendencies, was the master of Guatemala; the allegiances of the other states shifted with the fortunes of war. Through this confusion wandered Catherwood and Stephens, finding themselves arrested now by partisans of one group, now by those of the other, but always wiggling free on the strength of Stephens' diplomatic passport.

The venture into the jungle proved successful. Under great difficulties, the explorers reached the Mayan city of Copán, which is now known to have been built between the fifth and ninth centuries A.D. Stephens' account of his discovery of Copán is reprinted here. Crossing from Guatemala into Mexico, Stephens explored the ruins of Palenque, and in July, 1840, after ten months of exploration, Stephens and Catherwood returned to New York. The ruins had been found. Stephens had not accomplished much as a diplomat—"After diligent search, no government found," he informed Washington in explanation of his failure to present his credentials to anyone—but his explorational achievements were considerable.

Stephens produced a two-volume work, *Incidents of Travel in Central America, Chiapas and Yucatán*, with dozens of magnificent illustrations by Catherwood. Twelve printings were needed in three months. Poe reviewed it, calling it "perhaps the most interesting book of travel ever published." Poe may have been right. Stephens' narrative, which devotes as much space to the comic-opera political situation of Central America as it does to the exploration of ruins, is a masterpiece of low-keyed writing, sparkling with humor throughout. It remained in print for decades, and, indeed, is back in print today, in a handsome two-volume edition published by the Rutgers University Press.

In October, 1841, Stephens and Catherwood headed for Yucatán once again. They visited two more Mayan ruins—Uxmal and Mayapán, the latter once the Mayan capital—and set to work clearing the foliage from the buildings so Catherwood could draw them accurately. Accompanied by a young Harvard graduate, Dr. Samuel Cabot, Stephens and Catherwood spent six weeks at Uxmal before all three contracted malaria and were forced to withdraw.

Stephens' account of this second expedition, *Incidents of Travel in Yucatán* (1843) nearly equalled the popularity of his earlier book on the Mayan ruins. Catherwood also produced a book this time—a folio volume of plates of the ruins,

*Views of Ancient Monuments in Central America, Chiapas, and Yucatán* (1844).

To prove his assertions—for there were those who believed Stephens and Catherwood had invented their jungle temples from whole cloth—Stephens brought back an impressive array of Mayan relics, sculptures, vases, carved beams, and hieroglyphic inscriptions. These went on display at the Rotunda in New York and attracted excited attention. But they were soon destroyed, along with hundreds of Catherwood's drawings and water colors, by fire. Those few statuary pieces that survived the blaze can be seen today at the Museum of Natural History in New York.

After the disaster, Catherwood returned to the profession of architecture and journeyed to British Guiana to build a railroad there. Later, he invested in California real estate and railroading, then visited England, and was lost in a collision at sea while returning to the United States in 1854.

Stephens, too, had become involved with railroads. He built one in Panama and encountered his old friend Catherwood while engaged in the job. Then, becoming an agent for a steamship company, Stephens visited Europe for business reasons, and visited the explorer Humboldt, whom he called "the greatest man since Aristotle," at Potsdam. The gold rush of 1849 called Stephens to California where he went to supervise the construction of a railroad. In the west, he encountered a Sacramento-bound businessman named Heinrich Schliemann. Their conversations are not recorded, but perhaps Stephens' talk of cities in the jungles of Central America fired Schliemann's own archaeological enthusiasm. A recurrence of Stephens' malaria laid him low in 1852; he was hastily taken to New York where he died, at the age of 47. He was buried by mischance in the tomb of a family not his own and a century passed before his coffin was discovered.

Stephens was an explorer, not an archaeologist. But, like Belzoni and Layard, he did yeoman service in discovering the secrets of the past and laying the groundwork for the more systematic workers who followed after.

Sculpture at Top of Main Stairway at Copan, Honduras

# AN EXPLORER BUYS A CITY

Since the discovery of these ruined cities the prevailing theory has been, that they belonged to a race long anterior to that which inhabited the country at the time of the Spanish conquest. With regard to Copan, mention is made by the early Spanish historians of a place of that name, situated in the same region of country in which these ruins are found, which then existed as an inhabited city, and offered a formidable resistance to the Spanish arms, though there are circumstances which seem to indicate that the city referred to was inferior in strength and solidity of construction, and of more modern origin.

It stood in the old province of Chiquimula de Sierras, which was conquered by the officers of Pedro de Alvarado, but not one of the Spanish historians has given any particulars of this conquest. In 1530 the Indians of the province revolted, and attempted to throw off the yoke of Spain. Hernandez de Chaves was sent to subdue them, and, after many sanguinary battles, he encamped before Esquipulas, a place of arms belonging to a powerful cacique, which, on the fourth day, to use the words of the cacique himself, "more out of respect to the public tranquillity than from fear of the Spanish arms, determined to surrender," and, with the capital, the whole province submitted again to the Spanish dominion.

The cacique of Copan, whose name was Copán Calel, had been active in exciting the revolt and assisting the insurgents. Hernandez de Chaves determined to punish him, and marched against Copan, then one of the largest, most opulent, and most populous places of the kingdom. The camp of the cacique, with his auxiliaries, consisted of thirty thousand men, well disciplined, and veterans in war, armed with wooden

From *Incidents of Travel in Central America, Chiapas, and Yucatan* (New York: Harper, 1841) by John Lloyds Stephens.

swords having stone edges, arrows, and slings. On one side, says the historian, it was defended by the ranges of mountains of Chiquimula and Gracios a Dios, and on the opposite side by a deep fosse, and an intrenchment formed of strong beams of timber, having the interstices filled with earth, with embrasures, and loopholes for the discharge of arrows. Chaves, accompanied by some horsemen, well armed, rode to the fosse, and made sign that he wished to hold conference. The cacique answered with an arrow. A shower of arrows, stones, and darts followed, which compelled the Spaniards to retreat. The next day Chaves made an attack upon the intrenchment. The infantry wore loose coats stuffed with cotton; swords and shields; the horsemen wore breastplates and helmets, and their horses were covered. The Copanes had each a shield covered with the skin of the danta on his arm, and his head guarded by bunches of feathers. The attack lasted the whole day. The Indians, with their arrows, javelins, and pikes, the heads of which were hardened by fire, maintained their ground. The Spaniards were obliged to retreat. Chaves, who had fought in the thickest of the battle, was alarmed at the difficulties of the enterprise and the danger to the credit of the Spanish arms, but received information that in one place the depth of the ditch which defended Copan was but trifling, and the next day he proceeded to the spot to make an attack there. The Copanes had watched his movements, and manned the intrenchment with their bravest soldiers. The infantry were unable to make a lodgment. The cavalry came to their assistance. The Indians brought up their whole force, and the Spaniards stood like rocks, impassable to pikes, arrows, and stones. Several times they attempted to scale the intrenchments, and were driven back into the fosse. Many were killed on both sides, but the battle continued without advantage to either until a brave horseman leaped the ditch, and, his horse being carried violently with his breast against the barrier, the earth and palisadoes gave way, and the frightened horse plunged among the Indians. Other horsemen followed, and spread such terror among the Copanes, that their lines were broken and they fled. Copán Calel rallied at a place where he had posted a body of reserve; but, unable to resist long, retreated, and left Copan to its fate.

This is the account which the Spanish historians have given of Copan; and, as applied to the city, the wall of which we saw from the opposite side of the river, it appeared to us most meager and unsatisfactory; for the massive stone structures before us had little the air of belonging to a city, the intrenchment of which could be broken down by the charge of a single horseman. At this place the river was not fordable; we returned to our mules, mounted, and rode to another part of the bank, a short distance above. The stream was wide, and in some places deep, rapid, and with a broken and stony bottom. Fording it, we rode along the bank by a footpath encumbered with undergrowth, which Jose opened by cutting away the branches, until we came to the foot of the wall, where we again dismounted and tied our mules.

The wall was of cut stone, well laid, and in a good state of preservation. We ascended by large stone steps, in some places perfect, and in others thrown down by trees which had grown up between the crevices, and reached a terrace, the form of which it was impossible to make out, from the density of the forest in which it was enveloped. Our guide cleared a way with his machete, and we passed, as it lay half buried in the earth, a large fragment of stone elaborately sculptured, and came to the angle of a structure with steps on the sides, in form and appearance, so far as the trees would enable us to make it out, like the sides of a pyramid. Diverging from the base, and working our way through the thick woods, we came upon a square stone column, about fourteen feet high and three feet on each side, sculptured in very bold relief, and on all four of the sides, from the base to the top. The front was the figure of a man curiously and richly dressed, and the face, evidently a portrait, solemn, stern, and well fitted to excite terror. The back was of a different design, unlike anything we had ever seen before, and the sides were covered with hieroglyphics. This our guide called an "Idol;" and before it, at a distance of three feet, was a large block of stone, also sculptured with figures and emblematical devices, which he called an altar. The sight of this unexpected monument put at rest at once and forever, in our minds, all uncertainty in regard to the character of American antiquities, and gave us the assurance that the objects we were in search of were interesting, not only as the remains of an unknown people, but as works of art, proving, like newly-discovered historical records, that the people who once occupied the Continent of America were not savages. With an interest perhaps stronger than we had ever felt in wandering among the ruins of Egypt, we followed our guide, who, sometimes missing his way, with a constant and vigorous use of his machete, conducted us through the thick forest, among half-burned fragments, to fourteen monuments of the same character and appearance, some with more elegant designs, and some in workmanship equal to the finest monuments of the Egyptians; one displaced from its pedestal by enormous roots; another locked in the close embrace of branches of trees, and almost lifted out of the earth; another hurled to the ground, and bound down by huge vines and creepers; and one standing, with its altar before it, in a grove of trees which grew around it, seemingly to shade and shroud it as a sacred thing; in the solemn stillness of the woods, it seemed a divinity mourning over a fallen people. The only sounds that disturbed the quiet of this buried city were the noise of monkeys moving among the tops of the trees, and the cracking of dry branches broken by their weight. They moved over our heads in long and swift processions, forty or fifty at a time, some with little ones wound in their long arms, walking out to the end of boughs, and holding on with their hind feet or a curl of the tail, sprang to a branch of the next tree, and, with a noise like a current of wind, passed on into the depths of the forest. It was the first time we had seen these mockeries of humanity, and, with the strange monuments around us, they seemed like wandering spirits of the departed race guarding the ruins of their former habitations.

We returned to the base of the pyramidal structure, and ascended by regular stone steps, in some places forced apart by bushes and saplings, and in others thrown down by the growth of large trees, while some remained entire. In parts they were ornamented with sculptured figures and rows of death's heads. Climbing over the ruined top, we reached a terrace overgrown with trees, and, crossing it, descended by stone steps into an area so covered with trees that at first we could not make out its form, but which, on clearing the way with the machete, we ascertained to be a square, and with steps on all sides almost as perfect as those of the Roman amphitheatre. The steps were ornamented with sculpture, and on the south side, about half way up, forced out of its place by roots, was a colossal head, evidently a portrait. We ascended these steps, and reached a broad terrace a hundred feet high, overlooking the river, and supported by the wall which we had seen from the opposite bank. The whole terrace was covered with trees, and even at this height from the ground were two gigantic Ceibas, or wild cottontrees of India, above twenty feet in circumference, extending their half-naked roots fifty or a hundred feet around, binding down the ruins, and shading them with their wide-spreading branches. We sat down on the very edge of the wall, and strove in vain to penetrate the mystery by which we were surrounded. Who were the people that built this city? In the ruined cities of Egypt, even in the long-lost Petra, the stranger knows the story of the people whose vestiges are around him. America, say historians, was peopled by savages; but savages never reared these structures, savages never carved these stones. We asked the Indians who made them, and their dull answer was "Quien sabe?" "who knows?"

There were no associations connected with the place; none of those stirring recollections which hallow Rome, Athens, and "the world's great mistress on the Egyptian plain"; but architecture, sculpture, and painting, all the arts which embellish life, had flourished in this overgrown forest; orators, warriors, and statesmen, beauty, ambition, and glory, had lived and passed away, and none knew that such things had been, or could tell of their past existence. Books, the records of knowledge, are silent on this theme. The city was desolate. No remnant of this race hangs round the ruins, with traditions handed down from father to son, and from generation to generation. It lay before us like a shattered bark in the midst of the ocean, her masts gone, her name effaced, her crew perished, and none to tell whence she came, to whom she belonged, how long on her voyage, or what caused her destruction; her lost people to be traced only by some fancied resemblance in the construction of the vessel, and, perhaps, never to be known at all. The place where we sat, was it a citadel from which an unknown people had sounded the trumpet of war? or a temple for the worship of the God of peace? or did the inhabitants worship the idols made with their own hands, and offer sacrifices on the stones before them? All was mystery, dark, impenetrable mystery, and every circumstance increased it. In Egypt the colossal skeletons of gigantic temples stand in the unwatered sands in all the nakedness of desolation; here an immense forest shrouded the ruins, hiding them from sight, heightening the impression and moral effect, and giving an intensity and almost wildness to the interest.

Late in the afternoon we worked our way back to the mules, bathed in the clear river at the foot of the wall, and returned to the hacienda. . . .

In the morning we continued to astonish the people by our strange ways, particularly by brushing our teeth, an operation which, probably, they saw then for the first time. While engaged in this, the door of the house opened, and Don Gregorio appeared, turning his head away to avoid giving us a buenos dios. We resolved not to sleep another night under his shed, but to take our hammocks to the ruins, and, if there was no building to shelter us, to hang them up under a tree. My contract with the muleteer was to stop three days at Copan; but there was no bargain for the use of the mules during that time, and he hoped that the vexations we met with would make us go on immediately. When he found us bent on re-

CATHERWOOD D.                                    ANDERSON S.

maining, he swore he would not carry the hammocks, and
would not remain one day over, but at length consented to hire
the mules for that day.

Before we started a new party, who had been conversing
some time with Don Gregorio, stepped forward, and said
that he was the owner of "the idols;" that no one could go
on the land without his permission; and handed me his title
papers. This was a new difficulty. I was not disposed to dispute his title, but read his papers as attentively as if I medi-
tated an action in ejectment; and he seemed relieved when I
told him his title was good, and that, if not disturbed, I would
make him a compliment at parting. Fortunately, he had a
favour to ask. Our fame as physicians had reached the village,
and he wished remedios for a sick wife. It was important to
make him our friend; and, after some conversation, it was
arranged that Mr. C., with several workmen whom we had

hired, should go on to the ruins, as we intended, to make a lodgment there, while I would go to the village and visit his wife.

Our new acquaintance, Don Jose Maria Asebedo, was about fifty, tall, and well dressed; that is, his cotton shirt and pantaloons were clean; inoffensive, though ignorant; and one of the most respectable inhabitants of Copan. He lived in one of the best huts of the village, made of poles thatched with corn-leaves, with a wooden frame on one side for a bed, and furnished with a few pieces of pottery for cooking. A heavy rain had fallen during the night, and the ground inside the hut was wet. His wife seemed as old as he, and, fortunately, was suffering a rheumatism of several years' standing. I say fortunately, but I speak only in reference to ourselves as medical men, and the honour of the profession accidentally confided to our hands. I told her that if it had been a recent affection, it would be more within the reach of art; but, as it was a case of old standing, it required time, skill, watching of symptoms, and the effect of medicine from day to day; and, for the present, I advised her to take her feet out of a puddle of water in which she was standing, and promised to consult Mr. Catherwood, who was even a better medico than I, and to send her a liniment with which to bathe her neck.

This over, Don Jose Maria accompanied me to the ruins, where I found Mr. Catherwood with the Indian workmen. . . .

All day I had been brooding over the title-deeds of Don Jose Maria, and, drawing my blanket around me, suggested to Mr. Catherwood "an operation." (Hide your heads, ye speculators in up-town lots!) To buy Copan! remove the monuments of a by-gone people from the desolate region in which they were buried, set them up in the "great commercial emporium," and found an institution to be the nucleus of a great national museum of American antiquities! But quere, Could the "idols" be removed? They were on the banks of a river that emptied into the same ocean by which the docks of New-York are washed, but there were rapids below; and, in answer to my inquiry, Don Miguel said these were impassable. Nevertheless, I should have been unworthy of having passed through the times "that tried men's souls" if I had not had an alternative; and this was to exhibit by sample: to cut one up and remove it in pieces, and make casts of the others. The casts of the Parthenon are regarded as precious memorials in the British Museum, and casts of Copan would be the same in New-York. Other ruins might be discovered even more interesting and more accessible. Very soon their existence would become known and their value appreciated, and the friends of science and the arts in Europe would get possession of them. They belonged of right to us, and, though we did not know how soon we might be kicked out ourselves, I resolved that ours they should be; with visions of glory and indistinct fancies of receiving the thanks of the corporation flitting before my eyes, I drew my blanket around me, and fell asleep.

At daylight the clouds still hung over the forest; as the sun rose they cleared away; our workmen made their appearance, and at nine o'clock we left the hut. The branches of the trees were dripping wet, and the ground very muddy. Trudging once more over the district which contained the principal monuments, we were startled by the immensity of the work before us, and very soon we concluded that to explore the whole extent would be impossible. Our guides knew only of this district; but having seen columns beyond the village, a league distant, we had reason to believe that others were strewed in different directions, completely buried in the woods, and entirely unknown. The woods were so dense that it was almost hopeless to think of penetrating them. The only way to make a thorough exploration would be to cut down the whole forest and burn the trees. This was incompatible with our immediate purposes, might be considered taking liberties, and could only be done in the dry season. After deliberation, we resolved first to obtain drawings of the sculptured columns. Even in this there was great difficulty. The designs were very complicated, and so different from anything

Mr. Catherwood had ever seen before as to be perfectly unintelligible. The cutting was in very high relief, and required a strong body of light to bring up the figures; and the foliage was so thick, and the shade so deep, that drawing was impossible.

After much consultation, we selected one of the "idols," and determined to cut down the trees around it, and thus lay it open to the rays of the sun. Here again was difficulty. There was no axe; and the only instrument which the Indians possessed was the machete, or chopping-knife, which varies in form in different sections of the country; wielded with one hand, it was useful in clearing away shrubs and branches, but almost harmless upon large trees; and the Indians, as in the days when the Spaniards discovered them, applied to work without ardour, carried it on with little activity, and, like children, were easily diverted from it. One hacked into a tree, and, when tired, which happened very soon, sat down to rest, and another relieved him. While one worked there were always several looking on. I remembered the ring of the woodman's axe in the forests at home, and wished for a few long-sided Green Mountain boys. But we had been buffeted into patience, and watched the Indians while they hacked with their machetes, and even wondered that they succeeded so well. At length the trees were felled and dragged aside, a space cleared around the base, Mr. C.'s frame set up, and he set to work. I took two Mestitzoes, Bruno and Francisco, and, offering them a reward for every new discovery, with a compass in my hand set out on a tour of exploration. Neither had seen "the idols" until the morning of our first visit, when they followed in our train to laugh at los Ingleses; but very soon they exhibited such an interest that I hired them. Bruno attracted my attention by his admiration, as I supposed, of my person; but I found it was of my coat, which was a long shooting-frock, with many pockets; and he said that he could make one just like it except the skirts. He was a tailor by profession, and in the intervals of a great job upon a roundabout jacket, worked with his machete. But he had an inborn taste for the arts. As we passed through the woods, nothing escaped his eye, and he was professionally curious touching the costumes of the sculptured figures. I was struck with the first development of their antiquarian taste. Francisco found the feet and legs of a statue, and Bruno a part of the body to match, and the effect was electric upon both. They searched and raked up the ground with their machetes till they found the shoulders, and set it up entire except the head; and they were both eager for the possession of instruments with which to dig and find this remaining fragment.

It is impossible to describe the interest with which I explored these ruins. The ground was entirely new; there were no guide-books; the whole was a virgin soil. We could not see ten yards before us, and never knew what we should stumble upon next. At one time we stopped to cut away branches and vines which concealed the face of a monument, and then to dig around and bring to light a fragment, a sculptured corner of which protruded from the earth. I leaned over with breathless anxiety while the Indians worked, and an eye, an ear, a foot, or a hand was disentombed; and when the machete rang against the chiselled stone, I pushed the Indians away, and cleared out the loose earth with my hands. The beauty of the sculpture, the solemn stillness of the woods, disturbed only by the scrambling of monkeys and the chattering of parrots, the desolation of the city, and the mystery that hung over it, all created an interest higher, if possible, than I had ever felt among the ruins of the Old World. After several hours' absence I returned to Mr. Catherwood, and reported upward of fifty objects to be copied.

I found him not so well pleased as I expected with my report. He was standing with his feet in the mud, and was drawing with his gloves on, to protect his hands from the moschetoes. As we feared, the designs were so intricate and complicated, the subjects so entirely new and unintelligible, that he had great difficulty in drawing. He had made several attempts, both with the camera lucida and without, but failed to satisfy himself or even me, who was less severe in criticism.

The "idol" seemed to defy his art; two monkeys on a tree on one side appeared to be laughing at him, and I felt discouraged and despondent. In fact, I made up my mind, with a pang of regret, that we must abandon the idea of carrying away any materials for antiquarian speculation, and must be content with having seen them ourselves. Of that satisfaction nothing could deprive us. We returned to the hut with our interest undiminished, but sadly out of heart as to the result of our labours. . . .

The door of the hut looked toward the west, and the sun set over the dark forest in front with a gorgeousness I have never seen surpassed. Again, during the night, we had rain, with thunder and lightning, but not so violent as the night before, and in the morning it was again clear.

That day Mr. Catherwood was much more successful in his drawings; indeed, at the beginning the light fell exactly as he wished, and he mastered the difficulty. His preparations, too, were much more comfortable, as he had his water-proofs, and stood on a piece of oiled canvass, used for covering luggage on the road. I passed the morning in selecting another monument, clearing away the trees, and preparing it for him to copy. At one o'clock Augustin came to call us to dinner. Don Miguel had a patch of beans, from which Augustin gathered as many as he pleased, and, with the fruits of a standing order for all the eggs in the village, being three or four a day, strings of beef, and bread and milk from the hacienda, we did very well. In the afternoon we were again called off by Augustin, with a message that the alcalde had come to pay us a visit. As it was growing late, we broke up for the day, and went back to the hut. We shook hands with the alcalde, and gave him and his attendants cigars, and were disposed to be sociable; but the dignitary was so tipsy he could hardly speak. His attendants sat crouching on the ground, swinging themselves on their knee joints, and, though the positions were different, reminding us of the Arabs. In a few minutes the alcalde started up suddenly, made a staggering bow, and left us, and they all followed, Don Miguel with them. While we were at supper he returned, and it was easy to see that he, and his wife, and Bartolo were in trouble, and, as we feared, the matter concerned us.

While we were busy with our own affairs, we had but little idea what a sensation we were creating in the village. Not satisfied with getting us out of his house, Don Gregorio wanted to get us out of the neighbourhood. Unluckily, besides his instinctive dislike, we had offended him in drawing off some of his workmen by the high prices which, as strangers, we were obliged to pay, and he began to look upon us as rivals, and said everywhere that we were suspicious characters; that we should be the cause of disturbing the peace of Copan, and introducing soldiers and war into the neighbourhood. In confirmation of this, two Indians passed through the village, who reported that we had escaped from imprisonment, had been chased to the borders of Honduras by a detachment of twenty-five soldiers under Landaveri, the officer who arrested us, and that, if we had been taken, we would have been shot. The alcalde, who had been drunk ever since our arrival, resolved to visit us, to solve the doubts of the village, and take those measures which the presence of such dangerous persons and the safety of the country might require. But this doughty purpose was frustrated by a ludicrous circumstance. We made it a rule to carry our arms with us to the ruins, and when we returned to the hut to receive his visit, as usual, each of us had a brace of pistols in his belt and a gun in hand; and our appearance was so formidable that the alcalde was frightened at his own audacity in having thought of catechising us, and fairly sneaked off. As soon as he reached the woods, his attendants reproached him for not executing his purpose, and he said, doggedly, that he was not going to have anything to say to men armed as we were. Roused at the idea of our terrible appearance, we told Don Miguel to advise the alcalde and the people of the village that they had better keep out of our way and let us alone. Don Miguel gave a ghastly smile; but all was not finished. He said that he had no doubt himself of our being good men, but we were suspected; the country was in a state of excitement; and he was warned that he ought not to harbour us, and would get into difficulty by doing so. The poor woman could not conceal her distress. Her head was full of assassinations and murders, and though alarmed for their safety, she was not unmindful of ours; she said that, if any soldiers came into the village, we would be murdered, and begged us to go away.

We were exceedingly vexed and disturbed by these communications, but we had too much at stake to consent to be driven away by apprehensions. We assured Don Miguel that no harm could happen to him; that it was all false and a mistake, and that we were above suspicion. At the same time, in order to convince him, I opened my trunk, and showed him a large bundle of papers, sealed credentials to the government and private letters of introduction in Spanish to prominent men in Guatimala, describing me as "Encargado de los Negocios de los Estados Unidos del Norte," and one very special from Don Antonio Aycinena, now in this city, formerly colonel in the Central army, and banished by Morazan, to his brother the Marquis Aycinena, the leader of the Central party, which was dominant in that district in the civil war then raging, recommending me very highly, and stating my purpose of travelling through the country. This last letter was more important than anything else; and if it had been directed to one of the opposite party in politics, it would have been against us, as confirming the suspicion of our being "ennemigos." Never was greatness so much under a shade. Though vexatious, it was almost amusing to be obliged to clear up our character to such a miserable party as Don Miguel, his wife, and Bartolo; but it was indispensable to relieve them from doubts and anxieties, enabling us to remain quietly in their wretched hut; and the relief they experienced, and the joy of the woman in learning that we were tolerably respectable people, not enemies, and not in danger of being put up and shot at, were most grateful to us.

Nevertheless, Don Miguel advised us to go to Guatimala or to General Cascara, procure an order to visit the ruins, and then return. We had made a false step in one particular: we should have gone direct to Guatimala, and returned with a passport and letters from the government; but, as we had no time to spare, and did not know what there was at Copan, probably if we had not taken it on the way we should have missed it altogether. And we did not know that the country was so completely secluded; the people are less accustomed to the sight of strangers than the Arabs about Mount Sinai, and they are much more suspicious. Colonel Galindo was the only stranger who had been there before us, and he could hardly be called a stranger, for he was a colonel in the Central American service, and visited the ruins under a commission from the government. Our visit has perhaps had some influence upon the feelings of the people; it has, at all events, taught Don Gregorio that strangers are not easily got rid of; but I advise any one who wishes to visit these ruins in peace, to go to Guatimala first, and apply to the government for all the protection it can give. As to us, it was too late to think of this, and all we had to do was to maintain our ground as quietly as we could. We had no apprehension of soldiers coming from any other place merely to molest us. Don Miguel told us, what we had before observed, that there was not a musket in the village; the quality and excellence of our arms were well known; the muleteer had reported that we were outrageous fellows, and had threatened to shoot him; and the alcalde was an excessive coward. We formed an alliance, offensive and defensive, with Don Miguel, his wife, and Bartolo, and went to sleep. Don Miguel and his wife, by-the-way, were curious people; they slept with their heads at different ends of the bed, so that, in the unavoidable accompaniment of smoking, they could clear each other.

In the morning we were relieved from our difficulty, and put in a position to hurl defiance at the traducers of our character. While the workmen were gathering outside the hut, an Indian courier came trotting through the cornfield up to the door, who inquired for Señor Ministro; and pulling off his petate, took out of the crown a letter, which he said he was ordered by General Cascara to deliver into the right hands.

It was directed to "Señor Catherwood, à Comotan ó donde se halle," conveying the expression of General Cascara's regret for the arrest at Comotan, ascribing it to the ignorance or mistake of the alcalde and soldiers, and enclosing, besides, a separate passport for Mr. Catherwood. I have great satisfaction in acknowledging the receipt of this letter; and the promptness with which General Cascara despatched it to "Comotan, or wherever he may be found," was no less than I expected from his character and station. I requested Don Miguel to read

it aloud, told the Indian to deliver our compliments to General Cascara, and sent him to the village to breakfast, with a donation which I knew would make him publish the story with right emphasis and discretion. Don Miguel smiled, his wife laughed, and a few spots of white flashed along Bartolo's dirty skin. Stocks rose, and I resolved to ride to the village, strengthen the cords of friendship with Don Jose Maria, visit our patients, defy Don Gregorio, and get up a party in Copan.

Mr. Catherwood went to the ruins to continue his drawings, and I to the village. . . . My first visit was to Don Jose Maria. After clearing up our character, I broached the subject of a purchase of the ruins; told him that, on account of my public business, I could not remain as long as I desired, but wished to return with spades, pickaxes, ladders, crowbars, and men, build a hut to live in, and make a thorough exploration; that

I could not incur the expense at the risk of being refused permission to do so; and, in short, in plain English, asked him, What will you take for the ruins? I think he was not more surprised than if I had asked to buy his poor old wife, our rheumatic patient, to practice medicine upon. He seemed to doubt which of us was out of his senses. The property was so utterly worthless that my wanting to buy it seemed very suspicious. On examining the paper, I found that he did not own the fee, but held under a lease from Don Bernardo de Aguila, of which three years were unexpired. The tract consisted of about six thousand acres, for which he paid eighty dollars a year; he was at a loss what to do, but told me that he would reflect upon it, consult his wife, and give me an answer at the hut the next day. I then visited the alcalde, but he was too tipsy to be susceptible of any impression; prescribed for several patients; and instead of going to Don Gregorio's, sent him a polite request by Don Jose Maria to mind his own business and let us alone; returned, and passed the rest of the day among the ruins. It rained during the night, but again cleared off in the morning, and we were on the ground early. My business was to go around with workmen to clear away trees and bushes, dig, and excavate, and prepare monuments for Mr. Catherwood to copy. While so engaged, I was called off by a visit from Don Jose Maria, who was still undecided what to do; and not wishing to appear too anxious, told him to take more time, and come again the next morning.

The next morning he came, and his condition was truly pitiable. He was anxious to convert unproductive property into money, but afraid, and said that I was a stranger, and it might bring him into difficulty with the government. I again went into proof of character, and engaged to save him harmless with the government or release him. Don Miguel read my letters of recommendation, and re-read the letter of General Cascara. He was convinced, but these papers did not give him a right to sell me his land; the shade of suspicion still lingered; for a finale, I opened my trunk, and put on a diplomatic coat, with a profusion of large eagle buttons. I had on a Panama hat, soaked with rain and spotted with mud, a check shirt, white pantaloons, yellow up to the knees with mud, and was about as outré as the Negro king who received a company of British officers on the coast of Africa in a cocked hat and military coat, without any inexpressibles; but Don Jose Maria could not withstand the buttons on my coat; the cloth was the finest he had ever seen; and Don Miguel, and his wife, and Bartolo realized fully that they had in their hut an illustrious incognito. The only question was who should find paper on which to draw the contract. I did not stand upon trifles, and gave Don Miguel some paper, who took our mutual instructions, and appointed the next day for the execution of the deed.

The reader is perhaps curious to know how old cities sell in Central America. Like other articles of trade, they are regulated by the quantity in market, and the demand; but, not being staple articles, like cotton and indigo, they were held at fancy prices, and at that time were dull of sale. I paid fifty dollars for Copan. There was never any difficulty about price. I offered that sum, for which Don Jose Maria thought me only a fool; if I had offered more, he would probably have considered me something worse.

We had regular communications with the hacienda by means of Francisco, who brought thence every morning a large guacal of milk, carrying it a distance of three miles, and fording the river twice. The ladies of the hacienda had sent us word that they intended paying us a visit, and this morning Don Gregorio's wife appeared, leading a procession of all the women of the house, servants, and children, with two of her sons. We received them among the ruins, seated them as well as we could, and, as the first act of civility, gave them cigars all around. It can hardly be believed, but not one of them, not even Don Gregorio's sons, had ever seen the "idols" before, and now they were much more curious to see Mr. C.'s drawings. In fact, I believe it was the fame of these drawings that procured us the honour of their visit. In his heart Mr. C. was not much happier to see them than the old don was to see us, as his work was stopped, and every day was precious. As I considered myself in a manner the proprietor of the city, I was bound to do the honours; and, having cleared paths, led them around, showing off all the lions as the cicerone does in the Vatican or the Pitti Palace; but I could not keep them away, and, to the distress of Mr. C., brought them all back upon him.

Obliged to give up work, we invited them down to the hut to see our accommodations. Some of them were our patients, and reminded us that we had not sent the medicines we promised. The fact is, we avoided giving medicines when we could, among other reasons, from an apprehension that if any one happened to die on our hands we should be held responsible; but our reputation was established; honours were buckled on our backs, and we were obliged to wear them. . . .

That night there was no rain, and the next day, as the ground was somewhat dry, we commenced a regular survey of the ruins. It was my first essay in engineering. Our surveying apparatus was not very extensive. We had a good surveying compass, and the rest consisted of a reel of tape which Mr. C. had used in a survey of the ruins of Thebes and Jerusalem. My part of the business was very scientific. I had to direct the Indians in cutting straight lines through the woods, make Bruno and Frederico stick their hats on poles to mark the stations, and measure up to them. The second day we were thoroughly in the spirit of it.

That day Don Jose Maria refused to execute the contract. Don Gregorio was the cause. He had ceased to interfere with us, but at the idea of our actually taking root in the neighbour-hood he could not contain himself, and persuaded Don Jose Maria that he would get into difficulty by having anything to do with us; he even told him that General Cascara's passport was worthless, and that General Cascara himself had gone over to Morazan. He carried his point for the moment, but in the end we beat him, and the contract was executed.

After three days of very hard but very interesting labour, we finished the survey, the particulars of which I intend to inflict upon the reader; but before doing so I will mention the little that was previously known of these ruins.

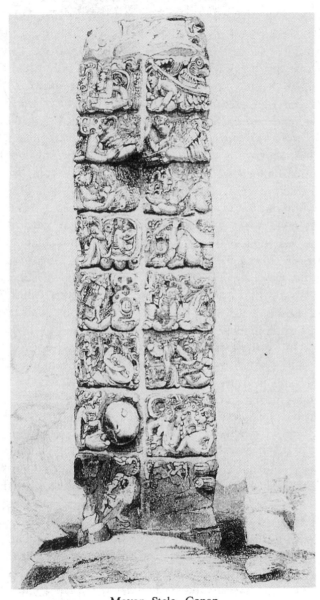

Mayan Stele, Copan

Huarros, the historian of Guatimala, says, "Francisco de Fuentes, who wrote the Chronicles of the Kingdom of Guatimala, assures us that in his time, that is, in the year 1700, the great circus of Copan still remained entire. This was a circular space surrounded by stone pyramids about six yards high, and very well constructed. At the bases of these pyramids were figures, both male and female, of very excellent sculpture, which then retained the colours they had been enamelled with, and, what was not less remarkable, the whole of them were habited *in the Castilian costume.* In the middle of this area, elevated above a flight of steps, was the place of sacrifice. The same author affirms that at a short distance from the circus there was a portal constructed of stone, on the columns of which were figures of men, likewise represented in *Spanish habits,* with hose, and ruff around the neck, sword, cap, and short cloak. On entering the gateway there are two fine stone pyramids, moderately large and lofty, from which is suspended a hammock that contains two human figures, one of each sex, clothed in the Indian style. Astonishment is forcibly excited on viewing this structure, because, large as it is, there is no appearance of the component parts being joined together; and though entirely of one stone, and of an enormous weight, in may be put in motion by the slightest impulse of the hand."

From this time, that is, from the year 1700, there is no account of these ruins until the visit of Colonel Galindo in 1836, before referred to, who examined them under a commission from the Central American government, and whose communications on the subject were published in the proceedings of the Royal Geographical Society of Paris, and in the Literary Gazette of London. He is the only man in that country who has given any attention *at all* to the subject of antiquities, or who has ever presented Copan to the consideration of Europe and our own country. Not being an artist, his account is necessarily unsatisfactory and imperfect, but it is not exaggerated. Indeed, it falls short of the marvellous account given by Fuentes one hundred and thirty-five years before, and makes no mention of the moveable stone hammock, with the sitting figures, which were our great inducement to visit the ruins. No plans or drawings have ever been published, nor anything that can give even an idea of that valley of romance and wonder, where, as has been remarked, the genii who attended on King Solomon seem to have been the artists.

It lies in the district of country now known as the State of Honduras, one of the most fertile valleys in Central America, and to this day famed for the superiority of its tobacco. Mr. Catherwood made several attempts to determine the longitude, but the artificial horizon which we took with us expressly for such purposes had become bent, and, like the barometer, was useless. The ruins are on the left bank of the Copan River, which empties into the Motagua, and so passes into the Bay of Honduras near Omoa, distant perhaps three hundred miles from the sea. The Copan River is not navigable, even for canoes, except for a short time in the rainy season. Falls interrupt its course before it empties into the Motagua. Cortez, in his terrible journey from Mexico to Honduras, of the hardships of which, even now, when the country is comparatively open, and free from masses of enemies, it is difficult to form a conception, must have passed within two days' march of this city.

The extent along the river, as ascertained by monuments still found, is more than two miles. There is one monument on the opposite side of the river, at the distance of a mile, on the top of a mountain two thousand feet high. Whether the city ever crossed the river, and extended to that monument, it is impossible to say. I believe not. At the rear is an unexplored forest, in which there are many ruins. There are no remains of palaces or private buildings, and the principal part is that which stands on the bank of the river, and may, perhaps, with propriety be called the Temple.

This temple is an oblong enclosure. The front or river wall extends on a right line north and south six hundred and twenty-four feet, and it is from sixty to ninety feet in height. It is made of cut stones, from three to six feet in length, and a foot and a half in breadth. In many places the stones have been thrown down by bushes growing out of the crevices, and in one place there is a small opening, from which the ruins are sometimes called by the Indians Las Ventanas, or the windows. The other three sides consist of ranges of steps and pyramidal structures, rising from thirty to one hundred and forty feet in height on the slope. The whole line of survey is two thousand, eight hundred and sixty-six feet, which, though gigantic and extraordinary for a ruined structure of the aborigines, that the reader's imagination may not mislead him, I consider it necessary to say, is not so large as the base of the great Pyramid of Ghizeh. . . .

To begin on the right: Near the southwest corner of the river wall and the south wall is a recess, which was probably once occupied by a colossal monument fronting the water, no part of which is now visible; probably it has fallen and been broken, and the fragments have been buried or washed away by the floods of the rainy season. Beyond are the remains of two small pyramidal structures, to the largest of which is attached a wall running along the west bank of the river; this appears to have been one of the principal walls of the city; and between the two pyramids there seems to have been a gateway or principal entrance from the water.

The south wall runs at right angles to the river, beginning with a range of steps about thirty feet high, and each step about eighteen inches square. At the south east corner is a massive pyramidal structure one hundred and twenty feet high on the slope. On the right are other remains of terraces and pyramidal buildings; and here also was probably a gateway, by a passage about twenty feet wide, into a quadrangular area two hundred and fifty feet square, two sides of which are massive pyramids one hundred and twenty feet high on the slope.

At the foot of these structures, and in different parts of the quadrangular area, are numerous remains of sculpture. At the point marked E is a colossal monument richly sculptured, fallen, and ruined. Behind it fragments of sculpture, thrown from their places by trees, are strewed and lying loose on the side of the pyramid, from the base to the top; and among them our attention was forcibly arrested by rows of death's heads of gigantic proportions, still standing in their places about half way up the side of the pyramid; the effect was extraordinary. . . .

At the time of our visit, we had no doubt that these were death's heads; but it has been suggested to me that the drawing is more like the skull of a monkey than that of a man. And, in connexion with this remark, I add what attracted our attention, though not so forcibly at the time. Among the fragments on this side were the remains of a colossal ape or baboon, strongly resembling in outline and appearance the four monstrous animals which once stood in front attached to the base of the obelisk of Luxor, now in Paris, and which, under the name of Cynocephali, were worshipped at Thebes. This fragment was about six feet high. The head was wanting; the trunk lay on the side of the pyramid, and we rolled it down several steps, when it fell among a mass of stones, from which we could not disengage it. We had no such idea at the time, but it is not absurd to suppose the sculptured skulls to be intended for the heads of monkeys, and that these animals were worshipped as deities by the people who built Copan.

Among the fragments lying on the ground, near this place, is a remarkable portrait, of which the following engraving is a representation. It is probably the portrait of some king, chieftain, or sage. The mouth is injured, and part of the ornament over the wreath that crowns the head. The expression is noble and severe, and the whole character shows a close imitation of nature.

At the point marked D stands one of the columns or "idols" which give the peculiar character to the ruins of Copan, the front of which forms the frontispiece to this volume, and to which I particularly request the attention of the reader. It stands with its face to the east, about six feet from the base of the pyramidal wall. It is thirteen feet in height, four feet in

West Side of Doorway Leading to the Inner Chamber
of the Temple at Copan, Honduras

front, and three deep, sculptured on all four of its sides from the base to the top, and one of the richest and most elaborate specimens in the whole extent of the ruins. Originally it was painted, the marks of red colour being still distinctly visible. Before it, at a distance of about eight feet, is a large block of sculptured stone, which the Indians call an altar. The subject of the front is a full-length figure, the face wanting beard, and of a feminine cast, though the dress seems that of a man. On the two sides are rows of hieroglyphics, which probably recite the history of this mysterious personage.

As the monuments speak for themselves I shall abstain from any verbal description; and I have so many to present to the reader, all differing very greatly in detail, that it will be impossible, within reasonable limits, to present our own speculations as to their character. I will only remark that, from the beginning, our great object and effort was to procure true copies of the originals, adding nothing for effect as pictures. Mr. Catherwood made the outline of all the drawings with the camera lucida, and divided his paper into sections, so as to preserve the utmost accuracy of proportion. The engravings were made with the same regard to truth, from drawings reduced by Mr. Catherwood himself, the originals being also in the hands of the engraver; and I consider it proper to mention that a portion of them, of which the frontispiece was one, were sent to London, and executed by engravers on wood whose names stand among the very first in England; yet, though done with exquisite skill, and most effective as pictures, they failed in giving the true character and expression of the originals; and, at some considerable loss both of time and money, were all thrown aside, and re-engraved on steel. Proofs of every plate were given to Mr. Catherwood, who made such corrections as were necessary; and, in my opinion, they are as true copies as can be presented; and, except the stones themselves, the reader cannot have better material for speculation and study.

Following the wall, at the place marked C is another mon-

ument or idol of the same size, and in many respects similar. . . .
The character of this image, as it stands at the foot of the
pyramidal wall, with masses of fallen stone resting against
its base, is grand, and it would be difficult to exceed the
richness of the ornament and sharpness of the sculpture. This,
too, was painted, and the red is still distinctly visible.

The whole quadrangle is overgrown with trees, and inter-
spersed with fragments of fine sculpture, particularly on the
east side, and at the northeast corner is a narrow passage,
which was probably a third gateway.

On the right is a confused range of terraces running off into
the forest, ornamented with death's heads, some of which
are still in position, and others lying about as they have fallen
or been thrown down. Turning northward, the range on the
left hand continues a high, massive pyramidal structure, with
trees growing out of it to the very top. At a short distance
is a detached pyramid, tolerably perfect, marked on the plan
Z, about fifty feet square and thirty feet high. The range continues for a distance of about four hundred feet, decreasing
somewhat in height, and along this there are but few remains
of sculpture.

The range of structures turns at right angles to the left,
and runs to the river, joining the other extremity of the wall,
at which we began our survey. The bank was elevated about
thirty feet above the river, and had been protected by a wall
of stone, most of which had fallen down. . . .

The plan was complicated, and, the whole ground being
overgrown with trees, difficult to make out. There was no
entire pyramid, but, at most, two or three pyramidal sides,
and these joined on to terraces or other structures of the same
kind. Beyond the wall of enclosure were walls, terraces, and
pyramidal elevations running off into the forest, which sometimes confused us. Probably the whole was not erected at the
same time, but additions were made and statues erected by
different kings, or, perhaps, in commemoration of important
events in the history of the city. Along the whole line were
ranges of steps with pyramidal elevations, probably crowned

on the top with buildings or altars now ruined. All these steps and the pyramidal sides were painted, and the reader may imagine the effect when the whole country was clear of forest, and priest and people were ascending from the outside to the terraces, and thence to the holy places within to pay their adoration in the temple.

Within this enclosure are two rectangular courtyards, having ranges of steps ascending to terraces. The area of each is about forty feet above the river. Of the larger and most distant from the river the steps have all fallen, and constitute mere mounds. On one side, at the foot of the pyramidal wall, is the monument or "idol" marked B, of which the engraving represents the front. It is about the same height with the others, but differs in shape, being larger at the top than below. Its appearance and character are tasteful and pleasing, but the sculpture is in much lower relief; the expression of the hands is good, though somewhat formal. The figure of a man shows the relative height. The back and sides are covered with hieroglyphics.

Near this, at the point marked A, is a remarkable altar, which perhaps presents as curious a subject of speculation as any monument in Copan. The altars, like the idols, are all of a single block of stone. In general they are not so richly ornamented, and are more faded and worn, or covered with moss; some were completely buried, and of others it was difficult to make out more than the form. All differed in fashion, and doubtless had some distinct and peculiar reference to the idols before which they stood. This stands on four globes cut out of the same stone; the sculpture is in bas-relief, and it is the only specimen of that kind of sculpture found at Copan, all the rest being in bold alto-relievo. It is six feet square and four feet high, and the top is divided into thirty-six tablets of hieroglyphics, which beyond doubt record some event in the history of the mysterious people who once inhabited the city. The lines are still distinctly visible, and a faithful copy appears in the following cut.

The next two engravings exhibit the four sides of this altar.

Each side represents four individuals. On the west side are the two principal personages, chiefs or warriors, with their faces opposite each other, and apparently engaged in argument or negotiation. The other fourteen are divided into two equal parties, and seem to be following their leaders. Each of the two principal figures is seated cross-legged, in the Oriental fashion, on a hieroglyphic which probably designates his name and office, or character, and on three of which the serpent forms part. Between the two principal personages is a remarkable cartouche, containing two hieroglyphics well preserved, which reminded us strongly of the Egyptian method of giving the name of the kings or heroes in whose honour monuments were erected. The headdresses are remarkable for their curious and complicated form; the figures have all breast-plates, and one of the two principal characters holds in his hand an instrument, which may, perhaps, be considered a sceptre; each of the others holds an object which can be only a subject for speculation and conjecture. It may be a weapon of war, and, if so, it is the only thing of the kind found represented at Copan. In other countries, battle-scenes, warriors, and weapons of war are among the most prominent subjects of sculpture; and from the entire absence of them here there is reason to believe that the people were not warlike, but peaceable, and easily subdued.

The other courtyard is near the river. By cutting down the trees, we discovered the entrance to be on the north side, by a passage thirty feet wide and about three hundred feet long. On the right is a high range of steps rising to the terrace of the river wall. At the foot of this are six circular stones, from eighteen inches to three feet in diameter, perhaps once the pedestals of columns or monuments now fallen and buried. On the left side of the passage is a high pyramidal structure, with steps six feet high and nine feet broad, like the side of one of the pyramids at Saccara, and one hundred and twenty-two feet high on the slope. The top is fallen, and has two immense Ceiba trees growing out of it, the roots of which have thrown down the stones, and now bind the top of the pyramid.

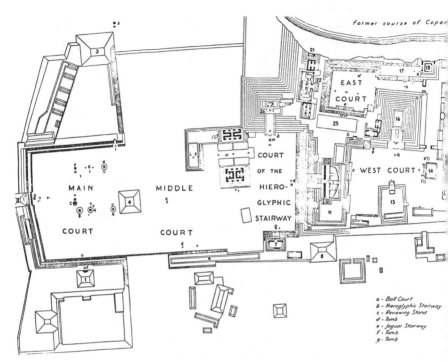

Plan of Copan, Honduras

At the end of the passage is the area or courtyard, probably the great circus of Fuentes, but which, instead of being circular, is rectangular, one hundred and forty feet long and ninety broad, with steps on all the sides. This was probably the most holy place in the temple. Beyond doubt it had been the theatre of great events and of imposing religious ceremonies; but what those ceremonies were, or who were the actors in them, or what had brought them to such a fearful close, were mysteries which it was impossible to fathom. There were no idol or altar, nor were there any vestiges of them. On the left, standing alone, two thirds of the way up the steps, is the gigantic head opposite. It is moved a little from its place, and a portion of the ornament on one side has been thrown down some distance by the expansion of the trunk of a large tree. . . . The head is about six feet high, and the style good. Like many of the others, with the great expansion of the eyes it seems intended to inspire awe. On either side of it, distant about thirty or forty feet, and rather lower down, are other fragments of sculpture of colossal dimensions and good design, and at the foot are two colossal heads turned over and partly buried, well worthy the attention of future travellers and artists. The whole area is overgrown with trees and encumbered with decayed vegetable matter, with fragments of curious sculpture protruding above the surface, which, probably with many others completely buried, would be brought to light by digging.

On the opposite side, parallel with the river, is a range of fifteen steps to a terrace twelve feet wide, and then fifteen steps more to another terrace twenty feet wide, extending to the river wall. On each side of the centre of the steps is a mound of ruins, apparently of a circular tower. About half way up the steps on this side is a pit five feet square and seventeen feet deep, cased with stone. At the bottom is an opening two feet four inches high, with a wall one foot nine inches thick, which leads into a chamber ten feet long, five feet eight inches wide, and four feet high. At each end is a niche one foot nine inches high, one foot eight inches deep, and two feet five inches long. Colonel Galindo first broke into this sepulchral vault, and found the niches and the ground full of red earthenware dishes and pots, more than fifty of which, he says, were full of human bones, packed in lime. Also several sharp-edged and pointed knives of chaya, a small death's head carved in a fine green stone, its eyes nearly closed, the lower features distorted, and the back symmetrically perforated by holes, the whole of exquisite workmanship. Immediately above the pit which leads to this vault is a passage leading through the terrace to the river wall, from which, as before mentioned, the ruins are sometimes called Las Ventanas, or the windows. It is one foot eleven inches at the bottom, and one foot at the top, in this form, and barely large enough for a man to crawl through on his face.

There were no remains of buildings. In regard to the stone hammock mentioned by Fuentes, and which, in fact, was our great inducement to visit these ruins, we made special inquiry and search for it, but saw nothing of it. Colonel Galindo does not mention it. Still it may have existed, and may be there still, broken and buried. The padre of Gualan told us that he had seen it, and in our inquiries among the Indians we met with one who told us that he had heard his father say that *his* father, two generations back, had spoken of such a monument.

I have omitted the particulars of our survey; the difficulty and labour of opening lines through the trees; climbing up the sides of the ruined pyramids; measuring steps, and the aggravation of all these from our want of materials and help, and our imperfect knowledge of the language. The people of Copan could not comprehend what we were about, and thought we were practising some black art to discover hidden treasure. Bruno and Francisco, our principal coadjutors, were completely mystified, and even the monkeys seemed embarrassed and confused; these counterfeit presentments of ourselves aided not a little in keeping alive the strange interest that hung over the place. They had no "monkey tricks," but were grave and solemn as if officiating as the guardians of consecrated ground. In the morning they were quiet, but in the afternoon they came out for a promenade on the tops of the trees; and sometimes, as they looked steadfastly at us, they seemed on the point of asking us why we disturbed the repose of the ruins. I have omitted, too, what aggravated our hardships and disturbed our sentiment, apprehensions from scorpions, and bites of moschetoes and garrapatas or ticks, the latter of which, in spite of precautions (pantaloons tied tight over our boots and coats buttoned close in the throat), got under our clothes, and buried themselves in the flesh; at night, moreover, the hut of Don Miguel was alive with fleas, to protect ourselves against which, on the third night of our arrival we sewed up the sides and one end of our sheets, and thrust ourselves into them as we would into a sack. And while in the way of mentioning our troubles I may add, that during this time the floor of the hacienda gave out, we were cut off from bread, and brought down to tortillas.

The day after our survey was finished, as a relief we set out for a walk to the old stone quarries of Copan. Very soon we abandoned the path along the river, and turned off to the left. The ground was broken, the forest thick, and all the way we had an Indian before us with his machete, cutting down branches and saplings. The range lies about two miles north from the river, and runs east and west. At the foot of it we crossed a wild stream. The side of the mountain was overgrown with bushes and trees. The top was bare, and commanded a magnificent view of a dense forest, broken only by the winding of the Copan River, and the clearings for the haciendas of Don Gregorio and Don Miguel. The city was buried in forest and entirely hidden from sight. Imagination peopled the quarry with workmen, and laid bare the city to their view. Here, as the sculptor worked, he turned to the theatre of his glory, as the Greek did to the Acropolis of Athens, and dreamed of immortal fame. Little did he imagine that the time would come when his works would perish, his race be extinct, his city a desolation and abode for reptiles, for strangers to gaze at and wonder by what race it had been inhabited.

The stone is of a soft grit. The range extended a long distance, seemingly unconscious that stone enough had been taken from its sides to build a city. How the huge masses were transported over the irregular and broken surface we had crossed, and particularly how one of them was set up on the top of a mountain two thousand feet high, it was impossible to conjecture. In many places were blocks which had been quarried out and rejected for some defect; and at one spot, midway in a ravine leading toward the river, was a gigantic block, much larger than any we saw in the city, which was probably on its way thither, to be carved and set up as an ornament, when the labours of the workmen were arrested.

Like the unfinished blocks in the quarries at Assouan and on the Pentelican Mountain, it remains as a memorial of baffled human plans.

We remained all day on the top of the range. The close forest in which we had been labouring made us feel more sensibly the beauty of the extended view. On the top of the range was a quarried block. With the chay stone found among the ruins, and supposed to be the instrument of sculpture, we wrote our names upon it. They stand alone, and few will ever see them. Late in the afternoon we returned, and struck the river about a mile above the ruins, near a stone wall with a circular building and a pit, apparently for a reservoir. . . .

Of the moral effect of the monuments themselves, standing as they do in the depths of a tropical forest, silent and solemn, strange in design, excellent in sculpture, rich in ornament, different from the works of any other people, their uses and purposes, their whole history so entirely unknown, with hieroglyphics explaining all, but perfectly unintelligible, I shall not pretend to convey any idea. Often the imagination was pained in gazing at them. The tone which pervades the ruins is that of deep solemnity. An imaginative mind might be infected with superstitious feelings. From constantly calling them by that name in our intercourse with the Indians, we regarded these solemn memorials as "idols"—deified kings and heroes—objects of adoration and ceremonial worship. We did not find on either of the monuments or sculptured fragments any delineations of human, or, in fact, any other kind of sacrifice, but had no doubt that the large sculptured stone invariably found before each "idol" was employed as a sacrificial altar. The form of sculpture most frequently met with was a death's head, sometimes the principal ornament, and sometimes only accessory; whole rows of them on the outer wall, adding gloom to the mystery of the place, keeping before the eyes of the living death and the grave, presenting the idea of a holy city—the Mecca or Jerusalem of an unknown people.

In regard to the age of this desolate city I shall not at present offer any conjecture. Some idea might perhaps be formed from the accumulations of earth and the gigantic trees growing on the top of the ruined structures, but it would be uncertain and unsatisfactory. Nor shall I at this moment offer any conjecture in regard to the people who built it, or to the time when or the means by which it was depopulated, and became a desolation and ruin; whether it fell by the sword, or famine, or pestilence. The trees which shroud it may have sprung from the blood of its slaughtered inhabitants; they may have perished howling with hunger; or pestilence, like the cholera, may have piled its streets with dead, and driven forever the feeble remnants from their homes; of which dire calamities to other cities we have authentic accounts, in eras both prior and subsequent to the discovery of the country by the Spaniards. One thing I believe, that its history is graven on its monuments. No Champollion has yet brought to them the energies of his inquiring mind. Who shall read them?

"Chaos of ruins! who shall trace the void,
  O'er the dim fragments cast a lunar light,
  And say 'here *was* or is,' where all is doubly night?"

In conclusion, I will barely remark, that if this is the place referred to by the Spanish historian as conquered by Hernandez de Chaves, which I almost doubt, at that time its broken monuments, terraces, pyramidal structures, portals, walls, and sculptured figures were entire, and all were painted; the Spanish soldiers must have gazed at them with astonishment and wonder; and it seems strange that a European army could have entered it without spreading its fame through official reports of generals and exaggerated stories of soldiers. At least, no European army could enter such a city now without this result following; but the silence of the Spaniards may be accounted for by the fact that these conquerors of America were illiterate and ignorant adventurers, eager in pursuit of gold, and blind to everything else; or, if reports were made, the Spanish government, with a jealous policy observed down to the last moment of her dominion, suppressed everything that might attract the attention of rival nations to her American possessions.

# 10. THOMPSON:

# *Into The Sacred Well*

Into this Well they have had and still have the custom of throwing men alive as a sacrifice to their gods in time of drought, and they believed that they would not die, though they never saw them again. They also threw in many other things like precious stones and things they prized, and so if this country had possessed gold it would have been this Well that would have the greater part of it, so great is the devotion that the Indians show for it.

—*Relación de las Cosas de Yucatán,* by DIEGO DE LANDA,
Archbishop of Yucatan (1566)

Temple of the Warriors, Chichen Itzá, Yucatán

Stephens had shown the way. The ruined cities of the Mayas became fair game for explorers and archaeologists. The most important, after Stephens, was Alfred Percival Maudsley, an Englishman who made seven expeditions to Central America between 1881 and 1894, and who brought out enough examples of Mayan art to put the study of the Mayan culture on a sound footing for the first time.

Among those youngsters of the 19th century who pored over the exciting reports of Stephens and Maudsley was New England-born Edward Herbert Thompson, who came upon Stephens' *Incidents of Travel in Yucatán* as a teenager and was thereupon committed to his life's work. Young Thompson had been chiefly interested in the Indians of North America until that time. He wondered whether the highly cultivated city-builders of Central America could be related to the simple hunting and fishing folk of the northern continent and decided that they could not. No, he declared, the city-builders were descendants of the inhabitants of lost Atlantis!

It was a theory that E. H. Thompson rarely advanced in his maturity. But in his youth, it fascinated him. In 1879, he published a magazine article, "Atlantis Not a Myth," which first brought his name before the public and set in motion the chain of events that built his archaeological career.

How Thompson came to go to Yucatán, and his exploits in the Sacred Well at Chichen Itzá, are told in the chapters reprinted here, which are drawn from his book of 1932, *People of the Serpent*. His exploration of the well, at a time when diving was a hazardous occupation even for professionals, is one of the most remarkable exploits in archaeological annals.

Thompson conducted his investigations in the Sacred Well from 1904 to 1907. He spent the remaining twenty-eight years of his life in Mexico, most of the time busily excavating. He served for more than two decades as United States Consul in Yucatán but ultimately left public service and dedicated himself to archaeology, purchasing extensive land holdings in the region of the Mayan ruins. As "Don Eduardo," he became a familiar and popular figure among the Mexican Indians, descendants of the great Mayas.

Thompson wrote only one popular book, *People of the Serpent,* but published a number of technical monographs on his work in Yucatán. His reports are marked by an exuberance and an enthusiasm that often led him far from reality, as when, discovering a series of superimposed graves in a pyramid, he immediately concluded that he had found the resting place not merely of a high priest, but of Kukulcan, the legendary hero-god of the Mayas. But such flights of fancy seem to be occupational hazards of archaeological pioneers—Schliemann was always quick to identify shields and masks as those of Achilles and Agamemnon—and need not be taken too seriously. Archaeological trailblazers often go their own way in casual disregard for the opinions of scholars and are sometimes, but not always, correct. Thompson's romanticism can be forgiven him since his discoveries were of unquestionable value regardless of the attributions he gave them.

Thompson turned the treasures of the Sacred Well over to Harvard and they can be seen today on the shelves of the Peabody Museum in Cambridge. This wholesale removal of national treasure caused no little distress in Mexico, which at the time had no legislation to prevent such things from happening. Though Thompson was greatly beloved in Mexico, he was criticized severely for his action, and antiquities laws were subsequently passed prohibiting such large-scale export of pre-Columbian artifacts.

Thompson had written, "With all the precious objects I have taken by force from the Rain God, I am very sure that I have wrested from him not a tenth of his jealously held treasure. There are many, many more golden ornaments hid away in the recesses of the uneven floor of the pit, and many, many things even more priceless than gold to the antiquarian."

This was borne out in 1960. In that year, the Peabody Museum voluntarily gave 94 objects from the Thompson collection to the Mexican National Institute of Anthropology and History, and the gift sparked a move to undertake fresh exploration of the Sacred Well. A group of Mexican divers and archaeologists, sponsored by the National Geographic Society and the Mexican National Institute of Anthropology and History, re-entered the Sacred Well and, utilizing modern diving equipment, harvested a yield nearly as great as that of Thompson half a century earlier.

## INTO THE SACRED WELL

I have referred before to an article, "Atlantis Not a Myth," written during my college days, and of the important bearing it had on determining my future course. It was while hunting up material for this article that I first came upon an old volume written by Diego de Landa, one of the earliest Spanish missionaries to Yucatan and later bishop of that diocese. Among other things recounted in quaint old Spanish in this book was a description of Chichen Itzá, the capital and sacred city of the Mayas. The wise priest laid special emphasis upon the traditions concerning the Sacred Well that lay within the confines of the city.

According to these traditions, as told to De Landa by his native converts, in times of drought, pestilence, or disaster, solemn processions of priests, devotees with rich offerings, and victims for the sacrifice wound down the steep stairway of the Temple of Kukil Can, the Sacred Serpent, and along the Sacred Way to the Well of Sacrifice. There, amid the droning boom of the *tunkul,* the shrill pipings of the whistle and the plaintive notes of the flute, beautiful maidens and captive warriors of renown, as well as rich treasures, were thrown into the dark waters of the Sacred Well to propitiate the angry god who, it was believed, lived in the deeps of the pool.

From the moment I read the musty old volume, the thought

From *People of the Serpent* (Boston and New York: Houghton Mifflin, 1932) by E. H. Thompson. Copyright 1932 by E. H. Thompson and re-printed by permission of and arrangement with Houghton Mifflin Company, the authorized publishers.

Chichen Itzá, Yucatán (an Aerial View)

of that grim old water pit and the wonderful objects that lay concealed within its depths became an obsession with me. Then, long years after, by what seemed to me almost an interposition of Providence, I became the sole owner of the great Chichen plantation, within whose confines the City of the Sacred Well and the Sacred Well itself lay.

For days and weeks after I purchased the plantation, I was a frequent worshiper at the little shrine on the brink of the Sacred Well. I pondered, mused, and calculated. I made measurements and numberless soundings, until, not satisfied but patiently expectant, I put my notebook aside and awaited the accepted time. It came when I was called to the United States for a scientific conference. After the session was over, at an informal gathering I told of the tradition concerning this Sacred Well of Chichen Itzá, of my belief in its authenticity, and the methods by which I proposed to prove it.

My statements brought forth a storm of protests from my friends.

'No person,' they said, 'can go down into the unknown depths of that great water pit and expect to come out alive. If you want to commit suicide, why not seek a less shocking way of doing it?'

But I had already weighed the chances and made up my mind. My next step was to go to Boston and take lessons in deep-sea diving. My tutor was Captain Ephraim Nickerson of Long Wharf, who passed to his reward a score of years ago. Under his expert and patient teaching, I became in time a fairly good diver, but by no means a perfect one, as I was to learn some time later. My next move was to adapt to my purpose an 'orange-peel bucket' dredge with the winch, tackles, steel cables, and ropes of a stiff-legged derrick and a thirty-foot swinging boom. All this material was created and ready for immediate shipment when ordered by either letter or wire.

Then, and not until then, did I appear before the Honorable Stephen Salisbury of Worcester, Massachusetts, and Charles P. Bowditch of Boston, both officers of the American Antiquarian Society and of Harvard University of which the Peabody Museum is a part. To them I explained the project and asked the moral and financial aid of the two organizations they represented. Although I had headed several important and successful expeditions under the auspices of these institutions, I found both of these gentlemen very reluctant to put the seal of their approval upon what they clearly believed to be a most audacious undertaking. They were willing to finance the scheme, but hesitated to take upon themselves the responsibility for my life.

I finally argued them out of their fears, and all other obstacles having been overcome, the dredge and its equipment were duly installed on the platform to the right of the shrine, and close to the edge of the great water pit, the Sacred Well.

During my preliminary investigations I had established what I called the 'fertile zone' by throwing in wooden logs shaped like human beings and having the weight of the average native. By measuring the rope after these manikins were hauled ashore, I learned the extreme distance to which sacrificial victims could have been thrown. In this way I fixed the spot where the human remains would probably be found. Regulating my operations by these calculations, I found them to respond with gratifying accuracy.

I doubt if anybody can realize the thrill I felt when, with four men at the winch handles and one at the brake, the dredge, with its steel jaw agape, swung from the platform, hung poised for a brief moment in mid-air over the dark pit and then, with a long swift glide downward, entered the still, dark waters and sank smoothly on its quest. A few moments of waiting to allow the sharp-pointed teeth to bite into the deposit, and then the forms of the workmen bent over the winch handles and muscles under the dark brown skin began to play like quicksilver as the steel cables tautened under the strain of the upcoming burden.

The water, until then still as an obsidian mirror, began to surge and boil around the cable and continued to do so long after the bucket, its tightly closed jaws dripping clear water, had risen, slowly but steadily, up to the rim of the pit. Swinging around by the boom, the dredge deposited on the planked receiving platform, a cartload of dark brown material, wood punk, dead leaves, broken branches, and other débris; then it swung back and hung, poised, ready to seek another load.

For days the dredge went up and down, up and down, interminably, bringing up muck and rocks, muck, more muck.

Once it brought up, gripped lightly in its jaws, the trunk of a tree apparently as sound as if toppled into the pit by a storm of yesterday. This was on a Saturday. By Monday the tree had vanished and on the pile of rocks where the dredge had deposited it only a few lines of wood fibre remained, surrounded by a dark stain of a pyroligneous character. Another time the dredge brought up the bones of a jaguar and those of a deer, mute evidence of a forest tragedy. And so the work went on for days.

I began to get nervous by day and sleepless at night.

'Is it possible,' I asked myself, 'that I have let my friends into all this expense and exposed myself to a world of ridicule only to prove, what many have contended, that these traditions are simply old tales, tales without any foundation in fact?'

At times, as if to tantalize me, the dredge recovered portions of earthen vessels undeniably ancient. I resolutely threw aside the thought that these might be the proofs I sought. Potsherds, I argued, were likely to be found anywhere on the site of this old city, washed from the surface deposits by rains. Boys are boys, whether in Yucatan or Massachusetts, and have been for some thousands of years. The instinct of a boy is to 'skitter' any smooth hard object, stone or potsherd, across smooth waters like those of the deep water pit and then it rests amid the mud and rocks at the bottom until brought up by the dredge. I could not accept these chance potsherds as the proofs that I required.

One day—I remember it as if it were but yesterday—I rose in the morning from a sleepless night. The day was gray as my thoughts and the thick mist dropped from the leaves of the tree as quiet tears drop from half-closed eyes. I plodded through the dampness down to where the staccato clicks of the dredge brake called me and, crouching under the palm lean-to, watched the monotonous motions of the brown-skinned natives as they worked at the winches. The bucket slowly emerged from the heaving water that boiled around it and, as I looked listlessly down into it, I saw two yellow-white, globular masses lying on the surface of the chocolate-colored muck that filled the basin. As the mass swung over the brink and up to the platform, I took from it the two objects and closely examined them.

They were hard, formed evidently by human hands from some substance unknown to me. They resembled somewhat the balls of 'bog butter' from the lacustrine deposits of Switzerland and Austria. There, ancient dwellings were built on piles in the midst of the lake to protect them against raiding enemies. The crocks of butter were suspended by cords let down between the piles and immersed in the ice-cold water for preservation. Despite all their precaution, raids did occur and the dwellings were destroyed by casual fires as well as by raids; so the crocks of butter fell unobserved from the charred piles down through the icy waters to rest unheeded in the increasing deposit until ages of time changed them into the almost fossilized material known to archæologists as 'bog butter.'

But these two nodules could not be bog butter, for unless the known data are strangely wrong, the ancient Mayas kept no domestic animals of any kind, much less cows or goats. They seemed to be made of some resinous substance. I tasted one. It was resin. I put a piece into a mass of lighted embers and immediately a wonderful fragrance permeated the atmosphere. Like a ray of bright sunlight breaking through a dense fog came to me the words of the old *H'Men,* the Wise Man of Ebtun: 'In ancient times our fathers burned the sacred resin—*pom*— and by the fragrant smoke their prayers were wafted to their God whose home was in the Sun.'

These yellow balls of resin were masses of the sacred incense *pom,* and had been thrown in as part of the rich offerings mentioned in the traditions. That night for the first time in weeks I slept soundly and long.

For a long time the belief had been growing in my mind that the scientific exploration of this Sacred Well of Chichen Itzá was to be the crowning event of my life-work, and that to do it as it should be done, I must give it all my time and attention. With the finding of these two nodules of incense and

Stela H. from Copan, Honduras

realization of what they indicated, this belief became a certainty. After much reflection I resigned my position as consul and devoted myself entirely to the work.

From that time on for months there was seldom a day when the dredge failed to yield objects of great scientific interest, earthen vessels, temple vases and incense burners, arrow-heads, lance-points finely shaped and chipped with wonderful skill, axes and hammer stones of flint and calcite. There were copper chisels, too, and disks of beaten copper covered with symbolical emblems and the conventionalized figures of the Maya deities, bells, disks, and pendent figures of low-grade gold, beads, pendants, and fragments of jade. Among the finds were the skeletons of young women, of thick-skulled, low-browed men. In every detail the old traditions were corroborated.

And now we come to the weirdest part of the weird undertaking, but, in order to put each thing in its proper place and make all matters clear, I must speak once more of the details of the sacrifices at this Sacred Well as reported in the ancient accounts.

The legend regarding the Sacred Well and the sacrificial rites performed therein was so clearly and yet so quaintly stated by the Alcalde of Valladolid, Don Diego Sarmiento de Figueroa, in 1579, that I am going to give his account here. Valladolid is the shire town of the *partido*, or county, in which Chichen is situated, and the *Alcalde* corresponds as nearly as possible to the officer we call mayor. This account is the official and authentic report rendered by the *Alcalde* to his sovereign, Carlos V. of Spain. He writes of the Sacred Well, called by him the *Cenote,* as follows:

> The lords and principal personages of the land had the custom, after sixty days of abstinence and fasting, of arriving by daybreak at the mouth of the *Cenote* and throwing into it Indian women belonging to each of these lords and personages, at the same time telling these women to ask for their masters a year favorable to his particular needs and desires.

The women, being thrown in unbound, fell into the water with great force and noise. At high noon those that could cried out loudly and ropes were let down to them. After the women came up, half dead, fires were built around them and copal incense was burned before them. When they recovered their senses, they said that below there were many people of their nation, men and women, and that they received them. When they tried to raise their heads to look at them, heavy blows were given them on the head, and when their heads were inclined downward beneath the water they seemed to see many deeps and hollows, and they, the people, responded to their queries concerning the good or the bad year that was in store for their masters.

I had some time before caused to be built a large, flat scow to serve me in the diving operations which I planned to carry on later and had lowered it by means of the derrick down to the surface of the well. There, moored to a rock shelf, it floated on the still water, awaiting the time for its use. One day I sat in it writing my notes and waiting for repairs that were being made on the dredge. The scow was moored ten feet under the overhang of the cliff-like wall and directly under the site of the derrick, sixty feet or more above. Looking casually over the gunwale, I saw that which gave me a thrill. It was the key to the story of the woman messengers in the old tradition.

The waters of the two great *cenotes* around which the ancient city was built are totally unlike. The water of one, called by the natives *Toloc,* and used by me as a bathing-pool, is dark blue by reason of depth, but is actually as clear and transparent, if not as cool, as the waters of a mountain lake. The water of the other, *Chen Ku,* or Well of the Sacrifices, is, on the contrary, dark colored and turbid, changing in hue at times from brown to jade-green and even to a blood-red, as I shall later describe, but it is always so turbid that it reflects the light like a mirror rather than deflecting it like a crystal.

Looking over the gunwale of the pontoon and downward to the water surface, I could see, as if looking down through great depths, 'many deeps and hollows.' They were in reality the reflections of the cavities and hollow places in the side of the cliff directly above me.

When they recovered their senses, the women had said: 'Below, there were many people of their nation and they . . . responded to our queries.' As I continued to gaze into those deeps and hollows, I saw below many people of their nation and they, too, responded. They were the heads and parts of the bodies of my workmen, leaning over the brink of the well to catch a glimpse of the pontoon. Meanwhile they conversed in low tones and the sound of their voices, directed downward, struck the water surface and was deflected upwards to my ears in words softly sounding in native accent, yet intelligible. The whole episode gave me an explanation of the old tradition that developed as clearly as the details of a photographic negative.

The natives of the region have long asserted that at times the waters of the Sacred Well turn to blood. We found out that the green color the water sometimes shows was caused by the growth of a microscopic algæ; its occasional brown hue was caused by decaying leaves; and certain flowers and seed capsules, blood-red in color, at times gave the surface of the water an appearance like that of clotted blood.

I mention these discoveries to show why I have come to believe that all authentic traditions have a basis of fact and can always be explained by a sufficiently close observation of the conditions.

The time finally came when the dredge no longer brought up valuable material from the bottom of the well. For weeks and months it had ceaselessly chewed its way through the thick deposit on the bottom within the area of the 'fertile zone.' For some time past the material that collected in the basin of the dredge was mostly a thin, watery mud, with only an occasional object of scientific value embedded in it. For a while the dredge doubled its trips and lessened the time of

The Red House at Chichen Itzá, Yucatán

making them by dumping the load into the waiting scow, where the contents were carefully examined and the tailings dumped on the shore of the Little Beach.

On the western side of the Sacred Well and nearly on a level with its waters, a rock shelf stands out from the cliff-like walls far enough to form a narrow beach and strong enough to support a thick clump of balsa-wood trees called by the natives *mash*. The interlacing roots of these strange trees, half-buried in the black mold about them and half-showing, darkly smooth and shining, seem like the writhing bodies of antediluvian reptiles. In the moist and darkly shadowed places beneath them can be seen the glistening eyes of giant toads, turtles, and lizards. This little beach is like a scene from the time when the world was young.

As each afternoon the tailings were thrown from the scow to the beach, the big lizards, their serrated backs bristling, would slink silently deeper into their holes, and the giant toads, their eyes blazing like diamond points in the darkness of their sheltered crannies, would cry out in deep-toned chorus: 'Don't Don't!'

At least so it seemed to me as, wet to the skin and plastered by sticky, black mud, I kept on throwing out the tailings.

When the dredge at the Sacred Well came up holding in its basin only the mud and sticks that had fallen into it from the loose material above; when the sharp-pointed steel teeth came up gritting with slivers of the rock bottom between them, we decided that our work with the dredge was finished. From now on human fingers must search in the crevices and the crannies of the bottom for the objects that the dredge could not reach to grasp. Nicolas, a Greek diver with whom I had previously made arrangements, arrived from the Bahamas where he had been gathering sponges. He brought an assistant, also a Greek, and we prepared at once for under-water exploration.

We first rigged the air pump in the boat, no longer a scow but once more a dignified pontoon, and then the two Greeks, turned instructors, taught a chosen gang of natives how to manage the pumps and send through the tube in a steady current the air upon which our lives depended and how to read and answer signals sent up from below. When they considered that the men were letter perfect, we were ready to dive.

We rode down to the pontoon in the basin of the dredge and, while the assistant took his place by the men at the pump to direct them, we put on our suits, outfits of waterproof canvas with big copper helmets weighing more than thirty pounds and equipped with plate-glass goggle eyes and air valves near the ears, lead necklaces nearly half as heavy as the helmets and canvas shoes with thick wrought-iron soles. With the speaking-tube, air hose, and life-line carefully adjusted, I toddled, aided by the assistant, to where a short, wide ladder fastened to the gunwale led down into the water.

As I stepped on the first rung of the ladder, each of the pumping gang, my faithful native boys, left his place in turn and with a very solemn face shook hands with me and then went back to wait for the signal. It was not hard to read their thoughts. They were bidding me a last farewell, never expecting to see me again. Then, releasing my hold on the ladder, I sank like a bag of lead, leaving behind me a silvery chain of bubbles.

During the first ten feet of descent, the light rays changed from yellow to green and then to a purplish black. After that I was in utter darkness. Sharp pains shot through my ears, because of the increasing air pressure. When I gulped and opened the air valves in my helmet a sound like 'pht! pht!' came from each ear and then the pain ceased. Several times this process had to be repeated before I stood on the bottom. I noted another curious sensation on my way down. I felt as if I were rapidly losing weight until, as I stood on the flat end of a big stone column that had fallen from the old ruined shrine above, I seemed to have almost no weight at all. I fancied that I was more like a bubble than a man clogged by heavy weights.

But I felt as well a strange thrill when I realized that I

was the only living being who had ever reached this place alive and expected to leave it again still living. Then the Greek diver came down beside me and we shook hands.

I had brought with me a submarine flashlight and a submarine telephone, both of which I discarded after the first descent. The submarine flashlight was serviceable in clear water or water merely turbid. The medium in which we had to work was neither water nor mud, but a combination of both, stirred up by the working of the dredge. It was a thick mixture like gruel and no ray so feeble as that of a flashlight could even penetrate it. So we had to work in utter darkness; yet, after a short time, we hardly felt the fact to be a serious inconvenience; for the palpic whorls of our finger-ends seemed not only to distinguish objects by the sense of touch, but actually to aid in distinguishing color.

The submarine telephone was of very little use and was soon laid aside. Communication by the speaking-tube and the life-line was easier and even quicker than by telephone. There was another strange thing that I have never heard mentioned by other divers. Nicolas and I found that at the depth we were working, from sixty to eighty feet, we could sit down and put our noses together—the noses of our helmets, be it understood—and could then talk to each other quite intelligibly. Our voices sounded flat and lifeless as if coming from a great distance, but I could give him my instructions and I could hear his replies quite clearly.

The curious loss of weight under water led me into several ludicrous mishaps before I became accustomed to it. In order to go from place to place on the bottom, I had only to stand up and push with my foot on the rock bottom. At once I would rise like a rocket, sail majestically through the mud gruel and often land several feet beyond where I wanted to go.

The well itself is, roughly speaking, an oval with one hundred and eighty-seven feet as its longer diameter. From the jungle surface about it to the water surface varied from sixty-seven to eighty feet. Where the water surface commenced could be ascertained easily, but where it left off and the mud of the bottom began was not so easy to determine, for the lines of demarcation did not exist. However, I can roughly estimate that of the total depth of mud and water, about sixty-five feet, thirty feet was a mud deposit sufficiently consistent to sustain tree-branches and even tree-roots of considerable size. About eighteen feet of this deposit was so compact that it held large rocks, fallen columns, and wall stones. Into this mud and silt deposit the dredge had bitten until it had left what I called the 'fertile zone' with a vertical wall of mud almost as hard as rock at the bottom and fully eighteen feet high. In this were embedded rocks of varied shapes and sizes, as raisins are embedded in plum puddings.

Imagine us, then, searching in the darkness, with these mud walls all about us, exploring the cracks and the crevices of the rough limestone bottom for the objects that the dredge had failed to bring up to the light of day. Imagine also that every little while one of the stone blocks, loosened from its place in the wall by the infiltration of the water, would come plunging down upon us in the worse than Stygian darkness that was all about us. After all, it was not so bad as it sounds. It is true that the big blocks fell when and where they would and we were powerless to direct or even to see them, but so long as we kept our speaking-tubes, air hose, and life-line and ourselves well away from the wall surface we were in no special danger. As the rock masses fell, the push of the water before and around them reached us before the rock did and even if we did not get away of our own accord, it struck us like a huge soft cushion and sent us caroming, often head down and feet upward, balancing and tremulous like the white of an egg in a glassful of water, until the commotion subsided and we could get on our feet again. Had we incautiously been standing with our backs to the wall, we should have been sheared in two as cleanly as if by a pair of gigantic shears and two more victims would have been sacrificed to the Rain God.

Before the dredge had even been installed and months before it brought up the first load, I had been told by a *H'Men,* pointing to a certain spot: 'There is where the Palace of the Rain God lies, as our fathers told us.'

That spot was out of the 'fertile zone,' and considerably to the right of it, but I determined to examine it. I found a deep natural depression in the floor of the pool that, so far as my observation could show, existed in no other place; and around the edge of that depression I found the outstretched skeletons of three poor women. Around the neck of one of them there were several jade beads as pendants. Portions of the garments worn by these victims preserved from decay in some strange way were secured for examination and study.

By what mode of reasoning did the *H'Men* or his predecessors select that special spot as the place where the Rain God dwelt? Its depth, if nothing else, made it physically impossible for a native diver to reach the place, spy it out, and return to the surface alive to tell of it. Who knows?

The natives for ages have believed that somewhere in those unknown depths the powerful God of the Waters had his home and that his anger caused the droughts, the pestilences, and the plagues of insects that from time to time descended upon the land. It was this belief that caused them to send messengers with supplications and rich gifts to propitiate the God. It can safely be inferred that the messengers were neither old women nor ill-favored.

The present natives of the region believe that big snakes and strange monsters live in the dark depths of the Sacred Well. Whether this belief is due to some faint remembrance of the old serpent worship, or is based upon something seen by some of the natives, can only be guessed at. I have seen big snakes and lizards swimming in these waters, but they were only snakes and lizards that in chasing their prey through the trees above had fallen into the pool and were trying to get out. We saw no traces of any reptiles or monsters of unusual size anywhere in the pool.

No strange reptile ever got me in its clutches, but I had one experience that is worth repeating. Both of us, the Greek diver and I, were busily digging with our fingers in a narrow crevice of the floor and it was yielding such rich returns that we neglected some of our usual precautions. Suddenly I felt something over me, an enormous something that with a stealthy, gliding movement was pressing down on me. Something smooth and slimy was pushing me irresistibly into the mud. For a moment my blood ran cold. Then I felt the Greek beside me pushing at the object and I aided him until we had worked ourselves free. It was the decaying trunk of a tree that had drifted off the bank of mud and in sinking had encountered my stooping body.

One day I was seated on a rock gloating over a remarkable find, a moulded bell of metal, and I quite forgot to open the air valves as I should have done. I put the find in my pouch and rose to change my position, when suddenly I began to float upward like an inflated bladder. It was ludicrous, but also dangerous, for at this depth the blood is charged with bubbles like champagne and unless one rises slowly and gives the blood time to become normal, a terrible disease called the 'bends' results, from which one can die in terrible agony. Luckily I had enough presence of mind to open the valves before going up very far and so escaped the extreme penalty, but I suffer the effects of my carelessness today in a pair of injured ear drums and greatly impaired hearing.

Even after I had opened the valves and was rising more and more slowly, I struck the bottom of the pontoon topsy-turvy, half-dazed by the concussion. Then, realizing what had happened and laughing at the thought of the fright my boys must have had when they heard me thump on the bottom of the boat, I scrambled from under it and threw my arm over the gunwale. As my helmet appeared over the side I felt a pair of arms thrown around my neck and startled eyes looked into the plate-glass goggles of my helmet, As they took off my diving-suit and I rested on a seat, getting back into normal condition and enjoying a cup of hot black coffee and the sunlight, the young Greek told me the story.

'The men,' he said, 'turned a pale yellow with terror when they heard the knock on the bottom that announced your unexpected arrival. When I told them what it was, they shook their heads mournfully and one of them, faithful old Juan Mis, said, "It's no use, *El Amo* the master is dead. He was swallowed by the Serpent God and spewed up again. We shall never hear him speak to us again"; and his eyes filled with tears. When your helmet came over the gunwale and he looked into its window, he raised both arms high above his head and said with great thankfulness, "Thank God, he is still alive, and laughing." '

As for the results of our dredging and diving into the great water pit, the first and most important is that we proved that in all essential details the traditions about the Sacred Well are true. Then we found a great store of symbolical figures carved on jade stone and beaten on gold and copper disks, copal masses and nodules of resin incense, many skeletal remains, a number of *hul chés,* or dart-throwers, and many darts with finely worked points of flint, calcite, and obsidian; and some bits of ancient fabric. All these had real archaeological value. Objects of nearly pure gold were encountered, both cast, beaten, and engraved in *repoussé,* but they were few in number and relatively unimportant. Most of the so-called gold objects were of low-grade alloy, with more copper than gold in them. That which gave them their chief value were the symbolical and other figures cast or carved upon them.

Most of the objects brought up were in fragments. Probably they were votive offerings broken before being thrown into the well, as a ritualistic act performed by the priests. The breaking was always in such a way that the head and features of the personages represented on jade plaque or gold disk were left intact. We have reason to believe that these jade pendants, gold disks, and other ornaments of metal or stone when broken were considered to have been killed. It is known that these ancient civilized races of America believed, as did their still more ancient forbears of northern Asia and as the Mongols to this day believe, that jade and other sacred objects have life. Accordingly these ornaments were broken or 'killed' that their spirits might serve as ornaments to the messenger, whose spirit would be appropriately adorned when it finally appeared before the *Hunal Ku,* the One Supreme God in the Heavens.

That this belief has come down through the ages to the present day is shown by this curious fact: A Maya noted for his knowledge of herbs and native medicines, not quite a *H'Men,* but respected among his people, lost his wife in childbirth and, as a particularly esteemed friend of the family, I was invited to the death feast, a ceremony much resembling the Celtic 'wake.' I was the only white man present.

The body of the beloved was dressed in new garments of white cotton cloth finely embroidered in the native fashion and handsome new shoes. I noticed first that the soles of the shoes had been cut in several places until the white stockings were to be seen between the slashes and then I saw that the new white garments had been similarly treated. I asked the husband the reason for this, and he answered:

'It is so that her soul shall appear before God dressed as the soul of my wife should be. If we had not done this, the spirits of the garments she wore would have remained in the coffin until the things rotted. Meantime the soul of my wife would remain without clothing, and that ought not to be.'

The value in money of the objects recovered from the Sacred Well with so much labor and at such expense is, to be sure, insignificant. But the value of all things is relative. The historian delves into the past as the engineer digs into the ground, and for the same reason, to make the future secure. It is conceivable that some of these objects have graved upon their surfaces, embodied in symbols, ideas and beliefs that reach back through the ages to the primal home of these people in that land beyond the seas. To help prove that is well worth the labor of a lifetime.

# INDEX